Intimacy and injury

Manchester University Press

GOVERNING INTIMACIES IN THE GLOBAL SOUTH

About the series

Governing Intimacies in the Global South deploys the categories of intimacy and governance to offer novel insights into the subjects, politics, cultures and experiences of the global south. The series showcases work that speaks to the affective and intimate worlds of communities located in Asia, Africa and Latin America while remaining attuned to governmental, social and other regulatory frames that undergird these worlds.

It seeks to bridge the gap between developmental analyses of the 'rest of the world', which theorise macro structures to the exclusion of the intimate, and historical and ethnographic records of micro-settings, allowing these to speak to larger structural conditions and constraints. Emphasising the postcolonial making of gender, sexuality and race as categories of meaning and power, this series views the relation between intimacy and governance from a position of theorising from the south, contributing to a reimagining of the idea of global south itself.

Intimacy and injury

In the wake of #MeToo in India and South Africa

Edited by

Nicky Falkof, Shilpa Phadke
and Srila Roy

MANCHESTER UNIVERSITY PRESS

Published by Manchester University Press
Oxford Road, Manchester M13 9PL
www.manchesteruniversitypress.co.uk

British Library Cataloguing-in-Publication Data is available

ISBN 978 1 5261 5762 1 hardback
ISBN 978 1 5261 7872 5 paperback

First published by Manchester University Press in hardback 2022
This edition first published 2024

The publisher has no responsibility for the persistence or accuracy of URLs for any external or third-party internet websites referred to in this book, and does not guarantee that any content on such websites is, or will remain, accurate or appropriate.

Typeset by Cheshire Typesetting Ltd, Cuddington, Cheshire

This book is dedicated to our mothers, with love and gratitude:
Bev Goldman, Shama Phadke and Reeti Roy

Contents

Part I Pre-histories

Part II #MeToo's silences

List of illustrations

Notes on contributors

Swati Arora is a lecturer in performance and global south studies at Queen Mary, University of London. Her work exists at the convergence of performance and visual culture, feminist theory, Black Studies, and dramaturgies of urban life. She has published essays in *Contemporary Theatre Review*, *New Theatre Quarterly* and *South African Theatre Journal*, and a manifesto to decentre theatre and performance studies in *Studies in Theatre and Performance*. She is working on her first book, on performance and resistance in Delhi.

Rupali Bansode is a Postdoctoral Fellow at the Indian Institute of Technology Bombay. She earned her PhD in Sociology from the Indian Institute of Technology Delhi in November 2020. Her research and teaching interests are in the fields of feminist anthropology and sociology of gender, caste and race.

Ragi Bashonga is a lecturer at the University of Johannesburg, pursuing a PhD in sociology at the University of Cape Town. Her research interests are in the areas of gender, the politics of identity, youth, and critical race studies. She contributes to this publication as part of an ongoing engagement with young people's efforts towards gender equality, particularly considering the pandemic of gender-based violence in South Africa. Ragi holds a Master's degree in Industrial Sociology and Labour Studies from the University of Pretoria, and is an alumnus of the Thabo Mbeki African Leadership Institute.

Jessica Breakey is an associate lecturer in the School for Electrical and Information Engineering at Wits University, where she teaches an interdisciplinary course on Science and Technology Studies. Jessica was awarded the Oppenheimer Memorial Trust Fellowship for her Master's degree at Wits and was a Chevening Scholar during her MPhil at the University of Cambridge. She has been awarded the Mandela Rhodes Leverhulme scholarship to pursue a PhD on questions of migration and borders at sea. She is co-author of the book *Moral Eyes: Youth and Justice in Cameroon, Nigeria, Sierra Leone, and South Africa* (HSRC press, 2018).

Nechama Brodie is a journalist and author based in Johannesburg. She holds a PhD in journalism and media studies from the University of the Witwatersrand, where she is also a lecturer. Her research focuses on the epidemiology and epistemology of fatal violence in South Africa and the global south, including developing tools that will allow violence researchers to build robust multi-use databases using news media and other archives. She is the author of *Femicide in South Africa* (Kwela Books, 2020), a monograph on female murder in the country.

Paromita Chakravarti (D.Phil, Oxon.) is Professor of English, and has been the Director of the School of Women's Studies, Jadavpur University, Kolkata. She teaches Renaissance drama, women's writing, sexuality and film studies and introduced the first Master's course in Queer Studies in India (2005). Her books include *Women Contesting Culture* (Stree, 2012) *Shakespeare and Indian Cinemas* (Routledge, 2018) and *Asian Interventions in Global Shakespeare* (Routledge, 2020). Dr. Chakravarti has served in the anti-sexual harassment cell in Jadavpur University for a decade. She also serves on the Internal Complaints Committee of several universities and corporates.

Louise du Toit is Associate Professor in the Department of Philosophy at the University of Stellenbosch in South Africa. She has been a rated researcher under the scheme of the National Research Foundation of South Africa since 2008. She is the author of *A Philosophical Investigation of Rape: The Making and*

Unmaking of the Feminine Self (Routledge, 2009); co-editor of *African Philosophy and the Epistemic Marginalization of Women* (Routledge, 2018); and guest editor for a special edition of the *Philosophical Papers* on 'The Meaning/s of Rape' (2009). She has held research fellowships at the University of Bristol Law School, the Center for Theological Inquiry in Princeton and the Stellenbosch Institute for Advanced Study.

Nicky Falkof is an Associate Professor in the Media Studies department at Wits University in Johannesburg. She is the author of *The End of Whiteness: Satanism and Family Murder in Late Apartheid South Africa* (Palgrave, 2015) and co-editor, with Cobus van Staden, of *Anxious Joburg: The Inner Lives of a Global South City* (Wits Press, 2020). She has been a visiting scholar at: the University of Dar-es-Salaam, Tanzania; Sussex University, UK; and UNAM, Mexico. Her research is concerned with race, anxiety and the media in the urban global south.

Amanda Gouws is Distinguished Professor of Political Science at the University of Stellenbosch, South Africa, where she holds a SARChI Research Chair in gender politics. Her research focuses on women and citizenship, women's representation, and gender-based violence. She is the editor of *(Un)Thinking Citizenship: Feminist Debates in Contemporary South Africa.* (UK: Ashgate and Cape Town: Juta, 2005), and co-editor of *Gender and Multiculturalism: North/South Perspectives* (Routledge, 2014). Recently she published 'Reducing Women to Bare Life: Sexual Violence in South Africa', *Feminist Encounters*, and an edited collection called, *The COVID Diaries: Women's Experience of the Pandemic* (Imball Academic Publishers, 2021). She was a Commissioner for the South African Commission for Gender Equality from 2012 to 2014.

Nithila Kanagasabai is an Assistant Professor at the School of Media and Cultural Studies, Tata Institute of Social Sciences, Mumbai, where she teaches courses in research methods and video production. She is also currently pursuing a PhD in Women's Studies at the same institute. Her areas of interest include: feminist media studies, feminist pedagogy, journalism studies, academic mobilities, research cultures, and digital media. Trained as a broadcast journalist, she has previously worked as a news reporter with NDTV and TIMES NOW covering news related to politics, health and environment.

Jamil F. Khan is a critical diversity scholar, columnist and author. They are currently enrolled for a PhD in Critical Diversity Studies at the Wits Centre for Diversity Studies. Their work explores multiple axes of difference including race, gender, sexuality and class. Their published work includes a socio-political memoir, *Khamr: The Makings of a Waterslams* (Jacana, 2020) – winner of best biography at the 2021 HSS Awards, book chapters on queer sex and subjectivity in titles published by Polity Press and Kwela and scholarly articles on the subject of queer ageing in academic journals, *Sexualities* and *Agenda*.

Zuziwe Khuzwayo is a feminist scholar whose interests include gender, sexuality and labour studies. She was previously a junior researcher at the Human Sciences Research Council (HSRC) and was involved in projects focusing on gender equality, HIV/AIDS and labour. She has published in the *Journal of International Women's Studies* and *Agenda* as well as the *South African Review of Sociology*. Her current PhD research focuses on how bisexual women construct their sexual identity in democratic South Africa looking at race, age, class and space.

Peace Kiguwa is Associate Professor in Psychology at the University of the Witwatersrand, South Africa. Her research interests include critical social psychology, affective politics of gender and sexuality, racism and racialisation and the nuances of teaching and learning. Her research projects include a focus on young women's leadership in Higher Education and the Destabilising Heteronormativity project. She is currently Editorial Board member on three accredited journal publications, the current Chair of the Sexuality and Gender Division of the Psychology Society of South Africa (PSYSSA), and recipient of the Oppenheimer Memorial Trust Rising Star Fellowship at Wits University.

Disha Mullick is the co-founder of Chambal Media, a company that produces feminist media for rural audiences. Chambal Media hosts the iconic rural news brand, Khabar Lahariya. When not sorting out financial and personnel crises at work, or shifting the dominant media voice in the country, Disha does some journalistic and personal writing and is currently participating in a South Asian writers' mentorship programme. She has a Master's degree in Gender Studies from the University of Warwick, and is an Acumen Fellow. She has worked in publishing and as a journalist before her journey with Khabar Lahariya.

Shilpa Phadke is a Professor at the School of Media and Cultural Studies, Tata Institute of Social Sciences, Mumbai. She is co-author of the critically acclaimed book *Why Loiter? Women and Risk on Mumbai Streets* (Penguin, 2011) and co-director of the documentary film *Under the Open Sky* (2016). She has published both academically and in mainstream media in the areas of gender and public space, ethnographies of feminism, feminist pedagogy, risk and the city, middle-class sexualities, middle classes and the new spaces of consumption, feminist pedagogies and feminist parenting. She is currently editing an anthology on friendship and its possibilities in South Asia.

Jhelum Roy is a PhD student in Jadavpur University, Department of English. Her MPhil thesis, completed in the School of Women's Studies, Jadavpur University, worked to rehabilitate the voices and testimonials of Naxalite peasant women into the historiography of the movement. She has also worked in research projects on issues of gender and sexuality.

Srila Roy is Associate Professor of Sociology and Head of Development Studies at the University of the Witwatersrand, South Africa. She is the author of *Remembering Revolution: Gender, Violence and Subjectivity in India's Naxalbari Movement* (Oxford University Press, 2012), editor of *New South Asian Feminisms* (Zed Books, 2012), and co-editor of *New Subaltern Politics: Reconceptualising Hegemony and Resistance in Contemporary India* (Oxford University Press, 2015). Her book on feminist and

queer feminist politics in liberalised India is forthcoming with
Duke University Press. At Wits, she leads the Governing Intimacies
project, which promotes new scholarship on gender and sexuality in Southern Africa and India, with support from the Andrew
W. Mellon foundation.

Rukmini Sen is Professor, School of Liberal Studies at Dr B.
R. Ambedkar University Delhi and currently Director, Centre
for Publishing. She is the recipient of the WISCOMP (Women
in Security, Conflict Management and Peace) SAAHAS awards
2020 recognising continuous engagements with curricula using
an intersectional lens. She was International Visitor Leadership
Programme on Human Rights Awareness (US State Department
of Education and Cultural Affairs) awardee in 2007. She has been
a member of Core Group on Women at National Human Rights
Commission, New Delhi since 2019; member of the Advisory
Board, Feminist Judgments Initiative, Gujarat National Law
University, India; and Life Member, Indian Association for Women's
Studies.

Jaya Sharma is a queer, feminist activist and writer based in New
Delhi. As part of a feminist NGO she worked on issues of gender
and education for over twenty years. She has also been intensively
involved in sexuality trainings for groups working with rural
women. As a queer activist she has co-founded and been involved
with queer forums in Delhi. Currently she is writing on issues of
sexuality and politics through a psychoanalytic lens.

Jyotsna Siddharth is an actor, artist, activist, writer and an intersectional queer feminist. Currently, they oversee Gender at Work
India. In the past, they have worked with several non-profits,
bilateral organisations, UN agencies on gender, gender budgeting,
inclusion, water and sanitation (WASH). Jyotsna's work spreads
across activism, theatre, development, caste-gender, feminist and
queer spaces. In 2020, Jyotsna was featured as 40 under 40 by
Edex and The New Indian Express. They are a founder of digital
social art projects Project Anti-Caste Love (2018) and Dalit
Feminism Archive (2019), and co-founder of Sive (2017). Jyotsna

holds a Master's in Development Studies from Tata Institute of Social Sciences, Mumbai and Social Anthropology from School of Oriental and African Studies, London. They are a recipient of the Chevening Scholarship (2014–2015).

Nosipho Vidima is a sex worker, human rights activist, black conscious feminist, HIV rights activist and wom_n rights activist. She previously worked at Sonke Gender Justice as a Sex Worker Rights Project Specialist, previously at SWEAT (Sex Workers Education and Advocacy Taskforce) as a Human Rights and Lobbying Officer and Programme Manager, Convenor of the Queer Feminist Film Festival, and Lead Researcher for the #SayHerName research study into SGBVF/IPV towards wom_n sex workers in South Africa.

Ntokozo Yingwana is a researcher and PhD candidate with the African Centre for Migration & Society (ACMS), at the University of the Witwatersrand. Her doctoral study is titled: 'Queering sex work and mobility in southern Africa: How does migration/mobility/movement influence gendered sexualities in sex work?' Yingwana's main passions are in gender, sexuality and sex worker rights' activism in Africa. She has worked for the Sex Workers Education and Advocacy Taskforce (SWEAT), and currently serves on its board. She occasionally consults for the African Sex Worker Alliance (ASWA), and the Global Network of Sex Work Projects (NSWP).

Acknowledgements

This book originated in a workshop held at Wits University, with the same title, jointly organised by Srila Roy, Shilpa Phadke and Crystal Dicks. Our thanks to the organisers and all the contributors who travelled from various parts of India and South Africa to be at this important event. Big thanks, also, to Yurisha Pillay who provided key logistical support to the workshop. For funding both the event and this publication, our thanks to the Governing Intimacies project (supported by the Andrew W. Mellon foundation and Wits University). Additional thanks for funding from the National Institute for the Humanities and Social Sciences.

The volume would not be possible without each of its contributors, who stuck with their research and writing in less than conducive pandemic times. For proof-reading and editing all chapters, our thanks to Caroline Jeannerat. The anonymous referees of both the proposal and the manuscript provided critical and generative feedback. It has been a pleasure to work with MUP, especially our editor Thomas Dark. Grateful thanks to SWEAT, Thandiwe Msebenzi, Blank Noise and Baaraan Ijlal for permission to include their powerful artworks.

Finally, we'd like to acknowledge the communities of feminist, queer and trans activists in both India and South Africa, who have shaped our understanding of gender-based violence and continue to deepen our commitments to building just feminist futures.

Introduction: intimacy, injury and #MeToo in India and South Africa

Srila Roy, Nicky Falkof and Shilpa Phadke

In a short period of time, we have witnessed both the seismic effects of the #MeToo movement and its ageing. We have felt the optimism that gathered as the hashtag travelled, while being sceptical about this particular wave of 'clicktivism'. Even as we saw how an individualised 'me' gathered and mobilised an ever-widening 'too' – exemplifying how a hashtag amalgamates individual experiences into a story of systemic harm and mobilises collective solidarity (Clark-Parsons, 2019) – worries accumulated. For every Harvey Weinstein who was stripped of power and influence, there was a Brett Kavanaugh who accumulated power and capital in spite of the force of women's testimony. Alongside the downfall of powerful men, women were implicated as aggressors (Filipovic, 2018; Gessen, 2018).

In the sustained afterlife of the movement, questions of coercion and consent, the blurring of intimacy and injury, the grey zones of intimate life – of 'what we want from intimacy' – seem not less but more obscure than ever (Padmanabhan, 2020).[1] Some worried whether these grey zones said something more fundamental about the nature of heteronormativity – the problem of 'bad sex' – than they did about male power and aggression (Chu, 2019). Feminist worries around #MeToo were also presented in generational terms, with 'older' feminists perceived to be cautioning against the excesses of online naming and shaming technologies, including their capacity to feed reactionary agendas. The movement shored up divides and acrimonies amongst feminists in other ways, with the strongest condemnation seeing it as an extension of forms of racialised and classed privilege – or 'political whiteness', as

Alison Phipps (2020) calls it. For Phipps, #MeToo epitomised how white feminism moulds itself through appropriating grassroots black feminist labour, incites a politics of neoliberal individualism, and sidelines minority voices, who are the worst casualties of carceral feminist agendas. Within heteronormative societies that emphasise binaristic gender, queer and trans people too felt erased and their narratives silenced – and so #MeToo was seen as a movement for cis women only. Added to this is the reality of 'digital feminist networks that reproduce colonial violence and oppression within mainstream neoliberal feminism and academia' (Trott, 2020: 16) and the acknowledgement that #MeToo has contributed to excluding 'marginalised communities and emphasising the individualised performance of trauma' (Loney-Howes et al., 2021).

These kinds of complexities – the grey zones of sexual violence, the tensions within feminism, the limited space for marginalised genders and sexualities – are often elided from transnational discussions of the contexts that this book is concerned with. The global south has historically functioned to confirm the fact of sexual violence, its stubborn endurance, its scale and lasting impact, in ways that leave one almost breathless. It has been seen less as a site of feminist struggle around such violence than as part of the making of feminist subjects elsewhere. Indeed, 'we' in the global south have been mined for the objects and ends of interventionist agendas located elsewhere but enacted in our name. Considerable energy has gone into debunking the assumption that feminism originates in the West and spreads as what Sara Ahmed (2017) calls an 'imperial gift' to the rest of the world.

And yet the loudest voices continue to belong to white feminists in the north, whose power derives in part from their capacity to exclude and appropriate, for the sake of claiming not 'me, too' but 'me, not you' (Phipps, 2020). Critical classifications of #MeToo as a white women's movement end up attaching it so closely to the white and mainstream Anglo-American experience that they cannot account for its varying travels, take-ups and consequences in the 'rest of the world'. On the contrary, they reinstate an affectively charged scalar politics in which the complexities of the south are flattened in the face of northern hegemony.

What would it mean to engage a different lens and politics? To view #MeToo from Egypt or Turkey, rather than the US and the UK, as its point of arrival if not origin? From its reverberations in Sweden and Norway on the one hand to India, South Korea, Japan and Egypt on the other, there was much to suggest that #MeToo was a 'transnational feminist consciousness-raising endeavour' (Ghadery, 2019: 254). Whether it named and vitalised pre-existing struggles or birthed entirely new ones, #MeToo 'allowed different groups of women in distinct places to take ownership of the individual manifestation of #MeToo in their specific context' (Ghadery, 2019: 254) and to expose 'deep structures of power and immunity' (John, 2020: 152). The Indian case, in particular, shows how feminist voices that are minoritised within the nation-state capitalise on transnationally circulating tools and affects to claim space against majoritarian voices (see Roy, 2017). Neither in the north nor the south, then, do feminists speak in one voice. That southern feminisms do not constitute an undifferentiated or homogeneous mass is also marked in the differential travels, take-up and even failure of the hashtag in specific contexts *within* the south, as this volume explores. Simplistic over-emphasis on #MeToo as a transformational moment of global feminist solidarity threatens to violently obscure the work and histories of feminist organising in our parts of the world; this is a trend we want to redress, by considering the manifestations of #MeToo in these contexts as well as its silences, weaknesses and incapacity to encompass the scale of longstanding local feminist work.

We can think of no better way to address the moment of #MeToo than taking comparative perspectives from different postcolonial sites, where we see the widespread impact of issues of sexual violence in vastly differing socio-political milieus. The kinds of questions being explored in this book can lead to a new set of interrogations, acting as an opening rather than offering straightforward answers and clear endings.

Issues surrounding #MeToo and gender-based violence (GBV) in the global south are hardly restricted to India and South Africa. Latin American nations like Chile and Guatemala are weighed down by impossibly high rates of femicide; sexual violence is commonplace in the post-conflict societies of east and southern Africa;

spousal abuse is rife in Pakistan; women face casual discrimination, daily violence and honour killings across the Middle East. India and South Africa are not special cases, not exceptional in their appalling statistics. What makes them valuable sites for this project, however, is their comparable role in the global imagination. Both are southern places that have heterogenous meaning in a transnational landscape. Unlike many countries in the south, the weight of history and media production means that they are not easily dismissed as simply locations of poverty. They connote glamour and development as well as disaster. Alongside this is their shared reputation as 'rape capitals' of the world. South Africa and India are places where both sexual violence in the south and resistance to that violence become particularly visible to a global audience. Indian and South African prehistories, manifestations and institutionalisations of #MeToo demonstrate important differences between their realms of gendered contestation. These events in the histories of postcolonial India and post-apartheid South Africa raise locally specific as well as globally resonant questions. They offer invaluable ways to think about the spread of #MeToo as a transnational and hypervisible idea.

The questions posed by this volume cannot readily be answered through national frameworks alone or by grappling with the centrality of the north in our analyses and imaginations. On the contrary, its comparative perspective undercuts the hegemony of the north while offering a different way forward, from a genuine feminist theorising of and from the south. In this introduction we take a broad approach to the problem of gendered violence in India and South Africa, considering representative cases, contexts, histories and politics. We hope to provide readers with a contextual frame that will cement the necessity of this distinctively south-south conversation.

#MeToo in India and Africa

For us in India and South Africa, #MeToo forced a reckoning that was not just familiar but also received with a degree of exhaustion. None of what was rendered visible and nameable under the hashtag, let alone the magnitude of sexual coercion that it exposed, was new to those of us who have been researching, campaigning or simply trying to understand the logics, workings and effects of power in these locales. Sexual violence has been the defining experience of gendered, sexualised, racialised, class- and caste-inflected lives in the postcolony.

Colonial tropes around victimised women in the global south persist. Even in heightened and visible moments of resistance, like the anti-rape protests in Delhi in 2012 and #FeesMustFall in South Africa, such tropes influenced how Western audiences consumed stories of rape and its resistance in the south (see, for instance, Roychowdhury, 2013). The dominance of colonial discourses when it comes to violence against women in these parts of the world should not, however, blind us to power relations that exist *inside* nation-states in ways that mediate the experience of victimisation and its representation. The resurgence of right-wing and religion-based populism is further constraining the field of public empathy when it comes to responding to and redressing violence. Long-standing fault lines and divergences in feminist thinking around the intersections of gender, sexuality, class-caste and race also mean that neither 'feminism' nor 'activism' are stable categories. Postcolonial, imperial and anti-apartheid legacies have meant a constant refashioning of feminist responses to sexual violence and gender-based inequality.

We know that rape was a key colonial technology of making not just gender and sexuality but also race: 'Sexuality [was] an important way in which the colonial Otherness was constructed', writes Amanda Gouws (2021: 5), drawing on the important work of Pumla Gqola (2015). In colonial India, female sexuality emerged as the ground not just for contests over sovereignty between colonial and indigenous patriarchies, but also for an entire edifice of 'modern social thought' (Mitra, 2020). The enduring quality of these ideas around gender, sexuality, race and caste meant that decolonisation in our contexts has had to contend with very specific structures of power and knowledge, which rendered rape as a 'way of life' (Gouws, 2021). Newly independent nation-states and local elites failed to take account of this, in spite of elaborate rhetorical commitments, leaving feminists to push for state and law to redress long histories of sexual violence. Political leaders and state functionaries – the police and the army – participated in an overall culture of normalising sexual violence and promoting a high tolerance for such violence over other crimes. Sexual violence has been at the heart of feminist concerns in India and South Africa and has offered activists complexly intersectional struggles rather than clear lines of resistance, which also acts as an important reminder that there can be no feminist resistance – no #MeToo – that is not intersectional. In both countries, caste and race have made the categories of rape, sexual harassment and GBV intelligible and governable.

In India, #MeToo was seen to bring new urgency to longstanding grievances and new tactics to existing repertoires of struggle, and even to make feminism newly relevant. The beginnings of India's #MeToo movement laid bare the issue of 'power and relationships in academia' (Sen, 2020); indeed, many chapters in this volume expose the university as an institutional site of gender and sexual politics of significant implications within and beyond India (see, especially, chapter 2 by Paromita Chakravarti and Jhelum Roy, chapter 9 by Rukmini Sen, Jessica Breakey's Reflection, and chapter 10 by Khuzwayo and Bashonga). A second wave had significant repercussions in the media and entertainment industries, where named sexual offenders faced losses that were social if not legal. The resignation of a minister of the Union government in India in the wake of multiple charges of sexual harassment was seen as a concrete victory for the movement. Nithila Kanagasabai's Reflection in this volume provides crucial insights into sexual harassment in the newsroom, while contending with the successes and limits of #MeToo's impact on this deeply sexist terrain. India's #MeToo also laid bare inequalities and differences as they exist within an Indian feminist community. Many contributions to this book reference the feminist arguments that erupted around the first iteration of #MeToo in India. Chapter 7, by Shilpa Phadke, centres not on the technology of naming and shaming itself, which was the source of the conflict, but the life of feminist contest in what she calls internet time and its implications for feminist solidarity-building. Like her, Jaya Sharma, in chapter 12, interviews feminist activists, mostly queer identified, to underscore queer critiques of #MeToo's sometimes flattening understandings of power and desire. Several critiques have pointed out that #MeToo in India erased the experiences of Dalit, trans, working-class and rural women as well as those of other marginalised groups (Ayyar, 2017; Akshaya, 2018; Sharma, 2018; Narayanamoorthy, 2021). A crucial aspect of the movement pertains to how anti-caste feminists made questions of caste privilege core to these new technologies of resisting sexual harassment. In underscoring the routine nature of sexual violence against Dalit women, chapter 4, by Rupali Bansode, shows how these women's testimonies were not always legible under #MeToo, even in the hands of anti-caste feminists.

In South Africa, #MeToo folded into new protest cultures around sexual violence, which also used online technologies to incriminate aggressors in the face of the limits of the state. Protests that spread virally escalated at the time of the 2015 student movement for removing university fees, encapsulated in the #FeesMustFall hashtag. Black women, trans and queer students made the issues of sexual harassment and rape culture in higher education central to these struggles, not least because of the harassment they faced from their own male comrades in movement spaces. Jessica Breakey's Reflection in this volume considers these complexities for feminists like herself, with resonances and ramifications that far extend the remit of this movement.

Feminist and queer politics were central to #FeesMustFall and other associated protest movements, employing both online and offline strategies. Chapter 8, by Amanda Gouws, discusses one of these hashtag campaigns, #EndRapeCulture, which predated #MeToo. It forced universities to take urgent institutional measures to combat the long-neglected normalisation of sexual violence on campuses. Some of these measures were discursive while others appeared at the level of policy. Zuziwe Khuzwayo and Ragi Basonga interview legal scholar Jackie Dugard, who was involved in the institutionalisation of sexual harassment redressal at the University of the Witwatersrand (Wits), to consider these practical and policy implications and consequences for students and others on campus. In both India and South Africa, then, the university was core to struggles around rape culture and sexual harassment well before the arrival of #MeToo; these tussles were energised in its wake.

Even as local activism was vitalised by the arrival of the hashtag – which also enabled some individual women to name harassment in the workplace – it is true that there was a limited take-up of #MeToo on the African continent. Many African feminists were wary that the newness of the moment would erase all that came before it and would recentre an optics controlled by and focused on the north. They responded to #MeToo less as transnational feminist activism than as a phenomenon from the US, steeped in the kinds of hierarchies and imperial logics that had plagued historical attempts to make feminism a global force. As Titilope Ajayi (2018) remarked:

> Spotlighting movements like #MeToo has a way of obstructing our vision of longstanding mobilisations on the ground in other parts of the world against the same issues. As much as transnational activism agendas are set in the 'West', a lot of significant movements tackling the same issues – even long before #MeToo – went on or are going on elsewhere.

Visibility has its own tensions, which are especially pronounced in forms of popular feminism that claim visibility as a goal in itself (Banet-Weiser, 2018). In India #MeToo made legible longstanding internal differences and inequalities within the local, while in some African countries, the transnational was experienced as eclipsing the local.

This book draws our attention to these politics of transnationalism: of how some forms of activism are truly transnational while others reinstate Western hegemony (see Tambe and Thayer, 2021). In South Africa, as some chapters in the volume show, #MeToo was a far from perfect lens to understand current feminist work, suggesting, instead, how global moments of feminist solidarity might well fail the global south.

Understanding sexual violence in India and South Africa

In 2013, well before #MeToo, two horrific killings occurred in India and South Africa, which became 'critical events' in their own right (Roy, 2014). Both involved the brutal gang rape and murder of a young woman at the hands of groups of young men, and both received enormous attention in countries where sexual violence is often dismissed as unremarkable and unworthy of public interest. The first was Jyoti Singh Pandey, a twenty-three-year-old student from India; the second was seventeen-year-old Anene Booysen from South Africa. While the murders had some similarities – their viciousness, their occurrence in countries with high rates of gendered violence, the youth of the victims, the wide media attention they received – their differences were significant, not least in the responses they engendered. In India, mass protests broke out in the wake of Jyoti's murder, making the 'Delhi rape' not just a critical event but a transnational one, as news of the gang rape and protests around it travelled globally (Roy, 2016).

In contrast, in South Africa, the public response to Anene's rape and death was sporadic and uncoordinated. Most of the responses came from established women's organisations, in contrast to India where the anti-rape protests were notable for galvanising diverse constituents, not all of whom self-identified as feminist or were part of the usual circles of activists and non-governmental organisations. Several rationales were offered as to why the public response to Anene's rape and murder was so muted in spite of the media coverage, with women's rights activists bemoaning how South Africans never had their 'Delhi rape moment' (Davis, 2014). Activists suggested that the media did not do enough to tell the story of who Anene Booysen really was, especially when compared to another murder victim who would dominate headlines a fortnight later, the model Reeva Steenkamp, killed by her celebrity boyfriend in a case that made global news (Watson and Lalu, 2014). Nechama Brodie, in chapter 1 of this volume, compares coverage of the two murders and, more tangentially, Reeva Steenkamp's, to suggest that the comparative lack of action around Anene's death may have been impacted by her classed and racialised identity: she was not 'one of us' and so was not mourned in the same way. And even as Jyoti's gang rape and murder were able to vitalise feminist protest in India, it was also true that she was more amenable to be read and mourned as 'one of us' than victims marginalised by class and caste (Roychowdhury, 2013; Shandilya, 2015).

The kind of violence that Jyoti faced was hardly new. Sexual harassment is part and parcel of Indian women's everyday experiences of public spaces. In their pathbreaking book, *Why Loiter?*, Shilpa Phadke, Sameera Khan and Shilpa Ranade (2011) argue that Indian women, even those who are class privileged, can only be in public through demonstrating purpose – either for education or for employment – which is synonymous with being respectable. Otherwise they risk losing respectability and invite the threat of violence. The typical public response to street harassment or even rape – from the state to individual families – is to further restrict women's freedom, to confine them in the home, in the name of their own safety.

Caging women also reflects cultural anxieties about female sexuality – that women might act in sexually 'immodest' ways if they are let loose on the streets, thus bringing shame and disrepute to their families. Keeping women safe not only controls their behaviour but also normalises violence. As elsewhere in the world, women in India are hardly safe at home. But 'confinement to the home' is itself a form of violence, as Kavita Krishnan (2020) powerfully shows. She provides data to show how little mobility and personal autonomy Indian women have, across classes, castes and communities, and how they live their lives basically 'in custody'. Women who exercise sexual autonomy or rights, by entering into consensual intimate relationships, do so at great risk, especially when these intimacies cross caste and faith lines. A shocking report by a mainstream Indian daily found that 'over 40% of what is classified as rape (in Delhi police files) is actually parental criminalization of consensual sexual relationships, often when it comes to inter-caste and inter-religious couples' (Rukmini, cited in Krishnan, 2020: 29).[2]

Underlying these pervasive social anxieties are the particular configurations around caste power in India, such that women's sexual autonomy comes to directly threaten the preservation of the caste system. Caste is, after all, maintained and reproduced by 'controlling women and ensuring they do not cross caste borders' (Krishnan, 2020). Village-based caste councils inflict violent punishment on individuals for transgressing such boundaries, akin to forms of 'honour killing' as they have come to be globally known.

Organised violence against women has reached new heights under the right-wing Hindu nationalist government, in its campaign, for instance, against the 'love jihad', intended to 'save' Hindu women from predatory Muslim men.[3] This has formed the perfect pretext for everyday vigilantism exercised by right-wing groups to victimise Muslim men and erode the sexual agency of consenting adult women.

Since the mass protests against the rape and murder of Jyoti Singh Pandey, feminist protests against restrictions on women's freedom and sexual autonomy have grown, but so have violent imperatives to keep women in line. Caste-based sexual violence is also on the rise, to which lower-caste and Dalit women are disproportionately vulnerable (see chapter 4 in this volume). The case of an unnamed nineteen-year-old Dalit woman who was gang-raped and murdered in northern India laid bare the intersections between caste and gender, and how sexual violence is a weapon of upper-caste privilege and power. 'Hathras, 2020', as this case came to be known, was seen by some to be 'a world apart' from Delhi 2012, because of caste prejudice that permeates Indian courts and communities (Chander, 2020). 'The system is moulded around the realities of caste and poverty, and the media or State rarely notice', write Disha Mullick and Khabar Lahariya (2020; see also chapter 5 in this volume).

Violence statistics and tales of women's lived experiences in South Africa are equally dire. Recent data show that a woman is killed on average every three hours, or around eight a day. More than half are murdered by current or former intimate partners (Brodie, 2020: 16). Even without considering the furthest extremes of femicide, the country's general statistics for GBV are shocking. Between 25 and 40 per cent of South African women experience physical and sexual intimate partner violence; just under half experience emotional or economic abuse; between 12 and 28 per cent of women report being raped; between 28 and 37 per cent of adult men report having raped a woman (SaferSpaces, n.d.).

Of course, it is not only women who are subjected to sexual or GBV. Jamil Khan's Reflection in this volume tells one painful, personal story of the violence that is casually meted out to queer people, who seldom gain recognition within discussions of gender-based harm. Louise du Toit, in chapter 6, foregrounds the experiences of male victims of rape, particularly within South African prisons. These men are subject to intense sexual violence but are almost entirely absent from discussions about it. Sexual violence is intimately connected to pathological performances of masculinity, so much so that this ongoing epidemic of violence against women has been ascribed to a South African iteration of the much-vaunted 'crisis of masculinity' (Payne, 1995). In this version of that convenient myth, young, particularly black, men have been let down by the ruling elite, socially disenfranchised and left behind in poverty despite the promises of the 'new' South Africa. While these claims are, of course, important, phrasing them as a contemporary crisis, and thus as exceptional rather than as structural, fails to account for the fact that GBV in South Africa – and, indeed, the instabilities in masculinity that apparently define this as a 'crisis' – have a much longer history. They also ignore the fact that women are murdered by men from all racial groups, and are sometimes poor, sometimes middle class or, in the case of Reeva Steenkamp, globally famous celebrities.

What causes violence in South Africa is a much more complicated question than the crisis approach suggests. Many scholars agree that rates of GBV are underpinned by powerful patriarchal attitudes inculcated in South African society across cultures and communities (see, for example, Gouws, 2016; Gqola, 2015; Ratele, 2008), which are next to impossible to unsettle without rigorous and well-funded state interventions that begin at the level of school and family. In a country riddled with corruption and failed service delivery, the possibility of such concentrated manoeuvres in early education and family support seems like a dream. Some researchers cite the patriarchal nature of 'traditional' South African families and societies, for example the current iteration of practices like *lobola*, or bride price, the payment of which is often seen as a justification for male physical abuse of women (Ludsin and Vetten, 2005: 24). Others link habits of violence directly to the ongoing consequences of the apartheid system: poverty, inequality and lack of opportunity; childhood exposure to violence and abuse; generational alcoholism and other dependences; the dissolution of familial structures (see Lamb and Snodgrass, 2013; Snodgrass and Bodisch, 2015). As Shanaaz Mathews, Rachel Jewkes and Naeemah Abrahams (2015) show in their study of men incarcerated for femicide, childhood trauma and poverty are only part of the picture. Their work reveals that 'the men sought to perform exaggerated versions of predominant ideals of masculinity, emphasising an extreme control of and dominance over women ... Killing [was] an ultimate means of taking back control in a context where gendered relationships legitimise men's use of violence to assert power and control' (Mathews et al., 2015: 107). In South Africa, GBV is tied to discursive, representational, traditional and institutional understandings of gender that are inherently patriarchal.

As with the hyper-vulnerability of Dalit women to caste-based violence in India, South African women face increased risks and different responses to their victimisation depending on how their positions are read. Despite the monopoly of the white middle class on the discursive field of fear of crime, both the fear and the reality of crime are greater among black South Africans (Mosselson, 2020), and public and political responses to these acts of violence are filtered through classed and racialised lenses. In August 2019, a twenty-year-old university student named Uyinene Mrwetyana was raped and murdered in a post office in Cape Town by a man who was an employee there. The killer later burned her body in a field. In a month of horrific killings, Nene, as she was known, became the latest poster child for South Africa's ongoing crisis of violence against women: she was memorialised in hashtags, marches, T-shirts, graffiti, artworks and on hundreds of posters. Her death, like Anene's, was particularly atrocious and led to a flood of media coverage. However, unlike Anene, who was from a poor and neglected community and who probably knew her murderers, Nene's personal life was not dissected in the press. She was swiftly anointed as an ideal victim and figurehead for burgeoning feminist protest. Both women were the victims of spectacular and appalling acts of violence, both of their young lives were cut short, both suffered at the hands of brutal men who laid claims to their bodies and their futures. However, the difference in the way they were remembered, and the differing manifestations they have had in popular culture, foregrounds the problem of selective empathy. In these two murders, we see again what the south has always underlined: that gender intersects with sexuality, race, caste and class. These are lessons southern feminists learned long before #MeToo.

Contesting GBV: old and new cultures of feminist resistance

Although the 2012 anti-rape protests were unprecedented in terms of scale and impact, they need to be contextualised within a longer history of women's activism around sexual violence in post-independence India. Indeed, it was the rape of a fourteen-year-old Adivasi woman, Mathura, at the hands of two policemen while in police custody that galvanised the mainstream Indian women's movement in the late 1970s. Women's groups appealed the decision of the Indian Supreme Court after it initially acquitted the policemen on the grounds that Mathura was lying and 'habituated' to sexual intercourse. The Mathura rape case eventually led to the amending of Indian law so that the burden of proof shifted from the accuser to the accused and custodial rape was made a punishable offense. It marked the beginning of a slew of legal reforms that would address domestic violence, sexual harassment and rape including, following Jyoti's case, the 2013 Criminal Law (Amendment) Act, which recognises a greater range of sexual offenses than before.

These two critical moments in the history of Indian feminism – the Mathura case in the late 1970s and the Delhi rape in 2012 – bookend a long history of feminist interventions into the realm of the law and the state. Yet critics argue that the strategy of legal reform has been limited (Menon, 2004). On a practical level, better laws have not improved the conviction rate for rape, which is still only 17 per cent in Delhi, largely due to deeply ingrained misogyny in the legal system and wider state apparatus (see Baxi, 2014). Additionally, legal reform has done little to change wider societal perceptions of the causes of violence against women or challenge the pervasive culture of victim-blaming that informs police and politicians alike. Chapter 9 in this book, by Rukmini Sen, maps changes to the legal landscape of sexual harassment in India, while also reflecting on the 'messiness' of complaints committees on university campuses. It was precisely this messiness that drove younger women and students to turn away from institutional redress to other kinds of protest technologies, as Paromita Chakravarti and Jhelum Roy show in chapter 2 on an important local movement around sexual harassment in eastern India. #MeToo landed on an affective terrain that was thick with disappointment and betrayal at patriarchal law, and ready to move beyond it.

In South Africa, too, institutional changes have not straightforwardly translated into changes at the level of culture and common sense, and the justice system appears especially broken when it comes to tackling GBV. This is despite the fact that South Africa has some of the most robust state-driven institutional mechanisms for gender equality in the world (such as the Commission for Gender Equality). The ruling African National Congress (ANC) recognised gender inequality as an area of state intervention early on, rolling out 'laws that not only introduced greater equality and rights within the family (including within customary law) but also recognised women's bodily autonomy and provided for positive measures to support women's employment' (Vetten, 2013). In the 1980s it closely collaborated with women's and civil society organisations, which formed the backbone of organising against gender inequalities in the post-1994 period.

In ensuing years, however, the ANC spectacularly failed to address the structural nature of women's oppression and the role that sexual violence plays within it. This was made evident in 2005 when Jacob Zuma, then deputy president of the ANC and future president of the country, was accused of rape by a young woman named Fezekile Ntsukela Kuzwayo, known to the South African public as 'Khwezi' to protect her identity. Not only was Zuma acquitted, but Khwezi faced such an intense backlash that she left the country and lived in exile until her untimely death (see Gqola, 2015; Hassim, 2009; Tlhabi, 2017). The Zuma rape trial was a powerful display of consensus around the normalisation of sexual violence and the victimisation of those most socially vulnerable – female, black and queer – by powerful men. The fact that the ANC's Women's League banded around Zuma showed the lack of autonomous women's mobilisation and the easy co-option of feminist struggles by the masculinist state. The ANC's Women's League 'were the stormtroopers of patriarchy,' writes Shireen Hassim (2017; see also Gouws, 2019; Hassim, 2014).

It was left to women in civil society organisations to hold the ANC to account (Gouws, 2019). In the wake of the Zuma trial, a new and assertive feminist movement began, with the women's rights organisation One in Nine formed expressly to support Khwezi (Hassim, 2017). As recently as 2015, four young female activists hijacked a high-profile speech that Zuma was making in front of mainstream media, holding up banners calling on the South African public to 'Remember Khwezi'. These queer black feminists, mostly university students, 'are part of a new moment that makes possible a new conversation' (Hassim, 2017).

Having said that, civil society mobilisations have struggled to sustain and extend themselves, worsened by the lack of resources. Like the NGO sector more broadly, South Africa's gender rights and LGBTI organisations have been weakened by an ongoing funding crisis. Service provision and staffing for rape survivors and abused women have been hit hard. The struggle to gain and keep funds also means there is little time and few resources for sustained activism. While recent years have seen new forms of actions and campaigns around sexuality and violence, these do not 'add up to a multi-layered, vibrant and diverse movement reflective of a range of women's concerns ... No nodes of engagement exist between parts, which resemble instead bounded spheres of disconnected organising and, with little ideological coherence evident, a very fuzzy – if not incompatible – politics' (Vetten, 2013).

It is also the case that South African civil society struggles to be free of co-optation from the ANC state, leaving activists to 'choose between civil society and party politics', as Philile Ntuli (2020) notes. Ntuli was writing in response to the 2018 #TotalShutDown marches against GBV, a nationwide series of strikes and marches that aimed to unite women in a new struggle against patriarchy. However, that movement was plagued by internal factionalism, prompting Ntuli (2020: 223) to remark that 'the most pressing challenge to the advancement of feminist agendas is not patriarchy ... Continued antagonisms, violence and inabilities to transcend differences threaten both the prospects of solidarity and the seriousness of women's movement demands'.

In both India and South Africa, the field of protest and activism in the name of women is fast changing at the hands of newer and younger activists, marginalised along the axes of caste, class, race, faith, gender and sexuality. GBV constitutes the ground for renewed feminist mobilisations in the public sphere, which draw on strategies such as online and offline protests, media advocacy, campaigns and casework. The digital, in particular, has changed the tenor of resistance to sexual violence, from something largely managed by organised women's groups in discussion with the state, to something that has more capacity than ever to spring up unplanned and explode into multiple possibilities. Many of the contributions to this book trace such 'new' feminist interventions. In chapter 3, Ntokozo Yingwana interviews activist Nosipho Vidima on the potential of new kinds of digital feminisms. Vidima discusses the #SayHerName campaign, launched in South Africa to memorialise and raise awareness of violence against sex workers, who are generally overlooked or abjected in South African public discourse. Chapter 5, by Disha Mullick, reveals how lower-caste women in rural India use technological skills and digital access to resist sexual harassment in a newsroom, complicating easy assessments of the digital as being accessible to metropolitan, middle-class feminists alone. These contributions show how online spaces are active as locations for feminist organising and resistance in sharply intersectional ways.

Much of this resistance involves sexual subalterns; transgender and non-binary people; younger women; black, 'coloured' and other racialised women in South Africa; and Dalit and Muslim women in India. These newer forms of feminist activism may cohere around hashtags but are expressed offline as well – through the making of new kinds of feminist 'noise', as Chakravarti and Roy call it in chapter 2. Despite the ongoing implications of the digital divide and the classed problem of data access, they can bypass some of the most potent critiques of digital feminism: that it is elitist and exclusionary; that it does not make space for the voices of the poor and marginalised; that it foregrounds certain voices to the exclusion of others. These mediated forms of communication have opened up the field of what it means to be a feminist in the global south.

But the digital is not, of course, the sole contemporary mode of protest and resistance. In order to fully understand iterations of #MeToo and beyond in India and South Africa, we must pay proper attention to their physical manifestations. Chapter 13, by Swati Arora, explores other modes of resisting sexual violence in both India and South Africa. These creative responses operate as archives of affect, care, community and politics, offering feminist resistance to GBV in conjunction with racism and casteism. Chapter 11, by Peace Kiguwa, equally foregrounds the affective dimensions of feminist movements against sexual violence in South Africa, highlighting four particular incidents that emphasise the power of rage, pain, love, shame, fury and resentment within feminist resistance. Finally, Jaya Sharma, in chapter 12, gets to the heart of the grey zone of intimacy and injury in mapping the psychic life of sexual politics in contemporary India, as laid bare by #MeToo.

Such intimate, affective and psychologically charged modes of protest are not readily found in archives of GBV in our parts of the world, which tend to privilege state responses. This despite the way in which, as Jyotsna Siddharth's Reflection in this book reveals, the state often mirrors the behaviour of the individual patriarchal predator rather than taking on the protective role it owes to female, femme and queer citizens. In the current context of heightened cultural and economic globalisation and religious and/or right-wing fundamentalisms, there is an urgent need to map two things at once: the ways in which state structures are shaping existing and new forms of patriarchal violence, and the ways in which this gives rise to multiple, unexpected and transverse forms of feminist resistance.[4] It is to these new possibilities of feminist world-making that this volume, in the wake of #MeToo in India and South Africa, gestures.

Conclusion

This book began its life as a workshop held at Wits University at the start of 2019, as part of Governing Intimacies, a project supported by the Andrew W. Mellon foundation and Wits, which aimed to nurture a new generation of feminist scholars in India and South

Africa. Many of the contributors first met and shared reflections on #MeToo in this space, which also afforded the possibility for genuine exchange on sexual harassment redressal work amongst academics in higher education. What struck us at the time – and has continued as this project developed – was the sense of discovery in a space populated by southern academic voices alone, with no mediation from anyone in a northern institution or locale. These spaces reminded us of the deeply entangled nature of our histories and contemporary problems, not least around GBV. This book, then, is also part of a wider imperative to build urgent epistemo-logical infrastructure in the south on the south, which is feminist in orientation and spirit.

The chapters included here present a broad variety of approaches to the problem of sexual violence, and to feminist responses to it, in India and South Africa. The contributions take three forms. First, using the varying approaches of scholarly research in multiple fields – psychology, philosophy, the law, the media, performing arts, history and literature – to think through the histories of, poli-tics around and resistances to sexual violence in our two contexts. Some of these chapters explicitly discuss elements of the #MeToo moment in India and South Africa; others consider pre-histories of #MeToo, locating this global movement within ongoing contexts and conversations on activism and organising in the south; still others use #MeToo as a frame to consider contemporary crises of GBV in India and South Africa. In taking these broad approaches, the chapters highlight both #MeToo's utility and its limits in south-ern contexts. The second type of contribution to this book is inter-views, in which scholar-activists undertake deep dive conversations with those working on the organisational front lines of GBV activ-ism in South Africa. These chapters reveal the pitfalls and pressures of feminist action, the sometimes insurmountable challenges as well as the enormous power and value of this work. The third type of contribution we have called 'Reflections': here feminist writers of different stripes tell their own stories or highlight their own con-cerns, moving from the scholarly to the personal in a way that has always been vital for feminist work.

In their multiplicity of approaches and perspectives, these chap-ters present new ways in which to think about GBV in India and

South Africa, not from the perspective of a developmental or NGO-ised or Western gaze but rather from an embedded position that centralises the voices of people in the south. These authors write not as imported 'experts' from the elite institutions of the north but rather as scholars, activists, journalists, people. Each contributor to this book is from either India or South Africa, and during the time of writing all were based at institutions in those countries. While the literature they cite may be broad and global, the perspectives they offer, the way in which they read southern lives, are inflected by their own positions. In that sense the existence of this book is an act of intersectional and transnational feminism: it foregrounds voices that are often neglected in the feminist canons of the West, shifting the sphere of analysis away from the centres of power and towards the life worlds of those who both live with this permanent threat of violence and whose critique and activism is most strongly directed towards it. It shows the deep generative possibilities of south-south collaborations and conversations in ways that re-energise and advance transnational feminist debates, politics and possibilities.

This book is a timely mapping of a transforming political field around GBV in India and South Africa. In proposing comparative, interdisciplinary, ethnographically rich and analytically astute reflections on #MeToo, it provides new and potentially transformative directions to scholarly debates, which are rarely brought into conversation with one another. It contributes, as well, to an ongoing reinvigoration of our commitments to redressing gender-based harm and instilling gender-just futures.

Notes

1 #MeToo's greatest legacy has been to explode the category of consent, by showing how it occupies a grey zone, is frankly unstable and therefore a poor indicator of women's desires and will.
2 Police and courts also act promptly when it comes to restoring members of same-sex couples to their families, in violation of their sexual rights, even as homosexuality is now decriminalised in India after decades of struggle.

3 Most recently, the government, under the leadership of Narendra Modi of the Bharatiya Janata Party, has rolled out anti-love jihad laws in some Indian states to effectively institutionalise what its foot soldiers had been doing all along, which is to criminalise Muslim men and control the sexuality of Hindu women.

4 For instance, at the end of 2019, for one hundred days and nights, hundreds of Indian Muslim women, some in their eighties, sat in a tent and braved an unusually bitter Delhi winter. They emerged as the unlikely face of a mass revolt against the Indian government's changed citizenships laws that threatened to disenfranchise religious minorities.

References

Ahmed, S. (2017). *Living a Feminist Life*. Durham, NC: Duke University Press.

Ajayi, T.F. (2018). '#MeToo, Africa and the politics of transnational activism', Africa is a Country. https://africasacountry.com/2018/07/metoo-africa-and-the-politics-of-transnational-activism. Accessed 1 January 2020.

Akshaya, V. (2018). 'Extending the Boundaries of #MeToo: Sexual Harassment in the Lives of Marginalised Women', *Economic & Political Weekly Engage*, 20 October, 53:42. www.epw.in/engage/article/extending-boundaries-metoo-sexual-harassment-marginalised-women. Accessed 20 February 2020.

Ayyar, V. (2017). 'Caste-Gender Matrix and the Promise and Practice of Academia', *Economic & Political Weekly Engage*, 16 December, 52:50. www.epw.in/engage/article/caste-gender-matrix-and-promise-and-practice-academia. Accessed 20 February 2020.

Banet-Weiser, S. (2018). *Empowered: Popular Feminism and Popular Misogyny*. Durham, NC: Duke University Press.

Baxi, P. (2014). *Public Secrets of the Law: Rape Trials in India*. New Delhi: Oxford University Press.

Brodie, N. (2020). *Femicide*. Johannesburg: Kwela Books.

Chander, M. (2020). 'Delhi 2012, Hathras 2020: A World Apart', Article 14, 4 October. www.article-14.com/post/delhi-2012-hathras-2020-a-world-apart. Accessed 20 October, 2020.

Chu, A.L. (2019). 'The Impossibility of Feminism', *Differences* 30:1, 63–81.

Clark-Parsons, R. (2019). 'I See You, I Believe You, I Stand with You: #MeToo and the Performance of Networked Feminist Visibility', *Feminist Media Studies*. https://doi.org/10.1080/14680777.2019.1628797.

Davis, R. (2014). 'Analysis: What can South Africa Learn from India's Response to Sexual Violence?' *Daily Maverick*, 10 July. www.dailymaverick.co.za/article/2014-07-10-analysis-what-can-south-africa-learn-from-indias-response-to-sexual-violence/#.VE_c5-cXGjU. Accessed October 2014.

Filipovic, J. (2018). 'When Women are the Bad Guys: Female Assaulters in the #MeToo Era', *Refinery 29*, 3 October. www.refinery29.com/en-us/2018/10/212614/metoo-movement-female-sexual-abusers. Accessed 5 May 2021.

Gessen, M. (2018). 'An N.Y.U. Sexual Harassment Case has Spurred a Necessary Conversation about MeToo', *New Yorker*, 25 August. www.newyorker.com/news/our-columnists/an-nyu-sexual-harassment-case-has-spurred-a-necessary-conversation-about-metoo. Accessed 6 May 2021.

Ghadery, F. (2019). '#Metoo – Has the "Sisterhood" Finally Become Global or just another Product of Neoliberal Feminism?' *Transnational Legal Theory* 10:2, 252–74.

Gouws, A. (2016). 'Women's Activism around Gender-Based Violence in South Africa: Recognition, Redistribution, and Representation', *Review of African Political Economy* 43:149, 400–15.

Gouws, A. (2019). 'Little is Left of the Feminist Agenda that Swept South Africa 25 Years Ago', *Conversation*, 5 August. https://theconversation.com/little-is-left-of-the-feminist-agenda-that-swept-south-africa-25-years-ago-121212. Accessed 10 January 2020.

Gouws, A. (2021). 'Reducing Women To Bare Life: Sexual Violence in South Africa', *Feminist Encounters: A Journal of Critical Studies in Culture and Politics* 5:1, 1–12.

Gqola, P.D. (2015). *Rape: A South African Nightmare*. Johannesburg: MFBooks Joburg.

Hassim, S. (2009). 'Democracy's Shadows: Sexual Rights and Gender Politics in the Rape Trial of Jacob Zuma', *African Studies* 68:1, 57–77.

Hassim, S. (2014). *The ANC Women's League: Sex, Gender and Politics*. Athens, OH: Ohio University Press.

Hassim, S. (2017). 'Why, a Decade on, a New Book on Zuma's Rape Trial has Finally Hit Home', *Conversation*, 5 October. https://theconversation.com/why-a-decade-on-a-new-book-on-zumas-rape-trial-has-finally-hit-home-85262. Accessed 20 January 2020.

John, M.E. (2020). 'Feminism, Sexual Violence and the Times of #MeToo in India', *Asian Journal of Women's Studies* 26:2, 137–58.

Krishnan, K. (2020). *Fearless Freedom*. New Delhi: Penguin.

Lamb, S. and L. Snodgrass. (2013). 'Growing Up with Normalised Violence: Narratives of South African Youth', *Commonwealth Youth and Development* 11:1, 4–21.

Loney-Howes, R., K. Mendes, D. Fernández Romero, B. Fileborn and S. Núñez Puente. (2021). 'Digital footprints of #MeToo', *Feminist Media Studies*. www.tandfonline.com/doi/abs/10.1080/14680777.2021.18861 42?journalCode=rfms20. Accessed 1 June 2021.

Ludsin, H. and L. Vetten. (2005). *Spiral of Entrapment: Abused Women in Conflict with the Law*. Johannesburg: Jacana.

Mathews, S., R. Jewkes and N. Abrahams. (2015). '"So Now I'm the Man": Intimate Partner Femicide and its Interconnections with Expressions of Masculinities in South Africa', *British Journal of Criminology 55*, 107–24.

Menon, N. (2004). *Recovering Subversion: Feminist Politics Beyond the Law*. Delhi: Permanent Black.

Mitra, D. (2020). *Indian Sex Life*. Princeton, NJ: Princeton University Press.

Mosselson, A. (2020). 'Inner-City Anxieties: Fear of Crime, Getting by and Disconnected Urban Lives', in *Anxious Joburg: The Inner Lives of a Global South Metropolis*, edited by N. Falkof and C. van Staden, 241–64. Johannesburg: Wits University Press.

Mullick, D. and Khabar Lahariya. (2020). 'An Attack in Hathras, and a Story of our Times', Article 14, 2 November. www.article-14.com/post/an-attack-in-hathras-and-a-story-of-our-times. Accessed 14 November 2020.

Narayanamoorthy, N. (2021). 'Exclusion in #MeToo India: Rethinking Inclusivity and Intersectionality in Indian Digital Feminist Movements', *Feminist Media Studies*, doi: 10.1080/14680777.2021.1913432.

Ntuli, P. (2020). 'Violence and/in the Feminist Movement: Reflections from the State', in *Living while Feminist*, edited by J. Thorpe, 215–29. Johannesburg: Kwela Books.

Padmanabhan, L. (2020). 'Facing Our Demons', Publics Books, 30 September. www.publicbooks.org/facing-our-demons/#:~:text=Michaela%20 Coel's%20new%20drama%2C%20I,on%20their%20most%20 intimate%20relationships. Accessed 1 October 2020.

Payne, L. (1995). *Crisis in Masculinity*. Grand Rapids, MI: Baker Books.

Phadke, S., S. Khan and S. Ranade. (2011). *Why Loiter? Women and Risk on Mumbai Streets*. New Delhi: Penguin Books.

Phipps, A. (2020). *Me, Not You: The Trouble with Mainstream Feminism*. Manchester: Manchester University Press.

Ratele, K. (2008). 'Masculinities, Maleness and (Illusive) Pleasure', Working Paper presented at the African Regional Sexuality Resource Centre, Institute of Social and Health Sciences, University of South Africa. www.arsrc.org/downloads/features/ratele.pdf. Accessed 11 March 2018).

Roy, A. (2014). 'Critical Events, Incremental Memories and Gendered Violence: The "Delhi Gang Rape"', *Australian Feminist Studies* 29:81, 238–54.

Roy, S. (2016). 'Women's Movements in the Global South: Towards a Scalar Analysis', *International Journal of Politics, Culture and Society* 29:2, 289–306.

Roychowdhury, P. (2013). '"The Delhi Gang Rape": The Making of International Causes', *Feminist Studies* 39:1, 282–92.

SaferSpaces. (n.d.). 'Gender-Based Violence in South Africa'. www.saf erspaces.org.za/understand/entry/gender-based-violence-in-south-africa. Accessed 21 October 2020.

Sen, R. (2020). 'Stay Home, Stay Safe: Interrogating Violence in the Domestic Sphere', EPW Engage. www.epw.in/engage/article/stay-home-stay-safe-interrogating-violence. Accessed 28 September 2021.

Shandilya, K. (2015). 'Nirbhaya's Body: The Politics of Protest in the Aftermath of the 2012 Delhi Gang Rape', *Gender and History* 27:2, 465–86.

Sharma, D. (2018). 'What's Missing in the #MeToo Movement?' *Economic & Political Weekly Engage*, 15 December, 53:49. www.epw.in/engage/article/what-is-missing-metoo-movement-limitation-law-justice. Accessed 20 February 2020.

Snodgrass, L. and A. Bodisch. (2015). 'Why Are We such a Violent Nation? The Legacy of Humiliation in South Africa', *Africa Insight* 45:3, 63–75.

Tambe, A. (2018). 'Reckoning with the Silences of #MeToo', *Feminist Studies* 44:1, 197–202.

Tambe, A. and Thayer, M. (2021). *Transnational Feminist Itineraries: Situating Theory and Activist Practice*, Durham, NC: Duke University Press.

Tlhabi, R. (2017). *Khwezi: The Remarkable Story of Fezekile Ntsukela Kuzwayo*. Johannesburg: Jonathan Ball.

Trott, V. (2020). Networked Feminism: Counterpublics and the Intersectional Issues of #MeToo. *Feminist Media Studies*, 1–18.

Vetten, L. (2013). 'Islands Adrift', Overland 213 Summer. https://overland.org.au/previous-issues/issue-213/feature-lisa-vetten/. Accessed 16 July 2021.

Watson, J. and V. Lalu. (2014). *Rupturing the Norms: The Social and Political Response to the Rape of Anene Booysen*. Cape Town: Heinrich Böll Stiftung. http://za.boell.org/sites/default/files/uploads/2014/09/rupturing_the_norms_saresponse_to_rape_anenebooysen_1.pdf. Accessed 16 July 2021.

Part I

Pre-histories

1

South Africa's own 'Delhi moment': news coverage of the murders of Jyoti Singh and Anene Booysen

Nechama Brodie

In order to understand the emergence of the #MeToo hashtag and its prominence as a global movement, it is important to review the contemporary archive of pre-#MeToo protests against gender-based violence (GBV), which show how prominent but otherwise unrelated cases of violence against women – even in different countries – could yield unexpected impacts on how these stories of violence were framed, and whose stories were seen to matter.

Indian journalist and researcher Sameera Khan (2010) observed that '"People like us" are the only ones that bleed.' She wrote this nearly a decade before the #MeToo movement would take off; and, even then, she was talking about a much older case, the molestation and subsequent harassment and suicide of teenager Ruchika Girhotra that had taken place in Haryana in the early 1990s.

'Overall, the media is attracted to the "people like us" stories', Khan continued, discussing media bias when it came to coverage of violent crime, an inherent preference for reporting on incidents 'where the main survivors or the main perpetrators are middle or upper class, and preferably urban'. Crime stories that had rural or tribal or 'poor' characters, she noted, were considered less likely to touch a chord with 'educated middle-class readers, viewers and advertisers' (Khan, 2010).

Media narratives of violent crime, particularly violence against women, have long arcs, and they are persistent in their preferences. Most often they show us divergence – the chasm between what is reported in black and white, and who lives and who dies every day. Occasionally, we also see convergence: where themes and stories combine, to create something that becomes more than just a story.

Sometimes it even becomes a movement. But the mechanisms of this are not always well understood. This chapter looks at the intersection of three prominent femicide cases in 2012 and 2013, one in India and two in South Africa, and shows how their reporting arcs intersected, and how the murders of two 'people like us' – one in Delhi and one in Pretoria – inadvertently and then directly boosted the media's coverage of a third incident, the killing of a marginalised woman in the Western Cape of South Africa.

On 2 February 2013, a seventeen-year-old named Anene Booysen was raped and murdered in the small town of Bredasdorp, South Africa. Booysen was assaulted on her way home from a tavern. She was discovered early the following morning at a construction site, still alive but very badly injured. It was reported that her intestines were hanging out of her body. She died in hospital several hours later.

At least 679 local news stories appeared either about or mentioning Booysen between the time of her death and August 2017 – making Booysen's murder the second-most covered South African femicide of the 2012/13 year, after the killing of celebrity and model Reeva Steenkamp.[1] Now, one might imagine it would be Anene's young age or the extreme violence meted out against her which resulted in such significant media coverage. But, sadly, her murder was not all that exceptional by South African standards. At the end of February 2013, twenty-eight-year-old Thandiswa Qubuda died in a Grahamstown hospital after being gang-raped and beaten so badly six weeks earlier that she had been left severely brain damaged and in a critical condition. Qubuda was mentioned in just thirteen media reports. The following month, in March 2013, fourteen-year-old Thandeka Madonsela was beaten, disembowelled and murdered in a patch of veld near Soweto. She was mentioned in just sixteen news reports.

This suggested that there were other factors which had triggered the almost unprecedented media response to Booysen's death. A reading of the first news articles that appeared about the case, starting four days after her death, reveal the answer: what made Booysen's murder notable was not the crime itself but, rather, its association with another rape-homicide that had occurred several weeks earlier and thousands of kilometres away. This was the killing of university student Jyoti Singh, also known as Nirbhaya, which took place in Delhi in December 2012.

Less than two weeks after Booysen's murder, South African model Reeva Steenkamp was shot dead by her celebrity sportsman boyfriend, in what would become one of the most highly publicised murder cases of the decade. While the Delhi rape-homicide amplified coverage of Anene's death because of similarities in the attacks, the murder of Reeva Steenkamp intensified media coverage of Anene because of the differences between the victims. A study of the intersecting media coverage of these three cases shows how certain global occurrences and campaigns can play a significant role in boosting the visibility of local events, magnifying or multiplying the perceived importance of incidents that otherwise might have gone relatively unnoticed.

Media and violence against women

In the wake of movements like #MeToo, it is important to understand how media reports of news events – including protests and activism related to violence against women – might interact with each other and influence which issues people think about or which issues they think are important. Media representations of violence against women form part of a complex and reciprocal relationship between media, society, crime and criminal justice. Seedat (1999: 132) explains that media 'not only constructs [a] violent event for the public but also informs the public on how to understand the violence'.

Although the definition of what constitutes 'news' is shifting, news media remain the primary source for public information about crime (Pollak and Kubrin, 2007; Tiegreen and Newman, 2009; Wozniak and McCloskey, 2010). However, as multiple studies have shown, media reports of crime typically do not match the actual rates or types of crime that are committed (Fairbairn and Dawson, 2013; McManus and Dorfman, 2003; Tiegreen and Newman, 2009; Wozniak and McCloskey, 2010), and there is no common 'functional truth' in journalism (McManus and Dorfman, 2005). Rather, the media acts as what Yvonne Jewkes (2004: 45) describes as 'a prism, subtly bending and distorting the view of the world it projects'.

Even in the case of homicide, not all murders that are committed are covered in the media (Schildkraut and Donley, 2012; Taylor, 2009), and those that are covered are not necessarily covered in the same way or to the same extent. Media processes of selection, exclusion and representation in crime reporting are, typically, obscure (in that they are not usually explained to readers/viewers/ listeners) and highly subjective, relying on many factors beyond the simple 'facts of a story', and include the beliefs of an individual reporter or editor (Taylor, 2009).

What newspaper crime reports represent are, simply, crimes that the newspaper has selected as being newsworthy. Nikunen (2011: 84) writes that 'some crimes are seen as important or interesting, while others are not. Since newspaper space is limited, it is impossible to give the same amount of attention to every news story'. These processes contribute to what Paulsen (2003: 289) describes as a 'socially constructed reality of homicide as portrayed by newspaper coverage of homicide incidents'. In turn, this construction can be seen to 'foster and reinforce particular perceptions of and attitudes toward violent crime' (Fairbairn and Dawson, 2013: 148).

Femicide in South Africa

South Africa has a femicide rate that is more than six times the world average[2] (UNODC, 2018; Wilkinson, 2019). Every year, between 2,500[3] and 2,900[4] women aged fourteen years or older are murdered, the majority of them killed by an intimate partner (Abrahams et al., 2013; Brodie, 2019; Wilkinson, 2019). Despite the prevalence of femicide, less than 20 per cent of these murders are ever reported in South African news media (Brodie, 2019; Brodie, 2020).

The use of the term 'femicide' has a perhaps surprisingly recent history – although the practice itself (the murder of women) is of course as old as the murder of men. Feminist academic, author, activist and sociologist Diana Russell used the term during her testimony at the International Tribunal on Crimes Against Women, held in Belgium in 1976, to describe not only female homicide but more specifically 'to suggest that when women are murdered, their femaleness is not incidental to the crime' (in Vetten, 1995: 78). The recognition that there was a gendered aspect to fatal violence emerged during a time when other terms like 'domestic violence' and 'marital rape' were also being tested out as new concepts within societies that viewed violence within the home as a private matter and not something where the state could or should intervene (Ertürk and Purkayastha, 2012).

Russell, in her own words, embraced the term 'femicide' (which she had picked up from another author) as 'a substitute for the gender-neutral word "homicide"'. She describes femicide as a hate crime against women – specifically, a 'hate killing of females perpetrated by males'. She later amended her definition of femicide as follows: 'the killing of females by males because they are female' (Russell, 2011). This definition is still used, particularly by agencies of state, and in this form might include things like intimate-partner homicide, rape homicides, killing of sex workers, so-called 'honour' killings and dowry killings, or killing a woman because of her sexual orientation.[5]

However, when working with actual murder cases rather than a hypothetical notion of femicide, this definition can also be quite limiting. First, in a large number of female homicide cases, we simply do not know who the perpetrator is. Under Russell's definition, we would have to exclude a large number of female homicides from being femicides simply because we cannot conclusively determine the killer or the motive. In countries like South Africa and other parts of the global south, which are often characterised by high rates of violent crime and low resources with which to combat crime, in those cases where a perpetrator is arrested and, more rarely, when he is convicted, the issue of motive is also often ambiguous. It is impossible to separate out the widespread, societal hatred of women from individual acts of violence against women.

In this chapter, the term 'femicide' refers to the illegal killing[6] of any woman aged fourteen years and older, by any perpetrator, for any reason, in line with definitions used by the South African Medical Research Council in two national autopsy-based studies into femicide (Abrahams et al., 2013; Mathews et al., 2004). While Russell had included the killing of female infants and the abortion of female foetuses as femicides, South African homicide studies (Abrahams et al., 2017; Mathews et al., 2013) indicate that the murders of girls under the age of fourteen have distinct features and a different epidemiological profile from those of women aged fourteen years and over – which is to say, the way that women are murdered once they start having or being subjected to relationships with men is quite different to the ways in which younger females are killed; and also that our definition of who should be defined as an 'adult' has more to do with social behaviours than with any specific idea of a legal majority. Shanaaz Mathews (2005) explains that 'the age category 14 years and older was used as the study aimed to determine the incidence of intimate partner homicide, as very little dating or few sexually intimate relationships occur before the age of 14'.

Using the South African media to study femicide

Media coverage of crime not only reflects and influences public perceptions and even fear of violence but also tells us about the society it reports on; and it can tell us about that society at particular points in time – a barometer and archive of the zeitgeist. By inclusion and exclusion, media coverage of crime tells us who matters, whose bodies matter, who is given the status of a legitimate victim, who is most-feared as a predator (Christie, 1986; Gillespie et al., 2013; Lindgren and Nikolić-Ristanović, 2011; Richards et al., 2014).

In addition, media coverage of crime can provide valuable information about crime itself. Even though media coverage typically has no correlation with the prevalence of crime, reports often add details that are not usually included in official data: news stories tell us not only how victims died but who they were and how they lived (Brodie, 2020). In countries where the state provides limited information about crime to begin with – and this includes South Africa and India – media coverage may also be one of the only publicly available sources there is and may include information about deaths that are *not* reported as murders (such as dowry killings in India).

In South Africa, a crime reporting year runs from 1 April to 31 March, which correlates with the financial reporting period of the South African Police Service (SAPS). By its own statistics, there were 16,259 murders across the country in the 2012/13 crime year, of which 2,587 were femicides – or an average of seven women killed every day.[7] Fewer than 450 of these murders were reported in the press (Brodie, 2019). This meant less than 20 per cent of femicides made it into the media at all.

The majority of cases that appear in the news receive very little coverage (most frequently only a single mention in the press, with a median number of three), while a smaller cluster receive more prominent attention – say, twenty articles or more. Only a handful of cases each year achieve fame or even 'notoriety', or what Soothill and his colleagues (2004) call 'mega cases'. In the 2012/13 crime year, just 6 of the 408 victims received coverage of more than one hundred articles each, and all of these victims were white – with one exception: Anene Booysen.

Before we examine how Jyoti Singh's murder directly influenced South African media coverage of Booysen's death, it is perhaps worthwhile pointing out that, even today, Singh's killing is still almost exclusively referred to as the 'Delhi Gang Rape'. Although a closer examination is outside the scope of this chapter, it is important to note the constant and repeated assertion, within broader studies of femicide and violence against women, that being raped is somehow a worse fate than being killed. Mason and Monckton-Smith's (2008) work carefully illustrates the tendency in media to sexualise female homicide, and for news coverage to perpetuate narratives that link sex and death in a way that effectively conflates the crimes of rape and murder. In this socially accepted form of storytelling, the act of rape is almost always depicted as potentially fatal (even when, patently, in most instances it is not); and, reciprocally, it implies that any sexual assault that is neither deadly nor extremely violent – thus leaving the affected woman at the verge of death – runs the risk of not being considered a 'real' rape. Surviving almost suggests the victim is complicit in her own rape.

South Africa was relatively late in picking up on the story of what, initially at least, was 'only' an extremely violent gang rape in India's capital. The first local news report about the then-unnamed victim appeared in the *Pretoria News* on 20 December 2012, four days after the assault. It should also be pointed out that early news coverage was linked to protests around the rape rather than coverage of the rape itself. Over the following weeks, there was frequent daily coverage of the Delhi case and the various demonstrations and marches it gave rise to – spiking shortly after the time of Singh's death at the end of December 2012 and continuing well into the new year.

Again, to get some sense of context, we can look at South African media coverage of Singh's death and compare it to two other prominent but relatively 'ordinary' local cases of femicide. On 19 January 2013, the partly naked body of twenty-year-old Lee-Ann Gordon was found in the bushes outside the Parkside Library in Gonubie in the Eastern Cape. That same day, ninety-eight-year-old pensioner and preacher Betty Titse was raped and strangled to death in Tloung Village in North West province. These two cases received a total coverage of just twelve and fourteen articles respectively. In contrast, between December 2012 and the end of January 2013, there were more than sixty South African news reports mentioning the Delhi case.

It was obvious that the incident in Delhi had struck a prominent chord with South Africa's own struggles with sexual violence – in particular that the mass action in response to the killing was something South Africans could learn from. In early January 2013, the Durban *Post* published a story about a 'sympathy march' that was scheduled to be held later that month (Durban is home to South Africa's largest Indian population), and included features about the 'outrageous scourge' of rape in India, together with a separate article with quotes and responses from Bollywood celebrities about the incident. A few days later the East London-based *Daily Dispatch* wrote a column titled 'A Lesson from India' (4 January 2013), which directly compared India's rape crisis with that of South Africa. In *The Star*, Dr Devi Rajab (8 January 2013) wrote that 'India's shame is every nation's shame' and that what had happened in Delhi was a 'lesson to all of us battling with gender relations'.

By the start of February, however, coverage of the case had started to drop off. This is typical of the news cycle and its relatively short attention span. But this changed after the first news reports were published about Anene Booysen's death. The very first report to appear in the media was on 6 February 2013, in the Afrikaans-language paper *Die Burger*, under the headline 'Meisie sterf na sy verkrag is' (Girl Dies After Being Raped). While there were some nominal similarities between the injuries sustained by Singh and Booysen – specifically, that they had been disembowelled or suffered severe internal injuries during their rapes, that they had died some time after the attack as a result of these injuries, and that they had lived just long enough to help identify their attackers – the cases were more strongly connected by the 'global movement' against rape that was growing in the wake of the Delhi case.

On 7 February 2013, five days after Anene's death, the spokesperson for the Congress of South African Trade Unions issued a statement to the press in which he specifically said: 'When a very similar incident occurred in India recently, there was a massive outbreak of protest; it was a big story around the world. We must show the world that South Africans are no less angry at such crimes' (Patrick Craven, quoted by Koyana, 2013). This set the tone for the mass coverage and op-eds that followed. Editors called for South Africa to 'find its India moment' (*Saturday Argus*, 9 February 2013) and to 'Let this be our own New Delhi moment' (*Cape Argus*, 14 February 2013); they traced Singh and Booysen's narrative 'From Delhi to Bredasdorp' (*Daily Dispatch*, 15 February 2013) or, as *The New Age* expressed it, 'From Delhi to Bredasdorp, rape outrage boils over' (18 February 2013). Within nine days of the first media story about Booysen's death, 129 news reports had been published about the incident in Bredasdorp. More than 10 per cent of these specifically cross-referenced India.

This kind of response was unprecedented in the South African media, particularly when it came to news coverage of the murders of poor, brown women. Even the high profile 1999 gang rape and murder of fourteen-year-old Valencia Farmer in Eersteriver in Cape Town – a case where three men were convicted, and the fourth and final perpetrator was only arrested and convicted of his crimes nearly seventeen years after the killing – appeared in fewer than 300 news clippings in the two decades after Farmer's death.

Framing news

The deliberate choice to frame Booysen's murder within the broader narrative of Singh's death was an important feature. Moody, Dorries and Blackwell (2008: 7, citing Bird and Dardenne's work on myth and the narrative qualities of news) explain how news reporting tends to 'reduce complex phenomena into neat mythical packages that reflect the ideological practices of news-making structures'. Media frames can be described in various ways: as principles of organisation; as mechanisms of selection (and thereby exclusion); and as a means of emphasis and presentation (Cacciatore et al., 2016; Gamson and Modigliani, 1987; Gitlin, 1980; Hawley et al., 2017; Matthes and Kohring, 2008). A frame can be a literalised focal device or an organisational device for narrative or meaning. As an extension of this, frames can take on broader narrative and supra-narrative functions as schemas within which meaning develops and can (or even must) be interpreted, namely: 'The act of reading a news article will determine which stored knowledge structure (or schema) becomes active. In turn, the activated knowledge structure will be used to interpret the news article' (Cacciatore et al., 2016: 16). This is to say that the rape and murder of Singh in India was invoked as a framework through which to read the rape and murder of Booysen in Bredasdorp, which conveyed, through news coverage, not so much that rape (and murder) was an individual event but that it was a societal problem, one which we experienced – and had to fight against – collectively.

The idea of 'social problems' being presented – or 'framed' – in particular ways is central to Entman's much-cited 1993 work, which attempted to clarify framing paradigms. Entman describes framing as predominantly about selection and salience. News frames typically: 'define a problem'; determine a causal agent or give a causal analysis; make a moral judgement to evaluate cause; and suggest a remedy to treat or fix the problem (Hawley et al., 2017). Entman (1993: 52) also writes that news frames can be examined and identified by 'the presence or absence of certain keywords, stock phrases, stereotyped images, sources of information, and sentences that provide thematically reinforcing clusters of facts or judgements'. Reese (quoted in Carter, 2013: 4) adds social dimension and duration, writing that 'frames are organising principles that are socially shared and persistent over time, that work symbolically to meaningfully structure the social world'. Hawley and her colleagues (2017: 5) propose that the 'success of any particular frame depends on journalists finding sources that will "sponsor" or endorse a frame' and on the frame being 'consistent and credible enough to endure through multiple reiterations and contestation'.

This can be related back to the earlier notion of 'mega cases'. Typically, mega cases are not only prominent at one point in time but are shared and become present and persistent over time, eventually becoming shorthand for everything we think we understand about femicide. In mega cases, the victims' names become so well know that we can refer to them by location, or without a surname, and the inference is understood (Brodie, 2020).

But Booysen's murder was not yet a mega case – although local news coverage of the incident peaked at nearly thirty stories on a single day (11 February 2013). It is possible, probably even likely, that, as with so many other murders, Anene's story would have gradually dropped off the radar – and, indeed, after its initial spike, news coverage of the Bredasdorp killing had started to decline, quite rapidly, to fewer than ten stories a day. But on Valentine's Day 2013, another event happened that changed the trajectory of coverage of Anene's case, when a gun-loving celebrity Paralympian shot his girlfriend, Reeva Steenkamp, to death. Within two days of the killing, coverage of that murder dramatically increased to thirty articles per day, then more than forty. Some newspapers would have three or four stories just on Reeva's murder in the same edition. While the press binged on Reeva and her killer, this had the effect of drowning out coverage of many other femicides. But, with Booysen, it had the opposite effect. In part, this was because the two victims were so different, except for their having being killed by violent men.

Booysen was poor, brown, a foster child who had left school in Grade Seven so she could work and help support her family. Steenkamp was a celebrity law graduate; she was white, beautiful and loved by her family. Where there had been a marginal correspondence between the coverage of New Delhi and Bredasdorp, there was an absolute contrast between Booysen and Steenkamp. And this then became the axis around which media coverage emerged – this tale of two women, completely unalike in dignity. And, as gross over-coverage of Steenkamp's death continued, coverage of Booysen's death and the subsequent trial of her alleged killers was positioned as a counterpoint. In part, this was an expedient attempt by the media to 'prove' that it did not only cover 'beautiful white women'. But it was also a genuine effort by many journalists and editors to maintain what they felt had been the start of something more significant. In the *Cape Times*, journalist Tanya Faber (28 February 2013) wrote a piece titled 'Two Killings Illuminate Two Worlds' in which she commented that, although it was human nature to be 'enthralled' by the circus that had sprung up around coverage of Steenkamp, the pulling of the trigger that had ended Steenkamp's life had also simultaneously ended what she believed was a rare moment of reflection around Booysen's murder, and whether *that* could have been prevented.

What we also see is that, after the middle of February 2013, South Africa's interest in Jyoti Singh declined – even after the trial and conviction of four of the men found guilty of her death. Narratively, of course, the Delhi rape and murder had been eclipsed by the two local cases, and there was no longer a need for an imported metaphor or a stand-in victim who represented a collective or shared idea of violence against women.

Conclusion

This chapter shows that unrelated but thematically resonant local and even global events can directly influence the potential prominence and salience of news reporting on violence against women – and that these events and intersections may have specific and particular resonance within the global south.

In the case of South African teenager Anene Booysen, local coverage of her rape and murder was amplified through its narrative association with the rape and murder of Indian student Jyoti Singh. This can be conceived of as one type of constructive interference pattern, where two stories (one globally important, the other locally resonant) are occurring at similar phases (the narrative framing or schema) and, when they meet, combine to increase their 'crests' or create more prominence. A second type of constructive interference that occurred with the case of Anene Booysen was the killing of Reeva Steenkamp – which, effectively, disrupted what was by then the already declining coverage of Booysen and, rather than cancelling out or simply amplifying coverage of Booysen, created two counterpoints or two different frequencies in the coverage of femicide in South Africa at that point in time.

These concepts – and their reciprocal, potentially negative or destructive interference (which can be seen through the effect of Steenkamp's death on all other femicides; thus, coverage of the celebrity case consumed almost all of the available media space, and directly contributed to a *decrease* in overall coverage of femicide as a result) – offer some important insights into how media functions as both a platform for and a driver of critical mass. Not just the critical mass required for mobilisation but also validation, as a way of legitimising an action or a struggle or even a hashtag.

While digital media studies might look at the frequencies of hashtags and words as proxies for meta narratives and global campaigns, when we look at news media coverage, we see that this is usually driven by individual incidents rather than generic moments or movements. It is obvious that the 'Bravehearts' or 'Damini' or 'Nirbhaya' case, as Singh's murder was referred to before her identity became known, had significant and specific purchase not only in India but also in South Africa, where the figure of a single prominent victim became a powerful local metaphor for the country's own long-standing rape crisis.

This may be important when it comes to understanding how and why certain events, certain incidents, certain victims gain media purchase when others do not. For example, are campaigns like #MeToo driven by the collective or by prominent individual cases – and, to what extent do individual accounts of violence need to be validated or legitimised within a broader schema in order for us to understand and accept them? Further, do 'movements' like #MeToo amplify individual cases or accounts of violence – or do they drown them out?

This final consideration is an important one and deserves more contemplation. Even a cursory survey of media coverage of other femicides at and around the time of Anene Booysen's death show that the amplifying effects of Singh and Steenkamp were not equally distributed – and that in fact the subsequent prominence of Booysen and Steenkamp may, ultimately, even have contributed to reducing or obscuring coverage of other cases and other individuals. While we can praise or acknowledge the importance of global movements and shared metaphors around violence against women, which is indeed a global problem, we should also be aware that the nature of these waves is that only some individuals, some cases, get promoted, while others disappear. In studying these cases, and these movements, we should be cautious not to confuse the prominent cases as being representative of the whole – rather, they may just be representative of the schema but not its components – and we should also be keenly aware that the majority of 'smaller' cases are shut out as a result.

In the case of South Africa, what is clear is that subsequent media coverage of the murders of Anene Booysen and Reeva Steenkamp had their own effects on the number of news reports of other femicides that took place around that time. While there was a brief uptick, in February 2013, in the total number of new femicide cases reported in the press, the following month, March 2013, saw the lowest number of new femicide reports for any of the previous twelve months (Brodie, 2019).

Acknowledgements

The author received funding from Governing Intimacies, funded by the Andrew W. Mellon Foundation.

Notes

1 Mentions of Reeva Steenkamp's murder by her celebrity Paralympian boyfriend received more than 1,827 matches on the Sabinet press clippings service alone. With online and other news sites included, this

figure would be expected to more than double – meaning that Reeva Steenkamp's murder was not only the most-covered death of 2012/13 but also that it received more coverage than all other femicides of that year combined.

2 According to the 2018 report by the United Nations Office on Drugs and Crime on 'Gender-Related Killing of Women and Girls', the 'global rate of female total homicide in 2017 was estimated to be 2.3 per 100,000 female population' (UNODC, 2018). For the 2017/18 year, Africa Check (Wilkinson, 2019) calculated that there were '15.2 murders for every 100,000 adult women in South Africa'.

3 This figure is based on data from 2012/13, supplied by the South African Police Service (SAPS) to the author. Official SAPS figures for 2012/13 for murders of women aged eighteen years and older is 2,266 femicides.

4 According to Wilkinson (2019), 2,930 women aged eighteen years and older were reported murdered to SAPS in 2017/18.

5 'Vienna Declaration on Femicide: Statement submitted by the Academic Council on the United Nations System, a Non-governmental Organization in Consultative Status with the Economic and Social Council', United Nations Commission on Crime Prevention and Criminal Justice, Twenty-second session, Vienna, 22–26 April 2013, p. 2.

6 'Murder' usually means the illegal killing of a person, as opposed to 'homicide', which may mean only the killing of a person. So-called 'legal' killings might include acts of self-defence, acts committed during war, and so on.

7 SAPS personal communication.

References

Abrahams, N., S. Mathews, C. Lombard, L. J. Martin and R. Jewkes. (2017). 'Sexual Homicides in South Africa: A National Cross-Sectional Epidemiological Study of Adult Women and Children', *PLoS One* 12:10, e0186432. https://doi.org/10.1371/journal.pone.0186432.

Abrahams N., S. Mathews, L. J. Martin, C. Lombard and R. Jewkes. (2013). 'Intimate Partner Femicide in South Africa in 1999 and 2009', *PLoS Med* 10:4, e1001412. https://doi.org/10.1371/journal.pmed.1001412.

Brodie, N. (2019). 'Using Mixed-Method Approaches to Provide New Insights into Media Coverage of Femicide', PhD diss., University of the Witwatersrand.

Brodie, N. (2020). *Femicide in South Africa*. Johannesburg: Kwela Books.

Cacciatore, M.A., D. A. Scheufele and S. Iyengar. (2016). 'The End of Framing as we Know it … and the Future of Media Effects', *Mass Communication and Society* 19:1, 7–23.

Carter, M.J. (2013). 'The Hermeneutics Framing: An Examination of the Media's Construction of Reality', *Sage Open* 3:2, 1–12. https://doi.org/10.1177/2158244013487915.

Christie, N. (1986). 'The Ideal Victim', in *From Crime Policy to Victim Policy*, edited by E. A. Fattah, 17–30. London: Palgrave Macmillan.

Entman, R.M. (1993). 'Framing: Towards Clarification of a Fractured Paradigm', *Journal of Communication* 43:4, 51–8.

Ertürk, Y. and B. Purkayastha. (2012). 'Linking Research, Policy and Action: A Look at the Work of the Special Rapporteur on Violence Against Women', *Current Sociology* 60:2, 142–60.

Fairbairn, J. and M. Dawson. (2013). 'Canadian News Coverage of Intimate Partner Homicide: Analyzing Changes Over Time', *Feminist Criminology* 8:3, 147–76.

Gamson, W.A. and A. Modigliani. (1987). 'The Changing Culture of Affirmative Action', in *Research in Political Sociology*, Vol. 3, edited by R. G. Braungart and M. M. Braungart, 137–77. Greenwich, CT: JAI Press.

Gillespie, L.K., T. N. Richards, E. Givens and M. D. Smith. (2013). 'Framing Deadly Domestic Violence: Why the Media's Spin Matters in Newspaper Coverage of Femicide', *Violence against Women* 19:2, 222–44.

Gitlin, T. (1980). *The Whole World is Watching: Mass Media in the Making and Unmaking of the New Left*. Berkeley, CA: University of California Press.

Hawley, E., K. Clifford and C. Konkes. (2017). 'The "Rosie Batty Effect" and the Framing of Family Violence in Australian News Media', *Journalism Studies* 19:15, 2304–23.

Jewkes, Y. (2004). *Media and Crime: Key Approaches to Criminology*, 3rd edition. Newbury Park, CA: Sage Publications.

Khan, S. (2010). '"People Like Us" Are the Only Ones that Bleed', in *Missing: Half the Story, Journalism as if Gender Matters*, edited by S. Kalpana. New Delhi: Zubaan Books. Available at http://asu.thehoot.org/story_popup/reporting-as-if-gender-matters-4710. Accessed 27 October 2021.

Koyana, X. (2013). 'More Arrests Expected in Murder, Rape Case', *Cape Times*, 7 February.

Lindgren, M. and V. Nikolić-Ristanović. (2011). *Crime Victims: International and Serbian Perspective*. Belgrade: Organization for Security and Cooperation in Europe, Mission to Serbia, Law Enforcement Department.

Mason, P. and J. Monckton-Smith. (2008). 'Conflation, Collocation and Confusion: British Press Coverage of the Sexual Murder of Women', *Journalism* 9:6, 691–710.

Mathews, S. (2005). 'Intimate Femicide-Suicide in South Africa: The Epidemiology of Male Suicide Following the Killing of an Intimate Partner', Master's thesis, University of Cape Town.

Mathews, S., N. Abrahams, R. Jewkes, L. J. Martin and C. Lombard. (2013). 'The Epidemiology of Child Homicides in South Africa', *Bulletin of the World Health Organization* 91, 562–8.

Mathews, S., N. Abrahams, L. J. Martin, L. Vetten, L. van der Merwe and R. Jewkes. (2004). *Every Six Hours a Woman is Killed by her Intimate Partner: A National Study of Female Homicide in South Africa*. Policy Brief No. 5. Cape Town: South African Medical Research Council.

Matthes, J. and M. Kohring. (2008). 'The Content Analysis of Media Frames: Toward Improving Reliability and Validity', *Journal of Communication* 58:2, 258–79.

McManus, J. and L. Dorfman. (2003). 'Distracted by Drama: How California Newspapers Portray Intimate Partner Violence', *Berkeley Media Studies Group* 13, 1–24.

McManus, J. and L. Dorfman. (2005). 'Functional Truth or Sexist Distortion? Assessing a Feminist Critique of Intimate Violence Reporting', *Journalism* 6:1, 43–65.

Moody, M.N., B. Dorries and H. Blackwell. (2008). 'The Invisible Damsel: Differences in how National Media Outlets Framed the Coverage of Missing Black and White Women in the Mid-2000s', paper presented at the annual meeting of the International Communication Association, Montreal, Quebec, Canada.

Nikunen, M. (2011). 'Murder-Suicide in the News: Doing the Routine and the Drama', *European Journal of Cultural Studies* 14:1, 81–101.

Paulsen, D.J. (2003). 'Murder in Black and White: The Newspaper Coverage of Homicide in Houston', *Homicide Studies* 7:3, 289–317.

Pollak, J.M., and C. E. Kubrin. (2007). 'Crime in the News: How Crimes, Offenders and Victims are Portrayed in the Media', *Journal of Criminal Justice and Popular Culture* 14:1, 59–83.

Rajab, D. (2013). 'India's Shame is every Nation's Shame', *Star*, 8 January.

Richards, T.N., L. K. Gillespie and M. D. Smith. (2014). 'An Examination of the Media Portrayal of Femicide-Suicides: An Exploratory Frame Analysis', *Feminist Criminology* 9:1, 24–44.

Russell, D.E.H. (2011). '"Femicide" – The Power of a Name', Diana E. H. Russell, PhD, 5 October. www.dianarussell.com/femicide_the_power_of_a_name.html. Accessed 10 December 2018.

Schildkraut, J. and A. M. Donley. (2012). 'Murder in Black: A Media Distortion Analysis of Homicides in Baltimore in 2010', *Homicide Studies* 16:2, 175–96.

Seedat, M. (1999). 'The Construction of Violence in South African Newspapers: Implications for Prevention', *Peace and Conflict: Journal of Peace Psychology* 5:2, 117–35.

Soothill, K., M. Peelo, J. Pearson and B. Francis. (2004). 'The Reporting Trajectories of Top Homicide Cases in the Media: A Case Study of the Times', *Howard Journal of Criminal Justice* 43:1, 1–14.

Taylor, R. (2009). 'Slain and Slandered: A Content Analysis of the Portrayal of Femicide in Crime News', *Homicide Studies* 13:1, 21–49.

Tiegreen, S. and E. Newman. (2009). 'Violence: Comparing Reporting and Reality', Dart Center for Journalism and Trauma, 18 February. https://dartcenter.org/content/violence-comparing-reporting-and-reality. Accessed 10 November 2018.

UNODC (United Nations Office on Drugs and Crime). (2018). *Global Study on Homicide: Gender-Related Killing of Women and Girls*. Vienna: United Nations Office on Drugs and Crime.

Vetten, L. (1995). 'Intimate Femicide', *Agenda* 11:27, 78–80.

Wilkinson, K. (2019). 'Five Facts: Femicide in South Africa', Africa Check, 3 September. https://africacheck.org/reports/five-facts-femicide-in-south-africa/. Accessed May 2021.

Wozniak, J.A. and K. A. McCloskey. (2010). 'Fact or Fiction? Gender Issues Related to Newspaper Reports of Intimate Partner Homicide', *Violence against Women* 16:8, 934–52.

2

Hokkolorob, campus politics and the pre-histories of #MeToo

Paromita Chakravarti and Jhelum Roy

Our current discussions on sexual harassment have become overdetermined by the #MeToo phenomenon. In India, Raya Sarkar's List of sexual harassers in academia has defined the terms of recent feminist debates on sexual harassment in academia.[1] The List and the extensive social media discussions generated by it have shifted our gaze away from other developments in Indian higher education institutions, which in some ways anticipated and set the stage for the List. This chapter examines this 'pre-history' by exploring how the discourse on sexual harassment has been shifting within student politics in India. Using the 2014 Hokkolorob student movement at Jadavpur University (JU), Kolkata, as a case study, the chapter analyses the discursive and ideological changes in how sexual harassment has been framed and how gender and sexuality have been engaged in campus politics over the last decade. It locates these shifts within a larger scenario of changing student demographics, the privatisation of education, increasing state intervention in public universities and funding cuts, amongst other factors.

The question of history

The question of history has been central to discussions of #MeToo, which has been celebrated, exceptionalised and attacked for effecting a discursive rupture in feminist struggles against sexual harassment. An online movement of 'metropolitan' 'cyberfeminists' who used the strategy of anonymously calling out perpetrators appeared to challenge the largely legalistic and institutional modes of countering sexual violence within the Indian women's movement. Queer scholar and activist Ponni Arasu (2017) speaks of #MeToo as a moment of necessary, even beautiful, 'destruction' by 'this large hammer ... destroying everything along the way. Chipping away – or perhaps making a biggish dent in patriarchy. But also destroying the structure we, as feminists, have built to address patriarchy – laws, institutions, languages, relationships, ways of being/working'. This 'destruction', she posits, forces us to contemplate the significance of the event in the history of our movements and think about starting afresh: 'So, what now? ... Where do we go from here?'(Arasu, 2017). On a more affirmative note, Nandita Badami (2017) quotes Rama Lakshmi's description of the List as inaugurating a new moment in the Indian feminist movement.

However, other feminists (Geetha, 2019; John, 2019; Roy, 2017, 2018; Vohra, 2018) have warned us against what might appear as apresentist bias in our evaluation of the #MeToo moment and have reminded us of continuities rather than ruptures in feminist mobilisations against sexual violence. Cautioning against the danger of trying to tell a 'single story' of Indian feminism and dividing feminists into generational binaries, Srila Roy (2017, 2018) has called for a re-evaluation of the Indian women's movement as a site of contradictions, multiple voices and contesting experiences.

But while it may be useful to situate the List in the history of the Indian women's movement, it is also important to contextualise it within the changing dynamics of student politics in Indian higher education institutions and the growing centrality of sexual harassment as an issue around which a new kind of gender and sexual politics is being articulated. The increasing visibility of middle-class, English-speaking, cyber-savvy female students on campuses, their often fraught relationships with the masculinism of established student organisations (usually on the left), the formation of breakaway, independent feminist collectives and their championing of issues of women's access to public spaces and freedom from violence, particularly harassment, has defined the recent political culture of many Indian universities (John, 2019). Referred to as the third (Roy, 2018) or even the fourth wave (Jha and Kurien, 2018) of Indian feminism, sometimes dismissed as 'clicktivists' (White, 2010) who are pursuing a neoliberal agenda out of touch with the Indian women's movement and its large constituency of working class women, these young women, nevertheless, have been putting feminist issues like sexual harassment at the heart of student activism and changing its discourse on Indian campuses. These developments have created a groundswell, a context in which both the Hokkolorob movement and the List had the impact and resonance that they did. This chapter attempts to trace some of these trends in the 2014 JU protests against the harassment of a female student, which grew into one of the largest student mobilisations, both online and offline, and fuelled some of the discursive shifts which later manifested in the controversy around the List. The next section explores the shifting dynamics of setting up sexual harassment policies and institutions in Indian universities and how these created antecedent conditions for the Hokkolorob movement and the List.

Sexual harassment and Indian universities: from *Vishaka* to ICC

Soon after the Supreme Court of India, in the *Vishaka* case in 1997, recognised sexual harassment in the workplace as a civil offence violating the fundamental rights to life, livelihood and equality of women workers (see chapter 9, this volume), many institutions, particularly public universities, created their own policies, procedures and bodies for gender sensitisation and redressal of harm. Several feminist academics helped set up democratic institutions which would be both autonomous of administrative interference and representative, sensitive rather than bureaucratic, to ensure gender justice on campus through due process of a formal enquiry. Their efforts were dedicated towards generating awareness about what constituted harassment and persuading a patriarchal institution to recognise and address it without engaging in protectionism or moral policing (Chakravarti et al., 2008; Menon, 2004). A significant contribution of these anti-sexual harassment committees was their sensitisation work, which effected shifts in ideas of safety, violence and women's sexual agency. Despite their failure to resolve all cases satisfactorily, due to legal and institutional impediments, the lasting legacy of the committees' decade-long work is a constituency of highly conscious and committed students who have taken up the struggle for a gender-just campus. This became evident in the widespread student protests triggered by the 2012 gang rape of the student Jyoti Singh on a Delhi bus, demanding safe and unrestricted freedom (*Bekhauf azadi*) for women to access public spaces without fear of rape and harassment. Students across India mobilised for campaigns such as Take Back the Night (Kolkata), Hyderabad for Feminism, and the 'Why Loiter?' groups (John, 2019; Krishnan, 2020; Phadke et al., 2011; Roy, 2018).

The government responded to the Delhi rape by setting up the Justice Verma Committee, tasked with drafting the Criminal Amendment Act (2013). It also made key recommendations to the Bill on sexual harassment which was later passed as the Sexual Harassment of Women at Workplace (Prevention, Prohibition and Redressal) Act (2013).The University Grants Commission (UGC) set up a task force in 2013 to conduct safety audits at Indian campuses. In their interviews with female students, the task force members found that sexual harassment was pervasive in higher education institutions and that teachers and administrations were either unaware of or insensitive to the need for gender justice. The Jyoti Singh case also produced a backlash, leading college authorities to curtail the rights of female students, impose stricter curfews in their hostels and police their movements, in the name of their safety (John, 2019). It is in this context that the Pinjra Tod (Break the Cage) movement gathered momentum across Delhi campuses, calling for an end to institutional patriarchy and gender discriminatory hostel rules and demanding effective and sensitive anti-harassment institutions (Gilbertson, 2018). Similar autono-mous feminist and queer collectives – the Tata Institute of Social Sciences (TISS) queer collective,[2] Saathi[3] at the Indian Institute of Technology in Bombay (Rosario, 2019) and Dhanak[4] at Jawaharlal Nehru University (JNU) (Ghosh, 2017) – formed on other campuses across India, which were critical not only of institutional poli-cies but also of the organised politics of male-dominated student unions. Even within student organisations, women became increas-ingly vocal, particularly on issues of sexual violence perpetrated by fellow party members. These developments are captured by the Anveshi Research Centre for Women's Studies in Hyderabad in a

2013 broadsheet on 'Sexuality and Harassment: Gender Politics on Campus Today', published after a midnight march in the town to demonstrate against sexual violence and for women's freedom of mobility in response to the Delhi rape (Anveshi, 2013). The articles in the broadsheet focused attention on everyday sexism, institutional patriarchy and violence against women, particularly sexual harassment, which emerged almost as a metonym for gender relationships, intersectional vulnerabilities and privileges of caste, religion, region, community, sexuality and a range of other inequities. Harassment cases became flashpoints reflecting

> concerns and conflicts (of identity/equality and difference, of administrative control and the freedom to grow, of normative privilege and lack, of love and hurt, of friendship and violence ...) ... Addressing these matters has led us into embattled terrains that flank the university today: caste assertions and conflict, 'efficient' hostel administration, 'criminalization' of student politics and, of course, apathy and antipathy towards gender justice. (Sinha and Rasheed, 2013: 2)

At a time when higher education campuses were simmering with anger against systemic apathy towards cases of harassment, the implementation of the Sexual Harassment of Women at Workplace Act (2013), instead of providing an antidote, only compounded the situation further. Under the new law, the democratically elected, feminist-led gender sensitisation and harassment redressal bodies, which had been constituted after the *Vishaka* judgement, were replaced by more bureaucratic internal complaints committees (ICC) nominated by institutional heads. Being nominated and appointed by the administration, rather than elected bodies voted in by the university constituencies of students, teachers and administrative staff, they lacked both autonomy and the confidence of the university community (Menon, 2018). The members of these ICCs, picked for their proximity to the university authorities rather than their experience and expertise in handling women's issues, were found wanting in credibility, contributing to students' disillusionment with their bureaucratic functioning – the ritualistic 'due process'. Increasingly students preferred to register cases with the police rather than lodge complaints with an ICC in which they had little faith. At JU, in recorded conversations, in their demands, in their slogans and posters, students repeatedly expressed their scepticism about the ICC which was seen to be doing to the bidding of the authorities and against the interests of justice.This dissatisfaction kept building up and became evident in highly publicised cases such as the one in which the Delhi police were forced to lodge eight harassment charges against JNU teacher Atul Johri at the insistence of an irate group of students (Menon, 2018; T. W. J. Desk, 2018). The JNU Student Union president, Geeta Kumari, alleged that the ICC, constituted by the university's vice chancellor, 'has no legitimacy among students. No one seems to have any faith in [the] ICC' (Vishwadeepak, 2018). The body, which had previously handled cases of sexism and sexual harassment – the Gender Sensitisation Committee against Sexual Harassment (GSCASH) – had been dissolved by the JNU vice chancellor. As described by a student from the university's School of Social Sciences, the lack of any credible or independent internal redressal system led many students to approach the police directly:

> Earlier, cases were resolved within the campus. GSCASH would have summoned both the sides and examined the case. If someone was found guilty, disciplinary actions such as banning them from classes were taken, but now students do not have any choice except reporting to the police because of the new VC [vice chancellor]. (Vishwadeepak, 2018).

In 2017 JNU teachers also protested the dissolution of the democratically elected GSCASH, seeing it as an attack on gender justice and as part of an ongoing attempt to curtail the space for democratic politics on university campuses and in the country at large (Loomba, 2017).

The right-wing national government under the Bharatiya Janata Party (BJP), which was voted into power in 2014, launched a systematic attack on left-leaning universities, such as the JNU, and sought to muffle voices of political opposition. The UGC, the government body which disburses funds to public universities, was threatening to slash budgets for any centres of learning associated with democratic dissent, such as schools for women's studies. By 2015, students were engaged in the Occupy UGC movement to protest against funding cuts, especially for research fellows (Pisharoty, 2015). At the JU School of Women's Studies, project staff resigned from programmes in anticipation of a curtailment of the activities of the school. Strong feminist institutions thus lost their voice and influence on campuses. Rightist student groups grew in strength and started campaigns to curb women's freedom and sexual agency. Moral police, later known as 'anti-Romeo squads', patrolled campuses to punish couples engaging in intimacy.[5] Presented as part of the BJP manifesto in the Uttar Pradesh state elections in 2015, the activities of these squads were described as being directed towards protecting women from sexual harassment (*Scroll*, 2017).

Even as the spaces opened up by the post-Jyoti Singh rape protests appeared to shrink, young women on and off campus resolutely resisted attempts to silence their dissenting voices. It is against this background that a sexual harassment case triggered one of the largest student mobilisations at Indian universities, lasting for five months and leading finally to the removal of the institution's vice chancellor.

Hokkolorob

On 20 September 2014, the streets of Kolkata were occupied by nearly 20,000 students chanting *hokkolorob* (let there be clamour) and demanding the resignation of the JU vice chancellor for unleashing police brutality on protesting students in campus. The city was abuzz with songs, posters and performances. While the core demand was the vice chancellor's resignation, the incident that initiated the protest was a case of sexual harassment. On 3 September 2014, a first-year history student complained of being molested in the male student hostel during the university fest.[6] Finding all campus toilets locked, she had gone into the hostel to use the facilities, accompanied by her boyfriend who was not a JU student himself but had been invited as judge for one of the music events being staged. As they entered the hostel, the male hostel residents encircled them, harassed the woman and locked up and assaulted her friend. The two were later rescued through the intervention of a senior student. The molested woman posted her experiences on social media. Outraged, the JU student community reached out to her and called a meeting to demand justice. Opinions, however, differed regarding how this was to be achieved – whether to ask for an ICC enquiry or to register a police case. Finally, it was decided that the case should be investigated by the university administration which, despite appeals for a speedy resolution, remained apathetic. The angry students started a sit-in demonstration, which escalated into a decision to *gherao* (detain) university officials. The vice chancellor, anticipating further trouble, called in the police, who brutally beat up the students in the early hours of 17 September 2014. This led to the launch of the Hokkolorob movement with the single agenda of removing the vice chancellor and restoring campus safety. In effect, the initial harassment complaint was forgotten. After the massive rally on 20 September, in which the students were accompanied by large numbers of citizens and support poured in from around the country and the world, the university's chancellor, who was also the governor of the state of West Bengal, met the students, but the vice chancellor remained intransigent. Eventually after several months of protests, sit-ins, marches and hunger strikes, on 12 January 2015 the chief minister of the state intervened to resolve the crisis. In an unprecedented move she arrived on campus and asked the vice chancellor to step down. Irregular as it was, students celebrated the action as marking their eventual victory. Yet, there were many students we interviewed for whom the movement had failed, as it had been unable to secure justice for the molested student. Despite this, the debates on gender, class, violence and sexuality that the Hokkolorob movement generated and the role of the institutional redressal mechanisms it exposed had lasting legacies. It is these discussions and discursive shifts which provide both a context and prehistory for the List.

Anticipating #MeToo

Both in impact and modalities, Hokkolorob anticipated some features of #MeToo and the List. These include: (i) an unprecedented large online mobilisation; (ii) the participation of and leadership by a group of young, middle-class English-speaking 'cyber feminists' (who before then had not had much visibility in JU campus politics, historically defined by left, male-dominated student unions); (iii) debates around the credibility of survivor narratives and related questions of due process; (iv) the failure of formal institutions of redressal and support, and the emergence of an autonomous feminist voice outside the purview of campus electoral politics, unaligned with organised political parties, challenging institutional patriarchies not always in a legible language of due process but more as a disruption or clamour, *kolorob.*

Hokkolorob was one of the first instances of a *campus* sexual harassment case which first broke on social media and for which much of the organising was conducted through Facebook.[7] Initially the mobilisation was not 'political' in a partisan sense and was led by a large number of digitally savvy, English-speaking middle- and upper-middle-class female students of JU's Arts Faculty, akin to a 'fourth wave' of cyberfeminists (Jha and Kurien, 2018). They empathised with the complainant's experience since they had had similar ones themselves. It was their collective outburst which drove the movement forward. Historically these women had never occupied the political centre stage on a campus dominated by left student groups since the late 1970s. The dominant left group on campus, the Students' Federation of India (SFI), is the student wing of the Communist Party of India (Marxist) (CPIM), which derived much of its power from its membership of the Left Front which ruled West Bengal for thirty-four years, from 1977 to 2011. Even after the Left Front was defeated in the 2011 student elections by the Trinamul Congress (TMC), it retained much power and influence at the university, which remains a largely left bastion as far as student politics is concerned. Other progressive and radical-left student groups at JU – like the Forum for Arts Students, the Revolutionary Students Front, the Democratic Students Federation and the All India Students' Association (AISA) – were critical of the CPIM and active in Hokkolorob.[8] But with the exception of AISA and some radical left organisations, these non-SFI left groups were not hospitable to female leaders. In West Bengal, the left political culture, although broadly progressive, has been blind to issues of gender and sexualities, has pitted class against gender and has failed to address patriarchy in society or even within its own organisations

(Loomba, 2019; Ray, 1999; Roy, 2012; Sinha Roy, 2010). Despite a large presence of women in left student organisations, few have been in leadership. There has also been a suspicion of middle-class metropolitan women who dressed or behaved in a particular way.

Madhuja, an erstwhile member of the SFI chapter at JU, pointed out in a personal interview conducted in October 2019 that women from upper-middle-class backgrounds who 'wore jeans, used lipstick and smoked' were not placed in the front line of left political organisations since they were considered too 'bourgeois'. They were considered a liability, with the potential of tarnishing the working-class image of the party and alienating cadres. Madhuja was told, by male party leaders, that while such women were useful for *janasanjog* (public outreach, a euphemism for recruiting new members), they could not be trusted with serious political matters. Hokkolorob, in contrast, had a large presence of, and leadership by, metropolitan, English-speaking, digitally equipped middle- and upper-middle-class women (and men) familiar with a global language of feminism, who had never previously been associated with JU student activism. A section of the media demonised them for their clothes, appearance and class, carrying forward this left legacy.[9] Media interviews with the alleged harassers underlined their rural, impoverished background and how their dreams of a better life were shattered by some middle-class urban girl's wild allegations and her refusal to 'settle the matter amicably': 'One of the two engineering students of Jadavpur University arrested … for allegedly molesting a girl on campus is a fisherman's son with five sisters to look after … Another student … set to join an IT company … fears being … arrested, a prospect that would shatter his dream of giving his ailing parents a better life' (Chowdhury, 2014). This politics of using class to delegitimise the claims of gender justice has been routinely used in Bengal's leftist political culture (Ray, 1999; Roy, 2012).

The credibility of the complainant's narrative was a major point of contention in Hokkolorob. The Faculty of Engineering and Technology Students' Union (FETSU), to which some of the accused male hostel residents were affiliated, issued a leaflet saying that they would support the complainant *if* her complaint was found true, causing outrage among other students, who were upset at the aspersions cast on the complainant' narrative. Some left student organisations went along with their description of the event as a 'misunderstanding' since the male student hostel was a vote bank for them. This was in line with the practice in left parties of treating middle-class women's testimonies of sexual abuse with suspicion (Roy, 2012). Many other students were sceptical because of the political proximity of the complainant's family to the ruling party, the TMC. Dibyokamal, a Hokkolorob student activist, reminisced about this in a personal interview in August 2018: 'Some people said it was a TMC thing, some said she was seeking attention, some said she was making out and got caught so she made up a story to hide it. People found so many reasons to say she was lying.'

Yet a significant section of students, mostly women, supported and believed the complainant. Arguments over the credibility of her narrative caused rifts in student organisations, leading to a realignment in campus politics. Within the Arts Faculty union, members were divided between those who wanted action against the accused based on the complaint, which it considered prima facie evidence, and those who insisted on a 'just and fair enquiry' to first establish the truth of the complaint. While the former put the onus of proof on the accused, the latter demanded a procedural enquiry conducted on the principles of natural justice – due process. The latter argued that 'we have to be neutral, we have to hold our patience, we have to wait for things to be done, we have to wait for a judicial probe, we have to wait for ICC' while the other side asserted 'we want justice right here, right now … [the] punishment of [the] perpetrators … [this side was] good at agitating' (Dibyokamal, personal interview, 2018).

When the students finally decided to have a procedural enquiry, a new crisis started. Doubts were cast on due process and the efficacy of the ICC, in which students were already losing faith. When the three months it had available to conduct its enquiry elapsed, the ICC filed an 'inconclusive report' and requested more time. By this point it had not yet interrogated the prime accused although the police had already arrested him in a case filed by the survivor's father. Even more distressingly, ICC members were allegedly involved in an irregular and even illegal act of threatening and blaming the complainant. Two ICC members visited the complainant's house and questioned her on what she was wearing and whether she was inebriated at the time of the attack, underlining the administration's victim-blaming attitude. The traumatised complainant registered a police complaint against them, and students demanded their removal from and the reconstitution of the ICC with gender-sensitive and legally aware members, including elected student representatives for greater accountability and transparency. In a referendum conducted by the movement, 97 per cent of students voted for the removal of the vice chancellor and 96 per cent voted for a new ICC with elected student members. The administration's refusal to listen to student demands intensified their disillusionment with due process. Parts of the media also shared this disappointment.

In a popular Bengali daily, Swati Bhattacharya wrote that the alleged victim-blaming by two ICC members appeared to be a continuation of older familial and social attitudes:

> For women, complaining about sexual harassment is like walking on broken glass. It is your fault if you cut yourself ... As a young girl complaining to her mother, she has heard, '[he] didn't do it to anybody else, why did he do it to you?' As a college student she was told that complaining was an excuse to increase her marks; at [the] office she was told that complaining was a way to cover up inefficiency ... Now there are committees and commissions, there are women members too, but nothing has changed. (Bhattacharya, 2014)

Significantly, one of the two ICC members who visited the complainant's house taught at the university's prestigious School of Women's Studies; she denied having asked offensive questions. Her colleagues at the school defended her by blaming the victim:

> Of course, the victim may have misunderstood something they [ICC members] said or she may be making it up ... Which bible of gender justice says that victims are incapable of lying? ... They deserve justice nevertheless. And it is because there are committees and laws that today's victims get the public attention they do and indeed deserve ... What shall we do? Do we dissolve all committees and bodies and abolish Women's Studies? (Facebook post, 2014).[10]

This defence foregrounds the problem that the ICC, as constituted under the new law, was throwing up in terms of its autonomy and acceptance by the larger university community. The role of the School of Women's Studies, often shoring up decisions by the administration against student demands for justice, appeared to stand in contrast to its critical, often combative,position vis-à-vis the authorities in earlier years. Before the ICC was formed, the school used to provide support for victims of harassment and a safe platform for feminist organising for women across political affiliations. But once the UGC threatened severe funding cuts from 2014, the school (and other similar centres at other universities) lost its autonomy and its influence on the university administration. The dismay felt by the feminist community, students and civic society at the position taken by these once vanguard JU institutions (Women's Studies and the Sexual Harassment Redressal Cell), built up through years of feminist struggle, anticipated some of the intergenerational tensions and polarisations, the sense of betrayal and the collapse of dialogue and solidarities experienced in the #MeToo and the List moments.

Hokkolorob also anticipated the disillusionment of the List survivors with due process, as it turned away from demanding an ICC enquirywhen it became evident that justice could not be secured for the complainant. It moved into the realm of what was seen not as an organised political response but more as a means of drawing attention to gender injustice by generating clamour. The JU student movement, #MeToo and the List all appear to have used a politics of noise and disruption in their efforts to seek attention and space.

Making noise to claim space: a new feminist politics?

Some accounts of Hokkolorob celebrate the fresh politics manifested in its large-scale online organising, its experimental language of protest drawn from popular youth culture, its pluralistic, inclusive and intersectional vision of gender justice and its non-partisan nature, equally critical of the right-wing central government, the populist state government and the parliamentary left (Dasgupta, 2014; Panjabi, 2015). It represented a spectrum of youth voices, broadly left and feminist – the *kolorob* being expressed both as clamour and polyphony. However, the novelty of the movement's goals and strategies, which seemed contingent and short term, and its leadership drawn from those seen as privileged students, particularly urban middle-class women, triggered debates on the idea of what constituted the legitimately political. Traditional left intellectuals like Ranabir Samaddar (2014) criticised the student movement as 'elitist'. Many saw it as a short-lived movement with limited objectives, started by privileged students who had no coherent ideological stance or class-based political vision for a long-term struggle for social change. The parliamentary left which has dominated West Bengal politics undermined the new gender-based fractious politics of the young, demonstrated in Hokkolorob, nostalgically lamenting the loss of the mass-based class struggles of the 1970s, which glossed over women's issues as being inconsequential. As Uditi Sen (2014) ironically suggests:

> The protesting young today fail to live up to the authentic radicalism of their elders … when student politics, organised under the banner of the organised left[,] took up real issues, such as those of the peasants and workers[,] and did not distract themselves with inequities closer to home. Such as, why women 'comrades' were expected to cook and clean and provide for their men, who led the vanguard. Those indeed were the days of glory … when the leaders … had no answers when a peasant woman asked, '*Why should my comrade beat me at home?*'

Supriya Chaudhuri (2019: 51), while acknowledging that Hokkolorob initiated a fight against male predatory behaviour, everyday sexism and curbs on women's access to the campus, nevertheless rehearses a similar nostalgia for what appears to be the more 'legitimate' realm of international politics, from which contemporary students' movements seem to be dissociated: 'Global issues, such as the wars in Iraq and Syria, refugees and citizenship, or catastrophic climate change, remain largely unaddressed – a strange realisation for my own generation of protestors against the Vietnam War and marchers for nuclear disarmament'. However, Chaudhuri deconstructs this notion of the political by evoking Ranciere's distinction of political speech and noise, demonstrating how the voices of 'women and workers' are denied 'politicity' and relegated to the realm of noise.

But despite the mourning over a lost vision of social transformation, the disruptive noise of a youthful plural politics caught the
imagination of the people – not just students but civil society as
a whole. This new articulation of the political was defined by the
presence and leadership of metropolitan women who were organising online, speaking a language of global feminism and claiming
sexual autonomy and unconditional access to public spaces (Jha
and Kurien, 2018).

This contestation for space is even more acutely felt within public
universities now. As the neoliberal state seeks to 'depoliticise' state-
funded higher education campuses[11] in order to prime them for
privatisation, political parties struggle to retain their fiefdoms and
vote banks, turning campuses into battlegrounds. As one of the
last bastions of affordable, inclusive and equitable quality education, these are also sites of increasing demographic diversity. The
growing presence of women, Dalit students and students from
historically marginalised north-eastern states is challenging the
hegemonies of androcentric, patriarchal and Brahmanical academic
structures on which liberal education has been based. In several
movements, like Pinjra Tod (Break the Cage), female students have
been asserting their right to equal access to libraries, laboratories,
canteens and hostels.[12] Dalit students, too, are battling for access
to institutional spaces. After Hyderabad Central University suspended hostel facilities for Rohith Vemula and four other student
activists of the Ambedkar Students Associations for their alleged
'anti-national' activities, Vemula claimed the site of their protest as
velivada – an embodiment of discrimination. Even after Vemula's
institutional murder, the authorities kept demolishing the *velivada*,
while students kept rebuilding it as a reminder of Dalit exclusion
from university spaces.

The molestation incident which triggered Hokkolorob also
underlined the question of unequal access. Finding no usable public
toilets on campus the complainant went into the men's hostel, an
action which the hostel residents saw as an 'encroachment' of their
private, all male space. The harassment could thus be read as a
reaction to women's assertion of their claim to the campus. The
indifference towards building or maintaining women's toilets highlights how apathetic, even unprepared many of our institutions are

for the growing numbers of women and trans users.[13] Hokkolorob recognised women's collective right to be

> safe to love ... walk ... speak and pee ... on the campus of an edu-
> cational institution. ... Could it possibly be a reflection of the same
> patriarchal mind-set that sees women as not really belonging to
> public spaces? Deserving to be locked up (for their own safety, of
> course) at night? (Sen, 2014).

The privatising of women's bodies and concerns is a strategy to remove them from the sphere of the political, which is marked as public and male. Hokkolorob opened up a space for discussing women's issues in public political discourse in an unprecedented way. This paved the way for the subsequent formation of a feminist students' group on campus called 'Periods', which focussed on the need to bring women's bodies and their natural functions into public and political discourse. Shortly after the Hokkolorob movement, in March 2015, and inspired by Delhi's 'Come See the Blood in my Skirt' campaign, Periods put up anti-patriarchy messages on sanitary napkins ('Pads Against Sexism') and displayed them prominently all over the campus.[14] Pads bearing messages like 'Victim Blaming is Sexual Violence' reminded people of the continuing significance of the sexual harassment issue which had remained unaddressed in the triumphalism surrounding the conclusion of the Hokkolorob movement. Shortly before that, in November 2014, while the Hokkalorob movement was happening, students started the *Hokchumbon* (Kiss of Love) protests at JU, in response to similar protests in Kochi.[15] This involved mass kissing on the streets to reclaim public spaces and free them from moral policing by the right-wing forces of the Sangh Parivar.[16]

The JU event was led by some of the Hokkolorob student activists who were publicly criticised for participating in an event which parts of the media and some intellectuals considered to be morally decadent and frivolous, undermining the Hokkolorob's serious purpose. A well-known editor of a paper sympathetic to the organised left felt that bringing an intimate act into the public domain was inappropriate and said that the Hokchumbon campaign would alienate public sympathy from Hokkolorob and 'disturb its focus'. Responding to the editorial, a Hokkolorob leader who participated in Hokchumban, Arumita, clarified that the protest was not just an exhibitionistic display of kissing – it was a strategy of resisting state repression and moral policing and claiming women's sexual autonomy in public spaces. The Hokchumban campaign was a defiance against Sangh Parivar's moralistic attacks on 'live-in relationships', 'jeans', 'Valentine's Day', 'kissing' – all symbols for women's choice. She clarified that while the Hokchumban protest was not a direct part of Hokkolorob, it was certainly not at odds with its fundamental aims and principles, since Hokkolorob started as a movement against sexual violence, victim-blaming and accusations of immorality raised against the survivor. Hokkolorob resisted police boots with guitar music; Hokchumbon challenged right-wing goons with barricades of love – what was obscene about this? (Mitra, 2015) Responding to comments that Hokchumbon was probably staged to derail and sabotage Hokkolorob, the administration of the Hokkolorob Facebook page said that although the Hokchumbon campaign was not planned as the next step after Hokkolorob, the two movements were connected in their goals of gender equality and resistance to moral policing, which is why perhaps both movements attracted the same people. It was also suggested that rather than focusing on the form of the protest, there was a greater need to think about the reasons that triggered the protest.

The debates generated around the Hokchumbon campaign revived many of the feminist concerns which had taken a back seat in Hokkolorob, once the demand to remove the vice chancellor had superseded the demand for justice for the sexual harassment complainant. The mass kissing event connected the movement with the post-Nirbhaya feminist mobilisations for *bekhauf azadi* (unconditional freedom) in public spaces, as well as with Hokkolorob, #MeToo and the List, which were also demands for space and access – for publicising incidents of institutional and individual abuse that had been silenced.

This politics of clamouring for space, both in Hokkolorob and later, the List was not just a plea for individual justice or for widespread social transformation but more a disruption, a call to change the discursive contours of what was considered legitimate student politics, to place feminist concerns at its heart and change the academic and political culture of higher education institutions which were keeping women and other marginal communities out of the mainstream. Hokkolorob signalled these shifts in campus politics, which were later manifested in the List and allowed it to have the impact it did. Some of these changes continue to have lasting legacies at JU and other institutions.

Legacies and aftermaths

A student activist described Hokkolorob as a movement which became successful exactly at the point that it ceased to be feminist: 'It failed to become the feminist movement it started off as ... the day the police were called in. The contradictions between complainant and her assaulters or between feminism and patriarchy was turned into one between students and authority' (Dibyokamal, personal interview, 2018). Since populist movements need a concrete and common enemy, the state and university administration proved to be much more effective mobilisers of emotions and energy than the abstract idea of patriarchy, whose ubiquitous presence precludes the easy demarcations of 'us' against 'them' needed to sustain movements. Students began asking for the vice chancellor's removal and with this the harassment incident receded into the background. However, the debates generated by the case remained alive – the limits of due process, the need to trust the survivors' narrative and to mobilise against sexist structures which enable harassment rather than focussing on individual complaints. There was sustained rethinking within student groups on systemic patriarchy, masculinist campuses, everyday sexism, feminist praxis and women's marginal roles in student politics. Some of these issues were also raised in the context of the List but discussions became polarised, often reaching a stalemate and endangering feminist friendships and solidarities.

When Hokkolorob started moving away from the harassment case, female students across diverse party affiliations reached out to each other and formed groups like Periods,[17] *Icarus*[18] and Iravan[19] to keep the feminist debate alive. They organised workshops, film shows and talks on gender issues, both during and after Hokkolorob, generating feminist conversations on campus.

The participation, albeit hesitantly, of engineering students in these events was a legacy of the unlikely friendships forged during Hokkolorob between arts students (dominated by middle-class English-speaking women) and engineering students (from the districts and vernacular-medium schools) – a divide which is not just disciplinary but of class, region, caste, gender and politics. It was initially assumed that since the complainant was an arts student and some of the respondents were from the engineering faculty, the latter's union would automatically protect 'their own'. However, FETSU took a much more nuanced stance, gauging the mood on campus and the firm resolve, in particular, of the arts faculty women. FETSU members spoke about how their initial responses had been modified by what they had learnt from 'these girls' about 'gender justice, feminism and patriarchy'. These dialogues led to new alliances and a growing recognition of gender issues in campus politics.[20] The entry of urban, middle-class women, who had earlier shied away from politics, into student organisations also changed perceptions of women's roles in politics. Dibyokamal commented:

> Women's participation in political movements earlier was restricted to following out orders or saying yes to male leaders, arranging fests or writing posters but never deciding what was to be written on the posters. … But during and after Hokkolorob women started yelling at General Body meetings. … [Earlier,] if you were to be taken seriously as a woman, you had to be somewhat masculine … carry yourself in a certain way. … If you showed up in a political meeting ten years ago in JU with red nail polish and a mini skirt, [people] would be like 'What?' But that has changed. … This was [earlier] seen as 'O my God, loose morality women pushing themselves into our working-class students' movements'. But this was a sham because students' movements were not working-class and the women wearing red nail polish were not always upper-class. (Dibyokamal, personal interview, 2018)

The entry of these women ensured that gender equality and women's safety, usable women's toilets and a functioning and credible ICC entered the manifestos of student organisations. Following Hokkolorob, one of the oldest left student outfits, the SFI, accepted the need for internal mechanisms to deal with sexual harassment complaints within the organisation.

But despite attempts to 'accommodate' gender concerns, women are still struggling to be heard in the mainstream student organisations and, in the aftermath of Hokkolorob, have formed breakaway feminist groups such as Women Against Sexual Harassment (WASH),[21] Waqif[22] and the JU Queer Collective.[23] These groups are united by their feminist ideology and their discontent with the organised left and its failure to address gender issues. Recently thirty-one SFI members quit the party over its mishandling of rape allegations against a leader (Mondal, 2020). In their collective resignation letter, they accused the organisation of consistent insensitivity to issues of gender, caste and class (in that order) – the consistent trivialisation of sexual violence against women, the support for leaders who attack feminism in their speeches, and the issuing of diktats against women wearing sleeveless dresses or smoking. Underlining the party's entrenched patriarchy, the letter pointed out that it was inimical to new thinking or revolutionary politics. The letter makes it clear that many of the issues experienced by women in left and Naxalite parties since the 1960s have remained unchanged. But queer and feminist perspectives have increasingly started to challenge traditional leftist positions on gender, sexualities and caste. In 2010, collectives of independent left students from JU and the Presidency University broke away from organised left student organisations and formed their own platforms, collaborating with queer groups particularly from marginal class and caste backgrounds on intersectional issues. It is these queer, feminist and independent left voices which are gradually finding articulation, even setting the political agenda on some West Bengal campuses now (Dutta, 2019).

In Presidency University – the erstwhile Presidency College, a prestigious colonial institution often placed in opposition to the nationalist JU and its long tradition of left politics – women challenged a popular student leader charged with multiple sexual harassment complaints. They mobilised across party lines to demand justice and expose the sexism in progressive political circles. Breaking away from established parties the women contested the elections as independent candidates in 2019. Their electoral promises included an effective Gender Sensitisation Committee Against Sexual Harassment and a queer-, disabled- and eco-friendly campus. In these elections, gender politics became a key issue and organisations competed with each other on their sensitivity to sexual harassment. One campaign leaflet said, rather honestly: 'Is there any organization without sexual harassment complaints? ... In our organization, there have been fewer complaints'.[24]

The increasing focus on sexual harassment on campus, not just as an individual wrong but as a symptom of systemic sexism in academia, appears to be a legacy of the debates around Hokkolorob. Chaudhuri (2019: 56) contends: 'It would be heartening to report that Hokkolorob instituted a lasting change in how sexual harassment is dealt with on campus ... but Jadavpur's own recent history will not bear this out'. Perhaps there is no change in how sexual harassment is 'dealt with' because the administration-nominated ICC has not changed. But there is a definite shift in how harassment is framed in campus politics and how students' understanding of consent, violation and gender justice have altered. Hokkolorob has exposed the patriarchies not only of academic institutions but also of liberal and progressive ideologies and ideologues who uphold them. These cannot be addressed simply by attempting to deliver justice to individual complainants through systems embedded in endemic structural inequities. As Nivedita Menon (2004: 155) said: 'It might be possible then, in the case of sexual violence, to see the feminist project, not as one of "justice" but of "emancipation"'. It is not so much a question of redressing individual complaints of harassment and more one of changing the structures which enables abuse – not due process to fix the patriarchal system but a liberation from it. No longer about this or that case, or about debating strategies and rules to strengthen the ICC, sexual harassment has now become a metonym for institutional exclusion and the thwarting of women's access, voice, participation and representation, which can be addressed by nothing short of a redefinition of academic spaces.

This change in how students frame harassment was evident in the 2017 Sushil Mandi case at JU. A member of a radical left organisation narrated on social media her experience of feeling harassed by a male colleague from another organisation while they were on an election campaign. The post baffled many because it bore no marks of being a proper complaint, demanding neither justice nor punishment. Her account refused to provide empirical detail and only registered a sense of violation at an inappropriate touch. But mostly it was a feminist critique of the masculine culture of left student politics which has been discussed earlier:

> Why is it that I was groped by a member of Radical, time and again, and the only response I got on complaining was 'why didn't you confront him?' ... Why, when I along with feminist allies etched the feminist symbol on one of the posters, did one of the candidates say something [like] 'we can't draw all the random symbols that come to our mind'? Your textbook Maoism does not have place for feminists who dress as they want, who speak their mind and are not humble servants of the communist cause? ... Your politics is an opportunist one that saw in feminism a rising interest of the student body ... There are lecherous misogynists within your organisation who have acted as though my body is accessible by them because I have protested alongside them ... Here's a big 'no' to you all. Maybe the next election, you will see an all-feminist organisation calling you out on the way you have paraded your pseudo feminism to call out the other pseudo leftists. Till then, I will continue being the violent opposition to you from within your circles. (Facebook post, 2017)[25]

Even when an organisational meeting was called to formally hear the complaint, the complainant was reported to have spoken 'for 98% of the time on feminism, providing no details of the incident' (Facebook post, 2017). Clearly all she wanted was an acknowledgement of her sense of violation, but only as a symptom of the structural misogyny that she was exposing, which frustrated those trying to address her complaint. This feminist project of radicalising the common-sensical understanding of harassment as individual harm and seeing it rather as a symptom of structural patriarchy was a lasting legacy of Hokkolorob, which rippled on to #MeToo and the List, all of which, despite failing to ensure justice for the individual complainant(s), redefined the terms of feminist political engagement with institutional sexism. Both Hokkolorob and the List appear to have achieved not so much a better or more efficient system to deal with sexual harassment in academia but rather to have transformed and expanded the ways in which we have so far understood harassment.

Hokkolorob marked several important shifts in Indian student politics. It signalled the growing dissatisfaction, particularly of a section of young middle-class women, many of whom had never participated in campus politics before, with left student organisations and their blindness to questions of gender, sexualities and caste. Politicised through the post-Jyoti Singh protests, they took up issues of equal and free access to public spaces, demanded a feminist understanding of discrimination and sexual harassment and formed their own collectives. Flamboyant, disruptive and noisy, they were inheritors of earlier campaigns like Blank Noise, Pink Chaddi, Why Loiter? and Take Back the Night, which were seeking to effect a discursive shift in how women's safety and freedom were framed (Mitra-Kahn, 2012; Phadke et al., 2011). Although broadly left in their orientation, they were critical of the parliamentary left groups, practised intersectional feminism, steered clear of electoral politics and demanded the recognition of women as equal stakeholders in student politics. Active in the cyberworld and familiar with the language of global feminism, they led movements like Hokkolorob, challenging both the language of the conventional left and that of the more established strands of the Indian women's movement which had negotiated with the law and the state. Mobilising across parties they realised that the political differences between the different shades of left and left-of-centre ideologies which characterise student organisations on campus are less critical than the ones between feminist politics and the masculinist political cultures pervading all parties. This shift in the political ambience of academic campuses brought about by young feminists were legacies of Hokkolorob that set the tone for the List and helped nurture the contemporary non-partisan and intersectional resistance movements led by women – for instance in the anti-Citizen Amendment Act protests in 2019–2020.[26] To mark continuities between these movements is to understand the relevance of earlier mobilisations. As Rupam Islam reminds us in his song celebrating Hokkolorob: *Andoloner shesh thaak-ena, thaake sudhu shuruwat* (Movements have no endings, only beginnings).

Notes

1 In October 2017 Raya Sarkar, a graduate student at the University of California, Davis, compiled a Facebook list of over 60 Indian male academics across 30 top institutions who were named as harassers by survivors of sexual violence. Although very few institutions took action against those named, the List generated intense debates about sexism in academia, the impunity of powerful male academics, particularly in progressive circles, and appropriate feminist responses to issues of harassment.

2 TISS Queer Collective was formed in 2015 as a support group to facilitate conversations on campus. The group lobbied for gender-neutral hostels and gender-neutral toilets.

3 Saathi was founded in 2011 in Indian Institute of Technology (IIT) Bombay as a support group.It also organised gender sensitisation events during orientation for incoming students.

4 Dhanak is a queer collective founded at JNU in 2012. JNU's first queer collective was formed in 2003, but this was forced to conceal its activities in the face of right-wing attacks and the abandonment by left organisations, which had failed to put up a unified resistance.

5 In 2014 students in the English and Foreign Languages University in Hyderabad protested against sexist rules on campus, and students at the Government Maharaja College Chhatarpur were suspended for protesting against moral policing by Hindu outfits at schools and colleges.

6 College fests are annual student union-organised cultural festivals including performances, lectures and competitions.

7 The Hokkolorob Facebook page, having served its purpose, is no longer active.

8 The position of the SFI was a contentious issue among the students who repeatedly called it out for its silence and for having been complicit with the university administration in 2005 when student protestors had faced a similar police attack under CPIM rule. In fact, one of the slogans in the movement was 'Alimuddin Shukiye Kath, Shotru ebar Kalighat', which roughly means that just as Alimuddin, the CPIM headquarters, had once faced the fury of the students so Kalighat, the residence of the state's chief minister, is now their enemy.

9 The newspaper *365 Din*, funded by the Trinamul Congress, ran cover stories on the loose morals of these women, describing them as wearing skimpy clothes and sleeping around. They carried pictures of women

wearing spaghetti-strap tops and of students hugging, talking to each other or sleeping side by side during the protest sit-in as examples of the obscenity that marked JU during the protests. It even carried the picture of a professor with a Mohawk haircut, along with the caption 'Professor Punku' (Screenshot by Rimi Chatterjee, 27 September 2014; the online access to the newspage is no longer active).

10 Name of person withheld for reasons of confidentiality.

11 Since 2006, the implementation of the Lyngdoh Committee recommendations saw first the depoliticisation and later the disbanding of student unions in favour of student councils. Fee hikes, police crackdowns, and the labelling of protesting students and teachers as 'anti-national' and 'urban naxals' have largely shut down dissent (DSU, 2014).

12 Examples are female students' protests at Aligarh Muslim University in November 2014 when they were not allowed to enter the library (Aligargh, 2014); the Pinjra Tod (Break the Cage) movement, which opposed curfews imposed on women's hostels (*Times of India*, 2018); and protests at Banaras Hindu University in September 2017 when a female student, pursued by bike-borne youths outside the university gate at 6 p.m., was warned by the hostel warden not to stay out 'so late' (Akash, 2017).

13 Toilets are a contentious gender issue in India: girls often drop out of school at puberty because there are no clean toilets for changing pads, and women are raped because they have to go out of the house at night to relieve themselves (Singh, 2017). Gender-neutral toilets have been a major demand of trans people. The government has been building toilets for poor women through Swachh Bharat (for critical commentaries of the government's attempts, see Krishnan, 2020; Phadke, 2014).

14 In 2015, Elone, a German student, began the 'Pads Against Sexism' campaign displaying sanitary pads with anti-patriarchal messages. This was taken up by students at Jamia Millia University, Jawaharlal Nehru University, the University of Delhi and Jadavpur University where they faced disciplinary action for displaying pads. A protest march was organised at the University of Delhi under the banner 'Come and See the Blood on My Skirt' (Pasricha, 2015; Vikram et al., 2015). Although labelled 'elitist', the campaign drew inspiration from the Napkin protest in Kerala in 2014 when 15 female employees of Asma Rubber Factory were strip searched after a used pad was found in the toilet (K., 2015).

15 In 2014 after a Malayalam news channel carried a story about a young couple kissing in a Kozhikode cafe, a mob affiliated to Bharatiya Janata Yuva Morcha vandalised the cafe. A public kissing campaign,

Hokchumbon, was organised in Kochi (Tharakan, 2014). Similar protests were organised in Kolkata by JU students (Zee News, 2014) and in Delhi (Press Trust of India, 2014).

16 Sangh Parivar(Sangh family, referring to the Rashtriya Swayamsevak Sangh organisation)is an umbrella term used to refer to Indian right-wingHindu nationalist outfits infamous for engineering pogroms, riots and the demolition of mosques.They are known for their regressive Brahmanical patriarchal views.

17 Periods was formed in 2014 during the Hokkolorob movement, mostly by students from JU's arts faculty as a forum for people to come together, and to hold discussions on issues of gender violence and measures that can be taken in the future to sensitise people and work towards a clearer, fairer understanding of feminism and gender in society.

18 *Icarus* was a small magazine run by the student's union of Jadavpur University's science faculty. It started in 2015 as a space for discussing science and literature and grew as a platform that engaged with gender issues.

19 Iraavan was an initiative by the Forum for Arts Students to hold discussions on issues of gender injustice and violence. It was formed in 2014.

20 After Hokkalorob, FETSU has been organising gender-neutral sports events to create more opportunities for women to participate. In 2019, a deputation of indignant arts faculty students (mostly women) chastised the organisers for failing to understand the difference between gender-neutral and mixed sports events and failing to be disabled- and trans-friendly. The organisers listened carefully and promised to make the suggested changes in future programmes. This willingness to listen is certainly new and an effect of the Hokkalorob conversations.

21 WASH was formed in 2017 when students from JU and the Satyajit Ray Film and Television Institute came together to create a forum to make noise about sexual violence in universities and workplaces.

22 Waqif is a Marxist feminist collective formed as a result of conversations emerging out of the #MeToo movement.

23 Jadavpur University Queer Collective was formed in 2018 as a platform that would act as a support group for queer students on campus and spread awareness on gender sexual minorities.

24 From a leaflet issued by the Independent Consolidation, a non-partisan student organisation, during the 2019 Union elections at Presidency University.

25 We have withheld the name of the person posting so as to protect the identity of the survivor. We are therefore unable to cite this in the reference.

26 Women, more specifically Muslim women, took centre stage in the recent protests against the Citizenship Amendment Act, which changes the very premise of granting citizenship on the basis of religion, akin to the Reich Citizenship Law of 1935 in Nazi Germany. Female students of Jamia Millia Islamia, JNU and Aligarh Muslim University have been at the forefront of these struggles, holding rallies and protest sit-ins and building campus resistance against Hindutva terrorism (BBC, 2020; Bose, 2020; *Outlook*, 2019).

References

Akash, K. (2017). 'BHU Protest: From "Sexist" Rules to Unruly Force and Political Mudslinging', *Business Standard*, 27 September. www.business-standard.com/article/current-affairs/bhu-protest-from-sexist-rules-to-unruly-force-and-political-mudslinging-117092500563_1.html. Accessed 3 February 2020.

Aligargh. (2014). 'AMU in Controversy over Denying Library Access to UG Women', *Outlook*, 11 November. www.outlookindia.com/newswire/story/amu-in-controversy-over-denying-library-access-to-ug-women/867399. Accessed 3 February 2020.

Anveshi (Research Centre for Women's Studies, Hyderabad). (2013). 'Sexuality and Harassment: Gender Politics on Campus Today', *Broadsheet on Contemporary Politics* 2:2&3. www.anveshi.org.in/wp-content/uploads/2013/12/sexuality-and-harassment.pdf. Accessed 3 February 2020.

Arasu, P. (2017). '#WHATNOW', *Kafila*, 31 October. https://kafila.online/2017/10/31/whatnow-ponni/. Accessed 31 January 2020.

Badami, N. (2017). 'Notes on a Feminist Crowdsourced List of Sexual Harassers', Kafila, 3 November. https://kafila.online/2017/11/03/notes-on-a-feminist-crowdsourced-list-of-sexual-harassers-nandita-badami/. Accessed 31 January 2020.

BBC. (2020). 'Shaheen Bagh: The Women Occupying Delhi Street against Citizenship Law'. BBC, 4 January. www.bbc.com/news/world-asia-india-50902909. Accessed 31 January 2020.

Bhattacharya, Swati. (2014). 'Kattababur Committee'. Anandabazar Patrika, 25 September. www.anandabazar.com/editorial/%E0%A6%95%E0%A6%A4–%E0%A6%A4-%E0%A6%AC-%E0%A6%AC-%E0%A6%B0-%E0%A6%95%E0%A6%AE-%E0%A6%9F-1.72244. Accessed 26 May 2020.

Bose, R. (2020). 'A Month after Seelampur-Jaffrabad Violence, Women Claim the Street to Protest against CAA'. News18. www.news18.com/

news/buzz/a-month-after-seelampur-jaffrabad-violence-women-claim-the-streets-to-protest-against-caa-2460039.html. Accessed 31 January 2020.

Chakravarti, U., P. Baxi, S. Bisht and J. Abraham. (2008). 'Reclaiming Spaces: Gender Politics on a University Campus', in *Constellations of Violence: Feminist Interventions in South Asia*, edited by R. Coomaraswamy and N. Perera-Rajasingham, 218–58. Delhi: Women Unlimited.

Chaudhuri, S. (2019). 'On Making Noise: *Hokkolorob* and its Place in Indian Student Movements', *Postcolonial Studies* 22:1, 44–58.

Chowdhury, S. (2014). 'The Nowhere Boys of JU', *Telegraph*, 29 September. www.telegraphindia.com/states/west-bengal/the-nowhere-boys-of-ju/cid/1286830. Accessed 31 January 2020.

Dasgupta, R. (2014). '#Hokkolorob – The Politics of Making Noise', *Kafila*, 29 September. https://kafila.online/2014/09/29/hokkolorob-the-politics-of-making-noise-rajarshi-dasgupta/. Accessed 15 May 2020.

DSU (Democratic Students Union). (2014). 'Why We Must Reject the Lyngdoh Committee Recommendations?' *Companion*, 19 September. https://thecompanion.in/why-we-must-reject-the-lyngdoh-committee-recommendations/. Accessed 3 February 2020.

Dutta, A. (2019). 'Dissenting Differently: Solidarities and Tensions between Student Organizing and Trans-Kothi-Hijra Activism in Eastern India', *South Asia Multidisciplinary Academic Journal* 20. https://doi.org/10.4000/samaj.5210.

Geetha, V. (2019). 'Speaking of Assault: Expressions and their Histories (Wednesday Talk as a Part of Changing India Series delivered on 20 March 2019). 49:15 min. http://eprints.nias.res.in/id/eprint/962. Accessed 31 January 2020.

Ghosh, G. (2017). 'JNU's First Queer Group Didn't Die; It was Forced to Invisibilise Itself', Youth ki Awaaz, 23 February. www.youthkiawaaz.com/2017/02/queer-collectvies-on-jnu-campus/. Accessed 16 May 2020.

Gilbertson, A. (2018). 'Between Inclusivity and Feminist Purism: Young Gender Justice Workers in Post-Nirbhaya Delhi', *Women's Studies International Forum* 67, 1–9.

Jha, S. and A. Kurien. (2018). *New Feminisms in South Asia: Disrupting the Discourse through Social Media, Film, and Literature*. New York: Routledge.

John, M. (2019). 'Sexual Violence 2012–2018 and #MeToo: A Touchstone for the Present', The India Forum. www.theindiaforum.in/article/sexual-violence-2012-2018-and-metoo. Accessed 20 October 2021.

K., J. (2015). 'Strip-Search in Rubber Firm: Exec Flooded with Used Pads', *DNA*, 1 January. www.dnaindia.com/india/report-strip-search-in-rubber-firm-exec-flooded-with-used-pads-2048558. Accessed 3 February 2020.

Krishnan, K. (2020). 'Kavita Krishnan Argues in her New Book that More Autonomy Means more Safety for Women in India', *Scroll*, 27 February. https://scroll.in/article/953499/kavita-krishnan-argues-in-her-new-book-that-more-autonomy-means-more-safety-for-women-in-india. Accessed 18 May 2020.

Loomba, A. (2017). 'The Assault on JNU's Sexual Harassment Panel is yet Another Attack on Democratic Spaces in India', *Scroll*, 23 September. https://scroll.in/article/851616/the-assault-on-jnus-sexual-harassment-panel-is-yet-another-attack-on-democratic-spaces-in-india. Accessed 2 May 2020.

Loomba, A. (2019). *Revolutionary Desires: Women, Communism, and Feminism in India*. New York: Routledge.

Menon, N. (2004). *Recovering Subversion: Feminist Politics Beyond the Law*. New Delhi: Permanent Black, 2004.

Menon, N. (2018). 'Statement by JNU Faculty against Targeting of Complainants of Sexual Harassment by ICC', *Kafila,* 15 December. https://kafila.online/2018/12/15/statement-by-jnu-faculty-against-targeting-of-complainants-of-sexual-harassment-by-icc/. Accessed 18 May 2020.

Mitra, A. (2015). 'Victory for Jadavpur Students' Hokkolorob Struggle', *Liberation* 2015–February. www.cpiml.net/liberation/2015/02/victory-jadavpur-students-hokkolorob-struggle. Accessed 31 January 2020.

Mitra-Kahn, T. (2012). 'Offline Issues, Online Lives? The Emerging Cyberlife of Feminist Politics in Urban India', in *New South Asian Feminisms: Paradoxes and Possibilities*, edited by S. Roy, 108–30. London: Zed Books.

Mondal, P. (2020). '31 Jadavpur University Students Quit SFI, Allege Sexual Abuse', *New Indian Express*, 7 January. www.newindianexpress.com/nation/2020/jan/07/31-jadavpur-university-students-quit-sfi-allege-sexual-abuse-2086122.html. Accessed 16 May 2020.

Outlook. (2019). 'Jamia Girls Lead Anti-CAA Protest'. *Outlook*, 20 December. www.outlookindia.com/newsscroll/jamia-girls-lead-anti-caa-protest/1690461. Accessed 2 May 2020.

Panjabi, K. (2015). 'Hokkolorob: A Hashtag Movement', *Seminar* #674. www.india-seminar.com/2015/674/674_kavita_panjabi.htm. Accessed 2 May 2020.

Pasricha, J. (2015). 'Come and See the Blood on my Skirt: Students Take Menstruation to the Streets', *Feminism in India*, 10 April. https://feminisminindia.com/2015/04/10/come-and-see-the-blood-on-my-skirt-students-take-menstruation-to-the-streets/. Accessed 3 February 2020.

Phadke, S. (2014). 'Better Toilets Won't Solve India's Rape Problem', *Al Jazeera,* 17 June. http://america.aljazeera.com/opinions/2014/6/better-toilets-wontsolveindiasrapeproblem.html. Accessed 18 May 2020.

Phadke, S., Sameera Khan and Shipa Ranade. (2011). *Why Loiter? Women And Risk On Mumbai Streets*. New Delhi: Penguin Books.

Pinjra Tod. (2016). 'No Nation for Women: A Statement by Pinjra Tod', *Kractivist*, 27 February. https://kractivist.org/we-wont-mother-india-nati onalism-cages-women-internationalwomensday/. Accessed 3 February 2020.

Pisharoty, S.B. (2015). 'What Lies Behind the "Occupy UGC" Protest', *Wire*, 24 November. https://thewire.in/education/what-lies-behind-the-occupy-ugc-protest. Accessed 18 May 2020.

Press Trust of India. (2014). '"Kiss of Love" Protesters Hold Demonstration Outside RSS Office in Delhi', *NDTV*, 9 November. www.ndtv.com/ delhi-news/kiss-of-love-protesters-hold-demonstration-outside-rss-of fice-in-delhi-690494. Accessed 3 February 2020.

Ray, R. (1999). *Fields of Protest: Women's Movements in India*. New Delhi: Kali for Women.

Rosario, K. (2019). 'Campus Change-Makers', Hindu, 22 March. www.thehindu.com/news/cities/mumbai/campus-change-makers/ article26602026.ece. Accessed 16 May 2020.

Roy, S. (2012). *Remembering Revolution: Gender, Violence and Subjectivity in India's Naxalbari Movement*. Oxford: Oxford University Press.

Roy, S. (2017). 'Whose Feminism is it Anyway?' *Wire*, 1 November. https:// thewire.in/gender/whose-feminism-anyway. Accessed 3 February 2020

Roy, S. (2018). 'MeToo Is a Crucial Moment to Revisit the History of Indian Feminism', *Economic & Political Weekly* 53:42. www.epw.in/ engage/article/metoo-crucial-moment-revisit-history-indian-feminism. Accessed 3 February 2020

Samaddar, R. (2014). 'Elitist Protest in Jadavpur University', *DNA*, 22 October. www.dnaindia.com/analysis/column-elitist-protest-in-jada vpur-2028218. Accessed 1 February 2020.

Scroll. (2017). 'BJP will Form an Anti-Romeo Squad to Protect Girls in Uttar Pradesh: Amit Shah', *Scroll*, 29 January. https://scroll.in/ latest/828024/bjp-will-form-an-anti-romeo-squad-to-protect-girls-in-uttar-pradesh-amit-shah. Accessed 18 May 2020.

Sen, U. (2014). 'A Reply To Ranabir Samaddar on Jadavpur', *Kafila*, 26 October. https://kafila.online/2014/10/26/a-reply-to-ranabir-samad dar-on-jadavpur-uditi-sen/. Accessed 1 February 2020.

Singh, S.N. (2017). *Toilet: Ek Prem Katha*. 155 min. Viacom 18 Motion Pcitures.

Sinha, M. and A. Rasheed. (2013). 'Editorial: Woman in the City', in 'Sexuality and Harassment: Gender Politics on Campus Today', special issue, *Broadsheet on Contemporary Politics* 2:2&3, 2–3. www. anveshi.org.in/wp-content/uploads/2013/12/sexuality-and-harassment. pdf. Accessed 3 February 2020.

Sinha Roy, Mallarika. (2010). *Gender and Radical Politics in India: Magic Moments of Naxalbari (1967–1975)*. Abingdon: Routledge.

Tharakan, T. (2014). '"Kiss of Love" Protests Rattle Modi's Conservative India', *Reuters*, 10 November. https://in.reuters.com/article/india-kiss ing/kiss-of-love-protests-rattle-modis-conservative-india-idINKCN0IU 1QB20141110. Accessed 3 February 2020.

Times of India. (2018). 'Pinjra Tod Storms Varsity Gate over DU Hostel Curfew Timings', *Times of India*, 8 September. https://timesofindia. indiatimes.com/city/delhi/pinjra-tod-storms-varsity-gate-over-du-hostel-curfew-timings/articleshow/66126109.cms. Accessed 3 February 2020.

T. W. J. Desk. (2018). 'Jawaharlal Nehru University Students Undeterred in Fight against Sexual Harassment by Faculty', *Woke Journal*, 19 March. https://wokejournal.com/2018/03/19/jawaharlal-nehru-univer sity-students-undeterred-in-fight-against-sexual-harassment-by-faculty/. Accessed 18 May 2020.

Vikram, S., R. A. Rahman and D. Sharma. (2015). 'Come and See the Blood on my Skirt: Statement from Organisers', *Kafila,* 8 April. https:// kafila.online/2015/04/08/come-and-see-the-blood-on-my-skirt-state ment-from-organisers/. Accessed 3 February 2020.

Vishwadeepak. (2018). 'JNU Sexual Harassment Case: Atul Johri Arrested, Students Allege ABVP Spreading Lies', *National Herald*, 20 March. www.nationalheraldindia.com/news/jnu-sexual-harassment-case-amid-vcs-silence-students-allege-abvp-to-spread-lies. Accessed 1 February 2020.

Vohra, P. (2018). 'Moments in a Movement', *mid-day.com*, 14 October. www.mid-day.com/articles/moments-in-a-movement/19888199. Accessed 1 February 2020.

White, M. (2010). 'Clicktivism is Ruining Leftist Activism', *Guardian*, 12 August. www.theguardian.com/commentisfree/2010/aug/12/clicktiv ism-ruining-leftist-activism. Accessed 1 February 2020.

Zee News. (2014). 'Kolkata Embraces "Kiss of Love", Says No to Moral Policing', *Zee News*, 5 November. https://zeenews.india.com/ news/west-bengal/kolkata-embraces-kiss-of-love-says-no-to-moral-policing_1494610.html. Accessed 3 February 2020.

3

Reading in-between the sheets: in conversation about SWEAT's #SayHerName

Ntokozo Yingwana and Nosipho Vidima

Sex workers in South Africa are confronted with high levels of violence, which rights groups – in particular the national movement of sex workers called Sisonke, and the Sex Workers Education and Advocacy Taskforce (SWEAT) – argue is the direct result of the criminalisation of the industry. SWEAT is a human rights-based non-governmental organisation, which advocates for the rights of adult, consenting sex workers in the country. Launched in 2016, the SWEAT #SayHerName campaign commemorates and honours womxn[1] sex workers who have violently lost their lives. It further promotes the recognition of sex workers' human rights, including the constitutional rights to healthcare, justice, labour law protection and, of course, freedom from violence. The campaign serves as an important curative in the global feminist discourse on sexual and gender-based violence (SGBV) – such as the #MeToo movement/moment – as it brings to the fore the all too often marginalised voices of African womxn sex workers. In this chapter, former SWEAT Human Rights and Lobbying Officer Nosipho Vidima – engages in a conversation about the #SayHerName campaign with the University of the Witwatersrand researcher Ntokozo Yingwana.

Selling sex in South Africa

Sex work can simply be understood as the exchange of sexual services for some form of monetary value. The Joint United Nations Programme on HIV/AIDS (UNAIDS, 2001: 13) defines sex work as 'any agreement between two or more persons in which the objective is exclusively limited to the sexual act and ends with that, and which involves preliminary negotiations for a price'.

Under Act 23 of the Sexual Offences Act (SOA) of 1957, sex work is fully criminalised in South Africa. This act is a remnant of the apartheid regime's Immorality Act of 1927, which criminalised sexual interactions across racial lines, specifically prohibiting sex between Black (African, Indian and Coloured) and White (Afrikaner and European) people. In 2007, the law was amended to include the purchasing of sex[2] – until then, only the selling of sex had been criminalised. Currently the sex worker, client and anyone living off the earnings of a sex worker are considered criminals. However, since it is difficult to prosecute someone for engaging in sex work (unless caught in the act), authorities tend to rely on entrapment, and municipal by-laws such as loitering, to arrest sex workers (Evans and Walker, 2018).

In 2002 the South African Law Reform Commission (SALRC)[3] embarked on the 'Sexual Offences: Adult Prostitution (Project 107)', a legislative reform process of the country's response to sex work (SALC, 2002). Sex worker activists and civil society organisations submitted recommendations to the Adult Prostitution Discussion Paper, which outlined the implications of full criminalisation, regulation, legalisation and decriminalisation of sex work. When the SALRC finally released its report on the country's proposed regulation of sex work in 2017, it rejected the decriminalisation model (DoJCD, 2017). Instead, the commission suggested either the continuation of the criminalisation of all aspects of sex work or the adoption of partial criminalisation (the so-called 'Swedish Model'). Partial criminalisation sees the client criminalised but not the sex worker. While purported to be in the interest of the sex worker, the 'Swedish Model' is designed to discourage the client or buyer in the hope of diminishing the sex work industry altogether, thus stripping sex workers of their livelihood.

Although sex work is criminalised in the country, it is still widely practised and tolerated by the general public; for while most people deem it immoral for religious or cultural reasons, many still consider it a 'necessary evil' (Gardner, 2009). According to the Quarterly Labour Force Survey (QLFS) of the first quarter of 2021, 'the official unemployment rate increase[ed] by 0.1% of a percentage point from 32.5% in the fourth quarter of 2020 to 32.6% – the highest since the start of the QLFS in 2008'; with about 7.2 million (out of a population of approximately 59.9 million) unemployed during this period (SSA, 2021a). This lack of unemployment is most notable amongst Black African women, whose unemployment rate is at 38.3 per cent, which is about 6 per cent higher than the national average (SSA, 2021b). Therefore, poverty is still highly feminised and racialised in South Africa. It should then be understandable that under such socio-economic conditions many Black African women decide to sell sex as the only (or most) viable option to make a living (Yingwana, 2018).

According to a 2013 estimate of the size of the sex worker population, there are approximately 153,000 sex workers in South Africa, with about 138,000 being women (which amounts to nearly 0.9 per cent of the country's female population), most of whom are Black and around 70 per cent street-based (SANAC, 2013: 4). In addition, according to a 2008 study, sex workers with a primary school education are able to earn nearly six times more selling sex than they would from formal labour, such as domestic work (Gould and Fick, 2008). The same study also notes that, on average, female sex workers support around four dependents, while their male colleagues about two.

SGBV and sex work

South Africa's progressive constitution recognises gender as a social act of expression and upholds the rights of all forms of gender expression.[4] However, the country's rates of SGBV are still among the highest in the world. A 2014 study found that 25.3 per cent of the surveyed women had suffered some form of sexual violence, while 37.4 per cent of the men admitted to having been violent (Vetten, 2014). According to the South Africa Demographic and Health Survey of 2016 (SSA, 2017), one in five (21 per cent) of ever-partnered women aged eighteen years and older reported having experienced domestic violence, while 8 per cent reported having experienced it during the twelve months preceding the study. Moreover, about 6 per cent of ever-partnered women reported they had experienced sexual violence by a partner, with 2 per cent of them having experienced that sexual violence in the previous twelve months (SSA, 2017). It is not known how many sex workers account for the above statistics, but based on another 2017 study, 53.8 per cent of sex workers in Soweto[5] had experienced intimate partner violence in the preceding twelve months (Coetzee et al., 2017). More research is needed on intimate partner violence among sex workers.

Like all forms of SGBV, the atrocities meted out against sex workers are deeply rooted in patriarchy. Sex workers (mostly women) tend to find themselves abused by clients (predominantly men), with few avenues for legal recourse. In addition, when police (also mostly men) enforce criminalisation, there is often a gender bias: they tend to detain the sex worker or ask for sexual favours, while letting the client go on a warning or bribe. A 2012 study by the Women's Legal Centre revealed that 70 per cent of the surveyed sex workers reported having suffered some form of brutality at the hands of the South African Police Service (SAPS) (Manoek, 2012). Therefore, when attempting to address SGBV in sex work, it is important to consider these gender and sexual dynamics that are at play under criminalisation.

In addition, a growing body of research has demonstrated how criminal responses to sex work tend to result in an increase in sex workers' vulnerabilities to rights violations (Richter and Delva, 2011). These include not only SGBV but also interpersonal violence (for example, exploitation by brothel owners and pimps), and structural violence (discrimination within and challenges accessing social services, such as healthcare, legal aid and education; Connelly et al., 2015; Richter and Vearey, 2016; Evans and Walker, 2018). In addition, studies also show that the violence which sex workers experience increases their risk of contracting STIs and HIV (Coetzee et al., 2017). These vulnerabilities, risks and violations are experienced by persons selling sex globally, but particularly in criminalised contexts such as South Africa (Sanders, 2005; Hendriks and Woensdregt, 2018).

In an attempt to humanise sex workers and raise awareness about their deaths, SWEAT and Sisonke launched the #SayHerName campaign in 2016. Since its inception the campaign has produced two reports on the killing of sex workers in the country. According to the first, during the 2014–2017 period, 'SWEAT received reports of 118 women who sell sex and who have died as a result of violence. More than 50 per cent of the deaths reported were as a result of murder' (Manoek, 2017: 6). The second notes that during the 2018–2019 period SWEAT logged 101 deaths of 'womxn' sex workers during this time and again found that nearly half (45 per cent) were probably attributable to murder (Vidima et al., 2020).[6] The following dialogue not only unpacks the campaign and the issues it illuminates, but also hopes to evoke the real human lives behind these overwhelming statistics.

The initial conversation between Vidima and Yingwana took place in 2019 as a session at a two-day workshop, which initiated this book project. In the following months the dialogue continued via telephone calls, emails, WhatsApp voice-notes and a final face-to-face interview on 19 February 2020 (Reef Hotel, Johannesburg). This chapter is the culmination of all these conversations.

Saying her name

Ntokozo Yingwana (NY): What is the #SayHerName campaign about? What inspired its initiation?

Nosipho Vidima (NV): This is how it started: *angithi* [isn't it that][7] every year SWEAT and Sisonke hold events in all provinces in commemoration of the International Day to End Violence Against Sex Workers, which is observed globally by sex worker groups on 17 December. At these events sex workers report deaths of their colleagues that happened during each year and have a moment of silence to remember their lives. This raised concerns for the apparent gap in our services, and the need to collect data about the deaths of sex workers. #SayHerName is actually drawn from an American social movement which seeks to draw attention to the murders of Black women who were dehumanised in the media, and whose deaths received very little attention – being framed in headlines only as 'woman found dead' or 'body found' – and never introduced as a human being whose loss is noted and mourned. So humanising sex workers, and ensuring that violence against sex workers is recognised and justice is sought, is an innovative way of addressing stigma and changing the way police investigate these crimes. It also encourages sex workers to report crimes they experience or witness.

NY: *What is the main purpose of the campaign?*

NV: Simply put, the purpose of our #SayHerName campaign is to bring public awareness to the issues faced by sex workers, to the extent that legal justice will inevitably follow. The campaign exists to honour womxn whose lives have been taken by way of violence. Ultimately it aims to protect and uphold sex workers' human rights.

NY: *How did SWEAT start going about collating these cases?*

NV: In 2014 we started collecting data relating to the deaths of sex workers. We created a report sheet which we shared with our partners. We collected the data in different ways. For instance, our Media Advocacy Officer and Media Liaison Officer pursued cases identified from the media by following up with journalists, as well as individuals identified in the articles – like investigating officers. We received reports from Peer Educators who conduct outreaches in areas where sex workers work, as well as facilitate creative spaces with sex workers.[8] We received reports from SWEAT's National 24/7 Sex worker Helpline. Oh, and, finally, our Human Rights Defenders reported where the deaths of sex workers had taken place.[9]

NY: *What are some of the type of deaths that are highlighted in the first 2017 report?*

NV: The first #SayHerName report analysed the deaths of 118 sex workers from 2014 to 2017. Of the cases we looked at 65 of the womxn were murdered, 26 died from natural causes, 15 were from unknown causes. Less than 12 were from suicide, accidents, peer- and drug-related causes combined. Based on these statistics, it is clear that sex workers are under attack, and are among the most vulnerable populations in South Africa. As stated in that report, 'given the high rates of gender-based violence (GBV) in South Africa, one in five South African women older than 18 has experienced physical violence, sex workers vulnerability to violence is compounded' [Manoek, 2017: 10]. Research shows that in some regions, mortality rates for sex workers are six times the general population [Goodyear and Cusick, 2007]. In the murders that were reported to us, many of the victims had also experienced sexual violence. The study found that clients of sex workers are the main perpetrators of the murders reported. But the findings also seem to suggest that sex workers are at greater risk of intimate partner violence. For instance, the report notes that three sex workers were killed by their partners, and two sex workers committed suicide due to continued violence and abuse at the hands of their partners. As for the brutality in the murders, it was reported that sex workers experienced mutilations, stripping of clothing, burning by acid, stabbing, and there was even one case of decapitation. These details are recorded not for sensational effect but as a means of exemplifying the hatred that people have against sex workers, and how these attitudes are carried out against them in the form of brutal violence.

Intimacy and injury

NY: You and I started this conversation at the Intimacy and Injury workshop last year, which focused on the #MeToo movements in India and here in South Africa. Would you say that SWEAT's #SayHerName campaign also speaks to the global #MeToo campaign or movement?

NV: With #MeToo the most apparent thing to me was how the campaign was centred around women actually speaking up against sexual abuse. You will find that in about 50 per cent of these murders, rapes happened first. Which is why at that workshop abstract *ngathi* [I said] 'Reading In-between the Sheets', because it starts as intimacy. The men are the same men that #MeToo speaks about. It's men who are close to us. It's men who are intimate with us. It's men who society sees as upstanding. There is no certain kind of client, just like there is no kind of perpetrator of rape. *Uyayibo* [you see]? The person who rapes in the township, who is your uncle, your reverend, your *wara-wara* [etc.], is the same person who rapes a sex worker and then murders her.

NY: But isn't sex work meant to be devoid of emotions and intimacy?

NV: *Kaloku,*[10] that's where the intimacy is. *Angithi?* [Isn't it?] The fact that you've allowed this person into your intimate space. And sometimes, *vele* [of course], it's not a client that you're seeing for the first time. Look at Zwelethu Mthethwa, Nokuphila's case. This was not a new client to the area where the sex workers work. This is a known client; they know this car, they know this guy. This is also not a new client for Nokuphila. It's a regular client. It is someone she has allowed a certain kind of intimacy. She knew him – she has been to his house. They had a certain kind of relationship of transactional sex working between them, but I don't think when Nokuphila saw Zwelethu Mthethwa crossing that road she got scared.

'My child liked pink and white flowers.' – Eva Kumalo (mother) (Vidima et al., 2020: 21)

In March 2017, globally acclaimed South African artist Zwelethu Mthethwa was found guilty of murdering 23-year-old Nokuphila Kumalo, who was a sex worker. Caught on CCTV camera, Mthethwa is seen beating and kicking Kumalo to death next to his Porsche, at a street in Woodstock, Cape Town, on 13 April 2013. Upon Mthethwa's sentencing to 18 years in jail, Western Cape High Court Judge Patricia Goliath proclaimed that '[t]he courts need to send a clear message to tackle gender-based violence. The killing of women in general will not be tolerated. The killing of sex workers in particular will not be tolerated' (Etheridge, 2017).

Figure 3.1   Nokuphila Kumalo's Keeping Memory Icon, 2020.

NV: It's a comment you will get with other cases in the #SayHerName campaign, where people are like, 'it was a regular client that used to pick her up. We don't know what happened that day.' Or, 'it's not a regular client for her, but we know this car. We know this guy. We've seen him before.' And there is even this thing of 'we didn't even suspect it, because he has been here. He has treated us nicely. He has paid nicely.'

NY: It seems as if some relationships between sex workers and their clients blur the lines between professionalism and intimacy. How does the campaign deal with this slippage? And how does this influence your interventions?

NV: Issues between clients and sex workers go far beyond the blurring of these lines. Instead, clients tend to cross the lines between assertion and control, between pursuit and obsession, between sex and rape, between rough and abusive. It is important that we aren't misinformed by the way the media portrays cases involving sex workers as they often feature headlines that dehumanise the victim and justify the brutal nature of the violence inflicted upon them. For example, in one case where a sex worker was brutally murdered, the news headline read 'Rough Sex Killed Prostitute', instead of 'name-of-the-murderer Killed Sex Worker'. By using the words like 'prostitute' and 'rough sex' in the headline, a negative connotation is placed on the victim and the focus is turned away from the perpetrator. This kind of misrepresentation is what leads to people believing that violence against sex workers can somehow be accidental or a by-product of 'rough sex'. It is not so much a slippage: clients intentionally and knowingly violate sex workers because they know they are vulnerable and are not likely to report abuse because of the risk of self-incrimination. One of the reasons the #SayHerName campaign was created was to highlight the ways in which things can go terribly wrong when sex workers' boundaries are violated. We have looked at cases where womxn are stalked by clients following an encounter, and due to the criminality and stigma surrounding sex work, perpetrators often do not stop the stalking. It leads to harassment, which can lead to assault, which can ultimately lead to murder. Our intentions as advocates for sex work have always been to emphasise professionalism of the industry, which is why one of our slogans is 'Sex Work Is Work'. But it is difficult to do under the current legal model, because society does not recognise something that is considered criminal as also being professional. Instead, society continues to ignore, exploit and abuse sex workers because they are not protected by the law. In short, our interventions always focus on the decriminalisation of sex work, followed by exposure of the issues faced by sex workers in an attempt to decrease victimisation.

Iconising the memories

NY: The #SayHerName reports have interesting graphics that go along with every person's commemoration. What's that all about?

NV: We call them Keeping Memory Icons. We contact either a friend or a family member of the sex worker that has passed away and ask for their permission to honour the memory of their loved one through the campaign. Of course, we also ask to use the person's real name, and we ask them to tell us something memorable

Figure 3.2 Nontobeko Valencia's Keeping Memory Icon, 2017.

Figure 3.3 Fikile Chauke's Keeping Memory Icon, 2017.

about their character, or what they loved most in their life. So, for instance, if you're looking at Nontobeko Valencia in the first report on page 14, you will see that the icon talks to her character: she was a humble, peaceful and sharing person; while Fikile Chauke's memory icon on the same page is a hand holding the word 'care', because according to her aunt the most loved thing in her life was her kids.

NY: *Speaking of the families and friends of the deceased, how have they responded to your request to have their loved ones' memories honoured? Have there been instances whereby a family has refused?*

NV: Most of the time it is not us approaching the family to let them know that the person who has died was a sex worker. Sometimes they find out through the police. When the police are reporting the murder, they will say that she was found dead this way and is known to be a sex worker, or we suspect that because she was a sex worker a person posing as a client killed her. But in cases where we've met up with the families, sometimes they are very receptive. We send out the Human Rights Defenders who go down there and, in a sensitisation training style, lay out the whole issue and make the family understand sex work in general while humanising the person, and make them realise the conditions that this person had to endure in order to put food on the table. We have cases where Malaika has assisted from beginning to end, and we have had cases where Lisa in East London has assisted through-and-through.[11] We have had cases where Sisonke members have worked with the family to the point of moving a body from one province to another province – this person was known to be a sex worker, and the family found out that they were a sex worker after they died. It is about reconciling the memory of a sex worker and destigmatising her in death. If the family has children that they need to look after, the stigma should not end up with the kids. But there have been a few cases where the family is not receptive at all. I remember at one point in Pietermaritzburg one of the sex workers ... I'm not even sure that her body ended up being picked up from the mortuary because the police had informed the family that this person had died doing sex work. When one of the Sisonke coordinators went to approach the family, they said that they were not willing to have the body buried within the family's fence.[12] They did not want the body next to the family. They did not want any kind of assistance; whether we are saying we are going to be paying half of the burial. They just resisted and said no, they don't even want that body there. They don't recognise that body, they do not recognise her, and they do not understand what she was doing in doing sex work. But obviously you jump through these hurdles and some-times you fight. You explain, you sensitise; and sometimes you win, sometimes you don't. Sometimes you really have to take your losses and move on, because there is nothing much that you can do. But in cases where we do get to sensitise the family, we've seen that we can go back at any time and ask them how the children are doing.

NY: *Do you find that most families already knew or suspected that their loved one was a sex worker, or was it upon their death that they found out? And how do the families feel about the campaign somewhat outing to the public that the person they have just lost was a sex worker?*

NV: I wouldn't say that the campaign actually outs anybody. It actually just brings families, sex workers and sex worker communities closer, because it's more a case of us coming in after the person has been reported dead in a sex work scenario by the police. The work that gets done is for us to leave the family having sensitised them to understanding sex work, so that the stigma does not carry on. So that the person's memory is not tainted by any stigma of sex work. And yes, the names we take and use for icons come from families that we've spoken to, or are in the public arena already, so it's not outing anybody. We do have ethics; where we have been told to not use the name, or we have been told not to give support, we stay away. We do not push it.

NY: *But if someone has never told their family that they sell sex, and did their sex work using a fake name, then perhaps we can assume that even in their death they wouldn't want their family or the public to know what they did for a living. How does SWEAT reconcile or justify saying her name, and telling the world through the #SayHerName campaign that the deceased was a sex worker? How do you navigate those ethics?*

NV: I believe that we're very ethical in our approach of the #SayHerName campaign. What we do is count numbers more than names. Where you see names of people, it's after we've talked to families or close friends. Because of working on the campaign for longer than five years, we've gotten to a point where we actually don't need to use the full name and surname of the person. We use the name only, the date, where they passed away – the area. If a family friend or a family member has talked to us, then we are able to create an iconic memorial for them. But like I said, it's done very ethically. When we're talking about numbers, statistics and data, we reduce it to people that have died through violence. The data is kept very confidential; it is shared with the people that work on the campaign only.

State and public engagement

NY: How have the police and the general public responded to the #SayHerName campaign?

NV: One of the comments was, *angithi* [isn't it], with *u*Nokuphila and with *u*Siam Lee, 'Wow! The guy smells so good' – the police said this. With Siam Lee's case there is even a video of the police. The investigating officer says: 'When we went and arrested him, we found a guy that was in a …' – he says a brand of a suit, these Italian tailored suits. 'And when we arrested him, were putting on handcuffs, he had this expensive aftershave that is just rich monies. And there were these cars in his yard. I thought to myself, "No, this can't be the man!"' [Multimedia LIVE, 2019]. Do you understand what I'm trying to say?

'You do not need to be small. You do not need to be delicate. Be loud, be passionate, because you'll regret minimizing yourself to please others' – Siam Lee (Vidima et al., 2020: 18)

The charred remains of twenty-year-old Siam Lee were found in a sugarcane field by a farmer and his grandson in New Hanover (Durban North), two days after she had been abducted by a former client, businessman Philani Ntuli. On 4 January 2018 Ntuli had taken Lee at gun point from where she worked as 'a sensual masseuse' and forced her into his black Mercedes-Benz Viano.[13] Lee's abduction followed a 'date' with Ntuli, after which she had told her mother that she 'never wanted to see that man again' (Govender, 2019). The family employed a private investigator to help find her. Ntuli's arrest came when an informant provided vital information, including his home address in the leafy suburb of Assagay (Shongweni). During his pre-trial, the court heard that Ntuli had previously raped another sex worker he had also found on the Red Velvet escort site and had a history of being abusive to his former fiancé (Mngadi, 2018). Ntuli died in June 2019 from skin cancer before his trial had officially begun (Wicks, 2019).

Figure 3.4 Siam Lee's Keeping Memory Icon, 2020.

NY: *And this is a police officer?*

NV: This is a police officer!

NY: *Clearly he has enough evidence to have been told, 'come and arrest this man'.*

NV: He has been investigating this case!

NY: *Oh, so he collected his own evidence but, he still can't believe it can be him?*

NV: *Mara* [but], he is expecting a certain type of man to be a rapist; to be someone who would rape, strangle, kill, burn a woman. Even with *um*Mthethwa, one of the leading things that his attorneys would try and bring up *ukuthi* [is that] he is a man of standards, of stature, of dressing good, of looking good, of having good etiquette in society. 'What are they doing even being close to a sex worker?' So they are expecting a *nyaope* boy.[14] It's the same when Karabo was killed here in South Africa. That guy was Forex, he had Armani suits, he had cars. He was – nobody was expecting – he wasn't the first suspect. We had looked somewhere else, because guys in Armani suits don't kill people, don't kill and rape women. *Nowakho angeke umbone ukuthi uyarayipha* [Your one, you will also not be able to see that he rapes].

> 'You know what *u*Karabo would have said if she was here ... "Forgive *u*Sandile. Pray for *u*Sandile"'. – Neo Mohlabane (friend) (*News24*, 2017)
>
> The killing of twenty-two-year-old Karabo Mokoena in 2017 'was used as a symbol of the wider violence faced by women in South Africa' (BBC News, 2018), even leading to the popularisation of the #MenAreTrash campaign in the country (Matebese, 2018). According to Twitter user Lilith's Kin (@bad_bunny97) 'people still don't know that #MenAreTrash is a # born out of a response

to high rates of femicide in SA, specifically sparked off by the murder of Karabo Mokoena'.

Mokoena was stabbed to death and burned by her ex-boyfriend Sandile Mantsoe, on 28 April 2017. However Mantsoe – a married father of three, who was estranged from his wife, and living with Mokoena at the time of the murder – maintained throughout his trial that she had committed suicide by stabbing herself in the neck; that he had merely found Mokoena bled to death at his residential building in affluent Sandton and, fearing the police would blame him, decided to dispose of her body by lacing it with a tyre and setting her alight (*Mail & Guardian*, 2018).

Indeed, CCTV footage from his building shows Mantsoe at the elevators wheeling his trash can at around 10 p.m. that night, driving out of the parking lot and then returning sometime after midnight (in the early hours of 29 April 2017) wearing blue cleaning rubber gloves and carrying a green rubbish bag. A post-mortem failed to deduce what had killed Mokoena as her body was too badly burnt and most of her internal organs were missing (Chabalala, 2018; Maughan 2018).

During the trial, photographs of Mokoena's battered face emerged (Hlatshwayo, 2017), and Mantsoe admitted that their relationship had been 'dramatic and violent at times' (Modise, 2018). On 3 May 2018 he was sentenced to 32 years in prison (Shange, 2018).

Effectiveness of SGBV hashtags

NY: Would you say that campaigns such as #MeToo, #SayHerName and #MenAreTrash still have a role to play in the work of SGBV movements, or have they started to reach a saturation point, which is making them lose their significance? Are these campaigns still effective; do they work?

NV: I don't know. When we say 'do they work?', are they reducing the violence? That we can never really answer. But do they work in terms of advocating and getting the message across? If you're looking at it from a social media point of view, it does make a reach. You do get the message out. But again, it's very nice to have these hashtags, just as it's very nice to have a gender-based violence act,[15] but unless there is implementation that is effective, we're still sitting with the same conversation. When will the government be accountable? And by accountable I mean, when will they stop not just using the hashtags? We see them using the hashtags in their messaging when they are talking about GBV. But the issue still is that a woman can die with a protection order in her hand. So they work in the sense that we get the messaging out. We start seeing the hashtags being popular, not just with women that have faced gender-based violence. We see people realising that gender-based violence is an issue. But it does not necessarily translate to police stations working faster when they get a call for GBV. Yes, it might alert the neighbour: 'a woman is crying, let me call the police'. But until the police are doing their jobs, until the ministry is actually putting in the money for these jobs to be done with efficiency, we are still facing a problem. We need accountability from government departments to start doing the work as well, and not just using the hashtags because they see us using the hashtags.

NY: What shifts or impact has the campaign had on the South African sex work industry; as in, how sex work is seen among the public, or how killings of sex workers are dealt with through the legal system?

NV: By spreading awareness of the violence experienced by sex workers and demanding that these cases not only receive media coverage but are represented accurately, we will hopefully be able to change the public view of sex workers and the industry as a whole. We hope that we can effect change in a way that will ensure that sex work is included in conversations about feminism, labour laws, healthcare, discrimination, motherhood and basic human rights. It is our hope that by putting the spotlight on the past cases of sex workers who have been harmed or murdered, we can decrease the number of future cases. Progress can be seen by the presence of sex work advocacy groups in parliament, the mention of sex worker cases in the media, and the growing presence and support from the public of events and campaigns held for the advancement of sex workers. President Cyril Ramaphosa has publicly addressed the topic of decriminalisation several times and has promised to make strides towards legal reform in terms of decriminalisation and the labour laws surrounding sex work. Unfortunately, there is still a lot of work to be done. In the meantime, sex workers continue to be taken advantage of by clients, police, healthcare providers and anyone else who preys on their vulnerability. Sadly, these stories are often never shared or reported. Social stigma around sex work is still prevalent, leaving many sex workers feeling alienated and discriminated against. It will take a large-scale change for things to really shift in a way that sex workers can feel free and safe in their communities. Decriminalisation will help jumpstart this process.

NY: *What is decriminalisation and how would it help deal with the killing of sex workers?*

NV: Our general understanding is that the decriminalisation of sex work means that there will be labour laws and better unionising of sex workers to work collaboratively. With better labour laws we envision that health and safety measures would be put in establishments where sex workers would be operating. And if they are working in co-ops, and have opened up their own flats, the standards would still apply because as long as it is a working place, and sex work is seen as work, certain standards, principles and procedures need to be applied when conducting sex work within that establishment or within that flat. Also, it means that sex workers in general would be recorded as workers, which means they will be paying tax and therefore known by the state. That would make it easier for us to know if a person is killed because they are a sex worker or while they were doing sex work; rather than [what we have] now when most of the cases we don't even get to find out about because people are not known to be sex workers. If the media is sending out headlines they would say 'woman found dead', but we then have to investigate and most of the time that means that we can't act-up or bring the perpetrators of violence or even murder to justice, even within the Hate Crimes Bill, for instance.[16] But if it was under a database or if sex workers were known and sex work is seen as work, we would be able to seek justice if instances of violence or murder happen. This is why we are asking for the decriminalisation of sex work.

Conclusion

The SWEAT #SayHerName campaign not only promotes the recognition of sex workers' human rights (specifically the right to life and freedom from violence), but also serves as an important curative in the global feminist discourse on SGBV (in particular the #MeToo discussion), as it brings to the fore the all-too-often marginalised voices of African womxn sex workers. And even though campaigns such as #SayHerName, #MenAreTrash and #MeToo may not – in themselves – result in the better implementation of existing SGBV-related policies or the reform of laws that are proving to be harmful to women (for instance, in the form of the decriminalisation of sex work), they certainly still have a powerful role to play, particularly by helping women globally to vocalise, mobilise and organise against SGBV. However, as stressed in this interview, it is not enough to simply have governments appropriating the hashtags for their politicking; accountability is still needed.

Notes

1 While we (the authors) are aware of the queer and feminist debates around the term 'womxn', in this chapter we deploy it to signal the inclusion of all forms of women (i.e. transgender and cisgender), but only where direct reference is made to the #SayHerName campaign and within the conversation itself. See https://yourdaye.com/vitals/cultural-musings/what-is-the-meaning-of-womxn, and www.girlboss.com/read/womxn-meaning. Accessed 2 June 2021.
2 Republic of South Africa, Criminal Law (Sexual Offences and Related Matters) Amendment Act, No. 32, 2007.
3 At the time (2002) it was referred to as the South African Law Commission (SALC).
4 See Section 9 (3) of the Constitution of the Republic of South Africa, 1996.

5 Soweto is a township in Johannesburg with an estimated population of about 1.57 million Black Africans. Its name is an English syllabic abbreviation for South Western Townships.

6 While the 2018/19 #SayHerName report makes reference to 'female and transwomxn' sex workers, the upcoming new edition will make use of the more inclusive term 'womxn'.

7 Where possible, words in isiZulu, isiXhosa (two of the eleven South African official languages) and colloquial language are translated into English.

8 Creative Spaces are support groups for sex workers that are organised by SWEAT and Sisonke. In these spaces sex workers collectively discuss their challenges, means of overcoming them, and are trained on how to access their health and legal rights.

9 Human Rights Defenders are sex workers who SWEAT has trained in human rights, in order to further empower their peers and assist them in accessing social and legal services.

10 *Kaloku* in English can loosely be translated to 'because', but its proper meaning is 'only possible in speech contexts' (Mini, 1995: 46).

11 Not their real names.

12 Traditionally South African farmers tended to bury family members on their farms. Farm workers and their families – who would have also lived with them on the farm – were also often buried on the farm. While this practice has died out in most farming communities, for cultural and religious reasons some families still bury their loved ones within their home yards (Agri Western Cape, 2015).

13 Lee was believed to have also been a sex worker, as she had featured in an advert on the Red Velvet adult website, alongside her mother, as 'Student in Training' (Mngadi, 2018).

14 *Nyaope* is a highly addictive narcotic substance, typically comprising heroin, marijuana and other substances, such as antiretrovirals and rat poison, which is smoked as a recreational drug in some parts of South Africa.

15 Vidima here refers to the Domestic Violence Act No 116 of 1998: www. gov.za/documents/domestic-violence-act (accessed 31 May 2021).

16 Here Vidima is referring to the Prevention and Combating of Hate Crimes and Hate Speech Bill B9-2018: www.gov.za/sites/default/files/ gcis_document/201804/b9-2018preventioncombatingofhatecrimeshat espeecha.pdf (accessed 31 May 2021).

References

Agri Western Cape. (2015). 'Protocol: Burial on Farms'. www.growing-greatness.co.za/wp-content/uploads/2015/10/Protocol-on-farm-burials.pdf. Accessed 22 July 2020.

BBC News. (2018). 'South Africa's Sandile Mantsoe Guilty of Karabo Mokoena Murder', *BBC News*, 2 May. www.bbc.com/news/world-africa-43979207. Accessed 11 April 2020.

Chabalala, J. (2018). '"I Put Petrol on Her and Walked Away" – Court Hears in Karabo Mokoena Murder Trial', *News 24*, 25 April. www.news24.com/SouthAfrica/News/i-put-petrol-on-her-and-walked-away-court-hears-in-karabo-mokoena-murder-trial-20180425. Accessed 11 April 2020.

Coetzee, J., R. Jewkes and G. E. Gray. (2017). 'Cross-Sectional Study of Female Sex Workers in Soweto, South Africa: Factors associated with HIV Infection', *PloS ONE* 12:10). https://doi.org/10.1371/journal.pone.0184775.

Connelly, L., L. Jarvis-King and G. Ahearne (2015). 'Editorial – Blurred Lines: The Contested Nature of Sex Work in a Changing Social Landscape', *Graduate Journal of Social Science* 11:2, 4–20.

DoJCD (Department of Justice and Constitutional Development, Republic of South Africa). (2017). 'MediaBriefing: Report on Sexual Offences: Adult Prostitution'. www.justice.gov.za/m_statements/2017/20170526-SALRC-Report.html. Accessed 1 April 2020.

Etheridge, J. (2017). 'Artist Zwelethu Mthethwa gets 18 Years in Jail for Brutally Kicking Sex Worker to Death', *News24*, 7 June. www.news24.com/SouthAfrica/News/artist-zwelethu-mthethwa-gets-18-years-in-jail-for-brutally-kicking-sex-worker-to-death-20170607. Accessed 1 April 2020.

Evans, D. and R. Walker. (2018). *The Policing of Sex Work in South Africa: A Research Report on the Human Rights Challenges across Two South African Provinces.* Sonke Gender Justice and SWEAT (Sex Workers Education and Advocacy Taskforce). https://genderjustice.org.za/publication/the-policing-of-sex-work-in-south-africa/. Accessed 9 December 2019.

Gardner, J. (2009). 'Criminalising the Act of Sex: Attitudes to Adult Commercial Sex Work in South Africa', in *The Prize and the Price: Shaping Sexualities in South Africa*, edited by M. Steyn and M. van Zyl, 329–340. Human Sciences Research Council Press.

Goodyear, M.D.E. and L. Cusick. (2007). 'Protection of Sex Workers', *BMJ* 334:7584, 52–3.

Gould, C. and N. Fick. (2008). *Selling Sex in Cape Town: Sex Work and Human Trafficking in a South African City*. Pretoria: Institute for Security Studies.

Govender, S. (2019). '"Nobody can Murder You, Rape You and Burn Your Body": A Visual Investigation into the Siam Lee Tragedy', *TimesLIVE*, 24 June. www.timeslive.co.za/news/south-africa/2019-06-24-watch-nobody-can-murder-you-rape-you-and-burn-your-body-a-visual-investigation-into-the-siam-lee-tragedy/. Accessed 5 April.

Hendriks, S. and L. Woensdregt. (2018). *Sex Work and Violence in Southern Africa: A Participatory Research in Botswana, Mozambique, Namibia, South Africa and Zimbabwe*. Aidsfonds. https://aidsfonds.org/assets/resource/file/Research%20report%20Handsoff%20Southern%20Africa.pdf. Accessed 2 June 2021.

Hlatshwayo, M. (2017). 'Bubbly Karabo Died on her Journey to Fighting Women Abuse', *Soweto Urban*, 17 May. https://sowetourban.co.za/36996/bubbly-karabo-died-journey-fighting-women-abuse/. Accessed 11 April 2020.

Mail & Guardian. (2018). '"I Thought No One Would Believe Me" – Karabo Mokoena Murder Accused', *Mail & Guardian*, 19 April. https://mg.co.za/article/2018-04-19-i-thought-no-one-would-believe-me-karabo-mokoena-murder-accused/. Accessed 11 April 2020.

Manoek, S. (2012). *'Stop Harassing Us! Tackle Real Crime!' A Report on Human Rights Violations by Police against Sex Workers in South Africa*. Women's Legal Centre, Sisonke and the Sex Workers Education and Advocacy Taskforce (SWEAT). http://wlce.co.za/wp-content/uploads/2017/02/210812–FINAL-WEB-version.pdf. Accessed 31 March 2020.

Manoek, S. (2017). *#SayHerName Report 2014–2017*. Cape Town: Sex Workers Education and Advocacy Taskforce (SWEAT). www.sweat.org.za/wp-content/uploads/2019/08/Sweat-Say-Her-Name-Report_HI-RES.pdf. Accessed 31 March 2020.

Matebese, S. (2018). '#MenAreTrash: What is this Movement really About?' Rhodes University, 26 July. www.ru.ac.za/criticalstudies/latestnews/menaretrashwhatisthismovementreallyabout.html. Accessed 11 April 2020.

Maughan, K. (2018). '"Her Heart was Missing": Cop still Believes Karabo Mokoena's Death a "Ritual Murder"', *TimesLIVE*, 9 May. www.timeslive.co.za/news/south-africa/2018-05-09-watch-her-heart-was-missing-cop-still-believes-karabo-mokoenas-death-a-ritual-murder/. Accessed 11 April 2020.

Mini, B.M. (1995). 'Lexicographical Problems in isiXhosa', *Lexikos* 5:5B, 40–56. www.ajol.info/index.php/lex/article/download/146398/135921/0. Accessed 1 April 2020.

Mngadi, M. (2018). 'Siam Lee Murder: Accused Got her Contact Details from an "Adult Website"', *News24*, 14 November. www.news24.com/ SouthAfrica/News/siam-lee-murder-accused-got-her-contact-details-from-an-adult-website-20181114. Accessed 5 April 2020.

Modise, K. (2018). 'Court Told Mantsoe and Mokoena's Relationship Was "Dramatic and Violent at Times"', *Eyewitness News*, 19 April. https:// ewn.co.za/2018/04/19/court-told-mantsoe-and-mokoena-s-relationship-was-dramatic-and-violent-at-times. Accessed 11 April 2020.

Multimedia LIVE. (2019). 'How a Gifted Young Girl was Kidnapped and Murdered: The Siam Lee Story', *Multimedia Live*, 24 June, 10:21 min. https://youtu.be/rWN_qK0oHU0. Accessed 22 July.

News24. (2017). '"Forgive Sandile, Pray for Him" says Karabo Mokoena's Close Friend', *News24 Video*, 18 May, 2:42 min. https://youtu.be/G_sHaJRAkbQ. Accessed 22 July.

Peters, D. and Z. Wasserman. (2018). *'What Happened to the Evidence?' A Critical Analysis of the South African Law Reform Commission's Report on 'Adult Prostitution (Project 107)' and Law Reform Options for South Africa*. Cape Town: Asijiki Coalition. https://asijiki.org.za/wp-content/ uploads/Refutation-Report-WEB.pdf. Accessed 2 June 2021.

Richter, M. and W. Delva. (2011). *'Maybe it Will be Better once this World Cup has Passed' – Research Findings Regarding the Impact of the 2010 Soccer World Cup on Sex Work in South Africa*. Pretoria: United Nations Population Fund (UNFPA) and SWEAT.

Richter, M. and J. Vearey. (2016). 'Migration and Sex Work in South Africa: Key Concerns for Gender and Health', in *Gender and Health Handbook*, edited by J. Gideon, 268–82. London: Edward Elgar Publishing.

SALC (South African Law Commission). (2002). *Media statement by the South African Law Commission concerning its investigation on Sexual Offences: Adult Prostitution (Project 107)*. www.justice.gov.za/salrc/ media/2002_pr107.pdf. Accessed 31 May 2021.

SANAC (South African National AIDS Council). (2013). *Estimating the Size of the Sex Worker Population in South Africa*. SWEAT and SANAC. www.sanacws.org.za/en/resource-centre/download/51fa5c1716341– sex-workers-size-estimation-2013-pdf. Accessed 8 December 2019.

Sanders, T. (2005). *Sex Work: A Risky Business*. Cullompton: Willan Publishing.

Shange, N. (2018). 'Sandile Mantsoe Sentenced to 32 Years in Jail for Karabo's Murder', *TimesLIVE*, 3 May. www.timeslive.co.za/news/south-africa/2018-05-03-sandile-montsoe-sentenced-to-more-than-3o-years-in-jail-for-karabo-mokoenas-murder/. Accessed 13 April 2020.

SSA (Statistics South Africa). (2017). *South Africa Demographic and Health Survey 2016: Key Indicator Report, Statistics South Africa*. www.

statssa.gov.za/publications/Report%2003-00-09/Report%2003-00-092016.pdf. Accessed 3 February 2020.

SSA (Statistics South Africa). (2021a). *Media Release: Quarterly Labour Force Survey (QLFS) – Q1: 2021*. www.statssa.gov.za/publicati ons/P0211/Media%20release%20QLFS%20Q1%202021.pdf. Accessed 1 June 2021.

SSA (Statistics South Africa). (2021b). *Statistical Release: P0211 Quarterly Labour Force Survey – Q1: 2021*. www.statssa.gov.za/publications/P0211/P02111stQuarter2021.pdf. Accessed 1 June 2021.

UNAIDS (Joint United Nations Programme on HIV/AIDS). (2001). *Regional Workshop on Situation Analysis of Sex Work in West and Central Africa, Abidjan, Côte d'Ivoire, 21–24 March 2000*. Abidjan: UNAIDS Inter-Country Team for West and Central Africa. www.who.int/hiv/topics/vct/sw_toolkit/workshop_on_situation_analysis_sex_work.pdf. Accessed 8 December 2019.

Vetten, L. (2014). *Rape and Other Forms of Sexual Violence in South Africa*. Policy Brief 72. Pretoria: Institute for Security Studies.

Vidima, N., R. Tenga and M. Richter. (2020). *#SayHerName: Female and Transwomxn Sex Workers Deaths in South Africa: 2018–2019*. Cape Town: Sex Workers Education and Advocacy Taskforce (SWEAT).

Wicks, J. (2019). 'Siam Lee Murder, Rape Accused Dies before Trial', *TimesLIVE*, 21 June. www.timeslive.co.za/news/south-africa/2019-06-21-siam-lee-murder-rape-accused-dies-before-trial/?fbclid=IwAR2x7nbAwa3HolMYEN9P00fmZCOXUN_i8iR1OMl23sRwPh2jFxxoSOFB8xs. Accessed 5 April 2020.

Yingwana, N. (2018). 'South Africa', in *Sex Workers Organising for Change: Self-Representation, Community Mobilisation, and Working Conditions*, by Global Alliance Against Traffic in Women (GAATW), 196–229. Bangkok: GAATW.

Reflection: 'When will the state be #MeToo'd?'

Jyotsna Siddharth

The discourse on #MeToo in India changed a few things. It gave upper-caste, upper-class, cis women in India a moment to express their agency to bring public attention to their sexual offender. It created, for them, a space to publicly express their anger offering a moment of celebration for the contemporary feminist movement. This moment may be seen to have brought some respite to this subset of women who experienced sexual harassment and violation. One might argue that this moment was useful but partial.

The LoSHA (List of Sexual Harassers in Academia) – a list of male academics accused of sexual harassment (discussed at length in other chapters in this volume) marked the beginnings of cancel culture within Indian feminism. Cancel culture, on which the #MeToo movement was built, made it almost impossible to ask difficult questions. Individuals, including feminists, were put on the spot and asked to pick sides. It became possible to 'call out' a person seen to be 'inadequately woke' at any given time, online or in person. Justice was sought through social media. It took individuals from their sociality and singled them out for public censure without creating a deeper sense of context, degree and intensity of sexual violations. A point of no return was established which allowed for no greys. Linear arguments pursued linear justice in a traditional, judgemental, casteist, sexist, homophobic and elitist Indian society. Vikram Aditya Sahai articulates the '#MeToo conversation as the most heterosexual conversation in the world – in which women are the subservient, sad, little victims and men are these dominant, abusive, harassing people – what you have done is made it impossible for any other frame of power to be acknowledged at all.' For Sahai, 'the movement has completely overlooked realities including caste, class, sexuality, ability, and age'.[1]

Even as it was limited to upper-caste, upper-class, cis women, the #MeToo discourse also shrank the focus on sexual violence, abuse and caste-based violence to the individual accused without reflecting on larger institutions and structures, especially the role of state.

The #MeToo discourse in India was riddled with amnesia – the criticality of state and its accountability to restore justice was forgotten. Individualistic assertions, which could with collective effort have been collaborative to amplify feminist voices that centred women, queer and trans people especially, from disadvantaged positions, were unable to do so and remained myopic in their demands. The Indian state in the #MeToo discourse was criticised for denying 'justice' in a court of law but never seen as a serial sexual offender itself. This overdependence and over reliance on the hetero patriarchal Brahmanical state to provide justice erased possibilities for indicting the state itself. There is a need to closely examine the brutalities meted out by the heteropatriarchal Brahmanical Indian state in nexus with the police, moneyed corporations, technocrats, and the political machinery and expose the state's role in sexual and caste-based violence against women, queer and trans people.

The state only performs justice: to pronounce a decree upon the sexual violator is designed to absolve the state of its complicity in the very violence that it intermittently pretends to prosecute. How did we forget to #MeToo the Indian state? What happens when the state manifests the tendencies of a sexual offender? Whom do we seek justice from when the putative purveyor of justice is the violator, oppressor and perpetrator? It is imperative, therefore, to expand the #MeToo discourse and interventions to foreground the role of the Indian state as the biggest sexual offender and abuser, as evident in historical and contemporary records.

One finds several testimonies of sexual violations of queer, trans and also women from disadvantaged castes and religious minorities, which record their reluctance to approach police stations or register First Information Reports. As significant as it is to challenge violations in personal and intimate spaces, it is crucial to contextualise them in a larger socio-political dynamic of power and privileges at play.

The experience of regions in India such as Kashmir, North East and Chhattisgarh has consistently shown the ugly face of the Indian state, which acts hand-in-glove with the police when it comes to sexually violating bodies of queer, trans and women from non-privileged backgrounds both in custody and outside. In spite of significant evidence, existing narratives of people's belonging to minority sections, and living bodies that carry the trauma, #MeToo has not picked up on voices against the Indian state.

In 2004, the state of Manipur became the site for an extraordinary abuse of the Armed Forces Special Powers Act (1958). As detailed in a Human Rights Watch report, a 32-year-old woman, Thangjam Manorama Devi, was brutally raped, tortured and executed by paramilitary personnel. In its ruling on the case, the Supreme Court wrote that 'a sex worker cannot file a case alleging rape if her customers refused to pay her. A bench of judges stated that while evidence submitted by a woman alleging sexual assault should be given significance, it cannot be regarded as the "gospel truth."'[2]

In another similar account, the Vakapalli gang-rape case was registered under the Prevention of Atrocities (Scheduled Caste and Scheduled Tribes) Act (1989), after 12 years. The article in *The Hindu* newspaper carried the news: 'on August 20, 2007, 11 Adivasi women of Vakapalli village in Nurmati Panchayat of G. Madugula mandal in Visakhapatnam Agency were allegedly gang-raped by 21 personnel of AP Special Police, who were on combing operation in the naxal-affected areas. Of the 21 accused, 13 were implicated in the case.'[3] Twelve years of consistent efforts on the part of these eleven brave Adivasi women (two of whom are now dead) brought the case to the final trial stage. These twelve years of sorrow, trauma and pain cannot be compensated for even if the judiciary gave a verdict in their favour. This active silencing of the assertions of Adivasi women, battling state-sponsored sexual violence and negligence, found no recognition in the #MeToo discourse either.

This is where we might find some hope in Dalit women's assertions, inevitably located at the margins, made, if at all, of the #MeToo conversations. In 1981, Phoolan Devi, a Dalit woman shot 22 Rajput men in Behmai Massacre in Uttar Pradesh for months of gang raping her. Sampat Pal belongs to Gulabi Gang, a vigilante group that continues to fight abuse and domestic violence against women in Banda district of Uttar Pradesh. In 2005, Anita Bharti and Rajni Tilak (my aunt and mother), both prominent names in anti-caste and feminist movements, took it upon themselves to barge into the launch of Dharamveer Bharti's[4] new book, *Premchand Samant ka Munshi* (Premchand – a feudal lord) at Rajendra Bhawan, New Delhi – one of many who regularly insulted and demeaned them and other women in their writings – and flung slippers at them, to mark their resistance.[5] Such assertions, along with everyday resistance of trans and queer women who do not sit around waiting to receive 'justice' from the sexual oppressor, mark moments of transformation in feminist activism and hopefully, in the eventual discourse. A lot of internal as well as external work needs to be done within the Indian activist and feminist spaces.

We must engage with the social, cultural norms and taboos that provide immunity to the Indian state. We need to join hands with people from minority and marginalised backgrounds – our demands and assertions cannot be solitary, individualistic and myopic in the face of the biggest violator of human rights and dignity in India. We must acknowledge the failure of mainstream assertions in forming collective resistance with non-normative communities against the Indian state. After decades of silencing, an anti-caste discourse has begun to make waves, the acknowledgement of trans people as humans with rights is fairly recent but we are far from achieving any kind of intersectionality in India.

Living as a minority in India has affirmed to me that justice is rarely offered easily, but must be demanded, sometimes snatched. Every day, new modes of survival are invented and imagined to negotiate with the precarities of caste system, misogyny, transphobia and religion-based apathy while also navigating intimate-partner violence, and the state's oppression. They are the outcastes amongst the outcastes, located at the margins of the margins, who rarely claim #MeToo. These women, these queer bodies that are alive today are fighters – each body that couldn't be killed, raped or murdered is the repository of lessons in resistance and hope.

If the #MeToo movement has failed to focus its attention upon the violence of the state, that task must be taken up by those of us who suffer and resist its violence.

Notes

1 Nandita Singh (2019) 'Hey #MeToo activists, there's a lot you don't know about sex and assault in India', *The Print*, 8 February. https://theprint.in/features/hey-metoo-activists-theres-a-lot-you-dont-know-about-sex-consent-and-assault-in-india/189485/. Accessed 30 November 2020.

2 Deya Bhattacharya (2016) 'SC ruling that sex workers can't cry rape is dictated by morality not legal reasoning', *First Post*, 13 October. www.firstpost.com/india/sc-ruling-that-sex-workers-cant-cry-rape-is-dictated-by-morality-not-legal-reasoning-3050044.html. Accessed 30 November 2020.

3 *The Hindu* (2019) 'Trial in Vakapalli case begins', *The Hindu*, 6 February. www.thehindu.com/news/national/andhra-pradesh/trial-in-vakapalli-case-begins/article26188072.ece. Accessed 30 November 2020.

4 A well-known Dalit Hindi critic and a civil servant.

5 Anita Bharti (2011) 'दलित महिला विरोधी डॉ. धर्मवीर?' (Is Dr. Dharamveer anti Dalit women?) http://oppressedworld.blogspot.com/2011/04/blog-post_28.html. Accessed 26 June, 2021.

Part II

#MeToo's silences

4

Moments of erasure of the testimonies of sexual violence against Dalit women

Rupali Bansode

This chapter attempts to bring into question caste-based sexual violence in India, generally understood as the violence committed by upper-caste men against lower-caste women, politically and socially identified as Dalit women. It builds on the case study of Satyabhama,[1] a Dalit victim of caste-based sexual violence, reported from the Chakur Taluka (administrative district) of the Latur district of the Indian state of Maharashtra, to highlight the moments in which Dalit women's testimonies of sexual violence get sidelined, erased or concealed. This erasure, sidelining or concealment of Dalit women's experiences of sexual violence is, at times, intentional and, at others, not. Further, the chapter discusses how India's #MeToo movement, although initiated by the Dalit-Bahujan feminists, also remains limited in engaging with the phenomenon of caste-based sexual violence.

The chapter is divided into four sections. The first details the caste atrocity committed against Satyabhama. The second discusses Dalit women's position in Indian society, which makes them vulnerable to sexual violence, and outlines how the nexus of society, state and law makes it difficult for Dalit victims/survivors of sexual violence to access legal and social justice. The third section engages with two movements – the Dalit movement and the women's movement – that have dealt with Dalit women's questions and examines their limitations in addressing caste-based sexual violence. The final section considers how India's #MeToo movement, although supported by the Dalit-Bahujan women, does not fully represent the heterogeneous nature of the Dalit and Bahujan groups. The movement also remains limited in its reach at the grassroots level in India as it fails to makes space for the testimonies of Dalit women victims of sexual violence from rural locales (see chapter 5 in this volume). I further argue that the method of naming the accused publicly, adopted in the India's #MeToo movement could have led to the victimisation of Dalit men.

Case of caste-based sexual violence against Satyabhama

On 5 February 2015, Satyabhama, a 50-year-old Dalit[2] woman from the Mang caste of Maharashtra (one of the Dalit communities in Maharashtra), was disrobed, paraded and beaten up by two Maratha[3] men and sixteen Mang men and women in the Khotgaon village of the Latur district of Maharashtra. A clash between Satyabhama and the group of Maratha men and Mang men and women had been ongoing for nearly two years. The village's *gram panchayat*,[4] which was then headed by the Maratha men, wanted to use the open space in front of Satyabhama's house to build a kitchen for the adjacent Annabhau Sathe temple, a space which mainly represents the Mang community of the village. For this, Satyabhama was asked to give up the entrance to her house, which she and her family had been using for the last twenty-six years. Not only her house but all other houses in Satyabhama's lane also had their entrances on this side but it was only Satyabhama who was asked to now use the rear side of her house. Despite Satyabhama's opposition to this demand, the panchayat, headed by the Maratha men, installed an iron fence in front of the entrance to Satyabhama's house. Satyabhama, in turn, sent petitions to the government offices in Chakur Taluka and the Latur district and went on a hunger strike. The Mahar community, a Dalit community, who lived adjacent to Satyabhama's house, supported her by joining the hunger strike and by visiting the offices with her. Satyabhama also received support from a local Dalit organisation in accessing the government and writing letters. Despite these efforts and the notice from the collector's office, the gram panchayat did not remove the iron fence. Instead, on 5 February 2015, Satyabhama was beaten up, disrobed, pulled by her hair and had caste slurs hurled against her.

When Satyabhama went to register her case at the Chakur police station, the upper-caste female Maratha officer on duty tried to persuade her to 'compromise' the case, asking her to settle it in the village and discussing the repercussions of filing the case. One of the Mahar community members, who had made a video to document the sexual violence against Satyabhama, was made to delete the video by the police officer on the pretext of preserving her 'morality'. Satyabhama was made to wait nearly five hours before her case was registered, and this was only done after she threatened to burn herself in the police station. Satyabhama believes that during these five hours as she was kept waiting the accused were allowed to escape the village and that the upper-caste female police officer played a role in this.

Caste and Dalit women's position

Satyabhama's case is an aberration in the Indian context. It is an aberration in the sense that among the many cases of sexual violence against women in India, particularly against Dalit women in India, it was actually registered (Baxi, 2014; Mangubhai, 2016). This was done under the Scheduled Castes and Scheduled Tribes (Prevention of Atrocity) Act of 1989 (PoA Act), which aims to protect Dalits against atrocities committed on them by non-Dalits, particularly upper-castes. To understand why Dalits need a law to protect them, we have to examine the caste-based social structure of Indian society.

Historically, Dalits were considered 'untouchables'. They occupied the lowest position in the caste hierarchy and were assigned to do menial work for the upper castes, which were above them (Ambedkar, 2014; Viswanath, 2014). Occupations in the caste hierarchy were assigned by birth, endogamy was strictly practiced and there were hardly any avenues to change this situation (Ambedkar, 2014). Dalits were considered impure by birth, which limited their access to public spaces like common water bodies, village streets or temples (Ambedkar, 2014; Chakravarti, 2003). Anyone who failed to adhere to this social hierarchy was punished on the basis of the position they occupied. But, where endogamy prohibited relationships between lower-caste men and upper-caste women (Chakravarti, 1993, 1995), upper-caste men had access to the labour of Dalit women, both physical and sexual (Rege, 1995, 1996; Chakravarti, 1995, 2003). Having to serve as 'unfree agricultural laborers' (Viswanath, 2014) on the lands of the upper-caste made Dalit women vulnerable to sexual violence at the hands of upper-caste men (Dube, 1996; Chakravarti, 2016). To curb the practice of untouchability against Dalits and to prevent caste violence against them, constitutional laws like the Untouchability Act of 1955 and the PoA Act were introduced. Although the PoA Act exists to protect Dalits against caste violence committed by non-Dalits, particularly upper-castes, the act includes several loopholes, which limits its implementation (Baxi, 2014) and leads to the erasure of Dalit women's testimonies, to which I now turn.

Patriarchal and casteist: society, state and law

Reports on sexual violence against Dalit women suggest that ten Dalit women are raped every day (Counterview, 2020). However, this data does not account for the numerous other acts of sexual violence like disrobing, parading naked, inserting objects into the vagina and cutting off of breasts and other body parts. Additionally, with the shame around sexual violence, cases of sexual abuse do not get reported by victims or their families. During my PhD fieldwork in Maharashtra, I also learned that many cases of caste violence were compromised – settled outside court between the victims and perpetrators – and thus never reported. If some of the cases, like Satyabhama's, did reach the police station, there were efforts from the police to get the case settled or compromised. The idea of compromise becomes important in the context of caste violence. Dalits not taking legal recourse for the violence committed against them and not talking about their humiliation outside the village is what compromise incorporates. 'Compromise', thus, takes advantage of the vulnerable position and helplessness of Dalit individuals. After the atrocity, Satyabhama was promised that the fence in front of her house would be removed as a compromise, an offer which she rejected. This offer of compromise did not consider the bodily and mental harm caused to Satyabhama or the public humiliation she had experienced. In fact, the offer normalised what Satyabhama had to endure. Many Dalits agree to compromise to save themselves from further violence or because of the difficulty in getting legal justice (Bansode, 2020). Compromises can be made for as little as INR 5,000[5] or, at times, a few hundred thousand, or sometimes for no money at all. When Dalits helplessly agree not to pursue a legal case or even take their cases back once they are registered, often the people they had accused file counter claims against them. Upper-caste perpetrators of caste violence and even caste-based sexual violence generally do not want the news about the case to reach Dalit activists and organisations, which might lead to the media highlighting the case, even supporting Dalit victims. So, they invest extensive efforts to conceal Dalit testimonies and to ensure that news about the incident does not go beyond the village. Perpetrators and their supporters use various methods like making threats, compromising the case (Baxi, 2014), filing false counter-claims against Dalits, running away from the village and persuading the police not to register the case. In Satyabhama's case, the compromise was made by the upper-caste woman police officer, who should have represented the law and the state that must function to protect Dalits. Instead, she ensured that the evidence (the video) was deleted; she pushed Satyabhama to accept the compromise; she delayed the process and thus helped the perpetrators run away. Thus, instead of fulfilling her official duties, the police officer becomes an agent, representative of upper-caste and other caste and gender perpetrators actively attempting to bury and hide the case.

Two years later, when I was staying with Satyabhama for my research on her case, she revisited her struggle at the police station. I asked her what made her decide on setting herself on fire. Satyabhama replied:

> What more was left of me? My honour was taken away in front of the whole village ... Beaten up, disrobed I went to the police station, that too in my petticoat, even the knot of the petticoat was broken ... running I went to the police station, holding my petticoat with one hand, hiding my chest [she was wearing a blouse] with the other. And then she [the upper-caste police officer] was refusing to take my case, giving me offers to compromise for money, an offer of getting the fence removed. I thought I am in such a worst condition and instead

of taking my complaint, this lady is asking me to compromise. I said I
want nothing. Just register my case. But she had some other plans ...
I felt helpless. I was angry. I could see no solution ... I thought even
if I die today, I will die in this police station. I will burn that police
station down with me ... I thought perhaps, at least then what happened to me, what was happening with me, shall come into the public
eye. I wanted the world to know what wrong had happened with me.

Satyabhama's resolve to have her case registered is not common
among victims of caste atrocity and sexual violence. Not many
victims can sustain the pressure or fear put on them by the various
parties – the upper-caste perpetrators, the police or other actors.
It requires determination and awareness of rights to get a First
Information Report[6] registered. Although Satyabhama was always
outspoken about her rights, the Dalit activists who were helping
her to write petitions or sitting on hunger strikes with her boosted
her confidence to stand against the injustice she was facing. The
support she received from various Dalit activists and organisations
in Maharashtra helped her to continue her fight. Satyabhama's
experience was covered by local Marathi newspapers. This led
many organisations from Mumbai and Pune to visit Khotgaon to
uncover the details of the case, to meet Satyabhama and to help her.

Satyabhama's case went on in the Latur sessions court for two
years, from 2015 to 2017. In this time, several court hearings were
cancelled. During my presence in the field, the hearing was cancelled three times, under pretexts like the judge's non-availability
or lack of authority to hear this case, the absence of the lawyer,
who was attending a marriage, or the need for the case to be heard
in a Special Court (this, when the case had been running in the
Sessions Court for nearly two years). It was a frustrating process for
Satyabhama, but she continued to lead the case.

Not many victims and witnesses are able to sustain the pressure
of the law and often turn hostile. Even in Satyabhama's case, the
witnesses, who mainly belonged to the Mahar community, turned
hostile in the court but continued to support Satyabhama in the
village. The caste atrocity committed against her had become
like a public secret in the village: everyone knew about it but no
one talked about it (Baxi, 2014; Zerubavel, 2006). Dalits were
scared of talking about it or even to speak to Satyabhama in

public as they could gain unwanted attention or be caught up in undesirable clashes with the upper-caste and Mang perpetrators. Committing sexual violence against Dalit women is also a form of punishing the whole community (Kannabiran and Kannabiran, 1991). It was not only Satyabhama who faced social boycott or spatial segregation in the village after the atrocity. Members of the accused families had also stopped talking with Mahar community members who had supported Satyabhama or were on talking terms with her. So the impact of caste violence has to be examined at two levels: the level of Dalits as individuals and that of Dalits as a community.

When Dalits in Satyabhama's village did speak about the atrocity, they also referred to earlier caste atrocities in the village or nearby villages. So, Dalit testimonies about one act of caste violence mirror the histories of violence they and the other Dalits have faced in the past. Simultaneously, the public silence about the violence and its disclosure only in the private space, in low, soft voices, shows that we have to read the silences, what is in-between the lines, what is left out. All these aspects open up multiple lived realities of Dalits and the multiple ways in which their testimonies of violence can and must be read.

Dalit movements and the women's movement of India

The two social movements that have dealt with sexual violence against Dalit women in India are the Dalit movement and the women's movement. Although both movements have been criticised for giving a secondary position to Dalit women and their issues (Guru, 1995; Rege, 1998), they are still crucial for fighting against caste and gender hierarchies. These movements are considered new social movements, which gained momentum in the 1970s and emerged from the active participation and politics of the two exploited groups in India (Omvedt, 1993; Ray and Katzenstein, 2005; Shah, 2004). A brief description of these movements is given below, followed by a discussion of the limitations of the movements in handling sexual violence against Dalit women.

While both the Dalit and the women's movements have existed for more than 100 years in various forms, under different ideologies and names (Krishnaraj, 2012: Waghmore, 2013; Roy, 2018), they gathered momentum in the 1970s. The women's movement dates back to the social reform movement in colonial India, which addressed issues like child marriage, the conditions of widows, women's education, and so on. These issues mainly concerned upper-caste, upper-class women and were fought for by men from upper-caste communities. Women were also part of India's independence movements but were given secondary positions. Their roles were mainly seen in connection with their men and the nation (Chatterjee, 1990). In postcolonial India, although on paper women had equal rights to men, the opportunities of education, employment and political participation remained limited to the few women coming from privileged upper-class, upper-caste backgrounds. During this period, many women were also part of the left movement in India; however, they simultaneously belonged to separate groups that specifically focused on women's issues. These groups gained momentum in the 1970s and 1980s when the women's movement highlighted issues that poor women, in particular, were facing.

The Dalit movement refers to various anti-caste movements like Bhakti movements, non-brahmin movements or Dravidian movements initiated by anti-caste activists in different periods in India (Omvedt, 1994). However, these movements were fragmented and did not exist as widely as India's independence movement or the left movement (Omvedt, 1994; Waghmore, 2013). In the 1970s, a young group of Dalit poets, scholars and activists emerged in Maharashtra. This group was inspired by the Black Panther movement in the US and hence named itself Dalit Panthers. They were influenced by the writings of social reformer B. R. Ambedkar[7] and Marxist thought. A difference of opinion over the use of violence for social justice led to a split of the Dalit Panthers in the late 1970s, but many of the leaders from these groups entered political parties and participated in elections. Although some Dalits have entered previously inaccessible spaces like academia, politics and other government and private offices, most Dalit communities remain downtrodden and face caste discrimination and exploitation at the hands of upper-castes (Guru, 1995; Rege, 1998).

The women's movement has been criticised for ignoring the caste question and giving precedence to class (Phadke, 2003). It has also been criticised for its innate elitism and upper-caste dominance, meaning Dalit women could not find their own spaces or felt alienated. Dalit feminists also feel that the feminist movement often ignores Dalit women, exemplified by its disregard of caste-based sexual violence (Ramdas, 2012). Dalit women also critique the Dalit movement for sidelining women's issues and the dominance of men in the movement (Pawar and Moon, 2008).

Interestingly, the Indian women's movement was galvanised by the protests and campaign against the rape of a tribal girl called Mathura, committed by two policemen in Gadchiroli district of Maharashtra in 1972. It was the first time in post-independence India that an anti-rape campaign was initiated by feminists against sexual violence. The case resulted in the legal provision of the Criminal Law Amendment Act 1983, which introduced custodial rape and shifted the responsibility of proof from the victim to the accused.[8] The subsequent struggle led by feminist organisations in the case of another gang-rape victim, Bhanwari Devi, in the *Vishaka* case in 1992 led to the conceptualisation of guidelines (called the Vishaka Guidelines) on how to deal with sexual harassment in the workplace as part of the judgement handed down. Bhanwari Devi, who worked as a state development worker, was gang-raped by upper-caste men for opposing child marriage. Devi and her family have since faced a social boycott in the village, and the District Court acquitted the accused. Her case is still in the courts. She speaks about the injustice she has met and continues to face.

Both Mathura's and Bhanwari Devi's cases are considered revolutionary for feminist politics and movements in India, but it is necessary to note that none of the victims in these cases have received legal justice. Their cases contributed to the shaping of the feminist movement, but the movement has achieved only limited success in reducing the hurdles these women were facing in their everyday lives. Interestingly, despite the fact that Mathura and Bhanwari Devi are lower-caste women, there are hardly any instances where Dalit movements have considered resistance against these caste-based sexual violence cases as part of their struggles. Not many Dalit activists and scholars, even on social media, discuss Bhanwari

Devi's and Mathura's struggles as much as they do of Phoolan Devi, another caste-based gang-rape victim who was raped by the upper-caste men in her village. Devi, popularly known as Bandit Queen, subsequently killed the upper-caste men who had committed the sexual violence against her. Why some women are recognised and celebrated but not others is a question the Dalit movement has not confronted yet.

Difference between Me Too and #MeToo: inspirations for Dalit movements

The preceding two sections discussed the different moments at the level of society and state institutions and even at the level of movements, where Dalit women's testimonies get erased or remain side-lined. But the histories of these erasures seemed to find a voice, or an inkling of justice, when it came to the fore that Raya Sarkar, who had collated and posted the List of Sexual Harassers in Academia (LoSHA) and was a leading figure in the #MeToo movement, was herself a Dalit.

Scholars have documented the LoSHA as the moment when Dalit, Adivasi and other marginalised community women finally initiated the discourse on sexual violence. However, there are many complexities to unpack while discussing the #MeToo movement of India. There is a need to understand the shape it took by situating the history of the movement in the US, its initiators' identities, the trajectory of the movement and the discourses it generated.

The MeToo movement in the US was initially started by African American activist Tarana Burke in 2006 to bring forth the voices of the victims of sexual violence and to generate awareness around sexual violence (see, for example, chapter 8 in this volume). Her movement did not receive media attention until 2017, when Alyssa Milano, a white actor and producer, used Burke's slogan Me Too as hashtag #MeToo on social media to call for women to share stories of sexual harassment. Burke's Me Too was acknowledged only when it was appropriated by Milano; despite the long history of black feminist movements in the US, the question of who spoke and who was heard was deeply influenced by race. This fact remains crucial when examining the #MeToo of India, particularly as the Dalit movements are inspired by the Black Panthers, Black feminist thought, womanism and intersectionality (Paik, 2014; Slate, 2012). Scholars have made several attempts to compare race and caste as two forms of inequality that create similar contexts for graded social domination with a specific gendered dimension, especially on women belonging to the lower ranks in these systems (Berreman, 1972). Black and Dalit women's bodies have been historically subjugated due to their race, caste and gender locations. These histories of inspirations become important at various junctures when we discuss the #MeToo movement in India.

Burke (2018a, 2018b, 2020) recognised the necessity of creating a space for the black and brown female victims and survivors of sexual violence for initiating a healing process. The healing process becomes important for survivors of any violence, but why it becomes particularly important for black women, according to Burke, is because the 'state-sanctioned' violence committed against black men makes it difficult for black women to talk about the violence they face from men within the community. Hence, for Burke, the MeToo movement opens up space for black girls and women to talk about the intra-community violence they face.

If India's #MeToo movement was inspired by Burke's movement, it would be easy to understand the former against a history of solidarity in which black movements have inspired Dalits (Slate, 2012). The MeToo movement of India would have talked about Dalit women's position in the caste hierarchy and the violence Dalit women face at the hand of both Dalit men and upper-caste men and women. But here I assert that India's #MeToo movement was not directly inspired by this history. In making this assertion I do not mean that Dalit-Bahujan women who were leading this movement lack knowledge of how black movements inspired Dalit movements or existing conceptualisations that draw parallel between Dalit women and black women. Here, I simply intend to point out that what sparked India's #MeToo movement by a few Dalit-Bahujan women was the #MeToo movement started in 2017 and not the MeToo movement of 2006 started by Burke. The fact remains that the Dalit and Bahujan movement led India's MeToo movement; however whether that categorises this movement as a

Dalit Women's Movement or another element of feminist movement is a crucial question for scholars of social movements to deal with. For me, the important contribution of MeToo movements all over the world, and particularly India is that it had inspired victims and survivors of violence to talk about the violence they had faced. But I also found the Indian #MeToo problematic at several points, as shown in the sections below.

The LoSHA and its impact on Dalits

The first problematic aspect of India's #MeToo movement was the creation of the LoSHA by a Dalit scholar and the support shown for it by several Dalit-Bahujan women without considering the impact this list could have on Dalit men and other marginalised communities in India. I appreciate that Sarkar initiated the #MeToo movement to make the voices of the victims of sexual violence heard, but from the very start the focus was on naming the harassers/perpetrator and not on the victims.

Unlike the claim made by feminists opposing the list, I do not think that the LoSHA 'enables the right wing to say that all anti-nationals are also sexual predators' (Menon, 2017), as the filing of false cases of sexual violence against Dalit men is a phenomenon that started well before the right-wing government took over in 2014. Highlighting the series of false accusations of sexual violence against Dalit men, Maharashtra activist Maya K. stated in her interview with me:

> Filing false cases of sexual violence, robbery, hooliganism against our [Dalit] men is not a new story … When there is a love affair between an upper-caste girl and a Dalit man, the girl's family objects to it, and then, in response, cases of sexual harassment or sexual violence are filed against the Dalit lover. I know so many such cases. [The] Dalit boy's life gets destroyed in such cases. But still, I would consider that it is a good thing that these cases are filed, and at least these boys are not killed on the streets then. … If cases are filed, you [the Dalit boy] might live. Yes, you might have to visit the court for trials, but the chances of lynching by the upper-caste goons are reduced to an extent; not completely but to an extent.

Speaking of a case in which three Dalit men allegedly raped and murdered an upper-caste fourteen-year-old girl, another Maharashtra activist, Pratigya, said:

> Most of the evidence, in this case, was tampered with and created to punish the alleged Dalit men. There are rumours that the deceased and an accused had an affair or something. We don't know that. ... I feel these accused are innocent ... but it is fine if they are in jail. At least they are alive in jail. If it is proved that they are innocent and come out of jail, they will be publicly lynched and killed by the upper-caste men. Do we want that? Of course not. Prison is safer for these men than in the village or any place else.

When read together, these excerpts reveal the vulnerable position Dalit men occupy in society. Burke reflects on the victimisation of Black men at the hands of the US state, which is similar to the status Dalit men occupy in India. In the ancient caste society, Dalits were severely punished even for petty crimes against the upper castes. For instance, if lower castes talked to upper castes in a language that the latter found insulting, then punishments like cutting out their tongues, thrusting an iron nail in their mouth or pouring hot oil into their mouth and ears were common (Bühler, 2008 [1886]: clauses 270, 271, 272). Although such punishments have been discontinued in contemporary times, beating, parading and murdering of Dalits remain common crimes committed against them. These crimes are committed against Dalits for downloading ringtones of songs that praise Ambedkar (Shanta, 2015), for entering a temple (Raju, 2020) or even for having an affair with an upper-caste woman (*Economic Times*, 2016). Filing of false cases against Dalit men, especially male activists, is a common practice.

These aspects show how the historical, social and political context of violence and the social location of the accused matter in incidents of violence. These social locations matter even in courts where upper-caste men enjoy impunity in the crimes they commit against Dalits, whereas lower-caste men are punished for petty crimes or become victims of false cases. The by-product of the impunity enjoyed by upper-caste men and the casteist and gendered nature of state institutions is the overrepresentation of lower-caste and marginalised people in Indian prisons (Wire, 2019).

If undemocratic methods of creating lists and naming accused are adopted and celebrated publicly, such as with the LoSHA, the risk is that victimised men of marginalised communities will bear the biggest brunt. Publishing the details of lower-caste men on public platforms (as in the case of the LoSHA) would make them and their families vulnerable to harassment and violence. Lynching, beating and killing of marginalised community men, particularly Dalit and Muslim men, occurs on a daily basis. It is not civility but the fear of the law that deters upper-caste mobs of men in India from violence against the marginalised.

Importance of the law for Dalits

After losing her case in the session court, Satyabhama filed it at the High Court. She was determined that if she were to lose there, she would apply to the Supreme Court. As long as the case continued in court, the perpetrators would restrain themselves, and this was how she could continue her life. While both supporters and opposers of the LoSHA recognised the correlation that exists between creating such a list on social media and the impact it could have on marginalised groups, neither paid attention to what meanings judicial processes have for subjects of different communities in India. The ignorance of the supporters of the list towards these realities leads to the sidelining of Dalit testimonies not only of direct violence, like beating, sexual violence or murder, but even of indirect, structural violence perpetuated at the level of state and its institutions.

However frustrating and imperfect, the law is the only mechanism that promises to protect Dalits, and Dalits have no other recourse (Wadekar, 2020). In the Hathras gang rape case of September 2020, four Thakur men allegedly gang-raped and murdered a nineteen-year-old Dalit woman in the Hathras district of the Indian state of Uttar Pradesh. While this violence is normalised in the case of Dalit women, what led to the protests by Dalit and feminist organisations across India was the burning of the dead body without the family's permission: the family of the deceased was barracked in its house while the police burned the body. In addition, the state government of Uttar Pradesh tried to divert the case by stating that it was not rape and that there was no caste angle to prevent the case from falling under the PoA act. The reason for discussing this case here is that the #MeToo movement of India did not take cognisance of the realities of Dalit women like in the Hathras case or even Satyabhama, who share a vulnerable position considering they live in the same localities where the perpetrators or the families of the perpetrators live. My ethnography revealed that the perpetrators imposed several spatial restrictions like disallowing access to certain streets or common water bodies to Dalit victims and their supporters after the atrocity.

Additionally, the victims also shared the burden of continuing their lives in the presence of the perpetrators. In these instances, calling out the perpetrators in public did not provide solace to the victims. Rather it is the following up of 'due process' – the legal process that helped victims to continue their lives. Here, the continuation of life does not mean the coming back of 'normal' times before the incident of caste atrocity (Das, 1995, 2006; Arif, 2016). Here the life post-atrocity is shaped by the memory and affect of it and with the legal proceedings that come with filing of the atrocity (Das, 2006; Arif, 2016; Baxi, 2014). The #MeToo movement of India fails to understand such complexities, which shape the decisions or journeys Dalits and Dalit women take while fighting against caste-based sexual violence.

#MeToo and Dalit women's 'speakability'?

In her paper 'In the Footprints of Bhanwari Devi: Feminist Cascades and #MeToo in India', Kannabiran (2018) rightly interrogates the 'Me' in the #MeToo movement in India: Is it all genders? Is it all 'women'? The answer to both these questions would be negative. #MeToo represented a faction of women from privileged communities, women who could afford to speak about the violence they faced, if not in public, then in private communication with Sarkar. It was commendable for these women to share their testimonies. But it leaves a number of questions open: Is the #MeToo movement, as initiated by a Dalit activist and supported by a few Dalit-Bahujan scholars and activists, a Dalit movement or a feminist movement? Scholars have contextualised India's #MeToo movement as a feminist movement led by Dalit-Bahujan women (Morais, 2020), but did these Dalit-Bahujan women in fact represent the voices of the majority of Dalit-Bahujan women or, indeed, those from marginalised communities?

In the initial phase of the movement in 2017, while I was conducting my fieldwork with victims of sexual violence and activists working on atrocities, I did not see many Dalit women support this movement. This was due to several reasons: many Dalit women or lower-castes, even victims of sexual violence, do not access social media (Sudhir, 2019) or are not aware of the existence of movements like #MeToo on social media. This reduces the possibility for Dalit women to write their testimonies in public (see chapter 5, this volume). For instance, the phone Satyabhama was using was an old basic Samsung, which could be used only for calls or text messaging, and she still does not use media like WhatsApp or Facebook. Sadly, testimonies of sexual violence from Dalit women tend to come to the public only when these women are dead. Their testimonies are not shared by the victim or their family members but are mostly spread by Dalits active on social media platforms. Second, many Dalit women activists could not identify or keep up with the ongoing debates on social media. For these activists, the academic and social media worlds are different from their world of the field. The field becomes the real space for them, and academia and social media are spaces that may be out there, removed from everyday reality. For instance, in the field, even I was looked at as a Dalit researcher. This defined me in terms of two identities: me as researcher involved in knowledge production but who does not have much knowledge of the field, and me as Dalit who understands exploitation and marginalisation. I was seen as both, a representative of the elite space of academia and a representative of the community within this space. Being from Maharashtra, I have lived in the field for many years of my life, was part of it; but my entrance into academia now made me both an outsider and an insider. Thus, identities and views existing among Dalits are heterogenous whereas perhaps in academic spaces, there are only a few marginalised communities and identities. Hence, where these communities and identities are studied and seen together in the academic sphere, internally, they are multiple. What brings these heterogeneous groups together living across India's vast landscape is the fight against inequality. Still, having only one homogenous voice could lose out on the crucial testimonies of Dalit women. So, even as the #MeToo movement came to be seen as representative of Dalit-Bahujan voices, it should be seen as just one part of India's heterogenous marginalised communities.

Towards a conclusion

By highlighting the limitations of India's #MeToo movement, I do not intend to delegitimise the movement. This movement emerged in reaction to the #MeToo movement that had started in the US. The study of the #MeToo movement of India and #MeToo movement of the US, their trajectories and histories reveal the connections and disconnections between these and even previous movements, like Burke's MeToo movement. The close study of these movements brings out their complexities and helps us address or make sense of them. For example, even though India's #MeToo movement was started and led by Dalit-Bahujan feminists, this movement did not limit its focus on Dalit women's testimonies. The leaders of this movement went beyond their caste locations to stand for the victims and survivors of sexual violence and called out their perpetrators. Moving beyond the barriers of caste to talk for and support the victims and survivors is commendable. But calling out perpetrators without thinking about the impact on subjugated masculinities can be dangerous. And the movement offered limited space to Dalit women from remote, especially non-metropolitan geographical locations. India's #MeToo movement offers new avenues to investigate how identity becomes a means to stand in for the marginalised. Yet, at the same time, the framework of identity politics can be limiting for analysing such a movement.

Acknowledgements

I would like to thank Professor Srila Roy for the constant support and guidance I received from her while writing this piece. I would also like to thank the reviewers for their comments on the drafts of this paper.

Notes

1 For my PhD I studied the caste and gender relations in the aftermath of the Satyabhama atrocity. I used an ethnographic approach to study Satyabhama's village, where the atrocity was committed, and to understand the existing face of the Dalit movement in Maharashtra. The fieldwork was formally conducted from June 2017 to December 2017 and September 2018 to November 2018. However, I carefully followed and studied all the happenings in the field during the course of two years, from June 2017 to June 2019. I interviewed activists and scholars working on caste atrocities. Excerpts from the interviews with two activists are included in the fourth section of this chapter. All interviewees are referred to by pseudonyms.

2 The ancient varna system hierarchically divided Indian society into four groups: Brahmins, Kshtriyas, Vaishyas and Shudras. There was another group, the 'Anti-Shudras' or 'Untouchables', who fell outside the caste hierarchy, but its position was still seen in response to the other groups. Each of the four groups was internally divided in castes and sub-castes. The group highest in the varna enjoyed the highest social, economic and political privileges, whereas the groups who were the lowest, Shudras and Ati-Shudras, were considered as service castes, tasked with serving as labourers for the other castes. The Ati-Shudras now politically and socially identify themselves as Dalits. They are recognised under the category of 'Scheduled Castes' in the Indian constitution with the Adivasi tribal communities recognised under the category 'Scheduled Tribes'. Dalits and Adivasi are considered the most vulnerable and exploited groups in India and hence the constitution protects them under several provisions. The traditional caste society also dominates many castes and communities in the Shudra category. The Dalits, Adivasis and Shudras together politically and socially identify and organise themselves under the term *Bahujan*, which in simple terms means 'the majority of people' (Karunakaran, 2016).

3 Marathas constitute a group of peasants who historically belonged to different communities in the state of Maharashtra but now claim themselves to be Kshatriyas, fighter castes, to which mainly the kings had belonged. They dominate Maharashtra politically, socially and economically today.

4 The *gram panchayat* is the government political body at village level.
5 INR 5,000 is about €57 or $67.
6 A First Information Report is the document written by a police officer on the basis of a complaint lodged by the victim or on behalf of the victim, orally or in writing (Logical Indian, 2017).
7 B. R. Ambedkar was a social reformer, philosopher, jurist and economist who fought for the rights of lower castes in India. After his death, his political and social-political thought has been a source of inspiration to Dalit and anti-caste activists and scholars.
8 Rape committed in government-controlled spaces like police stations or hospitals or in any other place by a public official (such as a police officer or army personnel) is known as custodial rape (NCW, n.d.). Baxi z(2014: 7) asserts the uniqueness of the Indian feminist 'conceptualisation of custodial rape' and considers it as one of the most significant contributions of the feminist movement of India.

References

Ambedkar, B.R. (2014). *Dr. Babasaheb Ambedkar: Writings and Speeches – Volume 17 (Part One)*. New Delhi: Dr. Ambedkar Foundation.

Arif, Y. (2016). *Life, Emergent: The Social in the Afterlives of Violence*. Minneapolis, MN: University of Minnesota Press.

Bansode, R. (2020). Re-casting the social in the aftermath of caste-based sexual violence: A study of gender and caste relations in Rural Maharashtra (Doctoral Dissertation, IIT Delhi).

Baxi, P. (2014). *Public Secrets of Law: Rape Trials in India*. New Delhi: Oxford University Press.

Berreman, G.D. (1972). 'Race, Caste, and Other Invidious Distinctions in Social Stratification', *Race* 13:4, 385–414.

Bühler, G. (2008 [1886]). *The Laws of Manu: Translated with Extracts from Seven Commentaries*. Hong Kong: Forgotten Books.

Burke, T. (2018a) 'Tarana Burke on what Me Too is Really About – Extended Interview'. Daily Show, YouTube video, 9:16 min, posted 4 June 2018. https://youtu.be/GfJ3bIAQOKg. Accessed 10 September 2020.

Burke, T. (2018b). 'Me Too is a Movement, not a Moment'. TEDWomen Talks, Palms Springs, California, November, YouTube video, 16:15 min, posted 4 January 2019. www.youtube.com/watch?v=zP3LaAYzA3Q. Accessed 11 Sepember 2020.

Burke, T. (2020). 'Tarana Burke: Full Address and Q&A'. Address given to the Oxford Union on 17 February 2020. YouTube video, 1:02:14 min, posted 13 April 2020. https://youtu.be/50wz6Xm9VYs. Accessed 13 Sepember 2020.

Chakravarti, U. (1993). 'Conceptualizing Brahmanical Patriarchy in Early India: Gender, Caste, Class and State', *Economic & Political Weekly* 28:14, 579–85.

Chakravarti, U. (1995). 'Wifehood, Widowhood, and Adultery: Female Sexuality, Surveillance and the State in 18th Century Maharashtra', *Contributions to Indian Sociology* 29:1&2, 3–21.

Chakravarti, U. (2003). *Gendering Caste: Through a Feminist Lens.* Calcutta: Stree.

Chakravarti, U. (ed.) (2016). *Fault Lines of History: The India Papers II.* New Delhi: Zubaan Books.

Chatterjee, P. (1990). 'The Nationalist Resolution of the Women's Question', in *Recasting Women: Essays in Indian Colonial History*, edited by K. Sangari and S. Vaid, 233–53. New Brunswick, NJ: Rutgers University Press.

Counterview. (2020). '10 Dalit Women Raped Every Day, Supreme Court Should Intervene: Dalit NGOs', Counterview, 12 October. www.counterview.net/2020/10/10-dalit-women-raped-every-day-supreme.html. Accessed 9 December 2020.

Das, V. (1995). *Critical Events: An Anthropological Perspective on Contemporary India.* Delhi: Oxford University Press.

Das, V. (2006). *Life and Words: Violence and the Descent into the Ordinary.* Berkeley, CA: University of California Press.

Dube, L. (1996). 'Caste and Women', in *Caste: Its Twentieth-Century Avatar*, edited by M. N. Srinivas, 1–27. New Delhi: Penguin Books.

Economic Times. (2016). 'Dalit Boy Killed over Affair with Upper Caste Girl; 7 Arrested'. *Economic Times*, 21 July. https://economictimes.indiatimes.com/news/politics-and-nation/dalit-boy-killed-over-affair-with-upper-caste-girl-7-arrested/articleshow/53314162.cms?from=mdr. Accessed 19 October 2020.

Guru, G. (1995). 'Dalit Women Talk Differently', *Economic & Political Weekly* 30:42/42, 2548–50.

Kannabiran, K. (2018). 'In the Footprints of Bhanwari Devi: Feminist Cascades and #MeToo in India', Prajnya Grit Working paper. www.csdhyd.org/gritwp18kk.pdf. Accessed 16 November 2020.

Kannabiran, V. and K. Kannabiran. (1991). 'Caste and Gender: Understanding Dynamics of Power and Violence', *Economic & Political Weekly* 26:37, 2130–3.

Karunakaran, V. (2016). 'The Dalit-Bahujan Guide to Understanding Caste in Hindu Scripture'. *Medium.com*, 14 July. https://medium.com/@Bahujan_Power/the-dalit-bahujan-guide-to-understanding-caste-in-hindu-scripture-417db027fce6. Accessed 3 June 2021.

Krishnaraj, M. (2012). 'The Women's Movement in India: A Hundred Year History', *Social Change* 42:3, 325–33.

Logical Indian. (2017). 'All you Need to Know about First Information Report (FIR) and its Importance'. Logical Indian, 24 February. https://the logicalindian.com/story-feed/awareness/fir/. Accessed 5 December 2020.

Mangubhai, J. (2016). 'Violence and Impunity in a Patriarchal Caste Culture: Difference Matters', in *Fault Lines of History: The India Papers II*, edited by U. Chakravarti, 257–90. New Delhi: Zubaan Books.

Menon, N. (2017). 'From Feminazi to Savarna Rape Apologist in 24 hours'. *Kafila*, 28 October. https://kafila.online/2017/10/28/from-feminazi-to-savarna-rape-apologist-in-24-hours/. Accessed 25 May 2021.

Morais, S. dos Santos Bruss. (2020). 'Queering Feminist Solidarities: #Metoo, LoSHA and the Digital Dalit', *Open Gender Journal*. https://doi.org/10.17169/ogj.2020.71.

NCW (National Commission for Women). (n.d.). 'Amendments to the Laws Relating to Rape and Related Provisions'. National Commission for Women, India. http://ncwapps.nic.in/frmLNewLaws.aspx#Amendments; http://ncwapps.nic.in/PDFFiles/Amendments%20to%20laws%20 relating%20to%20women.pdf. Accessed 14 September 2020.

Omvedt, G. (1993). *Reinventing Revolution: New Social Movements and the Socialist Tradition in India*. New York: M. E. Sharpe.

Omvedt, G. (1994). *Dalits and the Democratic Revolution: Dr Ambedkar and the Dalit Movement in Colonial India*. New Delhi: Sage.

Paik, S. (2014). 'Building Bridges: Articulating Dalit and African American Women's Solidarity', *Women's Studies Quarterly* 42:3, 74–96.

Pawar, U. and M. Moon. (2008). *We also Made History: Women in the Ambedkarite Movement*. New Delhi: Zubaan Books.

Phadke, S. (2003). 'Thirty Years On: Women's Studies Reflects on the Women's Movement', *Economic & Political Weekly* 38:43, 4567–76.

Raju, S. (2020). 'Dalit Boy Killed over Prayer at UP Temple'. *Hindustan Times*, 10 June. www.hindustantimes.com/india-news/dalit-boy-killed-over-prayer-at-up-temple/story-evS5ludyWjLWkJruO9Dk2J.html. Accessed 16 October 2020.

Ramdas, A. (2012). 'In Solidarity with All Rape Survivors'. Savari, 20 December. www.dalitweb.org/?p=1342. Accessed 6 January 2020.

Ray, R. and M. F. Katzenstein. (2005). 'Introduction: In the Beginning, There Was the Nehruvian State', in *Social movements in India: Poverty, Power, and Politics*, edited by M. F. Katzenstein and R. Ray, 1–31. Lanham, MD: Rowman and Littlefield.

Rege, S. (1995). 'The Hegemonic Appropriation of Sexuality: The Case of the Lavani Performers of Maharashtra', *Contributions to Indian Sociology* 29:1&2, 23–38.

Rege, S. (1996). 'Caste and Gender: The Violence against Women in India', EUI Working Paper RSC No. 96/17, European University Institute, 1–15.

Rege, S. (1998). 'Dalit Women Talk Differently: A Critique of "Difference" and towards a Dalit Feminist Standpoint Position', *Economic & Political Weekly* 33:44, 39–46.

Roy, S. (2018). '#MeToo is a Crucial Moment to Revisit the History of Indian Feminism', *Economic & Political Weekly* 53:42. www.epw.in/engage/article/metoo-crucial-moment-revisit-history-indian-feminism. Accessed 24 October 2020.

Shah, G. (2004). *Social Movements in India: A Review of Literature*. Delhi: Sage Publications India.

Shanta, S. (2015). 'Dalit Man in Ahmednagar Killed for Ringtone Praising Ambedkar'. Scroll.in, 22 May. https://scroll.in/article/729270/dalit-man-in-ahmednagar-killed-for-ringtone-praising-ambedkar. Accessed 12 August 2020.

Slate, N. (2012). 'The Dalit Panthers: Race, Caste, and Black Power in India', in *Black Power beyond Borders: The Global Dimensions of the Black Power Movement*, edited by N. Slate, 127–43. New York: Palgrave Macmillan.

Sudhir, S. (2019). 'Social Media, an Upper Caste Fort'. *Deccan Chronicle*, 22 October. www.deccanchronicle.com/nation/current-affairs/241019/social-media-an-upper-caste-fort.html. Accessed 4 June 2021.

Viswanath, R. (2014). *The Pariah Problem*. New York, NY: Columbia University Press.

Wadekar, D. (2020). 'What After Hathras? Episode#2'. Dalit Voices, YouTube video, 5:00 min, posted 29 October. https://youtu.be/QCTGrJ7nkIE. Accessed 5 December 2020.

Waghmore, S. (2013). *Civility against Caste: Dalit Politics and Citizenship in Western India*. New Delhi: Sage.

Wire. (2019). 'One in Every Three Under-Trial Prisoners in India is either SC or ST: Study'. Wire, 20 January. https://thewire.in/rights/one-in-every-three-under-trial-prisoners-in-india-is-either-sc-or-st-study. Accessed 15 November 2020.

Zerubavel, A. (2006). *The Elephant in the Room: Silence and Denial in Everyday Life*. New York: Oxford University Press.

5

#MeToo and the troubling of the rural public sphere in India: a feminist media house reports from the hinterland

Disha Mullick

Introduction: #MeToo and the universe of Indian media

The latter part of the twentieth century, synchronous with the women's movement in India and the second wave of feminism in Western countries, saw the entry of large numbers of middle-class women into certain domains of work. The news media and the entertainment industry in India, for instance, have been domains of work occupied by 'privileged' women, in terms of class, caste and mobility. Similar to other forms of public engagement, women's entry into a male-dominated space like journalism necessitated a constant proving of worth, of entitlement. This has been demonstrated in accounts by female journalists about having to hold the urge to pee for hours due to the lack of toilets in the field (Press Institute of India, 2004), having to normalise the sexist behaviour of male colleagues and supervisors, and having to 'accept' a workspace where sexualised banter and the objectification of women was a given aspect of office culture.

During the second half of 2017, women began to call out men in power in industries as influential as Hollywood. Closer to home, the List of Sexual Harassers in Academia (LoSHA) circulated on social media, setting in place a momentum that seemed unstoppable. Around October 2018 a few well-known journalists began to talk about experiences of sexual harassment within renowned media houses and called out men of considerable influence and power. A notable example was the accusation of long years of workplace harassment by prominent editor and politician M. J. Akbar. This naming and shaming, as a year earlier with the LoSHA, seemed like it would crack the foundations of the media industry (ripples of this 'MeToo moment' in India reached other industries, such as corporate India, but to negligible effect; see Nair, 2018). Senior journalists, editors, actors, directors and comedians were removed from their positions. Sexual harassment committees, a legal compliance, were revealed to exist on paper only, if at all, so that new ones were constituted at a fast pace. 'Training' was done on workplace etiquette; opinion pieces were written on how casual office flirtation was a thing of the past (Das, 2018). The number of accusations against Akbar resulted in his stepping down from his post in the Union cabinet as Minister of State for External Affairs.

As we know, the story has a blacker ending than the death of patriarchy. A 'call out culture' is predicated on the expectation (or assumption) that shame would induce a shift in norms, when it should be patently clear that gender and sexual norms have way more staying power than that. Influential male media persons have found themselves back where they were or have filed defamation cases against those who accused them, such as in the case of Akbar (Akbar notably lost this case in a February 2021 verdict issued by a Delhi court, Mohan J, 2021), journalist Gaurav Sawant, actor Alok Nath and artist Subodh Gupta (Sood et al., 2019). As this book goes to press, we are still holding our breath in cynical disbelief that the editor of the independent news magazine *Tehelka*, Tarun Tejpal, has been acquitted of sexual assault in a landmark case from 2013, after a strenuous eight-year trial (Baxi, 2021). YouTube channels have been created to put out 'evidence' and seek 'justice' for the reputations and lives that were 'ruined' (Deodhar and Manral, 2019).

But the #MeToo movement in India, significant as it has been in bringing an articulation of gender and patriarchy into contemporary publics, has been limited, perhaps by the same technologies that gave it sustenance. The voices that thickened the social media space were privileged ones: urban, upper-class and upper-caste (Padma Priya, 2019). This fact sometimes appeared in passing, as a reference to the many more women outside the cities who faced harassment and violence, but was rarely engaged with in a deep or meaningful way. For those of us who worked in the rural context, where 70 per cent of India's population is located, and confronted gender and patriarchy and the changes wrought by technology in a very particular way, this was a discomfiting negligence. This chapter documents my navigation of the #MeToo movement as an urban feminist working with a rural media collective, Khabar Lahariya. My location has been both inside and outside of this mo(ve)ment. I saw it as something precious in my trajectory as a feminist in India, a well-timed rupturing of the urban media space where I had been trained; but I also saw it as something that needed to be held to account, and questioned, by other feminisms lived elsewhere in the country.

On changing the subject: Khabar Lahariya, a new media voice in the digitalscape

On 12 October 2018, a local media organisation called Khabar Lahariya (News Waves) published an open letter (Khabar Lahariya, 2018a) in which it responded to the #MeToo movement from its own context: that of remote, rural central India. Emerging from a history of feminist education work in the region by a non-governmental organisation (NGO) called Nirantar – Centre for Gender and Education, Khabar Lahariya recruited local women from rural, marginalised and non-journalistic backgrounds (Naqvi, 2007). Khabar Lahariya, with which I worked in various leadership capacities from 2007, is located in Bundelkhand, a region of Uttar Pradesh state known for its droughts, outward migration, abiding feudalism and gang violence.[1] Between 2002 and 2015, Khabar Lahariya functioned as a chain of local language newspapers covering news from villages and small towns in Bundelkhand, distributed in a few districts of Uttar Pradesh.[2] Its objective was hyperlocal news in a hyperlocal language for a hyperlocal audience, created by local journalists most marginal to processes of media or knowledge production: women from Dalit, tribal or Muslim backgrounds.[3] At a microcosmic level, Khabar Lahariya attempted to shift deeply embedded and intersecting structures of power like gender, class, caste and ethnicity via the process of media production and consumption. It worked on breaking down and re/creating two products: the local news story and the local journalist. Both of these processes of production were stymied and shaped by forces of patriarchy, which drew the boundaries of what women could and could not do, and policed them via their male guardians – fathers, husbands, brothers, sons, in-laws, neighbours and the state.

The media landscape of India, even in the deep rural context where Khabar Lahariya was located, has changed at quite a significant pace. India began to be known as a major player in the mobile phone market, just behind China (*Economic Times*, 2018). Responding to these changes, as well as the changes in development funding, Khabar Lahariya in 2015 began to pivot its news production and distribution model from print to a digital-first one, and its journey away from a niche NGO project towards that of an exemplar digital media product. With the internet, the 'local' had gained significance in global politics, economics and media: it opened up ways in which reach and communication could become extremely contextualised, and yet audiences and markets could be accessed with much lower cost and effort. In 2015, at the time of planning pilot digital content, the number of mobile data subscribers in India was 245 million, and this was a buoyant upward trend (Kaushik, 2016). By February 2016, Uttar Pradesh East, the telecom circle in which Bundelkhand falls, had the largest number of active wireless (mobile) connections in the country – 91 million (TRAI, 2016). At the time of writing, almost 300 million of India's 600 million internet users are in its small towns and rural areas, with over 90 per cent accessing the internet on their mobile phones. And so, Khabar Lahariya prepared to enter a new world of power and male, upper-caste and upper-class privilege, to intervene in the new media narratives that existed there, via video reports published on a dedicated YouTube channel.

Between 2012 and 2019, Khabar Lahariya's YouTube channel published over 7,000 videos and garnered over 100 million views. Between September 2016 – shortly preceding state assembly elections in Uttar Pradesh – and 2019 – the year of the world's largest democratic election – views per month grew from 25,000 to 6 million. Thus, in parallel to a national harnessing of digital infrastructure to influence political narratives, a small, feminist media organisation set itself up to be part of this wave of change (Dixit, 2016; Ila, 2016). In doing so, it also brought into the space of social media discourse the issues of non-privileged subjects – both reporters and stories – and the pervasiveness of embedded social structures and systems, even in this new, virtual world.

When the teller changes the story: the Khabar Lahariya vantage point

Suneeta Prajapati, twenty-four years of age, is one of many young reporters in the Khabar Lahariya team.[4] A passionate print journalist, Suneeta has embraced Khabar Lahariya's digital/video avatar. She is from Mahoba district, around 100 kilometres from where Khabar Lahariya first put down its roots. It is similarly arid and drought-prone but is endowed with mineral resources which provide the opportunity of a double-edged livelihood for locals, laced with hazards of unsafe working conditions and exploitative wages. Its hilly terrain is mined for granite, diaspore and sand (Bundelkhand Research Portal, n.d.; Shukla, 2013). Suneeta's family lives at the edge of a stone quarry. Her village is coated with a thin white dust that comes from the continual 'blasting' of the quarry and from 'crusher' machines that dot the landscape. Her sister, like many others in the region, died of tuberculosis when she was young. Suneeta herself worked in the quarry as a young girl, putting herself through school with the money she was able to earn. She joined Khabar Lahariya in 2012, as an eighteen-year-old with ambitions beyond the debilitating labour her family had to do to survive, or not, as the case may be. As the head of its fledgling edition in Mahoba, Suneeta took keen interest in reporting on the disregard for labour or human rights in the process of mining in the district. This sprang from, and reiterated, the editorial standpoint that if Khabar Lahariya was started by and for women, it did not limit itself to covering 'women's issues' only but considered all issues were women's issues, and its journalists would cover 'hard' (crime, politics, economics) and 'soft' (culture and development) topics and everything in between, from their own perspective. Over the years, Suneeta has taken on the nexus between politicians, media and mining contractors, in order to expose the conditions of work in the mines. Over and over again, her stories have focused on issues like compensation for death due to hazardous working conditions and the lesser reported long-term health hazards to families living on the periphery of quarries, like her own. In her video reports, viewers are suffocated by the fine dust in the air, the circularity of the testimonies, and the feeling that the space between death by hunger or tuberculosis or fatal accident are all too close, and too inevitable (Khabar Lahariya, 2016, 2017a).

Khabar Lahariya has, over the years, directly raised issues around the misogynist nature of reporting on women, and especially crimes against women. Where rampant murders of women over dowry are grossly underreported (Dang et al., 2018) and sexual assault or long-term domestic violence either silenced or sensationalised to the extent of being pure misogynistic fiction, Khabar Lahariya has consistently brought reporting on violence against women, from women's perspectives, into the mainstream. In 2017, when the shift from print to digital media was at its peak, both nationally and in Khabar Lahariya's hinterland, a story about a young girl in Banda district of Bundelkhand caught the attention of the mainstream Hindi media. In a style which had already garnered notoriety as digital reporting of the 'viral' kind, the story that was published across print and digital platforms was far from the 'truth', and this had indirect correlation to the speed with which it travelled. In October 2017 the girl, tipped off that her absent lover was getting married, made her way to the site of the wedding and was shocked and angered to realise the story was true. The 'news report' that raced across the media later that day claimed that she had stormed into her lover's wedding and kidnapped him at gunpoint in a flashy SUV. The girl was quickly given the epithet of 'Revolver Rani' or 'Bullet Rani' (gun or bullet queen), and the stories were packaged with images from films similarly named. Kavita, Khabar Lahariya's co-founder and editor – in whose home town this story broke and took on a life of its own – resisted reporting on it for as long as she could, from the editorial point of view that women's personal lives should not be the material of newspapers. Soon she heard reports that both the local media and the police had been interrogating/ harassing the protagonist of the story in the local Banda police station. It was at this point that Khabar Lahariya began its investigation, uncovering how a fake news story gets created and how this kind of reporting on women's lives is itself a form of violence. The story was later picked up by other local and national media and contributed in some incremental way to shifting the knee-jerk style of reporting on news about women (Khabar Lahariya, 2017b).

Khabar Lahariya's audience engagement strategy has been rooted in the importance of closing the distance between the media producer and consumer. Maintaining a familiarity and an even gaze in its reporting, despite challenging social boundaries and structures, has been essential to the product, its voice, its distinction from the 'objective' (and, we could add, elite) point of view of other media. Its intimate engagement with its audience has sometimes meant reporters being threatened at gunpoint or mobbed by upper-caste readers assuming the political affiliation of the (Dalit) reporter and thus the editorial partisanship of the publication.[5] With the shift to digital and video reporting, the Khabar Lahariya reporters were much more visible as Dalit women in the public domain: their faces and opinions were visible in a new way. The reporters thrived on this long-desired visibility of their subjecthood and their citizenship. Upper-caste men who would have not known of their existence were now sparring with them as 'trolls' on Facebook, on issues of gender and caste. In many ways, Khabar Lahariya's public engagement with media and audiences on the 'Revolver Rani' story, and what this said about how content concerning women was consumed in the nascent digital landscape, was preparation for its distinct response to the global and national #MeToo movement which would break almost exactly a year later.

Calling out/on #MeToo from the margins

I'm anyway a very strange creature for these parts – a woman reporter … But, ever since I've gone digital, and come onto social media, I've had to deal with a lot more people, and in different ways. … People know us. So now I'm also in all these spaces that require me to also mingle, and I do. … Right now, my parents and I have negotiated these freedoms in my life. … If something like a photo of mine turning up in an unpalatable context can take away these hard-earned freedoms, and it totally can, then that ruins me and my life, doesn't it? ... Whatever I say to them will not go down well. *Unhe dhakka lagega* [they will feel the impact], and they will only react. Their dreams will shatter, it will be the end of the world for them. And by imposing restrictions on me, it'll become impossible for me also. ... For me [freedom] is essential to stay alive. It's like breathing.

Anyway, fear is an emotion exclusive to girls, right? (Unpublished interview with Khabar Lahariya reporter, 2018)

In 2013, in the context of the changing mediascape in small towns and rural areas of north India, a research project was designed by a Delhi-based NGO called the Women Media and News Trust on the experiences of journalists in small towns of Uttar Pradesh, Rajasthan, Madhya Pradesh and Bihar (WMNT, 2014). Through rich life stories, the negotiation of women from small towns with/in the structures of gender, class and caste in the process of navigating an oppressively patriarchal public domain, is brought to life. The study posits that the women embody a lived notion of citizenship by being active in a male public as reporters; and that this involves a daily performance and rejection of gender norms.

> Being women in this role, and most often the only women journalists in the area – their gender and sexual embodiment informed all their interactions: how they walked, talked, dressed, and with whom they interacted ... there was an awareness of how and why people looked and responded to them in the ways they did – paternalistic, protective, dismissive and leering. In our conversations, as in their lives and work, the reporters played multiple and contradictory roles: good journalists, good women, holding tight and then distancing themselves from their gender identity. (Mullick, 2015: 701)

When the stories of sexual harassment in newsrooms across the country began to travel via social media in late 2018 and jolt the mainstream media establishment (Datta et al., 2018), it took a while for us at Khabar Lahariya – a fairly unique urban-rural editorial team – to calculate a response. Solidarity was all very well, but discussions in our editorial meetings circled around the fact that the calling out of sexual violence in the workplace must be located in a specific historical and social context. The women of India's '#MeToo moment' – by and large urban, middle-class, English-speaking, upper-caste – who slowly came forward, on

Facebook and Twitter, in a nod to the global movement to visibilise sexual harassment in the workplace, to place their long-held trauma on record, were part of a public sphere where seeing women at work outside the home was not out of the ordinary any more. In metropolitan cities of the 2010s, English newsrooms, especially in terms of anchors and reporters, had an increasingly more balanced gender ratio (Byerly, 2011; Thomas, 2018). This was not the case further from the metro cities. In rural areas, and in rural north India specifically, women are visible as agricultural labour (especially poorer, more marginalised castes) or as field staff in government jobs, especially schools and hospitals. The 1990s saw legislation in the form of reserving positions for women in the panchayat system of local governance, and towards the formation of microcredit groups. The former, however, resulted in more male proxies in public rather than increasing women's participation; the latter moved women, as the savers in the family, from a private to a community resource. The Mahatma Gandhi Rural Employment Guarantee Act of 2009 (MGREGA), to ensure rural employment within villages, opened up employment opportunities for rural women – employment rates under MGREGA are 51 per cent compared to the overall rate for rural women at 27 per cent (Pande et al., 2016). The Right to Education Act of 2010 has incrementally increased the numbers of girls coming into the school system. However, in the still feudal context of rural north India, there is no notion of women having equal status to men in the public domain or having the freedom to explore occupations of their choice; their access and mobility is highly controlled (Devika and Thampi, 2011). In Khabar Lahariya's almost two decades of experience in rural north India, journalism, or any profession that required women to have unregulated mobility, access to and interaction with men, an ability to assert themselves in public and private spaces was still countered with fear and loathing, which often took the form of emotional and physical harassment (WMNT, 2014).

In this context, in the wake of the snowballing revelations of sexual harassment in newsrooms or news organisations across the country, Khabar Lahariya's politics and editorial strategy were at odds. We had an acute, bodily and social understanding of how patriarchal forces shaped the experience of working as journalists in

the public domain (Khabar Lahariya, 2019a). There was an instinc-
tive alignment with #MeToo; a deep sense of liberation in connecting experiences of women in different locations. However, we also
felt some concern about how the local audience would react if we
published stories about #MeToo. We were in agreement that it could
elicit a backlash from our predominantly male, upper-caste audience
who would argue that women should not be in the public domain
in this manner and that harassment was just due punishment. Many
members of our team, even senior journalists, still tread a very fine
line in their personal and professional lives, so that reporting or
writing opinion pieces on a movement that brought the harassment
of working women up for discussion was a risky proposition. For
someone like myself to push for the importance of recording or
reporting on this moment at Khabar Lahariya, for showing our solidarity as feminists, was to be insensitive to the journeys and contexts
which I had been part of and witnessed for many years.

One very vivid memory for the group was from 2015, when
Khabar Lahariya went public with a story of phone stalking that
had plagued the team for over nine months (Khabar Lahariya,
2015). A young man, eventually caught with over forty SIM cards,
repeatedly called six members of the team, some of whom were
experienced senior journalists. He had access to their locations
and, often, their daily schedules and routes. As if the fear of being
watched and harassed daily was not enough, the most scarring part
of the experience was the negligence and harassment at the hands of
the police, who quite openly placed the responsibility on the reporters themselves: why had they shared their numbers?; was this not
a natural consequence of life in the public domain? Going through
the process of filing police complaints necessitated the reporters
replaying the phone calls over and over, much to the mirth of the
police. The process mirrored the challenges they faced when they
reported on violence cases: often forcing the police to take note or
action. As women who had painstakingly established themselves as
professional journalists in the public domain for over a decade, the
process of accessing justice was humiliating, both locally and to the
larger public with which they shared their testimony.

In addition to this was the fact that access to personal mobile
phones and the internet made possible a new form of freedom for

the Khabar Lahariya journalists, as it had for millions of other young women in India (Doron, 2012; Tenhunen, 2018). It was freedom from a tightly surveilled offline existence, one where social identity constricted who, when and how one built relationships. It opened up access to a possibly more flexible existence: a space whose rules were yet to be determined. Facebook allowed for disguise and yet public displays of 'friendship'; WhatsApp chats allowed for a blurring of the boundaries between professional and personal that was all in the rules of the game; and then there were new apps for finding friendship: Like, Likey, Happn – the list was endless (Khabar Lahariya, 2019b; Mullick, 2017; Poonam and Bansal, 2020). This was something that neither our team, nor the other women coming online who did not have the privilege of urban women's sociocultural mobility, wanted to compromise on. A curtailing of hard-won, even surreptitious freedoms could be an unintentional side effect of discussing the circumstances of sexual harassment against women.

This was the personal and public context in which the strategy to respond to #MeToo was thrashed out in our newsroom. But, how could we *not* be part of this moment? The compromise we reached was to publish an open letter (Khabar Lahariya, 2018a), in a voice that trod between the urban and the rural, immersed in and shaped by the experience of rural female reporters yet with the distance to analyse this experience. The letter was addressed to the reporters' long-time male peers in the small towns of rural Uttar Pradesh, but also sought accountability from the hitherto predominantly urban #MeToo movement. We sought to ask, from a position of invisibility that rural women have in many contemporary conversations around gender (Roy, 2016), who would support rural women coming out with stories of harassment in the workplace – in the fields, in administrative offices, hospitals, schools, police stations? Would speaking out ensure a change in the way they were seen? Would speaking out change the cultural context in which laws against sexual harassment were embedded and flaunted?

> We feel relief that there is a platform and a movement that promises to expose the abuse that keeps us tied down, under the control of a powerful structure. But there is a dark place in our minds where this

relief refuses to reach – those of us who continue to fight, or those who have been defeated. The memory of a friend and colleague, a single woman trying to make it in the world of small-town journalism, and who was pushed into despair and a lonely death, only earlier this year, with no resonating cries off or online ... At the end of the day, our struggles are of lone women operating with few avenues to reach out, with little or no support structure to fall back on, at home or in the world. Whatever defence mechanisms we have, come from our own instincts, dressing down our personalities, keeping multiple SIM cards, or leaving a trail of breadcrumbs, creating our own informal networks for help when we're in danger. (Khabar Lahariya, 2018a)

The letter travelled across numerous English digital platforms. It resulted in interest and interviews with Khabar Lahariya journalists on their experiences of reporting in non-metro locations. It made, briefly, the discussions on news panels a fraction more inclusive of diverse experiences of navigating patriarchy in a digital age. Editors at Khabar Lahariya admitted that their male peers felt momentarily self-conscious sharing lewd content over Facebook or WhatsApp (Iyer, 2018). But like all viral content online, it had a limited shelf life. After the online storm, has the Indian #MeToo movement now become a force to reckon with outside of the urban Twitter room? Reading through the Tejpal judgement, which replays the crudity of rape trials in small town district courts, which put the survivor on the stand as entertainer and prosecuted (Khabar Lahariya, 2019a), there is an acute sense of fury of how limited the impact of this storm has been.

The open letter was only one strategy for us, addressing a political and an epistemological need to place the specific experience of entering the public domain as rural journalists who were women from marginalised communities, to add to the knowledge around women's experiences at work. The longer-term editorial strategy that accompanied this was to begin focused and regular reporting on women's experiences of harassment in the workplace in rural areas, in the form of a monthly video or audio series. With this series we wanted to break the silences and taboos around speaking about harassment; to break the stereotypes around what constitutes a workplace, a woman at work; and to expose the very complicated and fraught relationships that women navigate when they enter a public domain shaped by men, and with mostly men in power. How does a tribal woman construct a relationship with a police officer who can report her for 'illegally' collecting forest goods as a livelihood? How does a Dalit reporter negotiate a productive relationship with an upper-caste source of information in the local administration? How does a bonded labourer determine a relationship with an upper-caste contractor and moneylender, who ensures her entire family has work each year?

As a media organisation with a deep, working commitment to 'situated knowledges' (Harraway, 1988), our objective was to widen the narrative around sexual harassment in the workplace – from the perspective of geography, class, caste and religion/ethnicity. The strategy was to create detailed testimonies of women working in rural areas and small towns in order to understand the specificities of their experiences of work and navigating harassment. This would broaden local (rural, Khabar Lahariya's primary audience) knowledge about the barriers to women's participation in the public domain and their ability to interact with various institutions, as well as enabling women to speak/make visible these traumas and seek support if necessary. For all of us at Khabar Lahariya, it was clear that solidarity with a movement like #MeToo had to have a tangible local value, in terms of shifting the patriarchal narrative about women's roles in society.

#MeTooRural and teething pains

The actualisation of this editorial strategy, like the larger, long-term process of running a media institution set against the logic of media businesses – with women from the margins at the centre of news production, and poor communities as consumers of news – was challenging. As in many cases of structural violence that Khabar Lahariya reports on (for instance on migration, bonded labour or caste violence), subjects of stories that it covered as part of a new series entitled #MeTooRural would share their experience off record, or even on record, but would rescind their statements after the interview was over, or in a second or third conversation. In one case in Chitrakoot district, where Khabar Lahariya was founded, in the weeks between the recording of a reporter's testimony and publication of her story, the perpetrator of harassment, once her close friend and colleague, went to jail, was released, filed a case against her and decided to contest the general election for a new 'progressive' party. The reporter withdrew her statement and then, broken and betrayed, reapproached Khabar Lahariya for support in the form of justice and counselling. Unlike the perpetrator, she was out of work and discredited widely online and offline. This happened again and again in the #MeTooRural series. With Khabar Lahariya's embedded, invested local understanding of crisscrossing relationships, or those that sour and sweeten over time, holding an absolute version of the truth became too heavy a responsibility to carry.

The attempt did allow some powerful stories to emerge, however. One was the story of Neetu Shukla, a twenty-two-year-old constable posted in a remote police station in Banda district who allegedly committed suicide in September 2018 (Khabar Lahariya, 2018b). As Twitter erupted with #MeToo testimonies by urban media-persons in October and November, Neetu's alleged suicide was hotly reported in the regional news media. She had been jilted by a colleague; a 'blue' film had been shot and was about to be posted online; she was complaining about abuse by an older female colleague – the compulsorily sensational tone of reporting on violence against women in the Hindi news media had much material to use. *Hatya ya aatmhatya* (murder or suicide) is an all-too-common headline in the heartland press, given the norm of covering up the murders of women (Khabar Lahariya, 2017c). It seemed significant, then, for Khabar Lahariya to dive into the case as its first #MeTooRural investigation. It allowed us to speak to the many hurdles women in the rural workplace repeatedly confront, given the high stakes of losing a job, especially a permanent government job. The consequences of investigating or making public these stories of abuse could be more dire than being fired or suspended. In Neetu's case, it was death. Neetu's story became even more significant to me, against the background of the she-said-he-said on various Twitter handles. The dark and dubious information available about Neetu's life and death contrasted with the graphic and petty details of #MeToo testimonies in the urban context. Where both overlapped, however, was in the obfuscation of the structural underpinnings of the sexist workplace. The investigation of the death of a young police constable thus seemed a stark and significant way in which to pull a very different social location and experience into the purview of the #MeToo movement. Could this case, in a small town in rural India, have a #MeToo moment, or access justice through a digital exposé? Despite the impossibility of the investigation (relevant witnesses were transferred and inaccessible; police files were closed; neighbours and eyewitnesses refused to go on record, and those who did had versions which sounded like the crime thrillers they loved to watch), we still considered documenting and publishing this story an important way to expose how diligently harassment of women in a workplace can take place and be obscured, as though it was entirely fictional, a spurious news report.

Conclusion

The attempt to question or shift systems like patriarchy, or social structures like gender and caste that are embedded within it, requires more than the creation of subjects and products that can speak back to power. It is constant, strenuous investment to shift the landscape that the work is located within; it requires moving beyond the messages, into the context in which those messages are embedded.

Digitalisation of media opens up the possibility of countless narratives: unstable, contingent, mutable. The finality of print, even the reliable reference point of a face or opinion on television, no longer exists. It is tempting to think this is liberating and signals a democratising of the landscape and technologies of media. However, social structures and the institutions that they work through are more resilient than the scientific innovation of centuries; they adapt to our most shape-shifting technologies.

As the stories of women who had experienced sexual harassment snowballed towards the end of 2018 and start of 2019, digital media and social platforms began to turn on themselves with vivid accounts of more and more stories, polarised debates around the 'truth' of various testimonies, and snide commentary sensational-ised by the mainstream media (Singh, 2019). Khabar Lahariya's #MeTooRural series aimed to continuously nuance the context of accounts of sexual harassment in the workplace. The accounts were situated in the materiality of caste, gender, sexual norms, location and economic strife and the ways in which power within a patriar-chal system shifts between each of these layers of dis-privilege. The accounts of rural women's experiences hold a mirror to the #MeToo movement, and to society at large: that this was a systemic and urgent issue faced by many different kinds of women and men, one that required sustained investigation and action.

Khabar Lahariya's journalists and the microcosms of challenging patriarchy and institutionalised discrimination that they represent, as well as the reportage they produce, are instances of a kind of situ-ated knowledge that reflects the lacunae in even reflective, radical new media practice – whether in the creation of disruptive content, or in facilitating the naming and shaming of various forms of vio-lence and discrimination. New technologies and networks hold the potential to enable these hyperlocal narratives, and the disruptive processes involved in creating them, to travel: to enrich and compli-cate contemporary political understanding on these issues.

Notes

1 The region of Bundelkhand comprises thirteen districts of Madhya Pradesh and Uttar Pradesh. Socially, the region is diverse with a large Scheduled Caste population, a number of Scheduled Tribes and a large backward community, with the upper caste dominating through power, assets and leadership.

2 Khabar Lahariya was a project initiated by a Delhi-based NGO in 2002, in Chitrakoot district (then Banda, later divided into Chitrakoot and Banda) of Uttar Pradesh. The idea came from the success of a broadsheet, *Mahila Dakiya*, which included in its writing and production adult participants of a literacy intervention as a way for them to use their nascent literacy and information skills (Ghose and Mullick, 2015). This broadsheet, in Hindi and Bundeli, the local language, was intended for a predominantly local, female, neo-literate audience (although its readership soon swelled beyond this). It became so popular in the area that, after the educational

programme it was part of withdrew from the area, the female contributors and readers demanded it be reinstated. Khabar Lahariya was concep-
tualised as a local language newspaper that would be run by a team of
women journalists from marginalised communities and who had varying
levels of literacy. It was a way in which women could be part of produc-
ing reading material that would sustain their fragile literacy, but it was
also an attempt at subverting conventional gender roles and bringing
women out into the public sphere of information, news, governance,
politics and more.

3 Dalit, meaning 'broken/scattered' in Sanskrit and Hindi, is a self-assigned
   term mostly used by and for the communities considered the lowest, in
   fact outside of the fourfold varna or caste system of Hinduism.
4 Suneeta left Khabar Lahariya in Dec 2020, to work with its parent
   company, Chambal Media.
5 The Bahujan Samaj Party (BSP), a national political party in India, states
   that it represents the people at the lowest levels of the Hindu social
   system – those officially designated as members of the Scheduled Castes,
   Scheduled Tribes and Other Backward Classes – as well as other religious and social minorities. The core support group of the BSP consists
   primarily of Dalits, although over the last decade the party has made
   efforts to include 'general' or 'upper' castes into its voter base. Since the
   Khabar Lahariya journalists are predominantly Dalit, they are often seen
   as BSP supporters, especially during election reporting.

References

Baxi, Pratiksha (2021). 'For the Judge, It Was a Feminist Who Was on Trial,
    Not Tarun Tejpal. The Wire, May 29. https://thewire.in/women/for-the-
    judge-it-was-a-feminist-who-was-on-trial-not-tarun-tejpal. Accessed 29
    May 2021.
Bundelkhand Research Portal. (n.d). Mining and Quarrying in Bundelkhand.
    Accessed 1 December 2019.
Byerly, C.M. (2011). 'Global Report on Status of Women in the News Media',
    International Women's Media Foundation. www.iwmf.org/wp-content/
    uploads/2018/06/IWMF-Global-Report.pdf. Accessed 10 April 2020.
Chakravartty, P. and S. Roy. (2013). 'Media Pluralism Redux: Towards
    New Frameworks of Comparative Media Studies "Beyond the West"',
    Political Communication 30:3, 349–70.
Dang, G., V. Kulkarni and R. Gaiha. (2018). 'Why Dowry Deaths
    Have Risen in India?' ASARC Working Paper, 2018/3. Australia

South Asia Research Centre. https://crawford.anu.edu.au/acde/asarc/pdf/papers/2018/WP2018-03.pdf. Accessed January 2020.

Das, M. (2018). 'Flirting in in the Age of #MeToo', *Times of India*, 18 March. https://timesofindia.indiatimes.com/home/sunday-times/flirting-in-the-age-of-metoo/articleshow/63348492.cms. Accessed 9 April 2020.

Datta, D., S. Punj and C. Sinha. (2018). '#MeToo Hits Home', *India Today*, 22 October. www.indiatoday.in/magazine/cover-story/story/20181022-metoo-hits-home-1360419-2018-10-12. Accessed 1 December 2019.

Deodhar, N. and A. Manral. (2019). 'As Utsav Chakraborty calls #MeToo Allegations "Fabricated"; Mahima Kukreja Says He Needs to Own Up, Apologise', *First Post*, 25 November. www.firstpost.com/entertainment/as-utsav-chakraborty-calls-metoo-allegations-fabricated-mahima-kukreja-says-he-needs-to-own-up-apologise-7697521.html. Accessed 1 December 2019.

Devika, J. and B. V. Thampi. (2011). 'Mobility towards Work and Politics for Women in Kerala State, India: A View from the Histories of Gender and Space', *Modern Asian Studies* 45:5, 1147–75.

Dixit, P. (2016). 'India's Only All-Woman Rural Newspaper has a New Challenge: Cracking Digital Publishing', *Factor Daily*, 20 July. https://factordaily.com/khabar-lahariya-digital-publishing/. Accessed 9 April 2020.

Doron, A. (2012). 'Mobile Persons: Cell Phones, Gender and the Self in North India', *Asia Pacific Journal of Anthropology* 13:5, 414–33.

Economic Times. (2018). 'Smartphones Emerge as Bright Spot for Indian Manufacturing', *Economic Times*, 25 October. https://economictimes.indiatimes.com/tech/hardware/smartphones-emerge-as-bright-spot-for-indian-manufacturing/articleshow/66357164.cms?from=mdr. Accessed May 2019.

Ghose, M. and D. Mullick. (2015). A Tangled Weave: Tracing Outcomes of Education in Rural Women's Lives in North India', *International Review of Education* 61, 343–64.

Harraway, D. (1988). 'Situated Knowledges: The Science Question in Feminism and the Privilege of Partial Perspective', *Feminist Studies* 14:3, 575–99.

Ila, A. (2016). 'In a Cool Move Khabar Lahariya Goes Digital: What Does this Strategy Mean for its Largely Rural Audience?' The Ladies Finger, 17 August. http://theladiesfinger.com/khabar-lahariya-digital-first-strategy/. Accessed 9 April 2020.

Iyer, A. (2018). '#MeToo Reaches Rural India: "Men have Stopped Sending us Porn"', The Quint, 18 October. www.thequint.com/news/india/me-too-sexual-harassment-rural-women-khabar-lahariya. Accessed 1 December 2019.

Kaushik, V. (2016). 'India's Mobile Internet Usage Reaches New Heights', Think with Google, May. www.thinkwithgoogle.com/intl/en-apac/

trends-and-insights/india-mobile-internet-usage-reaches-new-heights/. Accessed 1 December 2019.

Khabar Lahariya. (2015). 'The Policeman Said: Why Don't You Tell Me what Gaalis He Whispers in Your Ear', Khabar Lahariya, September 14. https://khabarlahariya.org/the-policeman-said-why-dont-you-tell-me-what-gaalis-he-whispers-in-your-ear/. Accessed 1 December 2019.

Khabar Lahariya. (2016). 'These Mines Take the Lives of Labourers in Mahoba's Kabrai Village', Khabar Lahariya, YouTube video, 4:24 min, posted 22 March. www.youtube.com/watch?v=-IbAto1G3-8. Accessed 1 December 2019.

Khabar Lahariya. (2017a). 'Dirt, Dust and Disease: Kabrai's Residents Grow Sick and Tired of the Crusher Machines', Khabar Lahariya, YouTube video, 4:01 min, posted 26 April. www.youtube.com/watch?v=ia83tyTM5NA. Accessed 1 December 2019.

Khabar Lahariya. (2017b). 'Backstage with Revolver Rani', Khabar Lahariya, 12 October. https://khabarlahariya.org/backstage-with-revolver-rani/. Accessed 1 December 2019.

Khabar Lahariya. (2017c). 'The Price of a Woman's Life', Khabar Lahariya, 18 December. https://khabarlahariya.org/the-price-of-a-womans-life/. Accessed 1 December 2019.

Khabar Lahariya. (2018a). 'How Do You Silence a Ghost? You've already Done the Worst You Could', Khabar Lahariya, 12 October. https://khabarlahariya.org/how-do-you-silence-a-ghost-youve-already-done-the-worst-you-could-metoo/. Accessed 1 December 2019.

Khabar Lahariya. (2018b). 'Who Killed Neetu Shukla?' Khabar Lahariya, 31 December. https://khabarlahariya.org/who-killed-neetu-shukla/. Accessed 1 December 2019.

Khabar Lahariya. (2019a). 'Women at Work', Khabar Lahariya, 3 January. https://khabarlahariya.org/women-at-work-me-too-bundelkhand/. Accessed 1 December 2019.

Khabar Lahariya. (2019b). 'Love, Sex, Dhokha and Dosti: Episode 1', Khabar Lahariya, 26 October. https://khabarlahariya.org/love-sex-dhokha-dosti-ep-1/. Accessed 1 December 2019.

Mohan, J, Anand (2021). '#MeToo: Delhi Court Acquits Priya Ramani in Criminal Defamation Case Filed by MJ Akbar'. Indian Express. February 18. https://indianexpress.com/article/india/metoo-delhi-court-acquits-priya-ramani-in-criminal-defamation-case-filed-by-mj-akbar-7192384/. Accessed 30 May 2021.

Mullick, D. (2015). 'Playing Reporter: Small-Town Women Journalists in North India', *Journalism Studies* 16:5, 692–705.

Mullick, D. (2017). 'Freedom in a Chat Window', LiveMint, 10 February. www.livemint.com/Leisure/pFRy7l3fSAqPGgMxOhokKP/Freedom-in-a-chat-window.html. Accessed 1 December 2019.

Nair, S. (2018). '#MeToo in India Inc: Former Taj Hotels Staffer Speaks Out, Names then CEO', *Indian Express*, 1 November. https://indian express.com/article/india/metoo-in-india-inc-former-taj-hotels-staffer-speaks-out-names-then-ceo-5428268/. Accessed 1 December 2019.

Naqvi, Farah. (2007). *Waves in the Hinterland: The Journey of a Newspaper*. New Delhi: Zubaan Books.

Padma Priya, D. V. L. (2019). 'One Year On, #MeToo Has Run Out of Steam: Is the Failure to Include Marginalised Voices to Blame?' *Newslaundry*, 18 October. www.newslaundry.com/2019/10/18/one-year-of-metoo-but-structural-changes-are-a-long-way-away. Accessed 9 April 2020.

Pande, R., J. Johnson and E. Dodge. (2016). 'How to Get India's Women Working? First, Let Them Out of the House', IndiaSpend, 9 April. https://scholar.harvard.edu/rpande/news/how-get-india%E2%80%99s-women-working-first-let-them-out-house. Accessed 10 April 2020.

Poonam, S. and S. Bansal. (2020). 'Inside the Chinese Dating Apps Exploiting the Loneliness of India's Men', *Quartz*, 13 March. https://qz.com/india/1811151/chinese-dating-apps-are-exploiting-loneliness-of-indias-men/. Accessed 10 April 2020.

Press Institute of India. (2004). *Status of Women Journalists in India*. New Delhi: National Commission for Women.

Roy, S. (2016). 'Breaking the Cage', *Dissent*, Fall. www.dissentmagazine.org/article/breaking-cage-india-feminism-sexual-violence-public-space. Accessed 1 December 2019.

Shukla, N. (2013). 'Treasure Trove found at Bundelkhand', *Times of India*, 28 October. https://timesofindia.indiatimes.com/india/Treasure-trove-found-at-Bundelkhand/articleshow/24784926.cms. Accessed 16 July 2021.

Singh, S. (2019). 'Tanushree Dutta Blasts Neha Kakkar for Judging Indian Idol with #MeToo Accused Anu Malik'. ZeeNews, 18 November. https://zeenews.india.com/people/tanushree-dutta-blasts-neha-kakkar-for-judging-indian-idol-with-metoo-accused-anu-malik-read-full-state ment-2246952.html. Accessed 1 December 2019.

Sood, S., N. Singh, A. Mandhani and F. Khan. (2019). 'One Year after India's Big #MeToo Wave, a Reality Check', The Print, 12 October. https://theprint.in/features/one-year-after-india-big-metoo-wave-reality-check/304787/. Accessed 9 April 2020.

Tenhunen, S. (2018). *A Village Goes Mobile: Telephony, Mediation, and Social Change in Rural India*. New York: Oxford University Press.

Thomas, J. (2018). 'Women in Media: The Power and the Struggle', *Newslaundry*, 4 May. www.newslaundry.com/2018/05/04/women-med ia-gender-bias-power-indian-newsrooms-male-editors. Accessed 10 April 2020.

TRAI (Telecom Regulatory Authority of India). (2016). 'Press Release 26/2016: Highlights of Telecom Subscription Data as on 29th February, 2016', 26 April. https://main.trai.gov.in/sites/default/files/Press_Release_no26_eng.pdf. Accessed 1 December 2019.

WMNT (Women Media and News Trust). (2014). *Zile ki Hulchul: Conversations with Women Reporters in Small-Town India*. New Delhi: Women Media and News Trust.

6

Contesting the meaning/s of sexual violence in the South African postcolony: where are the male victims?

Louise du Toit

'n Oop hol is in die tronk soos 'n goudmyn – álmal soek 'n stukkie. (An open anus in prison is like a gold mine – everybody wants a piece of it.) (Sesant, 2020)

Under conditions of increased visibility of sexual violence crimes and victims speaking out, such as during the #MeToo and #SayHerName campaigns, patriarchal logic tends to change tack. No longer able to either deny its reality – or extent[1] – altogether (its first strategy) or to trivialise its destructive impact on victims (its second strategy), the focus shifts towards concurrently appropriating and distorting the meanings attached to the phenomenon (its third strategy). Feminist activists have to weigh in on this war of interpretations, in particular by drawing attention back to all of the actual victims' lived experiences themselves. This is especially important in colonial and postcolonial[2] contexts, where 'rape talk', thus the public ways in which rape is from time to time taken up as a matter of shared social concern, has mostly tended to serve racist colonial agendas. The aim of this chapter is to draw attention to the male victims of sexual violence in the South African postcolony. This might seem surprising, first, because male victims have been so effectively erased from public consciousness that the existence of the phenomenon itself may be questioned (first patriarchal strategy of erasure) and, second, because South Africans do in fact 'know' about its existence, judging from the pervasiveness of 'prison rape jokes' in social and other popular media (second patriarchal strategy of trivialisation) (see Maseko, 2015). We simultaneously know, and also 'do not know', that men are also victims of sexual violence.

One of the ways in which we 'do not know' is manifest in the absence of male victims from the South African #MeToo moment as well as other collective explosions of anger about sexual violence. The way that popular slogans (such as #MenAreTrash) polarise the sexes on this issue suggests that the erasure of male victims of sexual violence is one of the central weaknesses of this kind of hashtag activism.

My discussion places this wilful collective ignorance about male rape within the larger frame of public 'rape talk' in the South African postcolony, to show why and how male rape is either discursively erased altogether or its meaning distorted in the service of patriarchy. Contrary to what some feminist activists think (for example, Dolan, 2014; COFEM, 2017a, 2017b), I argue that the neglect of male victims of sexual violence ultimately serves patriarchal ends, and therefore requires urgent critical feminist attention. Moreover, this issue demands activism and vigilance on all three fronts: rendering it visible, acknowledging its harms, and feminists prevailing in the war of interpretations.

The first section examines the consequences that the colonial history of 'rape talk' has on postcolonial South Africa. The second section examines the lingering effect of the powerful colonial trope of unruly Black[3] male sexuality, even within the very attempts to overcome it, and links it to the calamitous failure of addressing sexual violence in the postcolony. The third section then examines in detail the consequences of the almost complete invisibility of male victims of sexual violence in mainstream 'rape talk' in South Africa.

The lingering effects of colonial rape talk

A number of feminist scholars have worked to show that sexuality and sexual politics have been of central importance to the colonial project everywhere (for example, Gqola, 2015; Graham, 2012; Lugones, 2007; Oyěwùmí, 1997; Ratele, 2009; Stoler, 1995, 2010). The main point to be drawn from this sexual-racial colonial history locally is that colonial and apartheid concerns about sexual violence were never focused on preventing direct harm to victims of sexual violence. Instead, given the colonial preoccupation of construing whiteness and preventing 'racial contamination', the overriding purpose of paying attention to sexual violence was to forestall threats to White male, heterosexual domination. Thus, 'rape talk' and sexual violence legislation tended to be limited to 'protecting' White female sexuality construed as particularly vulnerable, against a perceived 'predatory' Black male sexuality. This symbolic binary was mobilised to justify physical separation between the races, and the large-scale displacement of Black communities, for example through the historic Native Land Act of 1913 and the Immorality Act of 1927 (see Coetzee and du Toit, 2018; Gqola, 2015; Graham, 2012; Ratele, 2009). To be sure, not even White women's sexual integrity was properly protected in the process because victims' actual experiences of sexual attack would typically have to fit this particular mould of interracial transgression if they hoped to be taken seriously. And even then, the concern was not so much about the direct harm to the victim as about the implicit challenge to White men's sexual prerogative. This phenomenon falls under the third patriarchal strategy of neither erasing nor trivialising rape but, instead, appropriating and distorting its significance for racialised patriarchal purposes. Glaringly absent from this narrow, instrumentalist, interest and uptake, of course, are, amongst other factors, Black women as victims of sexual violence, and White men as its perpetrators.

Characteristic of this third patriarchal strategy of at once hijacking and distorting the meanings of sexual attack is that it appropriates the emotional energy attached to sexual assault – such as moral outrage, fear, anger and humiliation – for purposes often far removed from the experiences and interests of the primary victims. This is also why, as Linda Martín Alcoff (2018: 21) puts it, generally, 'there is less policing of rape than of rape victims' speech'. To the extent that women and girls are the vast majority of rape victims, this policing and appropriation of rape talk translates into a tacit social agreement to sacrifice the fundamental interests in sexual and bodily integrity of women and girls for purposes of patriarchal control. This phenomenon is by no means limited to colonial contexts: worldwide, 'rape talk' gets hijacked and activated for anti-feminist agendas such as xenophobic, imperialist and anti-immigration, racist, and homophobic and nationalist campaigns. One example will suffice. Sara Meger (2016: 154) writes that at the same time that the Australian and British governments were leveraging the reported use of sexual violence as weapon of war by ISIS, as a justification for their military intervention in Syria, they were withdrawing funds and closing down women's shelters and refuges in their own countries. Clearly, the main concern of these governments is not how to address the problem of sexual violence against women but rather how to mobilise the emotive power of rape talk for imperialist agendas.

European colonisation, the subjugation of foreign peoples and lands, taking place at the same time as the European Renaissance and Enlightenment, was not easily justified. Indeed, modern racism could be viewed as an epiphenomenon of European modernisation and colonisation, invented to justify the subjugation and exploitation of other nations reconstituted as 'other races'. Since sovereignty was both a masculine and sacrosanct notion in early modern Europe, colonial racism first and foremost targeted the Black man's sovereignty. In political theory, 'sovereignty' refers to the full right and supreme power of a governing body to rule over itself, within a given territory and without any outside interference (see Philpott, 2016). In Western philosophy, the notion of a 'sovereign individual' has also been prominent, representing the ideal of highest self-rule or autonomy being located in the person, for example in the work of Jean-Jacques Rousseau (see Bertram, 2020). In contrast, European colonisation required a complete disregard for the sovereignty of nations to be colonised, and thus a justificatory notion which lies at the heart of the colonial project is that non-European nations are *incapable* of ruling themselves. In the case of the Black man, in particular, this idea translated into the racist construct that the Black man is incapable of ruling himself because his sexual impulses are unruly and rampant and, as such, he must be externally controlled. In colonial-racist understandings, the inability of the Black man to control his own sexual impulses is inextricably linked with Black men's inability successfully to govern a nation. This is why the racial inferiorisation of the Black man cannot be meaningfully separated from the idea of a degenerate or perverse sexuality (see Coetzee and du Toit, 2018: 214).

Unfortunately, this racist-colonial figure of the Black man incapable of personal – especially sexual – and thus also national sovereignty has survived South Africa's transition to democracy and to political rule by a Black male elite. As Elizabeth Philipose (2009) shows, the trope of the sexually unwieldy Black man is a reliable figure waiting in the wings to continually justify Northern interference in the form of different kinds of 'legalist civilising missions' that disregard Southern nations' sovereignty. In fact, she says, this figure helps to prop up a two-tiered structure of national sovereignty after the Second World War: (i) the 'sovereignty inherent to European powers, thought to reflect their essential civilized nature' and (ii) the 'second-tier and contingent sovereignty granted to non-European states after decolonization and the decline of the European imperial order' (Philipose, 2009, 183). Being second-tier means that a state must continually perform its 'civilised nature' to a European audience, failing which, all kinds of intervention and external structuring are seen as justified. The crisis of sexual violence in post-apartheid South Africa is, therefore, likely to be couched in a similar discourse.

To give just two examples by way of illustration of the above, I first turn to Helen Frost's (2018) comparison between international and South African media responses to the gang rapes-and-murders of Indian national Jyoti Singh (in 2012) and South African national Anene Booysen (in 2013) (see also chapter 1 in this volume). The international media, she shows, used these high-profile cases to reactivate the all-too-familiar tropes around the unruly sexualities and masculinities of Black and Brown men populating colonial imaginaries, coupled with '[B]lack women's bodies [viewed] as sites of unrestrained sexualities' (Frost, 2018: 181). Frost sees in the twenty-five articles that she studied a significant shift in the meaning of the term 'rape culture'. In the North, it refers to structural arrangements that facilitate rape and impunity. In the South, it tends to criminalise racialised men and their unruly 'non-Western cultures' which fail to discipline them sexually. For Sabine Selkin (2004: 373), these media strategies ensure that 'victims and violators [are] othered, set off, while the subject [White, male and liberal] who assigns difference remains unmarked and unlimited in his possibilities'. Recall W. E. B. du Bois's famous ontological question: 'What am I other than a problem in white society?' (cited in Cornell, 2008: 106). These othering strategies in rape talk create the following effects: (i) the enormity of sexual violence in modern Western societies is denied (Frost, 2018: 182); (ii) the history of White men's violence (and White women's complicity) against women of colour is obscured (Frost, 2018: 182); and (iii) it becomes virtually impossible to address the greater sexual vulnerability of Black women in a place like South Africa. Once again, the primary victims of sexual violence get displaced in favour of an imperialist agenda.

The second example comes from inside South Africa. Similar to what we have seen in the Zapiro cartoons of then-president Jacob Zuma,[4] some of the liberal media in the country respond to horrific rape cases by metaphorising the actual incident and transferring its emotive power to other issues. The example, also discussed by Frost (2018), is Ranjeni Munusamy's (2013) article titled 'The Agony of South Africa's Daughter Anine Booysen: The Agony of South Africa' in which she writes: 'We are pounded daily with the rape of the public purse and the political elite using their positions to feather their nests'. The shock, aversion and indignation evoked by the terrible ordeal suffered by seventeen-year-old Anene Booysen are appropriated for other agendas in order to give them a transferred or stolen sense of urgency (see also chapter 1 in this volume). As Frost (2018: 191) writes, Anene Booysen 'becomes a mere cipher for abject and injured subjectivity' because 'the reading public is invited to imagine itself as violated'. However, the transfer is not to just any other issue, but, problematically, to criticism of the mostly Black, mostly male, government and governing party, thus implicitly linking the colonial figure of sexual abandon of the Black rapist with the shortcomings of the Black government. I have no qualms about criticising our government for its shortcomings and corruption, which were truly abundant during the Zuma era. However, there are two serious injustices lodged in forging this transfer between rape-murders and government corruption: (i) it deflects attention away from both the primary victims and the truly urgent crisis of sexual violence in the country, and (ii) it reactivates the problematic racist-colonial trope which conflates Black men's alleged lack of personal sovereignty with their alleged incapability of national sovereignty, thereby distorting both the phenomenon of sexual violence and the systemic failures in government. These symbolic strategies do not serve the feminist interest in keeping attention focused on the direct victims of sexual violence.

Defending Black male dignity

Rather predictably, given the tendency of some local and international commentators to portray the South African sexual violence crisis in racialised terms and to thereby cast doubt on Black men's ability to rule the nation, another strong voice in contemporary 'rape discourse' is the countervailing attempt to salvage Black male dignity. One example of where the chance for a national discourse on the rape crisis derailed through a racialisation of the issue relates to Brett Murray's controversial painting *Spear*, in the 2012 exhibition called 'Hail the Thief II'. The exhibition as a whole critiqued the corruption associated with then-president Zuma's government, and in this painting he is figured with exposed genitals. While clearly this could be read as a reference to the nakedness of the Emperor, it is equally clear that Zuma is depicted as hypersexual and driven by uncontrollable lust. The activation of the colonial figure of Black rapist is unavoidable, and sexual violence emerges as an aspect of the painting's meaning, whether intended (as metaphoric) or not. The response by Zuma and his supporters was immediate outrage: Zuma sued the gallery when it refused to take the painting down; there were death threats against the gallery owners and the painter; the painting was vandalised; and there were marches in support of Zuma's dignity, pitted against what was perceived as a purely racist attack (Hassim, 2014: 168). What we thus see is that the Black man's sexuality is directly linked with the corruption of power in these depictions of Zuma, which would have been completely arbitrary if his sex life had not been a constant topic in public life – including a very controversial rape trial before the start of his presidency (see Tlhabi, 2017).

What is thus very clearly playing out in the public clash over this painting (liberal defenders of free speech on the one hand

and defenders of Zuma's dignity on the other) is that even though the theme of sexual violence is clearly evoked by the painting, and by Zuma's personal history, it was not allowed to emerge as a serious issue in the national discourse. Instead, 'while Murray presented the president as the personification of hyper-masculinist elite power, the ANC presented him as the personification of [B]lack people' (Hassim, 2014: 171). Hassim (2014: 167) also notes that what was at stake in these debates were liberal political norms pitted against socially conservative populism and anxieties around citizenship and belonging. What was *not* included in the conversation was a discussion of patriarchal power, gender inequalities and sexuality in the postcolonial nation (Hassim, 2014: 180); thus, the ways in which feminists attempt to politicise sexual violence.[5] Thus, what the use of rape talk to undermine Black male sovereignty importantly shares with the defence of Black male sovereignty is a strategy of appropriating this discourse on sexual violence and deploying it for agendas far removed from the primary victims, in such a way that the latter disappear completely. Together, these two opposing strategies render it impossible to raise the issue of sexual violence in the country without it being assumed that the perpetrator is figured as a sexually unruly Black man, and we thereby inevitably find ourselves within the ambit of colonial racism.

The tone for this manoeuvre was already set before 2000, when then-president Thabo Mbeki responded to activist calls for government action around HIV, AIDS and sexual violence by labelling these calls 'racist'. Mbeki treated both these life and death issues as 'vectors for a defence of the sovereignty of African culture and for a racialized reading of African sexualities' (Hassim, 2014: 177). The irony is that sexual violence is a phenomenon that cuts across all South African divisions of race, class and culture, and that it is thus often the proponents of this distorting third strategy themselves, rather than the sexual violence activists, who keep alive the image of the sexual predator as a Black man.[6] Hassim (2014: 180) criticises this manipulative strategy for 'invoking' the 'archive of race' in order to 'close down discussions of gender and sexuality'. By making Black masculinities the focus of the conversation, what are ignored are the relationships between black men and black women, and between all women and all men. The colonial body is male; so too is the national subject male. The effect is to universalize the racial dimensions of the *Spear* image and to reduce the question of gender to the racialized, colonially shaped relationship between the white man and the black man. (Hassim, 2014: 174)

Frost (2018: 186) says about the same phenomenon that it evokes Black men's sexual dignity in order to 'foreclose public acknowledgements of gender inequality' in the country. It is sobering to recall here the talk in which Kimberlé Crenshaw (2016) reasons that when feminism and anti-racism respectively fail to display intersectionality, thus failing to take each other's justice concerns seriously, they often end up worsening the injustice that they ignore. In other words, feminist struggles, for example the suffrage struggles that ignored race, also reinforced racism and, equally, anti-racist struggles that ignored gender tended to reinforce patriarchy and sexism.

Male victims of sexual violence

The different parties in the dominant debate about sexual violence in South Africa seem to share the assumption (and assume that everyone else assumes) that the perpetrator of sexual violence is a Black man, and they all turn this into the most salient point of the crime. As discussed, because of the propensity of these participants on both sides to displace the actual, concrete *victims* of sexual violence from the discussion, in favour of a focus on the presumed *perpetrator* and the racialised colonial history of rape talk, which demonises the Black man's sexuality, the figure of the victim tends to dim and disappear from the public mind. Nevertheless, it is fair to say that the figure of the rape victim most likely implicit in the mainstream South African imaginary is that of the Black woman, who is likely to feature only as an anonymous, silent and passive 'site of unrestrained sexuality' (Frost, 2018: 181). Thus, not only is gender racialised – thus the key instrument of gender oppression, namely sexual violence, is interpreted only through the narrow lens of a racialised perpetrator – but race is also gendered in a way that bolsters patriarchy, in that it is only the Black man's race that is allowed to feature in the debate. This cluster of tendencies, ironically, is shared by colonial and anti-colonial discourses alike, and reinforced through their clash. As discussed above, 'the subject who assigns [racial] difference remains unmarked and unlimited in his possibilities' (Selkin, 2004: 373). Additionally, Black woman disappears from the ranks of both the colonised and the national, postcolonial body politic (Hassim, 2014: 174).

A classic example of these interpretative strategies is the way in which Jacob Zuma during his 2006 rape trial mobilised cultural defences for his behaviour towards Fezekile 'Khwezi' Kuzwayo, the complainant. As described by Tlhabi (2017), what was ignored in the trial was the fact that 'Khwezi', too, was a member of Zulu culture, she did not agree with his interpretations of the relevant cultural practices, and she had chosen to turn to the Western legal system rather than a traditional justice system in her search for justice. Similarly, what is ignored or erased when Black men's dignity is evoked and defended against gender activists trying to address sexual violence is the fact that the vast majority of victims are, in fact, Black women and not the White victims of the 'Black Peril' scenario. If anything, Black women have suffered more than Black men under colonial racism, having been relegated to the lowest rung of society, often below the reach of legal and civil protection; Gqola (2015) describes this situation as Black women being treated as 'unrapeable'. When their sexual integrity is treated in the postcolony with the same 'collective shrug' (Harding, quoted in Frost, 2018: 179) and systemic indifference that characterised colonial society, this must mean that the process of decolonisation has seriously derailed. Where do Black women's sexual dignity and bodily integrity feature in the mainstream debate in South Africa? They hardly feature at all[7] because of the emphasis on the alleged or imagined perpetrator, which paralyses attempts at institutional reform.

And yet, as vague and anonymous (silent and displaced) as the majority of female victims are within the prevalent discourses on sexual violence, I have claimed that the male victims of sexual violence are even less likely to feature. According to Rees Mann, founder of South African Male Survivors of Sexual Abuse,[8] one in five adult males in the country have been victims of sexual offences; in 2012, 19.4 per cent of all sexual abuse victims were male, but men are up to ten times less likely to report sexual violence against them than women (Maseko, 2015). We do not seem to have accurate South African statistics about male victims of sexual violence and rape, neither nationally nor related to the prison population. Moreover, as we have seen, when the topic of sexual violence in South Africa is raised, it is mostly assumed that the victims are female, and rape is typically discussed under the broader heading of violence against women and children. Rape talk featuring male victims is virtually absent in our context and, due to the context sketched above, likely to remain so. Male victims' stories indicate that they fear being laughed at, or that they had in fact been laughed at when trying to disclose their experiences of being raped (Louw, 2014; Maseko, 2015). The humiliation endured by the rape is perpetuated and intensified through the everyday responses to their plight. Maseko (2015) tells the story of an anonymous victim who tried to tell his closest male friends about being raped, who then just laughed and said, 'What, are you gay now?' and he responded with 'I am not gay. I was raped.' He then withdrew from his friends, believing there was no one who would respond differently. Even with regard to sexual attacks on gender non-conforming individuals, maybe because of the important activist work by someone like 'visual activist' Zanele Muholi on Black lesbians (SAHO, 2016), the perception exists that sexual attacks on gay men are relatively rare. However, in a 2003 study conducted by Out LGBT Well-Being and the University of South Africa Centre for Applied Psychology, researchers found that the percentages of gay men and women who had experienced sexual attack were similar (cited in Louw, 2014).

South Africa is not alone in this invisibilisation of male victims of sexual violence, and we can learn from other contexts. Laura Stemple (2008) writes that in international human rights discourse, the sexual violence focus has been almost exclusively on women and girls. Similarly, Žarkov (2007: 156) reports that in the war in the former Yugoslavia, both local and international media vastly underreported male victims of sexual violence, with academics following suit. Stemple (2008: 605) states, sexual violence against males continues to flourish in prison and other forms of detention. Men have been abused and sexually humiliated during situations of armed conflict, such as the highly publicised Abu Ghraib scandal in Iraq. Childhood sexual abuse of boys is alarmingly common; in fact, the vast majority of those abused at the hands of Roman Catholic clergy in the United States were boys. And sexual assault against gay men remains unchecked due to assumptions that, as was once commonly assumed about women, gay men who have been raped must have 'asked for it'.

Also in the US context, data on male rape is wanting, due to a combination of lack of societal uptake and the hesitancy of men to report. Stemple (2008: 606) cites the latest research, which suggests about 15 per cent of those who had experienced rape in their lifetime were men. Male rape is more likely to happen in institutionalised spaces such as prisons or prisoner of war camps, refugee camps and immigration centres, or within the army or navy, or in armed conflict – all contexts that are total institutions with limited chances of successful reporting.[9] A 2000 national US crime survey found that around 11 per cent of all sexual assault victims were male (quoted in Stemple, 2008: 607). Stemple (2008: 606) argues that this 'small but sizable' percentage of male victims should not be ignored by sexual violence activists and feminist theoreticians. Although feminists are sometimes reluctant to engage with the reality of male victims for fear of losing hard-won attention or funding for the plight of female victims, for Stemple there are solid feminist reasons for fully incorporating the male victims in our understanding of sexual violence and in our activist rhetoric. For example, by treating sexual violence as something that happens only to women, we tend to 'perpetuate norms that essentialize women as victims' and 'we impose unhealthy expectations about masculinity on men and boys' (Stemple, 2008: 606).

Because of a dearth of research on male rape, we have little reliable data and equally little serious academic discussion of the topic in South Africa. The context in which its reality is most likely to surface is in jokes related to prison rape. There is a widespread assumption in the country that men, especially certain kinds of men (effeminate, young and certain categories of criminals, such as child molesters) will routinely be raped in prison. This is often discussed

as if it were a completely legitimate supplement to legal state punishment (Gear and Ngubeni, 2002: 3). This trope is common in
social media whenever a publicly despised character is sentenced to
imprisonment, with a blatant revelling in the public's anticipation
of his prison rape. Prison rape is a human rights abuse, alarmingly
widespread, which has received very little attention from human
rights activists and scholars worldwide (Stemple, 2008: 608). Prison
populations, both in the US and in South Africa, are more than
90 per cent male, and thus men are overwhelmingly the victims
of this crime. In the US, one in five inmates reported pressured
or forced sexual experience while incarcerated (Stemple, 2008:
608). In one Californian study, moreover, gender non-conforming
prisoners made up 3.7 per cent of the state prison population but
accounted for 57.2 per cent of those reporting sexual assault in
custody (Stemple, 2008: 609). In South Africa, our knowledge
comes to us mostly through qualitative studies such as by the Centre
for the Study of Violence and Reconciliation (Gear and Ngubeni,
2002), some documentaries and anecdotal evidence, such as by
Siyabonga Sesant (2020) from *Die Son*, quoted at the start of the
chapter. Sesant and his informant, Anthony Oliphant, treat prison
rape – in this case at the St. Albans prison in Port Elizabeth – as an
established culture. Based on his experience of ten years imprisonment, Oliphant reports that 'die jong outjies' (the young guys) are
not only used as sex slaves but that their rectums are also used for
hiding cell phones and drugs. It seems to be only this latter usage
that lends the story its newsworthiness. Oliphant also explains that
'they take you for a woman' and then you have to do *'n vroumens
se werke* (a woman's work), especially forced sex work.

    In a recent article, Elizabeth le Roux and I (du Toit and le Roux,
2020) focused on the male victim in conflict-related sexual violence
(CRSV) and, arguably, many of those insights can be transferred
to domestic and peace-time male rape. We compared female and
male experiences of sexual violence in the context of Sri Lankan
security forces mistreating political prisoners, as compiled in the
Human Rights Watch report *We Will Teach You a Lesson* (HRW,
2013). Both genders reported deep feelings of shame, self-blame
and disgust about what had happened to them – the sexual element
of sexual violation ensured an enduring sense of stigma and an

accompanying need for self-censoring. Both genders experienced the sexual violation as a powerful lesson about domination, as a site of power transfer, with the victims feeling profoundly disempowered as a result. We concluded from this detailed analysis that male and female victims experienced many similar injuries to their sense of self in the world. The greater relative invisibility of male victims, we thus concluded, has less to do with degree or quality of the injury and more with a broad societal unwillingness to allow them to appear. We explained that

> the inclusion of male victims in our understanding and imagining of CRSV helps us to see more clearly how sexual violation in such a context serves the same primary function for male and female detainees, namely to cause long-term damage to their self-regard. When played out between male bodies, the power-political function seemingly becomes clearer because we are less tempted to see the sexual violence as an expression of ('natural', i.e. heteronormative, male) perpetrator lust. (du Toit and le Roux, 2020: 7)

Somehow, both the long-term destructive aims and outcomes of a sexual attack, as well as its power-dimension, are easier to 'see' when the victim is imagined as male, and it is precisely this powerful image of the humiliated male victim, I would argue, which makes societies so reluctant to allow this figure into the public discourse. Michel Foucault's (1978: 103) famous insight that sexuality is 'an especially dense transfer point for relations of power' tends to be obscured when women are imagined as natural, timeless and essential victims of sexual violence and men as natural sexual predators, immune to sexual humiliation. The 'spectacle' of the male rape victim brings home to everyone that sexual vulnerability is a social and political, and not a natural, condition. Prison rape, as discussed by the quoted articles, shows vividly how sexual prerogative or sex right (masculine, impenetrable, sovereign subjectivity), on the one hand, and sexual penetrability, exploitability (feminine subjectivity, stripped of all sexual sovereignty), on the other, do not pre-exist or cause sexual violence but are rather the dichotomous *outcome* of sexual violation.

To bring this back to the specifically South Africa context, then, in a strongly patriarchal society where there is a struggle over Black male sovereignty, as explained, and where the Black female victim is often glossed over, even as her plight is pushed into service of both sides in this struggle, there must be good, context-specific reasons why the Black male victim of sexual violation is kept almost completely under wraps. Returning to the three patriarchal strategies used to prevent sexual violence from becoming a rallying point for large-scale feminist resistance, we might conclude that when it comes to male victims of sexual violence, the situation is still successfully demobilised through the very first strategy, namely outright public denial. The first reason for the male victim's absence is the one just explained: male-on-male rape, especially maybe in the prison context that Gear and Ngubeni (2002) describe (where gangs regulate sex as a commodity and assign 'male' and 'female' status, as well as wifely status, hierarchically and arbitrarily to some of the male bodies), more clearly shows the extent to which sexual accessibility or inaccessibility is the result of patriarchal power, not nature. To bring into focus the logic of male-on-male rape is to illuminate the patriarchal symbolic machinery tirelessly at work to render women systematically vulnerable to sexual violence outside of prison and war, in the everyday, to destroy their sexual sovereignty and compel them into performing *'n vroumens se werke*.

Debra Bergoffen (2016: 137) explains that under patriarchy, sexual vulnerability becomes ideologically gendered; fundamentally distorting the human condition of ontological vulnerability, patriarchy designates female bodies as naturally sexually vulnerable and male bodies as inherently sexually invulnerable and threatening. However, in prison rape it becomes clear that is not the absence of a penis that renders one sexually vulnerable and thus violable with impunity; it may be something more like the absence of prison currency, such as cigarettes or powerful allies. Male-on-male rape thus exposes the lies that naturalise 'heteronormative' rape and shows the trappings of power that keep it alive. Yet this does not mean that male and female victims are now similarly positioned within the patriarchal symbolic. Instead,

given the *enduring* symbolic power of women's social subjugation expressed in pervasive sexual violence against them (perpetrated with impunity, institutionally embedded), it is not surprising that men are *sometimes* degraded and othered through this exact same template. To violate a man sexually, is to enact his social denigration, which under patriarchy automatically means he is designated as female because sexually vulnerable; he is symbolically castrated. (du Toit and le Roux, 2020: 9; emphasis added)

A second reason why the logic and the evocative power of male-on-male rape must be wrested away from the primary victims, for example through trivialising jokes, is discussed by Žarkov (2007: 160) who sees the heteronormativity of dominant patriarchal masculinity as threatened by any public discourse on the sexual violation of men. In our postcolonial situation, where, as we have seen, Black male sovereignty often experiences itself as beleaguered, this threat is doubled. Dominant patriarchy is threatened and, more so, Black men's presence within it, because the destabilising spectre of homosexuality rises up on both sides of the violation. It has the potential to demean both perpetrator (as bestial) and victim (as homosexualised), and this is why rape discourse pertaining to (mostly, but not exclusively, Black) male victims has to be even more vehemently policed – it tarnishes the idealised image of the 'naturally' sexually predatory, unified and impenetrable male body. Given that our prison population is both overwhelmingly male and Black, the acknowledgement of pervasive prison rape stands to demean the Black male body as homosexual and/or feminine/gay. If, on the other hand, the discourse rejects the spectre of homosexual lust and insists on prison sexual slavery as a purely power-political arrangement, then the overt comparisons to what happens to women outside of prison, in supposedly 'normal' heterosexual relations, become almost equally uncomfortable. This is especially true of the way in which prison sex slaves (those considered vulnerable in terms of the prison power economies, run by the gangs) are called 'women' or 'wives' (also called 'wyfies', which refers to female animals) and forced to do 'women's work', which is equated with sexual slavery. We thus see that the spectre of the Black male victim of sexual violation threatens the Black man's claim to sovereignty in the postcolonial state, and it threatens to reiterate the colonial trope that labels the Black man incapable of self-rule. But now, he is incapable of self-rule, not only because he cannot control his sexuality but, even more damagingly, because his sexuality is controlled from the outside, by another. He becomes Black woman, the anonymous and silenced body as 'site of [another's] unrestrained sexuality' (to reiterate Frost's phrase), the figure almost fully displaced from human society by colonial (and as we have seen, postcolonial) logic.

Conclusion

It should be clear from the discussion above that it is in the manifest interest of feminist activists in South Africa to place the plight of male victims of sexual violence firmly on the agenda. I explained in the introduction how patriarchy works to repress widespread sexual violence from being politicised for feminist aims, for example fighting for greater gender equality in all spheres of life. I claimed that patriarchy first tries to deny sexual violence altogether; when it comes to light, it secondly tries to trivialise it; and, if victims' testimonies blow holes in both these initial strategies, it tries to simultaneously appropriate its emotive energy and distort its meaning in the service of agendas far removed from the primary victims, its third strategy. I then showed that as far as female victims go, we find ourselves mostly within this last patriarchal strategy, with a masculine racialisation of the debate functioning as the main way in which the meanings and functions of sexual violence in society get distorted, and a feminist politics gets buried. In the final part of the chapter, I discussed male victims of sexual violence, of prison rape in particular, and made the case that it is as pervasive as it is ignored. In terms of patriarchy's three-tiered structure of repression, male victims are, in a sense, still stuck in the first two strategies: when their plight is not ignored, it is trivialised.

I argued that it is understandable, on a symbolic level, why the plight of especially Black male victims (the vast majority of the prison population) is not allowed to enter public rape talk. Facing their plight is experienced as deeply threatening on more than one level to a Black male sovereignty understood as beleaguered or at least challenged. At the same time, however, I have tried to show that facing their plight, and including it explicitly in feminist struggle, can actually serve feminist political ends (for her agreement with this point, see Stemple, 2008: 606). In summary, this is the case because, first, to include them is to work to denaturalise male-on-female rape. Second, their inclusion shows how the unequal distribution of sexual vulnerability is a function of social and political arrangements rather than bodily morphology or a natural dispensation. Third, the male rape victims in prison demonstrate, through their status as 'wives' who do women's work for the elite males, how closely sexual subjugation is related to all other forms of social (informal) subjugation, including labour exploitation. Fourth, the inclusion of male rape victims not only destabilises women's supposed 'natural' sexual vulnerability, but also destabilises men's supposedly natural sexual invulnerability, and shows sex right or its absence as contingently related to other forms of power, for example prison culture. It therefore destabilises the naturalised link between masculinity and sexual control; it exposes men's sexual vulnerability. Thus, fifth, the systematic inclusion of male victims in female theorising and activism helps illuminate the often hidden link between pervasive sexual violence and the masculinisation of public power. If there is a standing threat that a man may be demoted through sexual violation to the social status of a woman, then that is an indication that patriarchal values permeate society and keep women in their place. Men can only be threatened with such a degradation if most women already find themselves there.

Finally, with respect to our postcolonial context, one could say that prison rape provides a vivid counter-imaginary to the dominant colonial trope. If colonial discourse can only ever imagine the Black man as a sexual predator, the acknowledgement of Black men as victims of sexual violation disturbs this colonial imaginary at its core. If feminist activists were to place the Black male victim of sexual violence within the public domain, without appropriating or distorting his experience, this could do a lot to move the terms of the debate beyond the colonial Black Peril trope and, ideally, allow for more of the other obscured figures to also take their place within the debate: Black female victims, but also White male victims and perpetrators, and all female perpetrators and accomplices of sexual violence.

Notes

1 For statistics on sexual violence in contemporary South Africa, see the Introduction to the book.

2 I do not use this term to imply that in the 'postcolony' we have taken definitive leave of coloniality, as the rest of the chapter also shows. Its main significance is to refer to South African society after the political transition to democracy.

3 I capitalise the racial designators 'White' and 'Black' in order to acknowledge their artificiality and their labelling function, and to resist naturalising tendencies.

4 The best-known cartoon is labelled 'Rape of Justice' and appeared in the *Sunday Times* of 7 September 2008 (available at Zapiro, 2008).

5 The feminist attempt to politicise sexual violence must be understood in a threefold way: (i) to resist the traditional understanding of sexual violence as a private or domestic affair; (ii) to draw attention to how sexual violence functions to (re-)distribute personal and collective power on a fundamental, embodied level; and (iii) to illuminate the links between the pervasive threat of sexual violence and the ongoing masculinisation of public power.

6 It is important to note that, in South Africa, writers of different sexes and races take up either of these mainstream positions. In the case of Mbeki, Hassim (2014) uses as her primary examples the arguments made by two White women scholars, Gillian Schutte and Heidi Hudson.

7 There are some noteworthy counter-examples to a generally bleak picture. I want to give recognition to the courage of young Black women who publicly protest against this 'collective shrug', for example, with the topless female marches as part of the Fallist protests 2015–2017, with the 'Remember Khwezi' silent poster protest during Zuma's election speech of 2016, with the 2017 #MenAreTrash campaign in response to the murder of Karabo Mokoena, and with the 2016 'Rhodes Reference List' campaign (see https://mg.co.za/article/2018-07-06-00-rureference list-the-fear-of-repercussions-still-lingers/ Accessed 10 May 2021).

8 For the South African Male Survivors of Sexual Abuse, see www. samsosa.org.

9 In this regard, Gear and Ngubeni's (2002) report on prison rape in South Africa is interesting: it points to two institutional features that make official reporting of a rape complaint very unlikely, namely power dynamics among the inmates, and a combination of neglect and participation by wardens.

References

Alcoff, L.M. (2018). *Rape and Resistance: Understanding the Complexities of Sexual Violation.* Cambridge: Polity Press.

Bergoffen, D. (2016). 'The Flight from Vulnerability', in *Dem Erleben auf der Spur: Feminismus und die Philosophie des Leibes*, edited by I. Marcinski and H. Landweer, 137–52. Bielefeld: Transcript Verlag.

Bertram, C. (2020). 'Jean Jacques Rousseau', in *Stanford Encyclopedia of Philosophy*, Summer 2016 edition, edited by E. N. Zalta. https://plato.stanford.edu/archives/sum2020/entries/rousseau/. Accessed 12 May 2021.

Coetzee, A. and L. du Toit. (2018). 'Facing the Sexual Demon of Colonial Power: Decolonising Sexual Violence in South Africa', *European Journal of Women's Studies* 25:2, 214–27.

COFEM (Coalition of Feminists for Social Change). (2017a). *Funding: Whose Priorities?* Feminist Perspectives on Addressing Violence against Women and Girls Series, Paper No. 4.

COFEM (Coalition of Feminists for Social Change). (2017b). *Reframing the Language of 'Genderbased Violence' away from Feminist Underpinnings.* Feminist Perspectives on Addressing Violence against Women and Girls Series, Paper No. 2.

Cornell, D. (2008). *Moral Images of Freedom: A Future for Critical Theory.* Lanham, MD: Rowman and Littlefield.

Crenshaw, K. (2016). 'On Intersectionality', at Women of the World (WOW) conference. www.youtube.com/watch?v=-DW4HLgYPlA. Accessed 20 April 2021.

Dolan, C. (2014). 'Has Patriarchy been Stealing the Feminists' Clothes? Conflict-Related Sexual Violence and UN Security Council Resolutions', *IDS Bulletin* 45:1, 80–4.

du Toit, L. and E. le Roux. (2020). 'A Feminist Reflection on Male Victims of Conflict-Related Sexual Violence', *European Journal of Women's Studies.* https://doi.org/10.1177/1350506820904982.

Foucault, M. (1978). *The History of Sexuality Volume I: An Introduction*, translated by R. Hurley. New York: Pantheon Books.

Frost, H. (2018). '"There's Plenty of Rapists Here"; "Rape Culture" and the Representation of Anene Booysen's Rape in the International and South African Press', *Cultural Critique* 100, 176–95.

Gear, S. and K. Ngubeni. (2002). 'Daai Ding: Sex, Sexual Violence and Coercion in Men's Prisons', research paper written for the Centre for the Study of Violence and Reconciliation (CSVR). www.csvr.org.za/docs/correctional/daaidingsex.pdf. Accessed 10 May 2020.

Graham, L. (2012). *State of Peril: Race and Rape in South African Literature*. Oxford: Oxford University Press.

Gqola, P.D. (2015). *Rape: A South African Nightmare*. Johannesburg: MFBooks Joburg.

Hassim, S. (2014). 'Violent Modernity: Gender, Race and Bodies in Contemporary South African Politics', *Politikon* 41:2, 167–82.

HRW (Human Rights Watch) (2013). *'We Will Teach You a Lesson': Sexual Violence against Tamils by Sri Lankan Security Forces*. New York: Human Rights Watch. www.hrw.org/report/2013/02/26/we-will-teach-you-lesson/sexual-violence-against-tamils-sri-lankan-security-forces. Accessed 10 May 2020.

Louw, A. (2014). 'Men are also "Corrective Rape" Victims', 11 April, *Mail & Guardian*, 11 April. https://mg.co.za/article/2014-04-11-men-are-also-corrective-rape-victims/. Accessed 13 May 2021.

Lugones, M. (2007). 'Heterosexualism and the Colonial/Modern Gender System. *Hypatia* 22:1, 186–209.

Maseko, C. (2015). 'Male Rape still Considered a Joke in South Africa', *Health24*, 29 July. www.health24.com/Lifestyle/Man/Your-body/Male-rape-still-considered-a-joke-in-South-Africa-20150729. Accessed 10 May 2020.

Meger, Sara. (2016). 'The Fetishization of Sexual Violence in International Security', *International Studies Quarterly* 60, 149–59.

Munusamy, R. (2013). 'The Agony of South Africa's Daughter Anine Booysen: The Agony of South Africa', *Daily Maverick*, 8 February. www.dailymaverick.co.za/article/2013-02-08-the-agony-of-south-africas-daughter-anine-booysen-the-agony-of-south-africa/. Accessed 10 May 2020.

Oyěwùmí, O. (1997). *The Invention of Women: Making an African Sense of Western Gender Discourses*. Minneapolis, MN: University of Minnesota Press.

Philipose, E. (2009). 'Feminism, International Law, and the Spectacular Violence of the "Other": Decolonizing the Laws of War', in *Theorizing Sexual Violence,* edited by R. J. Heberle and V. Grace, 176–204. Abingdon: Routledge.

Philpott, D. (2016). 'Sovereignty', in *Stanford Encyclopedia of Philosophy*, Summer 2016 edition, edited by E. N. Zalta. https://plato.stanford.edu/archives/sum2016/entries/sovereignty/. Accessed 20 April 2021.

Ratele, K. (2009). 'Sexuality as Constitutive of Whiteness in South Africa', *NORA – Nordic Journal of Feminist and Gender Research* 17:3, 158–74.

SAHO (South African History Online). (2016). 'Zanele Muholi'. South African History Online, last updated 6 November 2020. www.sahistory.org.za/people/zanele-muholi. Accessed 13 May 2021.

Selkin, S. (2004). 'The Politics of the Strong Trope: Rape and the Feminist Debate in the United States', *Amerikastudien/American Studies* 49:3, 367–84.

Sesant, S. (2020). 'Père cash in op latte se stêre', *Die Son*, 27 April. www.son.co.za/Nuus/Ooskaap/pere-cash-in-op-latte-se-stere-20200427. Accessed 10 May 2020.

Stemple, L. (2008). 'Male Rape and Human Rights', *Hastings Law Journal* 60, 605–47.

Stoler, A.L. (1995). *Race and the Education of Desire: Foucault's* History of Sexuality *and the Colonial Order of Things*. Durham, NC: Duke University Press.

Stoler, A.L. (2010). *Carnal Knowledge and Imperial Power: Race and the Intimate in Colonial Rule*. Berkeley, CA: University of California Press.

Tlhabi, R. (2017). *Khwezi: The Remarkable Story of Fezekile Ntsukela Kuzwayo*. Johannesburg: Jonathan Ball.

Zapiro. (2008). 'Rape of Justice', cartoon. Zapiro, 7 September. www.zapiro.com/080907st. Accessed 10 May 2021.

Žarkov, D. (2007). *The Body of War: Media, Ethnicity, and Gender in the Breakup of Yugoslavia*. Durham, NC: Duke University Press.

7

Rebuilding precarious solidarities: a feminist debate in internet time

Shilpa Phadke

In October 2017, Raya Sarkar, a law school student in California, posted a crowd-sourced list on the social media platform Facebook of Indian men in academia who had been accused of sexual harassment by students. Within a day, a group of Indian feminists posted a statement on an online forum called Kafila, asking those who had posted the list to consider due process as a way to address sexual harassment, and requested that the list be taken down (Menon, 2017a). What followed was not so much a conversation on sexual harassment, as one might have expected, but a deeply fraught conversation between feminists engaging the terrain of feminism itself. This feminist battle lasted weeks and even today, more than three years later, there is still some hostility and acrimony in the air.

One interlocuter compared these disagreements to a feminist civil war (Ghosh, 2017). Another piece referred to it as a 'clear splintering within the Indian feminist movement' (Anasuya, 2017). A third suggested that it led to a loss of trust within feminist politics that would not be easy to rebuild (Menon, 2017b). It is to this sense of disquiet and perhaps hyperbole that I seek to respond. I locate this chapter around the idea of internet time and its capacities to reshape the trajectory of feminist debates. Given that the digital is here to stay, and that the digital has also given us exciting ways of engaging with feminism and with each other, how can we reflect on hostile and acrimonious debates between feminists which have taken place in these very public fora? I briefly discuss some of the arguments around this debate before I focus on the relationships between feminists. I argue that feminist politics is not so fragile that trust has been destroyed; it was merely shaken. Finally, I argue that feminist frictions are not new and are, in fact, a reassuring sign of a dynamic movement.

Writing about this fraught debate

Choosing to write about this fraught debate has not been an easy decision. Two days after the list was posted, an editor friend asked if I would write on it. Unable to wrap my head around the rage that was flying around and worried about getting caught in the crossfire, I declined. But now it feels like one might attempt to think through this conversation and the contestations in order to unravel some of the threads of the debates that took place at the time.

The list has variously been referred to as the List, with a capital letter; as the LoSHA, an acronym that has been read as List of Sexual Harassers in Academia (Wikipedia); as List of Sexual Harassment Accused (Rao, 2018); list of sexual harassers in Indian academia (Gajjala, 2018); and as List of Shame (Chakraborty, 2019). The responding statement has been referred to as the Statement, again with a capital letter, or as the Kafila Statement, based on the blog where it was posted. In this chapter, I use the terms 'list' and 'statement' to refer to them but without capitalisation so as to rather direct the attention to the feminist debates that followed. I also use the lower case as a political act, in the hope that Indian feminism and feminists can begin to work with the rage and pain that were generated, not forgetting it but accepting that we can talk, engage and even collaborate across the divides created. Deep emotions – of rage, shock, pain, betrayal, but also affection, friendship, solidarity – have been an integral part of this debate.

This chapter is part auto-ethnography, part online ethnography via participant observation, and part textual analysis of the conversation on social media, online portals and academic fora that followed the list and the statement.

I conducted eleven interviews with people from either side of the debate in late 2018 and early 2019, at least a year after the initial fraught debate. Many interviewees said that they would do things differently now. Many did not want to be quoted. Most were afraid of opening old wounds. I, too, am cautious about opening old wounds. I also feel the responsibility of representing accurately the voices of the people I interviewed. I quote from my interviews anonymously to protect people's identity.

This chapter focuses on feminist arguments, disagreements and solidarities in the wake of #MeToo rather than on the debates surrounding sexual harassment itself, which are addressed in other chapters in this book. I attempt to think thorough what it means to have an argument in internet time. What does it mean then to engage as feminists with each other in the online space? What are the specific pressures and anxieties produced by articulations and disagreements in online spaces? How might one reflect on the question of disagreement, especially disagreement with allies, in a time of social media? And how might one think of and construct the possibilities and circumscriptions of feminist solidarities in internet time, in messy circumstances?

I keep refreshing my screen

It is 24 October 2017: I am sitting at my desk trying to write when a former student sends me a link to a list on the social media platform Facebook. It is a long list of Indian academics, mostly from the humanities and social sciences, accused of sexual harassment. This is a simple list, recording the names only, providing no other details. My former student and I talk about sexual harassment in academia, our experiences and our choices of women mentors. We do not know it yet, but over the next week the two of us will have intense conversations, not on sexual harassment or the harassers but on feminist responses to what had just transpired.

At this point, little is known about this list other than that it was posted on the Facebook account of Raya Sarkar, about whom, again, little is known. There is a low buzz on my social media about the list, but even before the online universe can absorb it, on the very same day, a group of fourteen feminists posts a statement on a well-known left-leaning political blog called Kafila. This short statement of 216 words flags the signatories' long struggle to make sexual harassment visible and to put into place systems of accountability. It expresses dismay at the anonymous nature of the list and the lack of context or explanation. The authors acknowledge that institutional procedures are often 'often tilted against the complainant' but they nonetheless express a commitment to due process. They argue that such 'naming' could 'delegitimise the long struggle against sexual harassment' and appeal to those behind the initiative to withdraw the list, assuring them of support from the larger feminist community (Menon, 2017a).

A friend who signed the statement tags me on her link. I share it and add a comment. As my conversations grow, I edit the comment, multiple times. Eventually there is no comment left, just the statement hanging there. I do not know quite what to make of either the list or the statement because I am reeling under the response to the latter.

The contestation is pitched as a battle between the politics of naming and shaming on social media versus taking into account due process. The question of sexual harassment and the harassers recedes into the background. We are no longer talking about the names on that list but rather about feminists: about ourselves and about who is or is not a good feminist. There is intense activity on social media, including Twitter and Facebook, in regard to this list. Many of us sit refreshing our screen every few minutes, unable to do much else but follow the, often acrimonious, conversation.

As online battles over the question of what constituted 'good feminism' ensue over the next few days, I engage in multiple chat conversations (in various digital spaces as well as on the phone), most notably with two former students turned friends who had contributed to the list, one former student turned friend who was unconnected to the list, one young woman who has over the years become a kind of mentee, three friends who had signed the statement, one former classmate who had signed the statement, a mentor who had signed the statement, an activist friend with whom I had long conversations about the nature of the internet itself and, finally, a friend and collaborator with both of us shrieking into the telephone to make our point. In these conversations both I and my friends occupy multiple roles and shifting identities at different points. We are simultaneously feminist comrades and situational adversaries.

Like many other Indian feminists in India and globally, I spend those few days in a bit of a stupor, almost unable to take in what is happening. I have a deadline but I cannot write. I can only follow this conversation with mingled feelings of horror and bewilderment. I know there are many like me – I am talking to some of them. The emotions we feel span the gamut from rage, pain, betrayal, incomprehension to sorrow over the rift that was taking place.

These debates are far from the first time Indian feminists have disagreed. Until the 1990s, feminists in India refused to allow lesbian feminists to hold queer banners at women's marches, arguing that this would unnecessarily deflect attention from more important issues like poverty and health to sexuality (John and Nair, 1998; Menon, 2007). Today, of course, queer banners are ubiquitous at women's marches and the two movements are integral allies. There have been huge and continuing disagreements on the subject of sex work, for instance, with abolitionists on one side arguing against those seeking decriminalisation on the other (Datta, 2010 George et al., 2010; Kotiswaran, 2019; Shah, 2011), and those who see trafficking and force arguing against those who also see migration and choice. Transgender and transsexual concerns are also deeply contentious, not just in India but across the world (Camminga, 2020; Halberstam, 2018; Hines, 2020) and have produced hostile conversations.

These debates have also divided the movement and continue to divide it. This new divide, in India, – focused on the choice of publicly naming sexual harassers versus following due process within institutional structures – was defined as insurmountable. One of the things that made this debate different from those that had gone before was that it took place almost entirely on the internet, specifically on social media – Facebook and Twitter – and on blogs. I argue later in this chapter that internet time was crucial to the way in which this debate unfolded. But before that I trace some of the fault lines of the arguments made.

Framing the arguments

It seemed as if one of the core questions being addressed was in regard to the form of protest. How does one articulate protest? What is a feminist protest? What are the contours of a legitimate protest?

In relation to the list which was posted online, the first argument made by those who wrote the statement was that not following due process as established by universities and, moreover, using a medium such as Facebook, might damage the redressal processes which feminists had struggled for (Menon, 2017a; Ramdev and Bhattacharya, 2017). Those who curated the list responded by arguing that due process had not worked, that it existed at only a few central universities and that many universities did not even have a semblance of mechanism in place to address sexual harassment. Interestingly, fairly early in the debate Rina Ramdev and Debaditya Bhattacharya (2017) pointed out that most of those named on the list in fact belonged to institutions where some form of due process was indeed available, however flawed. They extrapolated that the presence of such mechanisms at the very least appeared to provide space for consciousness raising to take place, which would create the space for women to be able to report on sexual harassment. Yet others pointed out that one thing the list achieved was to demonstrate that powerful men did not have the same kind of impunity as they did before (Suneetha et al., 2017).

Another argument centred around the conflation of varied transgressions/crimes committed by those on the list. The argument was that by putting those men who had been convicted by their universities of sexual harassment alongside those who had never faced any official inquiry flattens the definition of sexual harassment itself (Menon, 2017b; Ramdev and Bhattacharya, 2017). Raya Sarkar had been quoted saying that she refused to provide more details about the complainants or the complaints 'to protect the identities of those who feared professional retaliation and retribution like we often see in academia' (quoted in Chatterjee, 2018). There were also discussions around the anonymity of the accusers, to which Chakravarty (2019) argues that discourses around sexual violence have been based on 'the presence of a victim, a surviving body as the evidence of survival' and that the list denied these voyeuristic pleasures, indeed subverted them.

Another argument was that the list was not intended to replace due process but rather resembled the 'whisper network' that had always existed to warn others of professors to be wary of. One argument against this form was that a focus on '"rumour and gossip" networks among women, over a feminist politics of women, standing up to and facing down sexually harassing men' (Menon, 2019a) would have the effect of putting the onus of keeping herself safe squarely back on the female student (Ramdev and Bhattacharya, 2017). Defending the idea of the whisper network, Gajjala (2018) argued that this requires a great deal of planning and bravery, as even in digital spaces the accusers' identities may be exposed.

The questions that arise from these debates are numerous and many of them are not going away anytime soon. What does it mean to publish a list of sexual harassers on a social media platform without any details? What is the function it performs for survivors who might not otherwise have a voice? What does this mean in terms of the capacity of those accused to defend themselves? Does the presence of such a list flatten the nuance needed to talk of sexual harassment and violence? What are the lines between a sexually coloured comment, a roving hand, sexual assault? What does the presence of the list mean for due process – is it undermined or, in the presence of adequate support, even buttressed?

Another line of argument was that it was particularly left liberal academics who were targeted by the list and that in the current political climate this might give right-wing political forces ammunition against left intellectuals who were already under attack (Ghosh, 2017; Gupta, 2017). Clearly it is not only liberal men who are sexual harassers. On the other hand, it is also true that being left or liberal or indeed an ally in other democratic struggles does not automatically mean that men are incapable of sexual harassment. However, the question is, should we refrain from naming left liberal men because there is a bigger enemy and because they are our allies in the struggle to save democracy in this country? There can be no suggestion that we subordinate concerns of gender and sexual harassment to another, better time; that time will be never.

A central thread of the debate was around the question of caste. The statement was seen as an intervention made by upper-caste feminists. The signatories challenged this, arguing that the caste identity of the signatories of the statement was not relevant as the complainants were likely to be from different caste backgrounds (Menon, 2017b). Others have argued that if we acknowledge that academic spaces are simultaneously sexist, classist and casteist, and that they maintain the hegemony of the English language, then we cannot perceive the caste of the signatories to be irrelevant to the discussion (Ayyar, 2017; Bargi, 2017; Chakraborty, in Gajjala, 2019).

Pallavi Rao (2018: 495) argues that a significant reason why the list was contentious was that it was hosted by a 'Dalit person outside India, with no networked caste affiliations to the savarna or "upper"-caste male professors on the LoSHA, nor to the universities where they taught and "allegedly" committed the acts'.

An acrimonious line of argument raised questions in regard to the actual caste identity of Raya Sarkar. Separately, another line of argument suggested male friends and colleagues named on the list were being protected by anyone who supported the statement. These were the subjects of a fair number of accusations being discussed on social media.

This also led to the suggestion that there was a generational divide between those who supported the list and those who supported the statement (Chadda, 2017). Others have argued that a generational lens is not helpful as it stifles the possibility of debates that might further the 'feminist political project' and simultaneously risk the erasure of complexity (Roy, 2017). Lukose (2018: 38) suggests that the media frames the debate as one between older feminists committed to due process and a language of sexual agency, who 'worry more about "sex panic" and regulation', and younger millennial feminists who are women 'speaking a language of sexual morality, righteousness and an excessive language of victimhood and exploitation'.

The aim in this section has been to present the debates that took place and the writing that has emerged reflecting these discussions. However, these are far from the only conversations that are relevant to this debate. Feminists have engaged in a variety of complex ways with the law. Flavia Agnes (1992) has reflected on how the law is inadequate by itself when not accompanied by a vigilant civil society. Similarly, Menon (2019b: 185), in engaging with sexual violence and the law, points out that 'few Indian feminists are under any illusion that the law is a genuinely transformative instrument' but rather see it as part of a larger strategy to create awareness and seek short-term redress. Menon's scepticism with the law here buttresses Agnes's argument that transformation can only come via a political feminist movement. Menon (2019b: 185) also points out that 'feminists work collaboratively with various political movements and have taken nuanced and often internally conflicting positions on issues pertaining to sexual violence in law and in the courts'. If we were to bring this scepticism to the way in which we view sexual harassment in the university and the structures to deal with it, we might find that our arguments over the list and the statement are not so conflicting after all.

Internet time

The list went up on a social media platform. It was shared with others on a social media platform and the conversations that took place also took place online – on blogs, on social media platforms and in comments to articles published online. The list went up on the internet, the statement was also posted on the internet – that is, it went up on a blog, not a newspaper where there would have been an editor. Interventions to the debate that were made in the form of emails were also circulated on social media with the permission of their authors. Emails written by scholars V. Geetha and Mary John thus appeared on the Facebook timelines of many invested in the debate. This movement from email to social media suggests that in order to substantively contribute to the conversation, interventions had to appear on social media. This is despite the fact that both of these email interventions were posted by the authors themselves on an Indian feminist email group.

The space of the internet, and the way in which the internet reconfigures time, I will argue, are central to understanding the debates following the list and the statement which took place almost entirely online and in what I call internet time. Internet time might be seen as ways in which conversations can take place over multiple geographical locations, can travel swiftly, produce rebuttals almost instantly. The space of Twitter or Facebook requires no editorial input; it permits self-publishing at a speed and volume never experienced before.

How might one reflect on this disagreement when one locates it within the frame of the space within which it took place – the internet and social media in particular – and the ways in which internet time itself is configured. Wendy Chun (2016: 104, 107) points out that in 'the mid-1990s, the Internet emerged as "cyberspace", a space of freedom and anonymity', though ironically the internet is one of 'the most compromised and compromising forms of communication'. Separately in a co-authored piece, Chun and Sarah Friedland (2015) pointed out, in relation to the narratives of fear, that women are taught, with regard to the online, that once they put something out there, it is there to stay and that they should be very careful about what they post. In contrast, they argue for a much more risk-taking attitude to the space of the internet. As feminists then, what does it mean to put out a disagreement of this kind into the space of social media? A space whose memory is long and where searches will yield detailed trajectories of hostility? Not only are the words and images one puts out into cyberspace there to stay, they also travel faster than ever before.

The context of digital space-time meant that all of this was happening far more rapidly than other debates had taken place in the past. One might see this thing called internet time as time simultaneously compressed and elongated: it allows for instant responses, amplifies things and creates contexts within which things, ideas and debates transform in ways that are particular to the capacity to respond instantly and publish to a fairly large group of people. Radhika Gajjala (2019: 47) quotes Maithrayee Chaudhuri who argues that the internet and new media involve a 'change in temporality' and indeed transform our 'experience with time' itself. Chaudhuri points out that information and images are being transmitted globally via a capitalist circulatory media in a 24 × 7 format. There is something of the 24-hour news cycle in the way in which social media operates. Menon (2017b), one of the signatories of the statement, invokes this sense of time when she uses the title 'From

Feminazi to Savarna Rape Apologist in 24 Hours' in her response to the backlash sparked by the statement. Digital space-time both creates a space within which one might speak and be heard and a space in which one might be misheard, re-heard, reinterpreted and reimagined. These conversations were challenging and messy precisely because so much was being reconfigured and reimagined within the space of the digital.

Internet time also meant that this conversation was taking place simultaneously across various continents, especially where there were Indians scholars at foreign universities. Two scholars of Indian origin and affiliated to US universities separately recounted to me a heated discussion they had witnessed as part of the feminist Pre-conference on Gender, Sexuality and Occupation at the South Asia Conference in Madison, Wisconsin, only two days after the list and the statement went up, on 26 October 2017. One of them pointed out that digital connectivity meant that Indian students continued to be deeply embedded in debates taking place in India. She pointed out that 'the distinctions between here and there are not really there anymore', suggesting that diasporic communities remain embedded in critical feminist discourses in their home countries via the internet. One might further argue that when both the list and the statement are posted online, there is no time lag in terms of access to information.

There is no doubt that internet time was central to this conversation. Most debates took place online. There is already a fair body of literature in relation to gendered experiences and spaces online as well as analyses of feminist mobilisation in the online space (Baer, 2016; Gajjala, 2019; Niranjana, 2010; Phadke, 2020) including specifically on mobilising around #MeToo (Mendes et al., 2018; Clark-Parsons, 2019; Loney-Howes et al., 2021) and the kinds of exclusions created by mobilising in online spaces (Narayanamoorthy, 2021).

When we look back at this conversation, or indeed at feminist debates taking place today we must not forget that it is deeply inflected by internet time. Disagreements in internet time taking place on social media produce specific kinds of traces and create particular kinds of archives. Even as such debates allow space for more voices to be heard, for diverse and sometimes disenfranchised groups a space to articulate dissent, they might also compel us to see only the fractures, and from here to assume that they are irreparable.

Pain, betrayal and possibilities of reparation

The first week after the list and the statement were published went by in a bit of a blur. Many were posting their feelings and opinions on social media. Some of these social media posts were then converted into articles for online portals. In hindsight, some of the people I interviewed say that they would have waited a while longer before they posted an opinion if they knew then what they know now about how the debate would unfold. And even three years later many acknowledge how difficult it is to talk across the divide, or even wonder whether a conversation on the list and the statement is possible.

Other interviewees posit that there is not necessarily a divide, as one feminist activist in her fifties argued in a phone conversation: 'I don't agree that it has fractured the women's movement. It may have created distances but … I felt it was necessary to talk about it, to get an understanding of what the list meant. But somehow that has not happened and that is the problem'. She continued: 'These splits take place on feminist platforms and platforms might split but some years down the line, while people might not be the best of friends, they might work together again'.

Menon (2019a) similarly suggested that the statement was in keeping with forms of feminist discussion and disagreement, such as the disagreement that erupted over the screening of the documentary *India's Daughter* on the 2012 gang rape on which feminists had a difference of opinion. Reflecting on the statement she wrote: 'There was no personal animosity – we disagreed, we debated, and continued to work together. The statement, therefore, was not senior academics addressing young students, but one feminist voice addressing another'. She added that the disagreement was not about whether sexual harassment existed but rather about how it might be dealt with. She seemed to suggest that the intention of the statement was a way of opening up rather than foreclosing conversation.

But this is not what happened. One scholar who teaches at a US university told me: 'Depending on how you feel about the list and the statement led to a fundamental divide. Strong solidarities were built on either side of the divide. I was asked to speak about this on a panel but said no as I am unable to keep my relationships out of this.' Another scholar of Indian origin also teaching at a US university pointed out: 'It's very difficult to talk or to voice disagreement, which is why I feel unable to touch it. One of the main tensions has been around challenging the work and integrity of people who signed the statement, which is unacceptable for me.' 'You feel watched', a feminist academic told me, 'especially on social media. Even when you don't take a position this way or that, you feel watched – by your students, and by your friends.' Later she added: 'One of my friends who signed the statement told me that she'd expected me to take a clearer stance in favour of the statement and was disappointed by my silence.'

Disappointment is a word I heard often during people's narratives – on all sides of the divide people felt disappointed, even betrayed and attacked. 'I felt betrayed that the women whose work had taught me about revolution refused to recognise ours', said a feminist journalist who supported the list. Another young feminist who was a student when the debate was taking place said: 'Many of us were disappointed, but those who had been taught by the feminists who signed the statement were literally heartbroken.' In a similar vein, Meghana T (2018) wrote:

> As I read the List of Sexual Harassment Accused (LoSHA), with every new name my heart sank further into my chest. The accused and their work was so deeply respected by me. ... As personally hurtful as reading the names on the List, was the hasty statement that soon followed: prominent feminists stating that this was going to invalidate all the work they had done and instead, we should follow 'due process'. Once again, I read name after name of the signatories and felt my heart sink. Here were feminists and scholars I deeply respected and I felt like they had rejected us in our time of need.

Shreya Ila Anasuya (2017) wrote: 'Many of us who understand why the list exists ... have been feeling deeply frustrated and betrayed by the *Kafila* reaction. I think we are legitimately furious at not being supported and at being condescended to by people who could very easily have chosen to do this differently.'

The disappointment is a common theme for both those who supported the list and those who supported the statement. Kavita Krishnan (2017) wrote:

> I am saddened that in the blink of an eye and a click of the mouse, those of us who have lost skin in innumerable battles supporting survivors against 'men of our own ideology/politics/milieu', who are the usual suspects supporting every such complainant and facing vicious hostility for so doing, are being pilloried and mocked on social media as 'establishment feminists protecting their own'. The statement I signed does not question the motives of 'younger feminists', indeed of anyone defending the list, but it does express uneasiness and respectfully make an appeal.

Monobina Gupta (2017) wrote in support of the statement:

> Name-calling and identifying an enemy – especially when the 'enemies' are feminists who have fought with blood and sweat to clear the way for you to raise your voice – in terms of class, caste, hierarchy, and privilege, is easy. It is easy to point a finger in anger instead of stopping to think about why some of the sharpest, most critical, most dissenting voices in a movement might be uncomfortable with your methods.

One activist in an interview with me pointed out how someone she knew used to be very active on social media, but after she was trolled for signing the statement had retreated into a radio silence. 'When did feminists become the main enemy? What happened to patriarchy, to misogyny?' another feminist scholar asked me when I described my project to document feelings around the new feminist fracture.

As the battle lines were drawn, and online hostilities played themselves out, one ended up having to belong to one or the other side. As Ramdev and Bhattacharya (2017) acknowledge, the very act of writing about it holds the risk of being seen to belong to one camp or the other.

There is often pain and bafflement on all sides. 'But how can "they" not see it', is a phrase I encountered more than once.

Feminist rage and pain have often been productive and for a while it felt like perhaps this time they were not, given that our rage was directed at each other. But, if we can see these emotions as productive, perhaps in the not too distant future we can sit together in a room and talk about them, in rage and in pain, but also in the hope that we can rebuild solidarities and trust. Can we imagine a space where we might have this conversation as feminists, in our diversities, but with the hope of being able to talk to each other again?

I don't want to be cancelled: feminist anxieties

Writing this piece caused not a little anxiety. As I navigated the arguments and the interviews, I trod carefully, attempting to represent all sides of the argument because all of them make sense. I see why due process matters so much in our struggle for gender equality, and a campus where sexual harassment is not tolerated. I also see why, when due process fails, students who do not have a voice feel compelled to seek other means. I hear students who feel they have little voice in the outcomes of sexual harassment cases. I also feel for the teachers who have struggled for decades to institute mechanisms for redressal of sexual harassment at their universities.

I have been in academia as student, as researcher and as teacher for nearly three decades. I have friends, mentors, students and colleagues on both sides of this feminist argument and they often occupy more than one of these roles in my life. I feel all of them looking over my shoulder as I write. I anticipate their comments. I worry that I might offend someone I have never met. Or worse, that someone I have deep affection for may feel I betrayed them in some way. In addition to this large, but nonetheless finite, group of friends, mentors, colleagues and students is the larger social media world out there. The debates around the list and the statement show just how quickly and how acrimoniously one could be taken to task and called out. As feminists we are afraid of being cancelled and called out and judged to be inadequate or bad feminists in the sense articulated by Roxanne Gay (2014).

Strong positions and articulations were assumed in the course of this debate. It is important to acknowledge that all of us are more than the positions we took then or continue to hold now; we are also more than the sum of our work. It is important to move forward, not by forgetting the rage and the pain but by remembering it and remembering that it is not about this one conversation but about the feminist movement. The relevant question then is: what are the possibilities opened up by feminist frictions?

Concluding thoughts

Feminist spaces are not utopian spaces of agreement or solidarity and they never have been. Feminist spaces, despite the broad commitment to social justice, are also hierarchical spaces that often do not reflect intersectional allyship. This is not new or unique to the Indian context. In the US context feminist organisations have confronted questions of implicit racism (Davis, 2010; Scott, 2000). In similar ways in the 1980s the Indian women's movement confronted differences in regard to questions of religion over the Shah Bano case (Phadke, 2003). Questions of caste have also been raised in relation to the women's movement in India (Guru, 1995; Rege, 1998; Raj, 2013), and in relation to specific moments like the discussion over bar dancing in Mumbai in 2005 (Gopal, 2012) and in relation to the to the Pinjra Tod movement (Lama and Maharaj, 2019). In May 2021, a senior feminist activist made trans-exclusionary comments, which became the trigger for a long discussion on trans questions in feminism, and a statement signed by several feminist activists and scholars asking for feminist accountability was released on a blog (Feminist Futures Collective, 2021). #MeToo itself has also produced similar feminist contestations and debates in the US, for instance around the accusations against Avital Ronell in 2017 (Greenberg, 2018) and Aziz Ansari in 2018 (Hindes and Fileborn, 2020) as well as a larger conversation on the rifts within feminism caused by #MeToo (Donegan, 2018) and as questions of race within #MeToo (Phipps, 2021).

Internet time has reconfigured feminism. It has enabled us to build new solidarities and to talk across geographical barriers. At the same time, it has enabled a public acknowledgement of larger fractures that are not new, that have always been there, including, though not limited to, those of race, caste and cis/trans-gender, physical ability among them. Feminist frictions and disagreements, I would argue, are the very substance of a democratic evolving movement. Differences – structural, ideological, and practical; named and unnamed – are central not just to the feminist movement but any movement for justice. They make for what might be painful and messy discussions and engagements but these are the signs of a robust movement that is willing to grow, unlearn and relearn. These disagreements and the rage, pain and conflict that they generate extracts a price in terms of the kinds of fractures it surfaces, but the point is that these fractures exist, they are not created by one particular disagreement. Acknowledging the presence of these fractures and even structural inequalities, is eventually a liberatory process that facilitates the naming of inequalities within our feminisms. These debates, then, are central to rethinking and restructuring our feminisms, to enabling the articulation of difference, and to the evolving project of solidarity building in precarious times.

Acknowledgement

I would like to thank Srila Roy, Nicky Falkof and the many friends (too many to name here) who read and commented on various versions of this draft.

References

Agnes F. (1992). 'Protecting Women against Violence? Review of a Decade of Legislation, 1980–89', *Economic & Political Weekly*, 27:17, WS19–WS33.

Anasuya, S. I. (2017). 'Why the Response to a List of Sexual Harassers has Splintered India's Feminist Movement', *DailyO.in*, 29 October. www. dailyo.in/politics/sexual-harassment-raya-sarkar-kafila-indian-feminism/ story/1/20291.html. Accessed 2 February 2020.

Ayyar, V. (2017). 'Caste-Gender Matrix and the Promise and Practice of Academia', *Economic & Political Weekly Engage*, 16 December, 52:50. www.epw.in/engage/article/caste-gender-matrix-and-promise-and-practi ce-academia. Accessed 20 February 2020.

Baer, H. (2016). 'Redoing Feminism: Digital Activism, Body Politics, and Neoliberalism', *Feminist Media Studies* 16:1, 17–34.

Bargi, D. (2017). 'On Misreading the Dalit Critique of University Spaces', *Economic & Political Weekly* 52:50. www.epw.in/engage/article/mis reading-dalit-critique-university-space. Accessed 20 March 2020.

Camminga, B. (2020). 'Disregard and Danger: Chimamanda Ngozi Adichie and the Voices of Trans (and Cis) African Feminists', *Sociological Review* 68:4, 817–33.

Chadda, G. (2017). 'Towards Complex Feminist Solidarities after the List-Statement', *Economic & Political Weekly Engage*, 52:50. www.epw. in/engage/article/towards-complex-feminist-solidarities-list-statement. Accessed 20 March 2020.

Chakraborty, A. (2019). 'Politics of #LoSha: Using Naming and Shaming as a Feminist Tool on Facebook', in *Gender Hate Online: Understanding the New Anti-Feminism*, edited by D. Ging and E. Siapera, 195–212. Cham: Palgrave Macmillan.

Chatterjee, R. (2018). 'I would Like to Credit Bhanvari Devi for Igniting the #MeToo Movement Years Ago', *Live Mint*, 15 October. www.live mint.com/Leisure/JYk9SoKvaPjeo9nevmUUPO/I-would-like-to-credit-Bhanvari-Devi-for-igniting-the-MeTo.html. Accessed 20 March 2020.

Chun, W. H. K. (2016). *Updating to Remain the Same: Habitual New Media*. Cambridge, MA: MIT Press.

Chun, W. H. K. and S. Friedland. (2015). 'Habits of Leaking: Of Sluts and Network Cards', *Differences* 26:2, 1–28.

Clark-Parsons, R. (2019). 'I SEE YOU, I BELIEVE YOU, I STAND WITH YOU': #MeToo and the performance of networked feminist visibility, Feminist Media Studies. www.tandfonline.com/doi/abs/10.1080/1468 0777.2019.1628797?journalCode=rfms20. Accessed 2 February 2020.

Datta, B. (2010). 'Her Body, Your Gaze: Prostitution, Violence, and Ways of Seeing', in *Nine Degrees of Justice: New Perspectives on Violence against Women in India*, edited by B. Datta, 285–316. New Delhi: Zubaan Books.

Davis, K. 2010. 'Avoiding the 'R-Word': Racism in Feminist Collectives', in *Secrecy and Silence in the Research Process: Feminist Reflections*, edited by Róisín Ryan-Flood and Rosalind Gill, 147–60. London: Routledge.

Donegan, M. (2018). 'How #MeToo Revealed the Central rift within Feminism Today', *Guardian*, 11 May. www.theguardian.com/news/2018/may/11/how-metoo-revealed-the-central-rift-within-feminism-social-individualist. Accessed 2 June 2021.

Feminist Futures Collective (2021). 'Call for Accountability in Feminist Circles', *Medium.com*, 20 May. https://feministfuturescollective.medium.com/call-for-accountability-in-feminist-circles-4b0ae9846787. Accessed 10 June 2021.

Gajjala, R. (2018). 'When an Indian Whisper Network Went Digital', *Communication, Culture and Critique* 11:3, 489–93.

Gajjala, R. (2019). *Digital Diasporas: Labor and Affect in Gendered Indian Digital Publics*. Lanham, MD: Rowman and Littlefield.

Gajjala, R. and A. Chakraborty. (2019). 'Dialogue Interlude with Arpita Chakraborty', in *Digital Diasporas: Labor and Affect in Gendered Indian Digital Publics*, edited by R. Gajjala, 204–6. Lanham, MD: Rowman and Littlefield.

Gay, R. (2014). *Bad Feminist: Essays*. New York: Harper Perennial.

George, A., U. Vinghya and S. Ray. (2010). 'Sex Trafficking and Sex Work: Definitions, Debates and Dynamics – A Review of Literature', *Economic & Political Weekly* 45:17, 64–73.

Ghosh, A. (2017). 'The Civil War in Indian Feminism – A Critical Glance', *Sabrang*, 7 November. https://sabrangindia.in/article/civil-war-indian-feminism-%E2%80%93-critical-glance. Accessed 2 February 2020.

Gopal, M. (2012). 'Caste, Sexuality and Labour: The Troubled Connection', *Current Sociology* 60:2, 222–38.

Gupta, M. (2017). 'Pointing Fingers, Dividing Feminists Will not Help the Fight against Sexual Violence', *Wire*, 29 October. https://thewire.in/gender/pointing-fingers-dividing-feminists-will-not-help-fight-sexual-violence. Accessed 2 February 2020.

Guru. G. (1995). 'Dalit Women Talk Differently', *Economic & Political Weekly* 30:41/42, 2548–50.

Halberstam, J. (2018). 'Towards a Trans* Feminism', *Boston Review*, 18 January.http://bostonreview.net/gender-sexuality/jack-halberstam-towards-trans-feminism. Accessed 2 February 2020.

Hindes, S. and B. Fileborn (2020). '"Girl Power Gone Wrong": #MeToo, Aziz Ansari, and Media Reporting Of (Grey Area) Sexual Violence', *Feminist Media Studies* 20:5, 639–56.

Hines, S. (2020). 'Sex Wars and (Trans) Gender Panics: Identity and Body Politics in Contemporary UK Feminism', *Sociological Review* 68:4, 699–717.

John, M. and J. Nair. (1998). 'Introduction', in *A Question of Silence: The Sexual Economies of Modern India*. New Delhi: Kali for Women.

Kotiswaran, P. (2019). 'Has the Dial Moved on the Indian Sex Work Debate', *Economic & Political Weekly* 54:22, 10–12. www.epw.in/journal/2019/22/alternative-standpoint/has-dial-moved-indian-sex-work-debate.html. Accessed 2 February 2020.

Krishnan, K. (2017). '"It's like Blackening Faces": Why I am Uneasy with the Name and Shame List of Sexual Harassers', *Scroll*, 25 October. https://scroll.in/article/855399/its-like-blackening-faces-why-i-am-uneasy-with-the-name-and-shame-list-of-sexual-harassers. Accessed 2 February 2020.

Lama, S. T. K. and S. Maharaj (2019). 'Statement: Why we Decided to Leave Pinjra Tod', *Roundtable India*, 19 February. https://roundtable india.co.in/index.php?option=com_content&view=article&id=9582:s tatement-why-we-decided-to-leave-pinjra-tod&catid=129:events-and-activism&Itemid=195. Accessed 2 February 2020.

Loney-Howes, R., K. Mendes, D. Fernández Romero, B. Fileborn and S. Núñez Puente (2021). Digital footprints of #MeToo, Feminist Media Studies. www.tandfonline.com/doi/full/10.1080/14680777.2021.18861 42. Accessed 10 June 2021.

Lukose, R. (2018). 'Decolonising Feminism in the #MeToo Era', *Cambridge Journal of Anthropology* 36:2, 34–52.

Meghana T. (2018). 'A Practitioner of Fingertip Activism Responds to Nivedita Menon', *Feminism in* India, 13 March. https://feminis minindia.com/2018/03/13/finger-tip-activism-response-menon/. Accessed 20 February 2020.

Mendes, K., J. Ringrose and J. Keller. (2018). '#MeToo and the Promise and Pitfalls of Challenging Rape Culture through Digital Feminist Activism', *European Journal of Women's Studies* 25:2, 236–46.

Menon, N. (2007). 'Introduction', in *Sexualities*. London: Zed Books.

Menon, N. (2017a). 'Statement by Feminists on Facebook Campaign to "Name and Shame"', *Kafila*, 24 October.https://kafila.online/2017/10/24/ statement-by-feminists-on-facebook-campaign-to-name-and-shame/. Accessed 2 February 2020.

Menon, N. (2017b). 'From Feminazi to Savarna Rape Apologist in 24 Hours', *Kafila*, 28 October. https://kafila.online/2017/10/28/from-feminazi-to-savarna-rape-apologist-in-24-hours/. Accessed 2 February 2020.

Menon, N. (2019a). 'How the Feminist Conversation around Sexual Harassment Has Evolved', *Wire*, 28 February. https://thewire.in/women/ how-the-feminist-conversation-around-sexual-harassment-has-evolved. Accessed 2 February 2020.

Menon, N. (2019b). 'Sexual Violence and the Law in India', in *Research Handbook on Feminist Jurisprudence*, edited by Robin West and Cynthia Bowman, 184–212. Cheltenham: Edward Elgar Publishing.

Narayanamoorthy N. (2021). 'Exclusion in #MeToo India: rethinking inclusivity and intersectionality in Indian digital feminist movements', *Feminist Media Studies*.www.tandfonline.com/doi/full/10.1080/146807 77.2021.1913432. Acessed 10 June 2021.

Niranjana, T. (2010). 'Why Culture Matters: Rethinking the Language of Feminist Politics', *Inter-Asia Cultural Studies* 11:2, 229–35.

Phadke, S. (2003). 'Thirty Years On: Women's Studies Reflects on the Women's Movement', *Economic & Political Weekly* 38:43, 4567–76.

Phadke, S. (2020). 'Defending Frivolous Fun: Feminist Acts of Claiming Public Spaces in South Asia', *South Asia: Journal of South Asian Studies*, 43:2, 281–93.

Raj, R. (2013). 'Dalit Women as Political Agents: A Kerala Experience', *Economic & Political Weekly* 48:18, 56–63.

Ramdev, R. and D. Bhattacharya. (2017). 'Sexual Harassment in the Academy: What the Hitlist Misses', *Kafila*, 29 October. https://kafila. online/2017/10/29/sexual-harassment-in-the-academia-what-the-hit list-misses-debaditya-bhattacharya-and-rina-ramdev/. Accessed 2 March 2020.

Rao, P. (2018). 'Caste and the LoSHA Discourse', *Communication, Culture and Critique* 11:3, 494–7.

Rege, S. (1998). Dalit Women Talk Differently: A Critique of "Difference" and Towards a Dalit Feminist Standpoint Position, *Economic & Political Weekly*, 33:44, WS39–WS46.

Roy, S. (2017). 'Whose Feminism is it Anyway?' Wire, 1 November. https:// thewire.in/gender/whose-feminism-anyway. Accessed 2 March 2020.

Scott, E. K. (2000). 'Everyone Against Racism: Agency and the Production of Meaning in the Anti-Racism Practices of Two Feminist Organizations', *Theory and Society* 29, 785–818.

Shah, S. (2011). *Sex Work and Women's Movements*. New Delhi: Crea.

Suneetha, A., U. Bhrugubanda, V. Nagaraj and L. Kutty. (2017). 'The "List" and the Task of Rearranging Academic Relationships', *Economic & Political Weekly*, 52:47, 25 November. www.epw.in/engage/article/ list-and-task-rearranging-academic-relationships. Accessed 20 March 2020.

Phipps, A. (2021). 'White Tears, White Rage: Victimhood and (as) Violence in Mainstream Feminism', *European Journal of Cultural Studies*, 24:1, 81–93.

Greenberg, Z. (2018). What Happens to #MeToo When a Feminist is the Accused? *The New York Times*, 13 August. www.nytimes. com/2018/08/13/nyregion/sexual-harassment-nyu-female-professor. html. Accessed 10 June 2021.

Reflection: progressive men and predatory practices

Jessica Breakey

The riot vehicles had made their way onto campus that night, like they had been doing almost every night since the start of the protests demanding free, decolonised, quality higher education in South Africa several weeks before. This time police were demanding students and staff evacuate the buildings they had occupied. The group, smaller than usual, split as some of us ran inside the building, barricading ourselves in with whatever chairs and tables we could find. The remaining students and sympathetic staff sat outside, blocking the entrance. Those who have been involved in this type of political organising and protest will know the adrenaline-induced haze that comes from such quick protest decision and action. The stack of tables blocking the doors had almost reached the ceiling by the time I took a breath and cleared the haze from my eyes. The room was almost entirely populated by men.

The police began by demanding our evacuation on their loudhailer, then arresting some of those who were blocking their entrance to the building. Finally, in a move we had grown to expect from them, they started throwing tear gas canisters through the window. Trapped, with our eyes burning, the only liquid we could find to relieve the pain was a litre bottle of Oros that someone found in the corner. Oros is an orange concentrate juice that is served at birthday parties, after school sports games and as a sweet celebration of a good school report, a ubiquitous marker of a South African middle-class childhood.

We passed the Oros around, gagging as the sticky sweetness clung to our faces. A few minutes later, I was assaulted by a comrade inside the room.

In late 2019, I presented a paper titled 'Progressive Men and Predatory Practices' at a workshop on sexual violence in the public sphere at the Centre for the Study of Law and Governance at Jawaharlal Nehru University (JNU). I use the term 'paper' here loosely. My colleagues presented papers, the results of rigorous research, offering deep analyses woven into appropriate theory. I, however, chose to use my paper to tell a personal story, to reflect on a moment years before that had caused me both psychological and intellectual unease. I had never recounted the story out loud before and it is still not entirely clear to me why I chose that specific setting to do it – a room filled mostly with strangers in a foreign country. It may be that I felt a sense of safety, such that I could finally share this story and my thoughts around it without the fear of a comrade overhearing, without speculation of who the 'perp' was, without bringing the public and private politics of a movement I still broadly supported into disrepute.

The retelling required me to piece together a narrative, to connect the dots not just of the event but of its political meaning. So, there I sat, in a stuffy seminar room in Delhi, sweating so much that my dress clung to the back of my seat, telling for the first time the story of my assault during the 2015 South African student movement. I spoke not of the details – I will not share those here either – but of the feminist and political tension, the internal tearing apart, that I felt afterwards. I am still not sure if anyone saw what happened; it feels hard to believe that no one did. I find it quite easy to justify that the chaos of what was happening around us meant that it was unlikely anyone saw, and even if they did, it was possible that the adrenaline haze made it difficult to make sense of what they had seen. Still, the years since that moment have been marked not with speculation on the actions of others but rather a coming to terms with my own action – or rather inaction – following what happened. I said nothing when it happened, and I had continued to say nothing.

In truth, it was not that I felt silenced but that I was wilfully choosing to forget what had happened. I exiled it from memory, asking what my individual story mattered when the broad political aims of the movement were those that I supported and that already occupied a vulnerable and turbulent space in South African political memory?

In *Remembering Revolution*, Srila Roy explores the underground, everyday gendered dynamics within the Naxalbari movement in India during the 1960s and 1970s. Roy reflects on how the 'forgetting' of the violence that was internal to the revolutionary community – those 'little violences' and acts of betrayal within interpersonal relationships *within* 'the movement' – was an act of repudiation more than of silencing, forgetting or erasure (Roy, 2012: 14). South African student protesters experienced severe state repression as riot police used rubber bullets and stun grenades to squash protests at universities around the country. The memory of this political violence endures while the women of the student movement struggle to name the violence experienced at the hands of their male comrades. Similarly, I felt that I did not want to damage the public political life of this student movement. I knew well that racist and conservative communities in South Africa were eager to tarnish and destroy it. Nor did I want to be responsible for contributing to the internal crumbling of the movement. So, I willed myself to remember the student protests the way I wanted them to be remembered by others.

The discussion that followed my talk at JNU taught me that this experience was not mine alone, nor was it rare; in fact, it was frighteningly common in progressive movements and spaces. For decades, JNU has been at the centre of leftist critique and activism in India. Recent years (and months) have seen increased political organising against anti-Muslim and fascist ideas and policies on the campus. The women in the seminar room, mostly students, shared with me their own experiences of navigating activist circles, publicly punted as feminist spaces but riddled with overt sexism, harassment and assault. When the enemy is so clear, in this case the right-wing Hindu nationalist government, it is easy for us to see the threat 'over there' and difficult to recognise (or reconcile) when it is 'right here', in our midst.

Those with experience in these student spaces will recognise a specific brand of 'leaderdom' as more the result of media portrayal than any kind of internal consensus. We have grown accustomed to broad, nuanced and politically evocative moments being remembered through the image of one man with his fist in the air. Perhaps he will have read a few pages of Kimberle Crenshaw's scholarship and will passionately spew a line or two about intersectionality before cornering you and shouting at you so loudly that the tiny hairs on your chin blow with his breath. Many of those who are publicly viewed as or become student leaders are, unsurprisingly, perpetrators of abuse; they are, if you want, 'progressive perpetrators'.

Though we may not agree with how these men found their way into this insidious kind of political stardom, we know that their fall from grace will almost always result in discrediting an entire collective, leaving one's own political work and sacrifice disregarded by mere association. Even if we wanted to 'out' these political men, these 'progressive' perpetrators, we are told, time and time again, that it would 'not be strategic', or that we need to 'keep our dirty laundry inside the movement'. In South Africa, these conversations happen not just in student activist spaces but in the spaces of well-funded NGOs, in influential trade unions, in university departments and in the highest public office. Political perpetrators remain protected by hollow progressive sentiment.

My intention with this reflection both at JNU and now is not to lament at my own guilt and indulge my own complicity, nor am I trying to provide any sort of road map or set of instructions on what women should or should not do when faced with the painful betrayal by a comrade. Rather, this writing serves as a process of thinking: a way for me to move away from the scream that sits lodged in my throat towards some kind of processing – a making sense of the timeless burden that political women carry, an ultimatum designed by political men such that we can choose to betray ourselves and our own bodies or betray 'the cause'.

As I observe the tidal wave of hyper-masculine fascism that is sweeping across the world, the cunning denial of climate change and pending ecological collapse, the rise of right-wing nationalisms and the closing in of borders, I hear the calls for an organised, transnational left to rise from its own ashes. The enemy is clearly marked and more dangerous than before – it is 'over there' and proudly announcing itself for the world to see. Of course I am afraid, afraid for the future of the planet, the future battles my body will have to endure, of economic depressions and growing inequalities, wildfires, rising water levels, pro-life policies and for-profit prisons. I am also afraid of all the sacrifices women will have to make in this political battle, the stories they will never tell.

Reference

Roy, S. (2012). *Remembering Revolution: Gender, Violence, and Subjectivity in India's Naxalbari Movement.* New Delhi: Oxford University Press.

Part III

Institutional locations: the university
and the state

8

#EndRapeCulture and #MeToo: of intersectionality, rage and injury

Amanda Gouws

We live a world that is saturated with sex. Imagery of sexual intercourse, sexuality and women's objectification can be readily accessed through advertisements, television series, online chat rooms and online pornographic sites. Sexual imagery in cyberspace rarely deals with erotica, women's sexual desire and consent. We also live in a world that is saturated with sexual violence against women, often graphically depicted in digital spaces, television series, social media, and normalised in pornography, where women's sexuality is portrayed through a male gaze. Sexual images are produced and reproduced for mass consumption, turning sex and sexuality into commodities, normalising in many ways sexual harassment and violence in the real world.

Given the pervasiveness of sexual harassment and sexual violence, women's pushback in 2017 came in a digital form when #MeToo allowed for the naming and shaming of men on social media platforms. Many men in power who got away with the most egregious types of violence were on the receiving end of women's rage. #MeToo also became a barometer of the pervasiveness of sexual harassment and rape. It told us a very familiar story – that due process and the law often fail women when they make claims about being sexually harassed or raped.

In South Africa visible resistance and protest against sexual harassment and the normalisation of sexual violence through rape cultures on universities campuses became a groundswell movement in 2016 with the #EndRapeCulture campaign. This campaign combined a digital dimension with direct protest action.[1] Young women, calling themselves radical intersectional African feminists pushed back against the pervasiveness of sexual harassment and rape at tertiary education institutions. It preceded #MeToo by nearly a year and forced universities to take note of rape cultures and failed policies and procedures dealing with sexual harassment and violence.

This chapter draws on analyses of #MeToo and #EndRapeCulture to show similarities and differences, centring South Africa as a postcolonial society where intersectional feminism and feminist anger at sexual violence, racism and patriarchy were foregrounded in women's digital protest as well as direct action through topless marches.

#MeToo

#MeToo as a digital campaign started in the US and Europe and circulated in eighty-five countries, spreading well beyond the global north (Gill and Orgad, 2018: 1317). It was effective in giving women space to articulate injury but at the same time invited criticism of a 'confession culture', or a 'call out culture', that has to stand in for legal measures dealing with sexual harassment and opening possibilities for men to be framed as victims.

#MeToo was a reckoning by women of men who got away with sexual harassment for a long time, some even for decades. Its breadth was determined by access to digital space and sites. Its impact was immediate (Gill and Orgad, 2018). Its support can be ascribed to its broad and inclusive appeal among women. While the digital campaign was started by heterosexual, white Hollywood celebrities, it developed into taking on board the experiences of queer people as well as women of colour outside the global north. Millions of women around the world participated in #MeToo by saying 'me too' on social media, and so the anger of women reverberated around the globe (see e.g. Chandra and Erlingsdottir, 2021).

The unprecedented speed of social media makes it indispensable for contemporary activism, but at the same time it creates opportunities in which certain discursive frames are amplified and others ignored (Salter, 2019: 2). Certain forms of expression that are not very salient or 'trending' may not receive a lot of attention. With regard to sexual harassment and violence, social media create spaces for 'speaking the unspeakable', where women who often are coerced into unwanted sex paradoxically state the obvious (the pervasiveness of sexual violence about which there is a silence) and speak the unspeakable (naming and shaming perpetrators) (Cooper, 2018: 1), making it possible to frame a confessional/ call-out narrative. The campaign also framed its concerns in terms of the relationship between sex and power and called for justice in relation to consent. Consent became a widely discussed topic, highlighting its conceptual shortcomings in law (Burgess, 2018; Cooper, 2018).

If women engaging with #MeToo assumed a universal experience and women's solidarity around sexual harassment and sexual violence, it took the corrective by black women to point out the lack of intersectional representation of women's identities and positionalities in relation to sexual violence. Foregrounding the experience of white women caused a certain invisibility/erasure of sexual violence experienced by black women. Tarana Burke, an African American woman, had already started a non-digital Me Too campaign in 2006, with which she attempted to empower young black women to deal with sexual violence. Digital #MeToo made invisible the unique form and specific vulnerability of black women to harassment (Onwuachi-Willig, 2018; see also Brajanac, 2019).

The call-out strategy of #MeToo also garnered critique about what some called 'mob rule' through the call-out culture (Mendes et al., 2018; Pipyrou, 2018). Those who are concerned with this aspect note the grey area around desire, the negotiation of sex and sexual intercourse that is often ambiguous, open to interpretation and misunderstanding, often difficult to distinguish from 'bad sex'.[2] Another concern was that calling out individual men makes visible the men and not the problem. Zarkov and Davis (2018) pose the question of whether visibility and exposure are the solution to sexual violence because #MeToo shapes a debate that leads to sympathy with victims in societies that are sexist, racist and classist, without positioning men and women in ways which show that not all women are victims and not all men are perpetrators (see also Gutting and Ruden, 2018).

#MeToo was also perceived as favouring a 'respectability' femininity of rich and powerful actresses (who are viewed as believable and trustworthy), rather than also giving visibility to the experiences of women who, for example, work as sex workers, strippers and in the adult entertainment industry (those who are deemed not worthy of respect). In the case of respectability femininity, sexual harassment is framed in relation to sex and power, but in the case of 'non-respectability' femininity, a frame of morality is used that makes power relations invisible. Furthermore, #MeToo initially created a binary, that harassment only takes place between men and women in the workplace (Gill and Orgad, 2018: 1319).

Demonising[3] men (such as calling them 'monstrous' or 'bad apples') was also challenged by some feminists because it does not account for systemic issues of sexual violence caused by the construction of masculinities that teach men to pursue women and not to take no for an answer. The contentious issue is that we cannot address men's behaviour in relation to women's sexuality without engaging men's socialisation and perceptions of issues of sex and sexuality and the normalisation of sexual violence through the media (Gill and Orgad, 2018: 1320; see also PettyJohn et al., 2019; Phipps, 2020).

#MeToo made visible a long history of feminists' questioning of the effectiveness of law in dealing with sexual harassment. Catherine MacKinnon's (1983, 1989) path-breaking work in this regard showed how difficult it is for women to get justice for sexual violence when the law trivialises and dismisses women's experience, through framing them as not believable or through secondary victimisation. Can a 'confessional culture', however, stand in for justice in other forms, such as legal justice, or restorative justice through processes of mediation (Jackson, 2018: 14)? Unlike evidence that is cross-examined in courts, confessional cultures work with the assumption that stories told from a subjective experience need to be accepted as evidence of injury. #MeToo, therefore, can be viewed as the extra-legal dimension of disclosure – the naming and shaming through social media, and individual and collective testimonies (Lukose, 2018: 40), not the official laying of complaints that will result in investigations, even though some women did lay complaints. The argument made in this regard is that while the focus is on epistemic authority and agency, the aim should not be the abandonment of existing legal channels, but rather their reform (Jackson, 2018: 16).

It is unclear if #MeToo has changed institutional cultures. For Gentile (2018), #MeToo is a cultural upheaval, but it still does not mean that we are dealing with the reconfigurations of institutional power in corporations or other organisations, such as universities. In the West, men continue to make women the agents of change for sexual harassment – they do not ask what has been done to women but ask what is being done to my career. (A good case in point is Cristine Blasey Ford's accusation in 2018 against US Supreme Court nominee Brett Kavanaugh (Pengelly, 2019).) This once again removes women from the picture. Gentile argues that women supporting #MeToo are accused of sowing moral panic (framing most men as sexual predators), but the moral panic is not about morality, it is 'heteropatriarchal panic'. As she puts it: 'Morality is the trope designed to hide the vulnerability and shame of heteropatriarchal masculinity when it faces any challenges' (Gentile, 2018: 243). To this we need to add corporations' fear of litigation rather than commitment to change (Harris, 2018: 254).

#MeToo created a crisis of the present, by making it possible for people to speak out against sexual harassment and assault, creating a break with the time before and disrupting taken-for-granted norms (Burgess, 2018: 354). As such, #MeToo occurred in a time that Pellegrini (2018) calls 'discursive displacement', created by the election of Donald Trump as president of the US. This is a time in which women want to deal with men like Trump, his 'pussy grabbing' comments and his creation of conditions of 'untruth', through rage and speaking out against injury. This rage is a consequence of the conditions created by non-truth and 'fake news' that suspend the lack of believability altogether. In this post-truth era Trump's scandals are not scandalous, as Burgess (2018: 356–7) puts it. Burgess is concerned that it gives space to the lie in public arenas of discourse without consequences and that it undermines our trust in the truth. The question then becomes: Why should anyone believe someone who claims sexual harassment? #MeToo claims the post-truth moment rather than critiquing it, and this has serious implications for due process where affective claims are interrogated in order to establish facts. Criticism was aimed at #MeToo because it deployed affective claims as truth claims. In post-truth logics, the expression of one's experience can serve as a demand to be believed, and in doing so the articulation of pain takes on the status of truth, placing truth beyond mediation, question and contestation (Burgess, 2018: 363). #MeToo shuts down any critique that will threaten the very premise of the movement – that women who speak out against sexual violence should be believed and that these beliefs cannot be contested. At the same time men who dispute their status as victims cannot be believed and therefore their claims should be contested (Burgess, 2018: 360).

As a confessional culture and with exposure of men who harass and rape, #MeToo made a significant contribution, and through feminist critique thereof opened spaces for debate of the complicated issues it raised, such as believing testimonial claims of sexual violence, consent and whether it is possible to reconcile epistemic justice based on women's voices with the due process of law.

#EndRapeCulture in South Africa

I now turn to the #campaigns in South Africa, which included #Rhodes MustFall, #FeesMustFall and #EndRapeCulture. I here discuss women's rage, the transnational circulation of ideas through the digital media that influenced students, the symbolism of their topless marches, and the call for epistemic justice for women in relation to sexual violence.

Preceding #MeToo by more-or-less a year, #EndRapeCulture started in South Africa on university campuses in tandem with the #RhodesMustFall and #FeesMustFall campaigns to 'decolonise' South African universities.[4] During 2015 university campuses all over South Africa erupted with the anger of black, mostly African[5] students, who claimed that institutional cultures reflect Western (read white) values, which alienate them. The protests were waged on a symbolic level against emblems of colonisation (such as the statue of Cecil John Rhodes, a notorious colonist, on the campus of the University of Cape Town), in what was known as the

#RhodesMustFall campaign. On the material level #FeesMustFall was waged against high university fees, which have a deleterious impact on the 'missing middle' (children of parents who earn too much to qualify for a scholarship, but too little to get a bank loan). These student movements coordinated their campaigns among institutions through social media, ensuring the fast spread of tactics. The campaigns showed deep levels of discontent among predominantly African students on all campuses. Their demands included institutional culture change, curriculum transformation and free tertiary education.

During this push back against hostile institutional cultures, sexual violence had an impact on the solidarity between male and female students when a female student was raped by a fellow activist in a university building during an all-night sit-in at the University of Cape Town (Mugo, 2015). At Rhodes University female students 'outed' eleven men as sexual violence perpetrators in what became known as the RU Reference List (Seddon, 2016). When the management at Rhodes University (renamed by the students as the University Currently Known as Rhodes [UCKAR]) refused to act against the alleged perpetrators until due process had taken its course, the #EndRapeCulture campaign was born and, through the use of social media (such as Whatsapp), spread to most universities in South Africa with great speed.

#EndRapeCulture used social media to call for protest and to distribute messages about where and when demonstrations and marches against rape culture would take place. It was therefore not only a digital campaign but also involved direct action. Female students used their bodies in the demonstrations, protesting with naked breasts or in their underwear. The digital campaign was in constant dialogue with the direct action of protest and demonstrations. Salter (2019: 2), drawing on Gerbaudo, calls this the 'choreography of assembly' in which he links the role of social media with political activism, and points out that this 'choreography is a process of the symbolic construction of public space' in which collective action can unfold in real world spaces. Students participating in #EndRapeCulture were angry about a colonial past and current conditions of violence, which rendered them voiceless in the public sphere.

The female students called themselves radical intersectional African feminists, with intersectionality referring to interlocking relations of dominant social, political, cultural and economic dynamics of power that are multiple and determined simultaneously (Bilge, 2010: 58). Lived experiences, structural systems of domination, sites of marginalisation, forms of power and modes of resistance occur in dynamic shifting ways in a matrix of domination (May, 2015: 21). In this matrix black and white people are differently located in terms of race, class, gender and other markers of identity (Gouws, 2017). In the case of #MeToo, intersectionality could not just be tagged onto the movement without, as Burgess (2018: 351) argues, thinking about how to centre the speech of marginalised groups. In the South African context, female students, embracing feminism, started out from the premise of intersectionality, grounding their claims in the lived experience (of 'black pain') of marginalised African and transgender students. The students attempted to change the language and the logics through which sexual violence is justified and resistance silenced. These women positioned the black woman's body as central to the infliction of sexual violence but marginal to institutional processes that are supposed to protect them from harm or alleviate the perpetration of sexual violence.

#EndRapeCulture managed to create feelings of solidarity, recognition and outrage among black female students. This included calls for men accused of sexual misconduct to be fired from their jobs, expelled as students, or professionally and socially ostracised, as a substitute for formal sanctions that often fail. The anger of students was aimed at institutions not dealing effectively with practices, beliefs and traditions that normalised whiteness and sexual violence against women. They were angry at institutions that were tone deaf to their pleas.

#MeToo and #EndRapeCulture – all the rage or just rage?

Underlying expressions of the pervasiveness of sexual violence of #MeToo and #EndRapeCulture is women's anger. This is anger stemming from often not being believed and being silenced when speaking out against men's sexual entitlement and the pervasiveness of sexual harassment. In the US, the case of Anita Hill against Supreme Court nominee Clarence Thomas in 1991, who despite her accusations was appointed to the position, is a good example of this (Barbaro et al., 2018).

#MeToo (as well as #EndRapeCulture) was a flashpoint of women's rage that made female anger legible as feminist rage (Orgad and Gill, 2019: 596). But rage cannot be disconnected from angry bodies. The white women celebrities who popularised #MeToo were angry, but their anger translated into passive action of saying 'MeToo', or clicking a link or emotional containment, as Orgad and Gill (2019: 599) show through an analysis of actress Uma Thurman's statement of anger about Harvey Weinstein on Instagram. It was not an 'uncontrollable discharge' but the anger was 'premeditated, focused and precise' – steering clear of the stereotypical hysterical woman. This is contained white anger that feeds into the patriarchal notion of reason – speaking calmly from a place of reason rather than with the aggression that would be fitting for sexual violation. This move is made because women's anger in the face of misogyny in patriarchal societies is viewed as unreasonable, crazy and, therefore, inadmissible. This type of containment, however, displaces the rage and individualises it. Orgad and Gill (2019: 601) call this waiting to feel less angry or 'cooling down' a safety valve for women's rage, that depoliticises it. This politics of respectability reflects #MeToo's initial focus on respectability femininity that expects women to show composure and not to have emotional rants that will make them unbelievable (Wood, 2019: 612).

Black women, on the other hand, are regularly seen as already angry (Orgad and Gill, 2019: 597) and the black body as charged with aggression. It is difficult for rage and respectability to co-exist (Wood, 2019: 612) and for this very reason black women may be able to use rage more effectively as visceral and transgressive. Miller (2016: 270, 273) likens #EndRapeCulture, featuring women's naked bodies and visceral anger and the radical politics of young women, to an 'ugly scream'. As she puts it, it was the ugly feminist turning up topless at the barricades to lament what happens to women's bodies and the social fabric of society. It was with militant irreverence and radical aggression that these women smashed through the barricades (Miller, 2016). It was a force of rage unleashed by urban black women, reminding of long histories of black women's rage expressed by, for example, Winnie Mandela in South Africa.

In postcolonial societies, black women's bodies are exposed to the colonial gaze and stereotypes based on colonial views of African women's sexuality (African women as hyper sexual, and slave women as the property of men who could rape them at any time). This led to a situation where they are simultaneously invisible (as people) and hypervisible (through their sexuality) (Toone et al., 2017: 208). It was violence/rape that kept colonial processes in place because the colonial forces subdued native men through spectacular violence and native women through rape (Gqola, 2015: 37–8). Anger for the black female students involved in #EndRapeCulture stemmed from the colonial continuities with current sexual violence against their bodies.

What was characteristic of #EndRapeCulture marches was the anger of women (and members of LGBTIQ/trans communities) brandishing sjamboks[6] (whips) to reinforce the promise that they will deal with perpetrators themselves. It also offered the politics of the spectacle of naked bodies in protest. Their protest challenged sexual objectification but also drew on disrobing as an African practice. In African culture, if women disrobe they show political agency that can involve both desperation and empowerment. It involves a dynamic cycle of power and vulnerability for the women and their targets (Naminata 2020: 6, 3). Invoking the 'genital curse' or 'genital shaming' often happens when women see no other option for action.[7] This defiant disrobing is almost always performed in a solemn mood, not joyful or festive (if compared, for example, to slutwalks, where women reclaim agency over their sexuality, which can be quite jovial)[8] (see Gouws, 2018). As Naminata (2020: 15) indicates, even if aggressive self-exposure, or what she calls 'naked agency', is a universal gesture, it is highly contextual, showing us what it means to be an acting agent in challenging material/political conditions. According to her (Naminata 2020: 146), disrobing in the case of #EndRapeCulture was an act designed to shame university officials, but also an act of exposing their bodies to protect their bodies – inviting violence to the self in order to protect the self from possible death, reinscribing vulnerability on the body.

The rage in both movements contrasts starkly with the shame and silence that normally accompanies sexual harassment for women. #MeToo expressed the pent-up anger of women who experienced harassment and/or witnessed harassment of other women and knew the price paid for silence. Women were not prepared to tolerate it any longer and used social media as an informal way of getting justice. In the case of #EndRapeCulture the same aspects apply, but here the colonial dimension of black women's pain is also important. Sexual harassment and sexual violence against black women's bodies are often trivialised in the South African context with its history of colonialism and apartheid. Gqola (2015) shows how the shame and debasement of slave women stigmatised black women's sexuality in colonial times but also under apartheid. It took more courage and determination to participate in protests that involved disrobing than merely saying 'me too' on social media. A number of female students in South Africa paid the price for their participation through being arrested by the police and/or facing disciplinary hearings at their universities (*News24*, 2017).

Transnational influences

Students involved in #EndRapeCulture were influenced by ideas that circulated through cyberspace from outside the borders of South Africa, such as feminist blogger Flavia Dzodan's slogan 'our feminism will be intersectional or it will be bullshit' from her blog Tigerbeatdown, Beyonce's album *Lemonade*, and Sara Ahmed's (2017: 113) notion of the 'feminist killjoy'. Ideas originating outside South Africa, especially in the US, had a strong appeal for students. At the same time, however, students built larger digital transnational networks and created counter-publics in South Africa that enabled them to voice resistant and critical speech that is often outside the public sphere (see Powell, 2015: 580). The use of social media by young women to resist rape culture 'produces, organises and deploys' a capacity to respond to cultures of harassment and sexual violence, or what Rentschler (2014: 69) calls networks of response-ability (the ability to respond) to hold perpetrators of sexual violence accountable. Communication technologies provide mechanisms to activists and some form of informal justice to victim/survivors of rape in the face of the failure of formal justice systems (Powell, 2015: 577).

Beyonce's album *Lemonade* was released during the time of the #EndRapeCulture campaign in 2016. Black female students who were involved in the campaign were influenced by this album and drew on 'misogynoir' – the hate of black women – as articulated through Beyonce's lyrics and echoed by the Black Lives Matter campaign. Beyonce was seen as introducing a different way for black women of being in the world – a positive aesthetic of tenacity and cultural originality as opposed to the stereotypical idea of black women as angry and uncouth (Gaines, 2017: 97). But, importantly, Beyonce does this with slavery as the origin of black women's oppression. Black female students in South Africa, in their quest for decolonisation through invoking black pain, could relate readily to *Lemonade*.

In the already tense and racially charged atmosphere of the Fallist movements, as they became known, the idea of the feminist killjoy was used as a narrative throughout the #EndRapeCulture campaign. The students used Ahmed's concept in relation to the lack of transformation (as regards race and gender) at South African universities. Ahmed makes the case from her own experiences, of being involved in institutional transformation, that universities do not necessarily want to transform and that anyone trying to engage transformation will be viewed as a killjoy. She argues that institutions are built on promises of happiness that cover up the violence contained in them (Ahmed, 2017: 257). What killjoys expose are the central feature of exclusion that determines these institutions which were created for only the privileged few. They also implicate the happiness myth of neoliberalism and global capitalism in institutions. In doing this, killjoys become viewed as the very cause of unhappiness. At many universities killjoys questioned the effectiveness and inclusivity of sexual harassment policies and grievance procedures because killjoys involved in universities are also required to expose the dishonesty of transformation strategies and narratives. Joy is killed when killjoys refuse to wilfully identify with institutions built on violence (Ahmed, 2017: 264). Intersectional African feminist students who were Fallists exposed the deeply problematic processes of racial transformation in tertiary institutions as well as their failure to deal with sexual harassment and violence.

The killjoy was employed to call out university cultures for their double standards around rape – for example expelling students for plagiarism but being unwilling to expel alleged rapists – and for their institutional racism. She was also used to call out black male students for their sexism and misogyny. As Salzano (2020: 49) argues, a killjoy is conscious of the limitations of superficial happiness that masks inequality. She is also aware of how it stifles the potential to create feminist politics. The killjoy is a historically important subject position for black women, creating knowledge designed to oppose racism, calling out the double standards of white feminists, even when it frames them (black women) as angry (Salzano, 2020: 50–1). It also makes visible the invisibility of whiteness as a dimension of intersectionality, when white feminists are complicit in silence regarding racist institutional cultures.

In 2016, I organised a public seminar for Stellenbosch University's diversity week with Panashe Chigumadzi, a novelist and then Master's student at the University of the Witwatersrand, as speaker. She is well known in South Africa for her radical views as an intersectional African feminist. During her presentation she used the notion of the feminist killjoy to refer to women who have exposed the rape cultures at their universities. The first person to pose a question after the talk was a black male student who accused black women participating in the topless marches of being 'un-African' and lacking self-respect. One after another six female African students got up and called him out for his lack of knowledge of African culture's naked curse and his sexism and for turning issues of power into an issue of respectability and would not continue with the event until he had left the venue. This incident confirmed the female students' fearlessness as well as their killjoy stance.

Black women operating as killjoys in a call-out culture around racism and sexism, however, found it difficult to foster racial solidarity with white female students around issues of institutional cultures, sexual harassment and violence that affect all women on campuses in South Africa. Many white students (women and men) could not relate to notions of decolonising universities (the power of privilege) and many white female students bought into the idea of 'respectability' femininity, not wanting to disrobe for the marches. It was black feminist killjoys who became the driving forces of the protest marches.

Epistemic justice

#MeToo and #EndRapeCulture were also about epistemic truth and epistemic justice. The significance of #MeToo rested on testimonies of survivors of sexual harassment and rape being believed in the online spaces they created. It gave credence to women's agency in producing knowledge about sexual violence. When women's testimonies are not believed, it is a form of epistemic injustice against those whose voices are not recognised. Believing testimonies is important because 'rhetorical spaces in which testimony is expressed are shaped by social scripts, attitudes, stereotypes and discourses which are culturally and historically situated' (Jackson, 2018: 5). Believing helps to undermine the stereotype of who fits the image of a 'real rape victim' and who does not. Those who are not believed are exposed to 'epistemic violence' and silencing because they are denied sympathy, emotional support and even access to due process (Jackson, 2018: 7). These victims, therefore, suffer in silence. #MeToo created spaces for mutual recognition of women's suffering at the hands of perpetrators of sexual violence and created the groundwork for a political movement by giving women epistemic agency (Jackson, 2018: 13).

In South Africa, the students' demands for epistemic justice were two-fold. They wanted the curriculum to be decolonised and to resist the dominant canons of hegemonic scholarship that do not reflect their own experience of being black in the world. Black female students wanted to be heard and believed on issues of sexual violence. Lewis and Hendricks (2017) draw parallels with the epistemic work that an older generation of feminists in South Africa did after the democratic transition. Then feminist scholars started epistemic projects in universities based on standpoint epistemology as articulated by feminist scholars such as Sandra Harding, Patricia Hill Collins and Chandra Mohanty, for example (Lewis and Hendricks, 2017: 5). They grounded their work in intersectionality and, in a sense, preceded the efforts of the Fallists. There were also similarities with highlighting the body in pain and how racist legacies are projected onto black bodies. The Fallists protests became a method of knowledge production.

Lukose (2018: 38) views generational differences as part of younger generations' 'fresh contact' with knowledge generated by older generations and giving it their own interpretation. What was remarkable is that these students caused greater attention to be given to their concerns and actions by university managements regarding rape culture and free education in a very short period of time, exactly because they were uncompromising. Many universities appointed Rape Culture Task Teams that investigated rape cultures and made recommendations for transformation (see chapter 10 in this volume). The task teams produced reports, fitting the context of each campus. In the implementation of the recommendations, however, some of these lost the radical edge of students' demands in the efforts of universities to find a balance between testimonial justice and the requirements of due process. Where due process dominates, victims/survivors run the risk of not being believed.

Conclusion

Both #MeToo and #EndRapeCulture (as all the Fallist campaigns) caused a crisis of the present, where what has gone before could not be continued afterwards as 'business as usual'. Men's impunity with regard to sexual violence, the complicity of institutional cultures in sexism and racism as well as the androcentricity of due process became part of the call-out culture of these campaigns.

In the case of #FeesMustFall and #EndRapeCulture, the decolonial moment was made intelligible through attempts to free the past of the hegemonic presentation of Eurocentric history and modern/colonial control over representation (Vásques, 2012: 7). What the students showed was the relationality of time and how a colonial and apartheid past actively constitutes the present. It enabled the students to create narratives that changed who is recognisable as someone who can make claims, who can create knowledge and who is entitled to epistemic justice for racism and sexual violence.

Both campaigns changed the landscape of how we think about sexual harassment, victim-blaming and consent. They introduced women's rage as legitimate in challenging due process that so often fails them when they are not believed. The campaigns also exposed the conspiracy of silence among men who know about abuse but keep silent. In centring intersectionality, #EndRapeCulture exposed the racial/heterosexual/androcentric prejudices of processes at tertiary institutions that are supposed to deal with sexual violence.

Notes

1 There have been many campaigns against sexual violence in South Africa, such as the One in Nine Campaign, or action orchestrated by women's organisations such as People Against Women Abuse (POWA). More recently in 2019 #TotalShutDown. #EndRapeCulture focused on universities specifically.

2 The Aziz Ansari case in the US was disputed as an incident of 'bad sex' (NPR, 2018).

3 In the South African context, there is a campaign called #MenAreTrash on Twitter.

4 #MeToo was not taken up to the same extent in Africa as in other parts of the world because of a strong patriarchal culture that stigmatises women who speak out and makes them more vulnerable. Women also do not want their families to know because families also blame victims (Gouws, 2019).

5 In South Africa, the apartheid era classified the population into four groups: white, coloured (mixed race), Indian and black (African). When I use 'black', it includes all three non-white groups. 'African' refers to African students specifically.

6 The sjambok or whip was used to control slaves and, later, by some farmers to control farm workers or to punish them for transgressions (a practice that has not abated). Under apartheid it was also used by the police. Its original use was for driving cattle.

7 See, for example, the case of Stella Nyanzi, professor and feminist activist at Makerere University in Uganda who was found guilty of cyber harassment of Ugandan President Yoweri Museveni through a poem she put on Facebook and sentenced to eighteen months imprisonment. She accused the magistrate of not listening to her pleas while she bared her breasts (see Asiimwe, 2019).

8 Slutwalks originated in Canada after a police officer told a group of female students that if they dressed properly they would not get raped. This caused such outrage that women organised 'slut walks' during which they dressed improperly to reclaim their bodies/sexuality, by arguing that it is not women's behaviour that should change but men's (women should be able to wear whatever they like without getting raped). Slutwalks became a global phenomenon.

References

Ahmed, S. (2017). *Living a Feminist Life*. Durham, NC: Duke University Press.

Asiimwe, D. (2019). 'Ugandan Don Gets 18 Months in Prison, Strips Naked in Court'. www.theeastafrican.co.ke/tea/news/east-africa/ugandan-don-gets-18-months-in-prison-strips-naked-in-court-1424128. Accessed 30 May 2021.

Barbaro, M., A. L. Young, N. Pathak, C. Toeniskoetter, L. Anderson and L. Tobin. (2018). 'Revisiting what Happened to Anita Hill', *New York Times*, 26 September, Podcast, 30:22 min. www.nytimes.com/2018/09/26/podcasts/the-daily/kavanaugh-anita-hill-clarence-thomas-hearings.html. Accessed 16 July 2021.

Bilge, S. (2010). 'Recent Feminist Outlooks on Intersectionality', *Diogenes* 57:1, 58–72.

Brajanac, A. (2019). 'Addressing Intersectionality in the #MeToo Movement', Master's thesis, University of Göteborg.

Burgess, S.K. (2018). 'Between the Desire for Law and the Law of Desire: #MeToo and the Cost of Telling the Truth Today', *Philosophy and Rhetoric* 51:4, 342–67.

Chandra, G. and I. Erlingsdottir. (2021). *The Routledge Handbook of the Politics of the #MeToo Movement*. London: Routledge.

Cooper, C. (2018). 'Speaking the Unspeakable? Nicola Lacey's Unspeakable Subjects and Consent in the Age of #MeToo', *feminists@law* 8:2, 1–19. https://doi.org/10.22024/UniKent/03/fal.669.

Gaines, Z. (2017). 'A Black Girl's Song: Misogynoir, Love, and Beyoncé's Lemonade', *Taboo: Journal of Culture and Education* 16:2, 97–114.

Gentile, K. (2018). 'Give a Women an Inch, She'll Take a Penis', *Studies in Gender and Sexuality* 19:4, 241–5.

Gill, R. and S. Orgad. (2018). 'The Shifting Terrain of Sex and Power: From the "Sexualization of Culture" to #MeToo', *Sexualities* 21:8, 1313–24.

Gouws, A. (2017). 'Feminist Intersectionality and the Matrix of Domination in South Africa', *Agenda* 31:1, 19–27.

Gouws, A. (2018). '#EndRapeCulture Campaign in South Africa: Resisting Sexual Violence through Protest and the Politics of Experience', *Politikon* 54:1, 3–15.

Gouws, A. (2019). '#MeToo Isn't Big in Africa: But Women have Launched their Own Versions'. *The Conversation*, 7 March. https://theconversati on.com/metoo-isnt-big-in-africa-but-women-have-launched-their-own-versions-112328. Accessed 30 November 2019.

Gqola, P.D. (2015). *Rape: A South African Nightmare*. Johannesburg: MFBooks Joburg.

Gutting, G. and S. Ruden. (2018). 'Taking the Measure of #MeToo: Two Views', *Commonweal* 145:5, 14–18.

Harris, A. (2018). 'Witch-Hunt', *Studies in Gender and Sexuality* 19:4, 254–5.

Jackson, D. (2018). '"#MeToo": Epistemic Injustice and the Struggle for Recognition', *Feminist Philosophy Quarterly* 4:4, 1–19.

Lewis, D. and C. Hendricks. (2017). 'Epistemic Ruptures in South African Standpoint Knowledge-Making: Academic Feminism and the #FeesMustFall Movement', *Gender Questions* 4:1. https://doi. org/10.25159/2412-8457/2920.

Lukose, R. (2018). 'Decolonizing Feminism in the #MeToo Era', *Cambridge Journal of Anthropology* 36:2, 34–52.

MacKinnon, C. (1983). 'Feminism, Marxism, Method and the State: Toward Feminist Jurisprudence', *Signs* 8:4, 635–58.

MacKinnon, C. (1989). *Towards a Feminist Theory of the State*. Cambridge, MA: Harvard University Press.

May, V.M. (2015). *Pursuing Intersectionality, Unsettling Dominant Imaginaries*. New York: Routledge.

Mendes, K., J. Ringrose and J. Keller. (2018). '#MeToo and the Promise and Pitfalls of Challenging Rape Culture through Digital Feminist Activism', *European Journal of Women's Studies* 25:2, 236–46.

Miller, D. (2016). 'Excavating the Vernacular: "Ugly Feminists", Generational Blues and Matriarchal Leadership', in *Fees Must Fall*, edited by S. Booysen, 270–91. Johannesburg: Wits University Press.

Mugo, K. (2015). 'When Comrades Rape Comrades', *Mail & Guardian*, 29 November. https://mg.co.za/article/201511-29-when-comrades-rape-comrades/. Accessed 15 May 2020.

Naminata, D. (2020). *Naked Agency: Genital Cursing and Biopolitics in Africa*. Durham, NC: Duke University Press.

News24. (2017). '#RhodesWar: Outcry after University Expels 2 Anti-rape Activists for Life', *News24*, 12 December. www.news24.com/news24/ SouthAfrica/News/rhodeswar-outcry-after-university-expels-2-anti-rape-activists-for-life-20171212. Accessed 24 May 2020.

NPR. (2018). 'The Fine Line Between A Bad Date and Sexual Assault: 2 Views on Aziz Ansari', NPR, 16 January. www.npr.org/2018/01/16/578422491/ the-fine-line-between-a-bad-date-and-sexual-assault-two-views-on-aziz-ansari. Accessed 23 May 2020.

Onwuachi-Willig, A. (2018). 'What about #UsToo? The Invisibility of Race in the #MeToo Movement', *Yale Law Journal Forum* 128, 105–20. www. yalelawjournal.org/forum/what-about-ustoo. Accessed 16 July 2021.

Orgad, S. and R. Gill. (2019). 'Safety Valves for Mediated Female Rage in the #MeToo Era', *Feminist Media Studies* 19:4, 596–603.

Pellegrini, A. (2018). 'MeToo: Before and After', *Studies in Gender and Sexuality* 19:4, 262–3.

Pengelly, Martin. (2019). 'Christine Blasey Ford Makes Rare Public Remarks, a Year after Kavanaugh Ordeal', *Guardian*, 18 November.

PettyJohn, M.E., F. K. Muzzey, M. K. Maas and H. L. McCauley. (2019). '#HowWillIEngage: Involving Men and Boys in the #MeToo Movement', *Psychology of Men and Masculinities* 20:4, 612–22. https:// doi.org/10.1037/men0000186.

Phipps, A. (2020). *Me, Not You: The Trouble with Mainstream Feminism*. Manchester: Manchester University Press.

Pipyrou, S. (2018). '#MeToo is Little More than Mob Rule//vs//#MeToo is a Legitimate Form of Social Justice', *HAU: Journal of Ethnographic Theory* 8:3, 415–19.

Powell, A. (2015). 'Seeking Rape Justice: Formal and Informal Responses to Sexual Violence through Technosocial Counter-Publics', *Theoretical Criminology* 19:4, 571–88.

Rentschler, C.A. (2014). 'Rape Culture and the Feminist Politics of Social Media', *Girlhood Studies* 7:1, 65–82.

Salter, M. (2019). 'Online Justice in the Circuit of Capital: #MeToo, Marketization and the Deformation of Sexual Ethics', in *#MeToo and the Politics of Social* Change, edited by B. Fileborn and R. Loney-Howes, 317–34. Cham: Palgrave Macmillan.

Salzano, M. (2020). 'Lemons or *Lemonade?* Beyoncé, Killjoy Style, and Neoliberalism', *Women's Studies in Communication* 43:1, 45–66.

Seddon, D. (2016). '"We will not be Silenced": Rape Culture, #RUReferencelist and the University Currently Known as Rhodes', *Daily Maverick*, 1 June. www.dailymaverick.co.za/opinionista/2016-

06-01-we-will-not-be-silenced-rape-culture-rureferencelist-and-the-university-currently-known-as-rhodes/. Accessed 15 May 2020.

Toone, A., A. N. Edgar and K. Ford. (2017). '"She Made Angry Black Woman Something that People Would Want to Be": *Lemonade* and Black Women as Audiences and Subjects', *Participations* 14:2, 203–25.

Vásques, R. (2012). 'Towards a Decolonial Critique of Modernity: *Buen Vivir*, Relationality and the Task of Listening', in *Capital, Poverty, Development,* edited by R. Fornet-Betancourt, 241–52. Aachen: Wissenschaftsverlag Mainz.

Wood, H. (2019). 'Fuck the Patriarchy: Towards an Intersectional Politics of Irreverent Rage', *Feminist Media Studies* 19:4, 609–15.

Zarkov, D. and K. Davis. (2018). 'Ambiguities and Dilemmas around #MeToo: #ForHowLong and #Where To?' *European Journal of Women's Studies* 25:1, 3–9.

9

From harassment to transgression: understanding changes in the legal landscape of sexual harassment in India[1]

Rukmini Sen

Introduction: pre- and post-#MeToo in feminist politics?

While there have been multiple ways in which feminist politics is experienced and transacted in the Indian context, #MeToo has undoubtedly transformed both the language and the practice of feminism. This chapter argues that the #MeToo moment in India became an important turning point for how the Indian women's movement engaged with legal processes. Rupan Deol Bajaj was the first woman in Indian legal history to secure a conviction against her perpetrator, by drawing on a law against the 'outraging of modesty' (S 354 Indian Penal Code (IPC)). The ruling was confirmed by the Supreme Court in 1995, seven years after she was sexually violated. India had to wait until 1997 for the inclusion of legal terminology around 'sexual harassment at the workplace', again through a Supreme Court judgement. More than two decades later, #MeToo poses new questions of sexual harassment.

It is a moment that foregrounded consent and the everydayness of gendered hierarchies in the workplace, which made sense of 'no', that developed listening practices, and that created caring spaces, outside of the law, in feminist politics. It is a moment which has brought to the table a renewed discussion of sexual harassment, somewhat differently from how it was conducted in the 1990s, and of the ambivalences of feminist negotiations with the law. The moment made use of social media platforms (sometimes critiqued as 'misuse') in multiple ways, gave new meanings to narratives and testimonials and, finally, led to a public discussion of the gendered workplace and the invisible (and overt) misogyny that prevails there. There have been multiple modes of articulating some of these injuries in social media spaces like Facebook, Twitter and Instagram, such as: naming the perpetrator but concealing the identity of the woman imposed on; naming both oneself and the perpetrator; or posting visual images on Instagram without naming anyone. Ranging from anonymity to naming and shaming, from reluctance to laying a complaint, to defamation suits – we saw it all between 2017 and 2020.

This chapter focuses on the specific site of Indian higher education institutions in the context of #MeToo. Based on an autoethnographic account of being a member of university committees framing anti-sexual harassment policies and dealing with complaints, I examine the role of care and conversation in feminist debates and their engagements with the law. I begin with a short description of the legal trajectory of sexual harassment in India.

From the *Vishaka* judgement to the Criminal Law Amendment Act of 2013

In 1992, a social worker of the Women's Development Programme, Bhanwari Devi, was gang-raped in Rajasthan while at work. Part of her job was to stop child marriages in her state. When she filed a rape case, she faced strong resistance from the attending police. When her case eventually went to trial, the High Court pronounced that rape could not be possible, as Bhanwari was a lower-caste woman and the perpetrators were upper-caste men. On the back of this atrocity, women's organisations filed a Public Interest Litigation against sexual harassment that women face in the workplace. This case, *Vishaka & Ors* v. *State of Rajasthan & Ors*, led to a landmark Supreme Court judgement on 13 August 1997 in support of the plaintiffs. In their opening statement, judges Sujata Manohar and B. N. Kirpal wrote:

> With the increasing awareness and emphasis on gender justice, there is increase in the effort to guard such violations; and the resentment towards incidents of sexual harassment is also increasing. The present petition has been brought as a class action by certain social activists and NGOs with the aim of focussing attention towards this

societal aberration, and assisting in finding suitable methods for realisation of the true concept of 'gender equality'; and to prevent sexual
harassment of working women in all work places through judicial
process, to fill the vacuum in existing legislation.

… The incident reveals the hazards to which a working woman
may be exposed and the depravity to which sexual harassment can
degenerate; and the urgency for safeguards by an alternative mechanism in the absence of legislative measures.

The judges called the suit a class action due to the fact that it had
been filed by a number of individuals and groups.[2] As they indicate
in their opening statement, they viewed their judgement as filling
a vacuum in the legislation regarding gender equality (a position
quite different from the #MeToo moment two decades later, which
indicted the limits of legal procedures).

Drawing on the UN Convention on the Elimination of All Forms
of Discrimination Against Women, the *Vishaka* judgement stated
that sexual harassment in the workplace can be humiliating to the
affected woman and may constitute a health and safety problem.
It added that it was discriminatory if the woman had reasonable
grounds to believe that her objection would disadvantage her in connection with her employment, including recruiting or promotion, or
when it created a hostile working environment. The judgement
called for the implementation of work, leisure, health and hygiene
conditions in the workplace for women; the workplace should not
be experienced as a hostile environment and there should be no
reasonable ground for women to believe that they are disadvantaged in their employment. It also called for the implementation of
effective complaints procedures and remedies, including compensation. In a section titled 'Workers' Initiative', the judges posited that
employees should be allowed to raise issues of sexual harassment at
workers' meetings and in other appropriate forums and that these
should be affirmatively discussed at employer-employee meetings.
They viewed women as a labouring community and argued for the
need to make the site of work gender-just and non-hostile.

The position that the judges in the *Vishaka* case took was very
different from the archaic 'outraging of modesty' provision contained in the IPC.[3] This is the provision that Bajaj had used in 1988
when she, an officer of the Indian Administrative Service, accused

the serving director general of the police of public misconduct. While the Chandigarh High Court, which first heard her case, found the accused not guilty, the Supreme Court overturned this judgement in 1995 and convicted him for committing a criminal offence under S 354 and S 509[4] of the IPC. In an interview, Bajaj said: 'Today the women speaking out have safety in numbers. When I called out the behaviour of Mr Gill [her assailant], I stood all alone, threatened with death [and] slander, given punishment postings and [subjected to] a blighted career' (Dogra, 2018). Despite this, Bajaj's case raised public awareness on the impunity powerful men enjoyed with regard to sexual harassment (Jaisingh, 2018).

Despite its path-breaking appraisal of women's situation in the workplace, the *Vishaka* judgement only had a limited effect: because it was not enshrined in law, employers were under no obligation to institute the suggested measures to prevent and redress sexual harassment. The judgement did, however, set in motion moves for new legislation. The Ministry of Women and Child Development drafted a bill that was based on *Vishaka*, circulated in 2007 with a request for public feedback and placed before parliament in 2010 as the Protection of Women against Sexual Harassment at Workplace Bill. The Bill took on the definition of sexual harassment[5] from the *Vishaka* judgement (which has since led to the implementation of anti-sexual harassment committees in higher education institutions in India, the focus of the next section).

The Bill was enacted in 2013 in the wake of the violent gang rape and murder of Jyoti Singh in Delhi in 2012. With the national outrage and protest about the rape, the government appointed the Justice Verma Commission to investigate reform of the country's anti-rape law. It submitted its Report on Amendments to Criminal Law in January 2013.[6] The Bill was enacted as the Sexual Harassment of Women at Workplace (Prevention, Prohibition and Redressal) Act, April 2013, making it mandatory for companies to create Internal Complaints Committees (ICCs). At the same time, the Justice Verma Report led to the amendment of the IPC's S 354 on 'Sexual Harassment and Punishment for Sexual Harassment', which came into force in April 2013. With these two laws, sexual harassment came into the legal landscape both in civil and in criminal law. The Preamble to the 2013 Act suggests that women have the right to a safe environment free from sexual harassment. The most important evidence that is necessary to prove or disprove sexual harassment is that the *act/action was felt/experienced as unwelcome* by the woman; and the ICC that 'enquires' into complaints of sexual harassment in a workplace has quasi-court authority. Although the Act takes the investigation and ruling out of the realm of the employer-employee relationship, sexual harassment can be treated as misconduct in accordance with the service rules.

In the progression from the IPC as it was in 1988, when Bajaj brought her case, to the two forms of legal provisions enacted in 2013, passing through the *Vishaka* judgement and the Judge Verma Report in between, we therefore see a shift from *outraging modesty* to *workplace harassment* to the *sexual intent* of the act becoming significant. The legal journey of gendered experience traverses from criminal law to equality/constitutional law and settles again in criminal law. With respect to the #MeToo moment, these developments raise three questions: a) What are the ways in which the law is creating a space for a specific gendered experience in the workplace? b) Is the law enabling the creation of a fair and accommodative complaints committee, which will be empathetic of the ways in which gendered experiences are narrated? c) How might these legal transformations impact on ways justice will be imparted through committees in workplaces, like colleges and universities? It is with these connections and questions that I now turn to my autoethnographic reflections on the gaps between politics and policies.

Committees, commitment and consciousness-raising

In this section, I look at the apparent dilemmas between institutional committees and consciousness raising objectives of Indian feminists with respect to sexual harassment. The politics around sexual harassment is connected to, and yet can be different from, the commitment of ensuring justice through a quasi-legal process. I try to reflect upon both. My involvement has been twofold. First, I was a member of a committee set up by a public university in Delhi to prepare the university's anti-sexual harassment policy. Second, I was an external academic expert on the anti-sexual harassment committee of another university in Delhi that heard testimonies of complainants and respondents and had to decide on the 'validity' and intensity of the complaint.[7] The main basis of my reflection is how 'messy' (O'Brien, 2009: 5) this committee-based work is, and challenging for a feminist sociologist to grapple with this complexity, contradiction and conflict. I approach this feminist messiness by examining certain conceptual and functional dilemmas.

On the one hand, stands the *power* that one potentially holds, as an expert (of doing work on gender-related matters), as a member of an enquiry committee, as someone empowered to 'interrogate' the complainant and the respondent, as someone authorised to reach a 'judgement'. On the other hand, is the fact that these anti-sexual harassment committees (since 2013 generally called Internal Complaint Committees (ICC), previously carrying university specific names) can only make recommendations to the university authorities, not binding rulings. It is important to keep in mind this paradox that the significant power held in the micro-setting is quite obtuse in the macro picture of the institution. A persistent anxiety held by university administrators in relation to anti-sexual harassment committees is that these should not over-power or challenge existing statutes or the sanctity of institutional structures – thus significantly limiting the functioning of these committees.

This raises a number of questions. First, is there any reason to assume that all members of these committees are feminists? And does feminist expertise always result in a fair assessment of the situation? Secondly, how should one deal with the contradiction between the need for *confidentiality* in the quasi-legal investigative process and the practicality, or sometimes even the necessity, for *public name calling* to challenge and break inherently discriminatory gender relations? It is absolutely vital to think about support structures for women who decide to write a complaint or to use social media to narrate their experiences, sometimes with or without naming their perpetrators. Confidentiality may not always work well (for a gender non-conforming, dalit or disabled woman student, for instance) in a non-supportive environment. I have experienced situations where the woman student, though able to share gendered experiences privately, does not feel confident enough to write a public complaint, worrying about the manifold ways in which the process would affect her/them. Thirdly, how does one navigate the path between the legal need for *evidence* and the psycho-social skill of *intuition* in a complaints committee? As a feminist pedagogue, I found this the most difficult part of being an expert in an enquiry committee. While one can empathetically understand the testimony and intuitively connect with the intensity of pain the complainant experiences, the committee's quasi-legal status makes it mandatory that one seeks more corroboration – either through written documents or other witnesses. While email exchanges, WhatsApp messages, or private messages on Facebook or similar social media may act as strong raw evidence, the question arises whether one also needs to take into account the alleged accused's patterns of behaviour. A complaints committee cannot act as a court room, which means that there has to be more space for ambiguity than in the latter. The quasi-legal sphere does not, however, provide great scope for messiness. How, then, does one draw conclusions based on the 'epistemology of the wound' (O'Brien, 2009: 7)? As an expert, I have been troubled by the complainant's expressions of woundedness and the inability of the process to provide any material confirmation for it. Fourthly, can one write a *conclusive* report at the end of an enquiry process? Is there space in it to discuss the complexity of consent? Can it suggest that the complainant experienced an event as a gender-based or sexual violation, even if it cannot provide evidence for sexual harassment in the specific ways in which the law defines sexual harassment? The necessity of writing an empathetic report is as important as the feminist ways in which the enquiry should be conducted.

Fifthly, are members of the complaints committee aware of and trained in the feminist debates that led to the very establishment of such committees within higher education institutions? Even if they are, it is important to reflect on the contradictions between feminist principles of *knowing* and (impartial) due processes of law. There are real dilemmas between propagating feminist principles of justice through politics and pedagogy and wanting to become members of committees such as these, within higher education institutions. Keeping confidentiality and knowing and working together with potential perpetrators, who may be faculty/staff colleagues, can lead to significant mental stress, in contexts that often provide no institutional spaces to have conversations about these kinds of fatigue and inner conflicts. Sixthly, how do complaints committees ensure that they *listen empathetically* to all, in a specific case? One has to be aware of what is one listening to – what is said but also unsaid, and perhaps expressed through the body rather than speech – because the latter cannot be captured in legal terms. How do questioning and listening co-exist and how is a synthesis arrived at between the need to reach the (messy) truth and the willingness to listen? It is important to never forget that the art of communication plays a significant role in any process of 'deposition'. There is speaking about the experience, disputing or countering that, hearing what is said, and listening to the unsaid or the ruptures between the different versions. Committee members need to process all of these voices and silences, the interplay of social locations, and the hierarchies in the gendered experiences; they need to arrive at a consensus on the complaint; and they have to pronounce a verdict/decision, which needs to be listened to by higher officials of a university.

Seventhly, from the perspective of an *institution* of higher education, the question arises of what is more valuable: having more complaints made to the complaints committee or fewer? How does the institution judge its stature and prestige through sexual harassment complaints and their resolution? Institutions are concerned that these committees could be potential troublemakers and that there could be 'false' accusations. A feminist understanding would consider an increase in cases as a sign of a rising awareness among students of what kinds of sexual violations they will not tolerate, but neither all members of a complaints committee nor the institution may necessarily think along the same lines. Finally, to what extent can members of complaints committees appreciate the nature of *intimacies* that students in higher education institutions explore – sometimes consensually and at other times through transgressions? The question to reflect upon is not only whether the members are trained to make interpretations of the law but also whether they are connected to the multiple social realities of intimacies made and relationships ended among young people in higher education. The ways in which the student population today creates or disrupts intimacies might need to be a significant aspect of an enquiry process. Conservatism about adult intimacies or ridicule towards 'love gone wrong' can prove both detrimental and insensitive to the one who has come with a complaint.

I close this section with the suggestion that the formation of committees is not an end in itself; rather, it is the beginning of another journey – of sustaining an environment of dialogue rather than discipline, enabling rather than constraining, preventive and not punitive, transparent (with anonymity) and not secretive (with procedural delay). Committees like these are a product of years of women's movements, feminist pedagogies and practices within and outside university spaces. They are now mandatory within higher education institutions as university grants committees (UGC), mandated as per the 2016 UGC notification. But it is necessary that their official capacity does not erase the history through which they came into being. Just as a 2013 report into gender relations on campuses (the Saksham report; more below) highlighted the complexity of higher education institutions – as much a workplace as an educational space – my autoethnographic reflections point to the dilemma between commitment to a juridical process and the practice of feminism as a pedagogy in an enquiry committee (as opposed to the classroom). In the final section I propose the importance of creating conversations and caring networks, and thus moving away from a culture of complaint, beyond the #MeToo moment.

Complain, converse and care: the new challenges in feminist debates

In 2017, Raya Sarkar posted on her Facebook timeline a crowd-sourced list that identified by name men in higher education institutions around the country alleged to have committed sexual harassment (List of Sexual Harassers in Academia, also known as LoSHA). The list contained the names of numerous influential and renowned Indian intellectuals and professors. It is seen as a precursor to the #MeToo moment in India. It drew a lot of condemnation, including a statement signed by fourteen Delhi-based feminists, the Kafila Statement.[8] I wrote my first tentative response to LoSHA in a Facebook post where I suggested the need to create an ethics of teacher-student relationships within academic spaces and where

I began to interrogate whether, at this moment of rupture, the feminist 'we' was an already formed community – was it disintegrating or being re-constituted? The 2013 Saksham report might help us chart a path beyond the apparent fracture to feminist politics that India witnessed in 2017.

Saksham (which stands for 'capable' or 'empowered') was a task force set up by the main regulatory authority of higher education in India to 'review the measures for ensuring the safety of women on campuses and programmes for gender sensitization'. It submitted its report in October 2013, entitled 'Saksham: Measures for Ensuring the Safety of Women and Programmes for Gender Sensitization on Campus'.[9] The Saksham report acknowledged that 'very few colleges have committees functioning according to clear guidelines and face shortcomings in their functioning … Several institutions declared that the absence of a complaint of sexual harassment implied that they were gender equal institutions' (UGC, 2013: 2). Despite the recommendations given in the *Vishaka* judgement in 1997, the Saksham task force identified that there was still a widespread absence of functional committees in institutions of higher education. This is an unfortunate feminist political reality that needs to be taken into account to make sense of the questions raised by the #MeToo movement about the limits of law. The task force laid down broad principles and guidelines that should be followed when dealing with sexual harassment in institutions of higher education:

> *Confidentiality* (both with regard to the details of the complaint and the identity of the complainant the absence of which is the biggest impediment to coming forward), providing a context of *non-coercion* as well as interim relief, *fair enquiry* in terms of procedures and the composition of the complaints committee, including recognizing that existing rules will require updating from time to time to be in consonance with the law of the land, and an approach that is oriented towards redressal and being *educational*. (UCG, 2013: 5, emphasis in original)

While the report emphasised confidentiality, it also underlined the need for ICCs to build a sense of confidence in university employees and students that their institutions were ensuring equality and freedom and were taking into account everyone's citizenship rights in an equal manner. In this context it is valuable to consider the reflections raised by scholar and publisher, V. Geetha, in reaction to LoSHA and the fractures between feminists it marshalled around speech, sexual harassment and the cultures of citizenship at institutions of higher education:

> We need to ... think of how we enable speech about sexual harassment and violence that is not about law and justice alone, but about social relationships and the power invested in those who defined the terms of the latter, on account of their class, caste and authority as intellectuals. Would it not be more useful, therefore, to ask questions of the nature of intellectual life in universities, on mentorship, and what young people experience, when they confront dazzling scholarship combined with questionable ethics, brilliant minds that are insensitive to the lived realities of class, caste and gender, and intellectual acumen that is not always capable of self-reflection? So the question is not what naming in the university can achieve – it might or might not achieve legal redress, but it is the barest acknowledgement that those who take their authority for granted be shown up for what they are. (Geetha, 2017)

It seems that where the Saksham report pointed to what is desirable for committees to do, the LoSHA moment alerted us to the impossibilities of doing so, and V. Geetha guided us towards introspection on how hierarchies are constituted. The Saksham report made a significant, separate assertion about research scholars: 'Given the singular power that such faculty can have over the future of such students, an *ethics of supervision* that prevents the abuse of power through sexual harassment is required' (UCG, 2013: 5, emphasis in original). This is particularly important to build upon in future discussions on sexual harassment; the #MeToo movement in higher education has indeed brought to light the complexity of the supervisor-supervisee relation. Is this relationship one of respect, awe, submission, or even obedience in the garb of being intellectually (and even affectively) intimate and equal? How do we engage with gendered hierarchies of power through which these relationships are structured as we consider charismatic, trustworthy, indulgent and supportive teachers/supervisors? The report also separately considered students, teachers and staff in the natural sciences where:

the perceived gender neutrality in the teaching practices of the sciences can make it harder to recognize social problems and power relations. Research undertaken in a collaborative mode, involving significant funding can also compound dependency on supervisors which is open to the abuse of power. Working in laboratories with long hours and in relatively isolated conditions requires measures that render it safe for women to work in with a sense of security. (UGC, 2013: 6)[10]

In their study of universities in the UK and the US, Whitley and Page (2015: 40) suggest that:

the supervisor may be the only person reading the student's work, the only person meeting with them to discuss their ideas and the only person providing feedback and guidance throughout the process of writing-up. The fear of losing this academic support can be a powerful motivator for accepting abusive behaviour.

Thus, what is assumed as a consenting relationship is set in a graded reality that makes the complaint of any transgression so much more difficult. Whitley and Page indicate an important aspect of the complaint mechanism:

The complaint, instead of being seen as the identification of a problem, is seen as responsible for setting off a chain of reactions which leads to the interruption of teaching, and is therefore the cause of the problem. By treating a reported incident of sexual harassment as a singular, one-off event, perpetrated by a singular (and excisable) member of staff, the university can maintain its reputation. All it needs to do to address the problem is to censure or remove one individual. (Whitley and Page, 2015: 45)

Too much reliance on the complaint mechanism thus risks, on the one hand, reinforcing the model of the individual complaint and, on the other, ignoring the underlying structural aspects of misogyny, thus leading to a culture of silence. Chatterjee affirms that:

the way in which silence is mobilized within the university, who chooses to remain silent and about what, coupled with the precarity complaint creates for the student, illustrates that sexual harassment in the university needs to move beyond being thought of as discrete incidents and rethought as a larger, more encompassing culture of sexual power and misconduct'. (Chatterjee, 2018: 103)

Whitley and Page (2015: 38) echo this insight: 'there is an institutional form to the way sexism operates, perpetuated at the individual and organisation level through concealment within culture, policies, the hierarchies that exist within how institutions are structured and regulated, and how responsibility is allocated'. Ahmed (2019) similarly reflects on both the impossibility of complaining and the inner conundrums of a complaint culture:

I have been learning how complaint means committing yourself, your time, your energy, your being, to a course of action that often leads you away from the work you want to do even if you complain in order to do the work you want to do (as many do). A formal complaint can lead you into the shadowy corners of an institution, meeting rooms, corridors; buildings you did not have any reason to enter before become where you go; what you know. We can learn from this: how trying to address an institutional problem often means inhabiting the institution *all the more* ... So *why complain?* She complained because she '*wanted to prevent other students from having to go through such practice*'. By the reproduction of culture, we are talking about practices: we are talking about what people are routinely doing; how they are behaving; what they are saying; what they are allowed to do and to say (even when what they do and say contradicts commitments made in official policies on equality and diversity and dignity at work). (Ahmed, 2019, emphasis in original)

The concerns that Ahmed raises are echoed in my autoethnographic reflections about the absence of supportive and caring networks and the importance of listening. This ethics of listening and caring, of creating an enabling feminist support system to hold the pain attached to these gendered experiences, and of those quasi-legal enquiries, need to be acknowledged and addressed.

As a feminist, influenced by the loss and recovery of law as a subversive site, having myself gone through the experience of lodging a complaint at a former workplace and being merely offered appeasement, not even a verbal apology, in front of the one member-constituted committee, I can only underline the importance of more open conversations within institutions, which can then impact the listening practices within committees. The individual complaint cannot be taken as the sole solution to a gendered reality, as it keeps the institutional foundation in place. What are the spaces on campus where we can have conversations on the ordinariness of (sexual) transgression? I conclude by emphasising the need to craft cultures of conversations – between students, between faculty, between faculty and students, between administrative staff – that move beyond a culture of complaint. Organising film screenings, reading groups, discussions and debates on the complex questions around desire, secrecy, consent, love, promises to marry, betrayal, power wielded by academic faculty and present in our everyday social contexts may go some way in generating critical insights into these questions. This is by no means a suggestion that these conversations have not happened earlier or can easily transpire now. Networks of care will be created and identified only when these conversations are made possible. Unless spaces to talk intimacy are created, transgressions will not be expressed without fear of power. Till that happens, a complaints committee applying the legal definition of sexual harassment will not be limited to apply a social justice framework. The way forward, post-#MeToo, lies in creating democratically enabling spaces for conversations which, though difficult, may not be impossible.

Notes

1 An earlier version of this chapter was presented at the 'International Conference on Intimacy and Injury: In the Wake of #MeToo in India and South Africa', organised by the Governing Intimacies project at the University of the Witwatersrand, South Africa, in February 2019. I would like to thank the editors for their detailed comments on the first draft of this chapter. Various conversations around #MeToo with many students at Dr B. R. Ambedkar University Delhi have been extremely helpful in developing my ideas.
2 Incidentally, in the US, the first specific discussion on sexual harassment happened when eleven female mine workers filed a class action law suit in Minnesota in 1984. It took fourteen years until Eveleth Mines Company finally paid a total of US$3.5 million to the women in 1998. See Bingham and Gansler's *Class Action* (2003) and the film *North Country* (2005), both based on the events.
3 Section 354 Assault or Criminal Force to Woman with Intent to Outrage her Modesty: Whoever assaults or uses criminal force to any woman, intending to outrage or knowing it to be likely that he will

thereby outrage her modesty, shall be punished with imprisonment of either description for a term which may extend to two years, or with fine, or with both.

4 Word, gesture or act intended to insult the modesty of a woman – whoever, intending to insult the modesty of any woman, utters any word, makes any sound or gesture, or exhibits any object, intending that such word or sound shall be heard, or that such gesture or object shall be seen, by such woman, or intrudes upon the privacy of such woman, shall be punished with simple imprisonment for a term which may extend to one year, or with fine, or with both.

5 The Bill defined that the act of sexual harassment includes such unwelcome sexually determined behaviour (whether directly or by implication) as: a) physical contact and advances; b) a demand or request for sexual favours; c) sexually coloured remarks; d) showing pornography; e) any other unwelcome physical verbal or non-verbal conduct of sexual nature.

6 The main recommendations of the Verma Committee in relation to the anti-sexual harassment bill were the following:

- The inclusion of domestic workers into the purview of the Bill.
- The Bill should not require the complainant and the respondent to first attempt conciliation. This is contrary to the *Vishaka* judgement which aimed to secure a safe workplace to women.
- The employer should pay compensation to the woman who has suffered sexual harassment.
- The Bill should not require the employer to institute an internal complaints committee to which complaints must be filed as this defeats the purpose of the Bill. Instead, it should require the establishment of Employment Tribunals to receive and adjudicate complaints.

7 My involvement in these committees took place between 2012 and 2016. The first university replaced its ICC and the policy I helped develop in 2020; the second university replaced its ICC in 2017. There is a lot of debate around replacing university specific anti-sexual harassment committees with ICCs after the passing of the 2013 Act, which goes beyond the remit of this paper.

8 The signatories of the Kafila Statement felt the need to remind those who posted the LoSHA of a history they considered the latter not to know. The Kafila Statement was formulated in terms of a collective 'we': we – 'as feminists', we – 'are dismayed', we – 'too know', we – 'remain', we – 'appeal' (Menon, 2017).

9 The Saksham report is extremely comprehensive, having reached out to numerous institutions in Delhi, Kolkata, Hyderabad and Kerala, where it conducted open forums and discussions with students, faculty and staff. It also sent questionnaires to additional institutions across the country, of which 1,300 were returned and included in the analysis. A nation-wide discussion of this nature specific to questions of sexual harassment, gender sensitisation, and the presence of committees and their functioning, had not been undertaken before.

10 In this context, it may be worthwhile to remember the complete absence of ethical codes (as different from moral codes) guiding professional relationships between colleagues, research scholar and supervisors within institutions of higher education. Other than a 1989 Code of Professional Ethics, prepared by yet another UGC-created task force, there is nothing on ethical guidelines. As per this code, teachers should adhere to a responsible pattern of conduct and demeanour expected of them by the community. They are expected to respect the rights and dignity of the student in expressing their opinion and also be affectionate to the student.

References

Ahmed, S. (2019). 'Why Complain?' Feministkilljoys, 22 July. https://feministkilljoys.com/2019/07/22/why-complain/. Accessed 16 July 2021.

Bingham, C. and L. L. Gansler. (2003). *Class Action: The Landmark Case that Changed Sexual Harassment Law*. New York: Anchor Books.

Chatterjee, S. (2018). 'Speculations from the Borderlands of Knowledge and Survival in the Academy', *Annual Review of Critical Psychology* 15, 100–14. www.academia.edu/37728680/ARCP_15_Sex_and_Power_in_the_University_2018_?auto=download. Accessed 9 October 2020.

Dogra, C.S. (2018). 'A Retired IAS Officer on how the #MeToo Movement can Use her Case against K. P. S. Gill', *Wire*, 15 October. https://thewire.in/women/rupan-deol-bajaj-kps-gill-case-me-too. Accessed 8 May 2020.

Geetha, V. (2017). 'Important to Name Perpetrators, says V Geetha on Raya Sarkar's Crowd-Sourced List of Sexual Harassers'. *New Indian Express*, 27 October. www.newindianexpress.com/nation/2017/oct/27/important-to-name-perpetrators-says-v-geetha-on-raya-sarkars-crowd-sourced-list-of-sexual-harasser-1684340.html. Accessed 30 September 2020.

Jaisingh, I. (2018). 'On Eulogies and Obituaries', *Leaflet*, 24 May. http://theleaflet.in/on-eulogies-and-obituaries/. Accessed 8 May 2020.

Menon, N. (2017). 'Statement by Feminists on Facebook Campaign to "Name and Shame"', Kafila, 24 October. https://kafila.online/2017/10/24/statement-by-feminists-on-facebook-campaign-to-name-and-shame.

North Country. (2005). Film, directed by Niki Caro, 126 min. USA: Participant Productions.

O'Brien, J. (2009). 'Sociology as an Epistemology of Contradiction', *Sociological Perspectives* 52:1, 5–22.

UGC (University Grants Commission). (2013). 'Saksham: Measures for Ensuring the Safety of Women and Programmes for Gender Sensitization on Campuses'. New Delhi: UGC.

Whitley, L. and T. Page. (2015). 'Sexism at the Centre: Locating the Problem of Sexual Harassment', *New Formations* 86, 34–53. www.lwbooks.co.uk/new-formations/86/sexism-at-centre-locating-problem-of-sexual-harassment. Accessed 10 October 2020.

10

Feminism and Fallism in institutions: in conversation with Jackie Dugard

Zuziwe Khuzwayo and Ragi Bashonga

South Africa is known for having one of the highest rates of rape globally (Moyo et al., 2017). Gender-based violence (GBV)and femicide are rife, and have been largely attributed to patriarchal and sexually oppressive beliefs, which directly impact on women's freedom to exist in both private and public space (Fakunmoju et al., 2021). The 'Victims of Crime Survey Data' of 2018/19, conducted by Statistics South Africa, revealed that the fear of crime significantly impacts women's ability to meaningfully engage in various daily activities; this is true in the context of higher education as well (Stats SA, 2018).

Historically there has been some ignorance, coupled with denialism, of the reality of GBV on university campuses, both globally and in the South African context (Dugard and Finilescu, 2021). The issue of sexual violence on campus has long been an issue at institutes of higher education in South Africa. There is a record of student activism against its occurrence from as early as the 1980s (SaferSpaces, n.d.). However, since 2012 there has been a notable increase in concern over sexual harassment on campuses (Omar, 2019). In 2016, this concern intersected with numerous student protests across the country (SaferSpaces, n.d.) which have come to be known as Fallism. In our earlier work we define Fallism as 'a moment depicting young, predominantly black people's struggles against various forms of colonial, racial and gendered oppression in post-apartheid SA. The movement is notable for the centrality of social media in campaigning and the engagement of publics on these issues' (Bashonga and Khuzwayo, 2017: 37). In this chapter, we zoom in on these Fallist protests relating, in particular, to rape and sexual harassment on campus, the most prominent of which were #RUReferenceList and #RapeAtJunction. #RUReference list is a protest which occurred in response to the publication of a list of alleged perpetrators of sexual violence by students at Rhodes University in Grahamstown (currently Makhanda), in the Eastern Cape of South Africa. Feelings that the university response to this list was inadequate resulted in the publication of the list on social media, and ultimately had the effect of rallying support from other universities and society more broadly (Section 27, 2017). Not long after the online protests gained momentum, there was a rape reported at the Junction student residence at the University of the Witwatersrand (Wits), in Johannesburg, South Africa. The incident came to be known as #RapeAtJunction. Responses to this incident by university management were published on social media by students, who called them both inadequate and insensitive (Davison, 2016). These protests were pivotal in gaining resonance at other campuses that led to sister protests such as #UWCRapeAlert,[1] #Iam1in3[2] and #NMMUShutDown.[3] As these protests took place both physically and on social media, they have been central to publicising the problem of sexual violations on campus, bringing this to the attention of the media and society at large. Importantly, the conversation on institutional responses to sexual violations was brought into scrutiny as a result of severe discontent with responses from management and provision in existing policy. In our earlier article (Bashonga and Khuzwayo, 2017), we show how university policy is generally perceived as reactive rather than proactive and as protecting perpetrators rather than victims; and that staff are generally viewed as lacking sensitivity in their approaches to responding to incidents of sexual violation. We argue that the pervasive nature of sexual violations on campuses as well as the lack of confidence in the institutional response is a reflection of rape culture and patriarchy in South African society more broadly. The February 2019 Wits workshop titled *Intimacy and Injury: In the Wake of #MeToo in India and South Africa* drew on perspectives of researchers, writers, journalists, artists, activists and academics with the aim of teasing out and exploring sexual violence in the world's 'rape capitals', India and South Africa. Conversations that took place in formal sessions and in more casual interactions with the participants shed light on the journeys and struggles of fellow feminists. Despite the strides that have been made in various institutions and across different levels of society, there was, for us, something of a newfound cognisance of the labour it takes, physical and emotional, to do the work of dismantling patriarchy and dealing with issues of sexual violence in public institutions. We listened in on discussions regarding the process of developing and improving policies, working through challenges and pursuing the feminist ideals through policy and legislation; and, of course, how these processes are shifted, enhanced and sometimes even complicated by social media and 'social media activism'.

For us, the workshop presented another important opportunity not only to share the process and findings of our research on rape at South African universities but also to reflect and deeply engage with one of the central aspects that emerged in our analysis: perceptions of the failure of policy on sexual violence. Being located at Wits, engaged in these conversations, demanded from us that we consider what had, in 2014, gone into the process of developing Wits' Sexual Harassment Policies and the establishment of the Gender Equity Office (GEO), an integrated office that deals with all aspects of gender-based harm and the advancement of gender equity in the institution. This is significant as it was the first office established at a tertiary institution in the country that dealt with sexual harassment and violence cases occurring on the campus. Professor Jackie Dugard was the inaugural head of GEO and we thought it critical to get her thoughts and perspectives on it, historically and currently, and to consider how it has been influenced by the #MeToo movement, which has contributed towards the raised awareness of sexual harassment and violence against women and girls on a global scale.

After attending this workshop, we developed a set of questions that would help us interrogate the role of GEO at Wits. This was done with the intention of reflecting on our earlier paper (Bashonga and Khuzwayo, 2017), which perused a number of university policies on sexual harassment and presented perceptions on these policies and university responses to incidents of sexual or gendered violations. By holding an interview with an official GEO representative, the idea was to gain a better understanding of the process of developing sexual harassment policies at institutions and to grapple with the complexities of what is an adequate response. The interview was conducted by Zuziwe Khuzwayo, who spoke to Jackie Dugard about how feminism has influenced different aspects of her work, about the establishment of GEO and the Sexual Harassment Policy at Wits, and the successes and failures of GEO in light of #RapeAtJunction.

Reflecting on this interview, we note a few key lessons about pursuing effective sexual harassment policies in institutions of higher education; or perhaps even in institutions more broadly. Jackie demonstrates her own journey within feminism – having grown into a greater awareness of gender issues and patriarchy over the years by learning from lessons at work in various institutions. She advocates for a similar pattern of learning and revision in her approach to the work of GEO. Jackie shows the importance of reviewing and revising policy to reflect approaches that are sensitive to the needs of the complainant. This, however, does not occur in a vacuum. The conversation with Jackie demonstrates that although Wits came under fire for seemingly protecting the rights of perpetrators over those of the complainants, there is a delicate and complex balance between meeting the needs of the complainant and pursuing procedures that are legally sound. However, perceptions of ineffectiveness by students expressed on social media were instrumental in highlighting areas across the institution, not only GEO, which did not conform to the ideals of gender equity.

Zuziwe Khuzwayo (ZK): *I know that you have a background in law and human rights. How do you think this influenced your perspective in your previous position as the Head of the Wits Gender Equity Office?*

Jackie Dugard (JD): I have always considered myself to be a human rights or social justice activist. I didn't start out working on gender, I always worked on socio-economic rights. I come from a human rights-oriented family. My father was a human rights scholar and academic of human rights law. He played this role under the wicked legal system of apartheid and became one of the leading scholars within South Africa. Obviously he was white, and spoke out against the ways the law was used in apartheid, but also about the things people could do with the law even under a wicked and oppressive system such as apartheid. So I guess I come from a background in which there is a tradition of using the law to advance justice however you can, and I think that has very much influenced me. I ended up working at the Centre for Applied Legal Studies [CALS],[4] which is the organisation he founded in 1978, and during my time there I saw things around class, and so class was the main struggle for me.

ZK: How did that perspective influence your gender work?

JD: I worked for CALS for six years and then, together with [former CALS executive director] Stuart Wilson, founded SERI [Socio-Economic Rights Institute].[5] SERI was concerned exclusively with socio-economic rights but almost immediately became embroiled in civil and political rights. All the communities we served were being arrested and put into detention because of the protesting they were doing around socio-economic rights. Throughout my time in CALS and SERI it became more and more apparent to me that the people that were most affected were women. Most of our clients were women, and through exposure to their stories I became aware of the structural role of patriarchy. I hadn't worked specifically on gender and, looking back, I regret that we didn't explicitly mainstream gender into our work in the ways which I would have liked.

It was really serendipitous that around that time when I was thinking of leaving SERI – because I had been there for three years – Wits had just undergone a crisis of exposure in 2012 [around issues of sexual harassment of students by lecturers][6] and they were at the point when they needed somebody to come and create an office and machinery [to address the problem], and so I was asked to come in for six months to do that. That was the first time I worked explicitly on gender. There wasn't any office then, so I was hired to set it up. I employed the staff and my main job for three years as the director of that new office was to establish the systems, policies, procedures, protocols, etc. There was one policy that existed at that time which had just been brought into circulation by a very nascent sexual harassment advisory committee that had been set up in the midst of the crisis, just prior to me coming into the office. The policy was there from 2013. I started in February 2014 and set up the structure.

ZK: What was your biggest motivation in deciding to be part of establishing GEO?

JD: I have always enjoyed starting things. I enjoyed starting SERI and that's why I stayed there for three years, but I felt that it was about creating something and then handing it over to other people to carry on. So I thought that starting GEO was an opportunity to get into the gender space and to be more directly aware of that critical fault line. I always say to people, on reflection, I think that when I got into the space I was extremely ignorant: I thought gender was a bit of a false consciousness – I always thought class was the number one issue. I always say to people that from day one in that office, I realised how absolutely wrong I had been and what an extraordinarily prevalent fault line it is. I will always feel extremely grateful that I had the opportunity to work directly in that space, to learn. I saw it as a challenge. I was lucky that I was given that opportunity, especially given the lack of direct experience I had. The experience that I brought was that I had worked in academia, civil society and in social justice for a long time. I had set up an organisation, and I think I had a reputation as somebody who isn't afraid of authority and will do what it takes. I think that those were the qualities that made me well-suited to the job. But it was a really steep learning curve for me to experience on a daily basis how patriarchy manifests.

ZK: Can you explain the policies and procedures that existed during your tenure for addressing sexual harassment and violence on campus?

JD: There was one policy when I got into the space, which they had to quickly establish in order to create the office. There had already been an independent inquiry, which Bonita Meyersfeld had done,[7] which effectively said that there needed to be one stand-alone office that would deal with everything comprehensively, ranging from [offering] psycho-social support to being complainant-driven and a hundred per cent focused on complaints, regardless of what or where the harm occurred and who had perpetrated it. It also had to focus on what the complainant wanted. If the complainant wanted nothing done, then that should normally be the end of the story. We did retain the rights to take it further in the interest of the university community as a whole if it was an extremely serious case, but overall the approach was always to be complainant driven.

One of my main tasks in those three years was establishing procedures and other policies. We established the procedure for dealing with gender-based misconduct, which came into effect in mid-2015. We established a relationship policy between students and staff and a disclosure policy. The disclosure policy dealt with if you are a supervisor or a manager of a student or staff member, you should not be having a sexual relationship with that person. That's considered to be a conflict of interest, so part of the policy addresses this. We then realised that there is a whole other factor in a university which has to do with abuse of power; so then we brought into effect another policy saying that even if you are not supervising a student, you may not have a relationship regardless of what position you are in at the university. You may not have a relationship with an undergraduate or postgraduate student because of the asymmetrical power dynamic. So these policies took a hell of a long time to formulate as there was not much for us to go on. At the time there were a whole lot of misconduct inquiries at Ivy League universities in the USUnited States[8] and I happened to be in the US and had the opportunity to speak to people at Yale, Harvard, Columbia universities and NYU etc. and to learn from their experiences. And so we drafted these policies based on, but adapted to, our circumstances. Those policies and procedures then had to go through committees required in Wits in order to be approved.

ZK: How did your office [GEO] respond to cases of sexual harassment and violence on campus?

JD: We had a dedicated counsellor, and we would let the complainant see the counsellor as soon as possible, obviously only if the complainant wants to. The counsellor was there to provide the necessary support but also to start to probe a little bit, depending on the circumstances, where the complainant is at and what she wants to do in this space. That may not happen at the first session, it may happen thereafter, and we never put a cap on the number of sessions; it would always be what the complainant wants. At some point there would be a discussion about what she wants to do and the various options. If the complainant wanted to pursue something like a disciplinary [procedure], there would be a discussion at which point either the director or the investigative officer would be brought in to talk about how that would play out.

ZK: What were your biggest achievements as head of GEO?

JD: Creating the office, creating the procedures and the policy, and moving things forward in South Africa. I think that what GEO did and what it represents is a bold and necessary move. Wits at the time was the only South African university to have created an office of this kind and that led to some of the challenges, which of course is the disadvantage when everything you do is new, particularly in the legal sphere. When it is all about precedence and you don't have it, and you are trying to do something new, then it is very hard. You have to constantly try to get more and more and more legal opinions to support you. I think we did a lot, and the credit here goes to the independent inquiry and Bonita Meyersfield for really figuring out that this was what was necessary. I just then implemented it. But I think I have a lot of pride about what Wits did collectively. I think it was the right and brave thing to do.

ZK: Why do you say that?

JD: I think that having one office dealing with everything, making sure that if you are a complainant, if you have experienced gender-based harm – whether it happened when you were back home, whether it happened on campus, whether it was your boyfriend, regardless – you can come to us, we will then bring the cocoon around you: we will hold you, we will support you, we will talk you through. We can't take it [the experience] away, we can't take the bullet for you, but we can support the person, we can be there for them. And I think that is the number one thing that someone needs in that space. We can support them regardless of their decision, we can support them even if they sometimes want to make a formal complaint and sometimes they don't, they are having second thoughts about the ramifications: we are just there for them in a non-judgemental and completely supportive way. I think it is the right thing to do.

I think that having GEO is [having] one space where you have both the psycho-social support, the disciplinary process and advocacy. A space where everything is dealt with is the way forward as well because I think everything is able to inform each other and although, like I said, there might be some friction sometimes between counselling and litigation. I think this is a creative and necessary space in order to move things forward systemically and, most importantly, for the complainant.

ZK: What were some of the challenges that you faced in this role?

JD: I think the biggest challenge was that I had underestimated the pushback. I remember that it was Nomboniso Gasa[9] who pointed out to me that, in the institutional environment where Wits was taking this bold step with GEO, [it] didn't mean that every space in Wits was progressive. I think realising how patriarchy clamps down and protects its space was challenging. It's a dilemma that feminists face in deciding on whether you have a standalone separate gender office, or you mainstream, or do you do both and how do you do it? What I realised then, and I do still think is the right thing to have done, is to have a separate office that can be sort of ring-fenced and the rest of patriarchy carries on in all the other spaces, so that became an awareness. While I think that we had done something very progressive and innovative and the work was necessary, the rest of the space was carrying on as business as usual; so that was an ongoing challenge which I think has continued now even more than ever. I think the pushback has been more and more profound. I faced a concrete challenge with a particular case that occurred in the context of #FeesMustFall,[10] at one of the residences where a rape had occurred: this hit the media and that was my biggest challenge of how to manoeuvre, because once it hits that space [the media], things shut down and then it became politicised. We tried to protect the complainant in an overexposed space; not only that, but the perpetrator's identity was known to students and then other students came for him. It became very, very, very fraught, so that was a huge direct challenge in how to manoeuvre in that institutional environment.

ZK: *Did you find any challenges with students raising their issues and the follow-up with disciplinary cases?*

JD: It's very difficult because we wanted to create a relatively non-legal process. We were very aware about how procedure and over-legalisation, and especially a criminal justice framework, act to the disadvantage of the complainant's cause. They are always on the back foot: it's very hard to prove things and it drags things out and makes it much, much, much more difficult. So we tried to be as non-legal as we could be. But, you know, I have realised in the years since that it's not possible. I think that you can provide a complainant a supporting environment and that is absolutely essential and that you have to have an office that's safe for the complainant. But you also have to ensure that your procedures are a hundred per cent procedural: you have to cross every T and dot every I, otherwise the respondent is going to nail you on that and then you lose everything. Cases will be overturned if you've made one procedural misstep. Procedure becomes doubly important when you are trying to do something ahead of the curve.

Part of this question relates to a climate where students distrust management, a climate where students, understandably, feel that the university has done too little too late and then want to know what's happening with this case, what's happening with that case. It's extremely hard to do what you want to do, which is to tell people everything that's going on, but you can't, so it's very difficult. You feel like you're having to fight with one or two arms tied behind your back. It is a hard space but, you know, these are things we have to figure out; it's not to say that it's too hard, we give up, no! We have to figure out how we can be as transparent and communicative as much as possible; how can we keep people with us while still protecting the spaces both for the complainants, primarily from the complainant's perspective, but also so that we keep that space untainted. You can't have that tainting of the disciplinary space. So, a big lesson has been the importance of being extremely procedurally strong and trying to figure out how to protect a procedural space in which it's fair and there is justice for the respondent while still supporting the complainant.

ZK: Based on your experience as the head of GEO, what are your key recommendations for improving the functioning of these sorts of offices?

JD: I do think it's an iterative process. It is innovative stuff and, particularly when you are going ahead of the mainstream, I think you need to review, reflect; and I do think that GEO has been doing that. I think that it's an ongoing process and so I think we can always collectively learn how to do things better, sympathetically and ultimately more effectively.

ZK: Now, shifting away from your former role as the head of GEO, I know you are also part of the Wits Sexual Harassment Advisory Committee [SHAC]. Do you think this committee has been helpful in trying to address sexual harassment and violence on campus?

JD: I am a co-chair with Nompumelelo Seme.[11] SHAC is a committee that exists across the university. The idea on the creation of SHAC was to have experts on gender work together to provide advice to the university and to the Gender Office when it's necessary. Also, in terms of the procedure, we [at SHAC] have a specific role which is that in all disciplinary hearings there should be a SHAC member or a gender expert. If a SHAC member is not available, then an external gender expert must come in. So that's a very important mandatory role because hearing panels are independent from GEO; GEO sets them up, but there's obviously no way that GEO could also sit on the panels as that would mean that GEO is judge and jury. SHAC members sit on these committees in order to ensure appropriate gender input. So the committee plays more of an indirect role.

ZK: I want to talk about your experience in all these different spaces you have mentioned, and how they fall into the broader Fallism protests. In the wake of the protests, Wits came under fire because there was a rape that happened at the Junction student residence. The university was subsequently accused of not handling the situation properly. What are your thoughts on the concerns raised or presented by the students?

JD: That's the incident I was talking about earlier. I think it is very difficult for me to comment because, first, in a way I am implicated, so it is difficult for me to comment objectively. I would say that I feel that we were complainant-oriented in that case and I think that it is very difficult for people on the outside to understand precisely what's going on in cases, for good reasons, including the protection of the complainant. I think [this] was not really understood by the students – which I understand, because they didn't have all the facts. I will say that I felt upset for the complainant because I think that her experience was propelled into a political domain and I don't think it did her any good. I think the students were interested in political points against university management, which I also understand, but I think that she became collateral [damage] and in that sort of a situation I will just say that I think everybody loses.

ZK: Do you feel students were justified in using social media or protesting on campuses in order to bring about a response from the university?

JD: Oh yeah, I think that it's often extremely necessary to go to the media. In fact, I always say that it's thanks to brave women going to the media in 2012 that things moved at Wits. You can say the same about the Rhodes University crisis where students went to the media to raise the issue of sexual violence and harassment on campus and how management was doing nothing about persecuting perpetrators. These are the reasons people go to the media, to call out the injustice. It's not unique to Rhodes or Wits; it's not unique to South Africa. In the world people don't generally act against these things until there is a crisis, and often not until there's a set of crises which are reported on do people [i.e. the institutions] begin to make the necessary changes.

ZK: Do you feel like these protests were taken into consideration by SHAC and GEO in that they influenced policies and procedures on campuses?

JD: I think the exposure that occurred in 2012, as mentioned earlier, was fundamentally revolutionary and I think it had positive spin offs because of the independent inquiry we ended up having. I do think from an outside perspective, the Rhodes protests exposed some problems and failures to act and failures of systems which were similar to what Wits had experienced. I do think that the specifics around the attention of the Junction rape is of a different sort: it was a specific thing where I don't think the main attention was where it needed to be.

ZK: Do you think that these protests impacted on how you have written the policies and procedures?

JD: Oh yes! As I said, if what happened in 2012 at Wits was not reported and protested by students, then I don't think we'd be sitting here now with the gender office. The same could be said of the protests around sexual violence on campus that occurred during #FeesMustFall.

ZK: To what extent do you think the global #MeToo movement has influenced the #FeesMustFall South African student movements in raising the issue of sexual violence and harassment on campus?

JD: We always knew that with the establishment of the GEO office the amount of complaints would go up and we always thought that would be the case. We always thought that would be an indicator of our success. It's one of those confounding things where more complaints probably means you are doing a good job because people are coming forward. So it would be difficult to segregate the impact of #MeToo because I think the complaints were going up anyway as people became aware of the office and, hopefully, began to trust it. What I do think has happened is that there has been a backlash and a pushback. I think that we are in a moment where men are feeling threatened and challenged by the #MeToo movement. What we've seen at Wits is men getting into a sort of crisis mode about their identity and about how women are coming for them, because everybody is having a #MeToo moment and that's going to mean all men. Probably most men feel 'gosh is that thing that I did two years going to get me in trouble?' So there is now a heightened sense of anxiety by men about whether they are going to be 'targeted'.

ZK: *Do you think that the #MeToo movement has forced particularly South African society to engage with the issue of sexual violence and harassment more?*

JD: Definitely!! Obviously, you know, there have been some flashpoints, like the murder of Uyinene[12] recently, which has galvanised people around this issue of sexual violence and harassment, and I think there has been more consolidation and collaboration which seeks to fight for better prevention methods.

If there's one thing that it has done, it's that it has made it clear to people how pervasive gender inequality is. I think that hashtag was absolutely brilliant because it effectively communicates that it's a 'me and me and me and me and me, it's all of us.' There is probably not a woman who doesn't have a story, and I think that is the importance of the movement. I'd hope that it has begun to dawn somewhere in masculine culture, and in positions of power, how pervasive it is and that it's not just about a single incident. You could be a patriarch without having had non-consensual sex, you can be a patriarch without having pushed your wife around, this issue [gender inequality] is everywhere.

Conclusion

The establishment of GEO is significant as it is a critical juncture in Wits' history of pursuing means to adequately address issues of sexual harassment and violence on campus, by providing an institutional body for students to raise their cases and concerns. The office has made notable contributions, particularly in establishing mechanisms and setting policies for addressing sexual violence. Yet, despite these significant strides, problems still persist. Students' trust in the office to resolve sexual violence and harassment cases fairly, and the implementation of policy for the benefit of students and staff, remains an institutional challenge. This, unfortunately, mimics the reality of reporting on and addressing sexual violence in broader society. GEO continues to be an important blueprint used by universities across the country for establishing offices to address sexual violence and harassment on campuses. Institutions of higher education may benefit from more nuanced engagements with students and staff as well as civic organisations. There remains room for investment in research on the subject of appropriate institutional responses to sexual violence if we are to begin to see more effective response in these contexts.

Notes

1 #UWCRapeAlert is a Twitter hashtag started by students of the University of the Western Cape (UWC), South Africa, to raise the issue of rape on their campus.
2 #Iam1in3 is a Twitter hashtag highlighting the high levels of rape experienced by women and girls in South Africa.
3 #NMMUShutDown is a Twitter hashtag started by students at Nelson Mandela Metropolitan University (NMMU) in Port Elizabeth, South Africa (now called Nelson Mandela University), calling for the shutdown of the university because of university fees as well as the lack of proper response by management to sexual harassment and violence on campus.
4 CALS was founded as a legal resource unit affiliated to Wits.
5 SERI is an independent human-rights non-profit organisation located in Johannesburg.
6 The crisis was triggered by students going to the media to report on occurrences of Wits students being subjected to sexual harassment by lecturers (Mtshali, 2013; Tshandu, 2014).

7 Bonita Meyersfeld is Associate Professor at the School of Law
   at Wits. She was appointed to conduct an inquiry into the sexual
   harassment cases that had been reported to the media, as previously
   stated.
8 For the misconduct inquiries at the US Ivy League universities, see
   Perez-Pena (2015) and Anderson (2016).
9 Nomboniso Gasa is Adjunct Professor of Law at the University of Cape
   Town (UCT). She is a gender researcher and analyst.
10 #FeesMustFall is a student movement that falls under the broad
   umbrella of Fallism as defined in the introduction.
11 Nompumelelo Seme is a lecturer at the School of Law at Wits.
12 Uyinene Mrwetyna was a nineteen-year-old student at UCT. She was
   raped and murdered in August 2019 by a postal clerk when collecting
   a package from Clareinch Post Office.

References

Anderson, N. (2016). 'These Colleges Have the Most Reports on Rape',
   Washington Post, 7 June. www.washingtonpost.com/news/grade-point/
   wp/2016/06/07/these-colleges-have-the-most-reports-of-rape/. Accessed
   31 March 2020.
Bashonga, R. and Z. Khuzwayo. (2017). '"This Thing of the Victim has to
   Prove that the Perp Intended to Assault is Kak!" Social Media Responses
   to Sexual Violence on South African University Campuses', *Agenda*
   31:3–4, 35–49.
Davison, J. (2016). '#RapeAtJunction Activists Confront Residence
   Management', *Student News Grid,* 18 November. https://studentnews
   grid.com/2016/11/rapeatjunction-activists-confront-residence-manage
   ment/. Accessed 31 March 2020.
Dugard, J. and Finchilescu, G. (2021). 'Experiences of Gender-Based
   Violence at a South African University: Prevalence and Effect on
   Rape Myth Acceptance', *Journal of Interpersonal Violence* 36:5–6,
   NP2749–NP2772.
Fakunmoju, S.B., T.Abrefa-Gyan, N. Maphosa, and P. Gutura (2021).
   'Rape Myth Acceptance: Gender and Cross-National Comparisons
   Across the United States, South Africa, Ghana, and Nigeria', *Sexuality
   and Culture* 25:1, 18–38.
Moyo. N., E. Khonje and M. Brobbey. (2017). *Violence against Women in
   South Africa: A Country in Crisis.* Johannesburg: Centre for the Study
   of Violence and Reconciliation. www.csvr.org.za/pdf/CSVR-Violence-
   Against-Women-in-SA.pdf. Accessed 10 August 2020.

Mtshali, N. (2013). 'Wits Fires Third Sex Pest', *IOL*, 6 September. www. iol.co.za/news/south-africa/gauteng/wits-fires-third-sex-pest-1574108. Accessed 31 March 2020.

Omar, J. (2019). 'Protecting the Learning Space: The Case for the Regulation of Staff-Student Relationships at University Campuses in South Africa', *South African Journal of Higher Education* 33:2, 123–41. https://doi.org/10.20853/33-2-2794.

Perez-Pena, R. (2015). '1 in 4 Women Experience Sexual Assault on Campus', *New York Times*, 21 September. www.nytimes.com/2015/09/22/us/a-third-of-college-women-experience-unwanted-sexual-contact-study-finds.html. Accessed 31 March 2020.

SaferSpaces (n.d.). 'Gender-Based Violence at Higher Education Institutions in South Africa', Safer Spaces. www.saferspaces.org.za/understand/entry/gender-based-violence-at-higher-education-institutions-in-south-africa1. Accessed 16 July 2021.

Section 27. (2017). 'Education and Policies are Vital in Fight against Rape Culture', Section 27, 26 July. http://section27.org.za/2017/07/education-and-policies-are-vital-in-fight-against-rape-culture/. Accessed 31 August 2020.

Stats SA (Statistics South Africa). (2018). *Crime Against Women in South Africa: An In-Depth Analysis of the Victims of Crime Survey Data 2018*. Report 03-40-05. Pretoria: Statistics South Africa. www.statssa.gov.za/publications/Report-03-40-05/Report-03-40-05June2018.pdf. Accessed 23 August 2020.

Tshandu, P. (2014). 'Wa Mamatu Apologizes after Year of Denial', *Wits Vuvuzela*, 1 September. http://witsvuvuzela.com/2014/09/01/wa-mamatu-apologises-after-a-year-of-denial/. Accessed 31 March 2020.

Reflection: beyond the media storm – on sexual harassment in the news and the newsrooms

Nithila Kanagasabai

On 21 May 2021 the District and Sessions Court at Mapusa, Goa acquitted journalist Tarun Tejpal, the Editor-in-Chief of *Tehelka* magazine, who was charged, in 2013, with the rape, unlawful confinement and sexual harassment of a young female journalist working at the magazine. One of the most high-profile cases of sexual harassment in journalism, the investigation took eight years, with a 'fast track' court taking almost four years to commence trial; and despite the more-than-adequate evidence against Tejpal – including his apology emails in which he admitted to non-consensual conduct towards the survivor – he was acquitted of all charges. The survivor, on the other hand, was discredited, with her sexual history being invoked (though such a move is deemed to be unlawful according to Indian law), and accused of not doing enough to protect herself and of not looking sufficiently traumatised after the event. Coming more than nearly two years after #MeToo went viral in October 2018, a year after the news of Hollywood producer Harvey Weinstein's sexual crimes broke, this judgement typifies so much of what is wrong with legal redressal of sexual violence.

In 2018, Indian journalism was forced to publicly confront what industry insiders had known, and experienced, for decades. Numerous female journalists – mostly urban and belonging to English-language media – recounted on social media their experiences of harassment and predatory behaviour in interactions with their colleagues. While some of them went on to file legal cases, most did not. Some female journalists compiled accounts of harassment, protecting the identities of survivors who wished to remain anonymous; and coordinated legal and mental health resources for them. Questions were raised: How does one address complaints from over two decades ago – legally or otherwise? Should they even be addressed? Can one trust the naming-and-shaming lists with anonymous complainants? Why are privileged women the only ones complaining? Was this a concerted attack against 'progressive' men? Is this problem endemic to the media and entertainment sectors? While reams of newsprint, hours of broadcast, and numerous webpages debated these issues, with news coverage relating the #MeToo in newsrooms with accusations against academics a year earlier, or with the global movement, little attention was paid to the long history of journalists complaining about gendered workplace harassment or the structural specificities of the current mo(ve)ment.

In her book *Making News: Women in Journalism* (2000), based on interviews of over two hundred female journalists across India, Ammu Joseph records multiple experiences of sexual harassment in newsrooms. In a chapter called 'The Enemy Within', she writes that female journalists unanimously agree that most cases of discriminatory behaviour they encountered have been internal to media organisations rather than external, and that colleagues – more than unsupportive families, a conservative society or dismissive sources – have caused the greatest grief. Drawing on personal accounts starting from the 1980s, Joseph documents a range of gendered harassment in the newsroom – from the telling of sexually explicit jokes to lewd telephone calls, from unsolicited comments about the way one looks or dresses to being asked 'So you don't mind being raped?' when offering to do night duty. The chapter underlines the tendency of management to underplay incidents and avoid taking serious action, and documents a few cases where the women took official or legal routes to fight harassment. Statistical data supports Joseph's claim that sexual harassment of varying levels was so pervasive that it was thought of as an 'occupational hazard'. In 2002–2003, a national-level survey (PII, 2004) found that nearly a quarter of the 410 respondents surveyed stated on record that they had been sexually harassed *at* work, or *in connection* to their work; but a mere 15 per cent of them lodged a formal complaint.

In 2012, a decade after Joseph's book was published, I interviewed seventeen women in English-language print and television journalism based in three Indian metropolises – Mumbai, Chennai and New Delhi – on the gendered nature of the profession. Much had changed in the meantime: the media had witnessed tremendous growth in the early 2000s, a process that had been kick-started post-liberalisation but scaled new heights around this time, resulting in more attractive salaries and better perks. At the same time, contractual employment was already introducing an element of precarity. Robust press unions had become a thing of the past. Women had entered the profession in very large numbers, allowing the newsroom to become a site of mythical celebratory postfeminist narratives. Individualism, choice and agency became the dominant modes of engaging questions of gender and journalism, and this was accompanied by a silencing of structural inequities.

Much also remained the same. Speaking at a time when most media houses did not have the recommended internal complaints committees (ICC),[1] or had one only on paper, journalists I interviewed gestured at the prevalence of sexual banter in the newsroom, often considered a far more 'liberal, informal or permissive' workspace than your traditional corporate office. While the starkly illuminated workspace, its location in high-rises and strict organisational structures made it like any other corporate workplace in a highly globalised world, the open-floor office landscape, the frequent casual conversations and the influx of young blood lent a certain informality and egalitarianism to the newsroom. This, then, shaped it as both a space of transgression and one of oppression. It was a space that allowed overstepping conservative social norms; but it also meant that women were implicitly told to be careful not to be 'misunderstood' and thereby lose respectability or credibility. My interlocutors recognised the need to differentiate between unsolicited sexual banter and physical harassment, but also pointed out that the former could, at times, be a precursor to the latter.

My interest in questions of harassment in the workplace stems from my experiences in the newsroom. I know, first-hand, how futile it can be to approach an ICC. In 2009, the organisation I worked for was one of the few that had acted upon the Vishaka Guidelines[2] and had put a system in place to address sexual harassment at work. It organised bi-annual workshops on how to 'tackle' sexual harassment, and all employees were briefed about the process of filing a complaint. But when I filed one against a colleague for verbal harassment, it took three emails to the editorial and human resource departments for the organisation to respond. After keeping me waiting for a month, an informal meeting was arranged 'to sort out the problem'. I was talked into settling for a written apology, which I never received. I was also asked 'not to make a big deal of the issue'. My editor later told me that he could not do much about it because the harasser was 'a good reporter who added value to the team'. My interviews with journalists led me to believe that such incidences were far from rare in news organisations.

Many participants in my research were unwilling to approach the ICC at their organisations because they thought it would have a negative impact on both their personal and professional lives. While the ICC brings the resolution of the issue of sexual harassment within the ambit of the workplace, the site at which the problem occurs, it also allows for the targeting and vilification of the complainant and slipshod investigations. Employers are hesitant to implement the grievance procedures, and employees fear using them as they feel it often hinders the complainant's career path rather than that of the accused.

In December 2012, even as I was wrapping up my interviews with journalists, a 23-year-old physiotherapy intern was beaten and gang-raped on a bus in Delhi. The woman died from the injuries thirteen days later. The incident sparked nationwide protests. Thousands of people took to the streets demanding security for women in public spaces; and the media followed this relentlessly. This hastened the enforcement of the Sexual Harassment of Women at Workplace (Prevention, Prohibition and Redressal) Act, 2013. It had taken the Indian state over fifteen years since the Vishaka Guidelines to finally pass this.

It is now 2021. Much has changed. The world is in the grip of a pandemic, work is being conducted via phone or video, scores of journalists have been asked to resign with offered terms or their employment has been terminated, bureaus are being shut and, belatedly, precarity is being addressed from within the professional community. Amidst this, sexual harassment is finally inching towards becoming more a part of the discourse *within* newsrooms than of the news being reported. At the same time, not much has changed. It is being reasoned that, in the recent layoffs, departments that typically employ more women – the features or editorial-marketing sections – have been the first to be closed down. Regional-language newsrooms seem to be worse hit than English-language newsrooms, which continue to be largely upper-class and almost fully upper-caste. Powerful men are still being allowed to twist the very laws that ensure the protection and privacy of survivors to serve their own ends. In a report released by Gender at Work and the Network of Women in Media, India in March 2020, based on an online survey of 456 cis and trans media women, including journalists, journalism educators, trainers and researchers, over a third of the respondents reported having experienced sexual harassment in the workplace. More than half of them did not report it to anyone. Of those who did approach the ICC with their complaints, more than 70 per cent reported that they were not 'completely satisfied'. And most importantly, merely a quarter of those surveyed reported feeling safe at their workplace (Murthy et al., 2020).

When the dust around the #MeToo media storm had finally settled, journalists and academics alike questioned if there had been any *real, tangible* impact. Or was this just a blip in the grand scheme of things? The return of many of the accused perpetrators to work and the continuing mistrust of due process often lead to a narrative that marks the moment as futile. However, seeing #MeToo in the context of the larger women's movements in the country – as a small, but important step towards creating a collective consciousness, which could possibly fuel the slow, painstaking work that goes into building a more equitable society – opens up possibilities. When read against the longer, fractured history charted out here, it is possible to imagine that many female journalists saw 2018 as a moment in which, supported by colleagues, they could publicly out their harassers, if only anonymously. There was a chance that their grievances could be redressed and solidarities established, even if only partially and momentarily. And they were taking it.

Notes

1 None of the journalists I interviewed were aware of a functioning ICC in their organisation, though most of them knew about the Vishaka Guidelines, which had recommended such committees be set up. Most also admitted to having personally witnessed or heard of a sexual harassment case at their workplace.

2 The Vishaka Guidelines, a set of procedural guidelines for use in cases of sexual harassment, were promulgated by the Indian Supreme Court in 1997, the outcome in the case of the gang-rape of Bhanwari Devi, a village-level worker in a government-initiated development programme in Rajasthan. The guidelines were superseded in 2013 by the Sexual Harassment of Women at Workplace (Prevention, Prohibition and Redressal) Act, 2013.

References

Joseph, A. (2000). *Making News: Women in Journalism*. New Delhi: Konark Publishers.

Murthy, L., A. Aggarwal, R. Karthikeyan, A. Joseph and S. Kundu. (2020). *Creating Safe Workplaces: Prevention and Redressal of Sexual Harassment in Media Houses in India*. Gender at Work and the Network of Women in Media, India. https://genderatwork.org/wp-content/uploads/2020/03/Creating_Safe_Workplaces.pdf. Accessed 15 October 2020.

PII (Press Institute of India). (2004). *Status of Women Journalists in the Print Media*. New Delhi: National Commission for Women. http://ncwapps.nic.in/pdfReports/Status%20of%20Women%20Journalists%20in%20India.pdf. Accessed 10 September 2020.

Part IV

Affect and aesthetics

11

Fury, pain, resentment … and fierceness: configurations of con/destructive affective activism in women's organising

Peace Kiguwa

You need only claim the events of your life to make yourself yours. When you truly possess all you have been and done … you are fierce with reality. (Scott-Maxwell, 1968: 42)

This chapter explores the role and function of affect in women's activism against sexual and gender violence in South Africa through a focus on the use and effect of emotion work in galvanising social response, as well as in the circulation of emotion between bodies. In so doing, I make an argument for a more concentrated look at the place of emotions to show how social movements take on a life of their own and achieve multiple and often unforeseen effects that attest to their unpredictability. This argument rests on a view of emotions as more than just interior life, which engages emotions as never residing inside or outside of bodies but rather circulating within an assemblage that includes human and non-human actors.

In South Africa, activism around #MeToo has intersected with configurations of race, class, gender, sexuality and geographical contexts amongst other social signifiers that attest to the country's complicated social and political history and present. Given this, it is not surprising that different registers of affect have become attached to specific bodies which indicate hierarchies of power and privilege. These hierarchies, in turn, have influenced how certain affective registers have been taken up within the broader social and psychical sphere. #MeToo's roots and its unfolding in the US and Europe have played out significantly differently in Africa where the movement has failed to take as deep and entrenched a hold as it has in the US. While South Africa has engaged much more publicising around the movement than elsewhere on the continent, this engagement has encompassed less direct galvanising under the banner of #MeToo, favouring alternate formations (Gouws, 2019).[1] This lack of galvanising around #MeToo does not mean that there has been no active or coordinated social organising of women around gender-based violence (GBV) and harassment, either on the continent or in the country more specifically. On the contrary, the much-publicised rise and organising around #MeToo worldwide – perhaps given its roots in the Western context – have sidelined important histories of social organising and protest by women around the continent. I explore some of these configurations of social organising, which, while not directly tied to the #MeToo movement, share some significant politics of galvanising around gender and violence.

The chapter commences with an outline of some of the prominent features of affect as discussed by scholars in the field, illustrating the utility of thinking with affect for understanding how bodies are organised. I then explore the place of affect in social movements and discuss its capacity to mobilise bodies in particular ways, with a focus on key dimensions of social organising and activism as these have emerged in South Africa. In exploring the capacity of affective activism in South Africa, I discuss four events that highlight the collective imaginary and its potential for participation, including the manner in which the original event inscribes us and directs our bodies towards and away from imaginations of freedom. To do this, I identify and discuss affective registers of *rage*, *pain*, *love*, *shame*, *fury* and *resentment* as they emerged within the movement. It is my contention that these different registers of affect illustrate both constructive and destructive functions to social organising and to the movement in particular. In so doing I ask: What does affect do for social organising? What are its fault lines and successes?

Affective activism and the work of assembling

What is affect's role in social organising? In considering this question I adopt Brian Massumi's (2002) assertion of the potential of bodies to affect others in particular ways. However, affect is more than just about bodies affecting other bodies. It is also about the circulation

of emotions and what they do in the public domain. These circula-
tions of emotions and capacity of bodies to affect each other operate
within an affective economy that is, in turn, marked by racial,
gendered and classed formations (Brown and Pickerill, 2009).

In the aptly titled 'Poem About My Rights', June Jordan laments:

> I have been raped
> be-
> cause I have been wrong the wrong sex the wrong age
> the wrong skin the wrong nose the wrong hair the
> wrong need the wrong dream the wrong geographic
> the wrong sartorial I
> I have been the meaning of rape
> I have been the problem everyone seeks to
> eliminate by forced
> penetration with or without the evidence of slime.

This lament becomes her warrior cry toward a reclamation of
power that involves a refusal to accept a status quo that diminishes
her worth and dignity:

> I am not wrong: Wrong is not my name
> My name is my own my own my own
> and I can't tell you who the hell set things up like this
> but I can tell you that from now on my resistance
> my simple and daily and nightly self-determination
> may very well cost you your life. (Jordan, 2005: 105, emphasis in
> original)

In considering exactly what it is that affects do, Jordan's rallying
words engage a number of affective devices that I argue are present
in the different practices of gender activists. In that cry there is an
explicit acknowledgement and taking up of grief, pain and rage as
necessary responses to discrimination, oppression and violence.
It is in the reclamation of these emotions that Jordan resists and
speaks back to domination and violence. In that cry Jordan invites
us to consider what it might mean for women to engage violence's
reach with a responding rage and violence that is righteous. In that
cry a haunting addresses melancholic loss and rage. In that cry the
political act of naming our loss and rage becomes its own activism.
I am interested in what such a cry does as part of a process of social

organising and galvanising for social justice. Exploring the affective meaning of such a cry is not only to consider the work of emotions and how they circulate but also to consider these registers of loss, rage and grief as part of an attempt to speak back/against society. As Goodwin et al. (2001: 9) observe: 'Protest can be a way of saying something about oneself and one's morals, of finding joy and pride in them'.

Affect then is transmissible (Brennan, 2004): it circulates in, amongst and through bodies so that it is impossible to think of the skin as bounded. Sara Ahmed and Jackie Stacey in *Thinking Through the Skin* (2001) argue for an approach to theorising bodies that not only posits bodies as already imbued with meaning but also considers bodies as agentic in the imagination of new and different social arrangements. I am interested in how gender activisms can produce affective reactions on a broader scale and in a way that actively *haunts* and ignites response, a sense of *urgency*. Mobilising Deleuze and Guattari's analytic of assemblage we might ask: How are gender activisms simultaneously brought into 'being, stabilised, dissolved, and re-assembled' (Bansel and Davies, 2014: 2)? Deleuze and Guattari (2004: 265) note that 'affect is not a personal feeling, nor is it a characteristic; it is the effectuation of a power of the pack that throws the self into upheaval and makes it reel'. From this we can think of bodies and their capacity to affect in terms of their qualities, speeds, flows, forces. Indeed, for Bansel and Davies, affective assemblages must be read in terms of their continuous becoming, with no intent to arrive at any final point. Through multiple encounters affective assemblage may be defined not by what they are but what they can do, or become. Goodwin et al. (2001: 9) thus invite us to consider identity's emotional character in social movements: 'What is difficult to imagine is an identity that is purely cognitive yet strongly held. The "strength" of an identity, even a cognitively vague one, comes from its emotional side'.

In considering the work of assembling in social organising I ask: Who and what gets assembled? How this assembling is inflected with race, gender and class registers and other inclusion and exclusion markers is important. Through this, we can begin to think of the bodies we do not see, the voices that get sidelined and the privileging of narratives that reinforce binaries of gender and sexuality. In framing this, I am at pains to avoid the tendency toward mere discursive and social representation of in/exclusion via language registers. Instead I want to argue that affective assemblages are crucial to the formation of *feeling* bodies that have rights and those that do not. For example, in considering rage as affect we explore not only what is made possible via the register of rage but also what gets forestalled in the emergence of rage in gender activism.

To do this, Deleuze and Guattari's (2004) diagrammatic approach to assemblage is useful in its drawing together myriad interconnecting dimensions of the affective. They conceptualise assemblage in terms of two axes: the horizontal and the vertical. The horizontal axis incorporates both an *assemblage of content* or *machinic* assemblage (concerned with the materiality of bodies and their web of interrelation) and an *assemblage of expression* (concerned with language and the discursive). Machinic assemblages highlight those features of affective parts that have to do with body movement in space and how they are made legible in discourse. They relate 'not to the production of goods but rather a precise state of intermingling of bodies in a society, including all the attractions, repulsions, sympathies, antipathies, alterations, amalgamations, penetrations, and expansions that affect bodies of all kinds in their relations with one another' (Deleuze and Guattari, 2004: 99). Bodies engaged in protest and other action, bodies narrating their stories of sexual and gender violence, discrimination and oppression, passionate bodies, desiring and desirous bodies, are far from neutral. They are infected with the racial, gendered, sexual, classed histories of a society that influences these affective assemblages and how they are made intelligible. Subjects with differential speaking and acting rights emerge within this assemblage of power matrices. This emergence is especially possible because power matrices produce 'incorporeal transformations attributed to bodies' (Delueze and Guattari, 2004: 98).

The vertical axis of assemblage highlights the capacity for affective force to shift and move between bodies in three particular ways: *territorial*, *deterritorial* and *reterritorial*. Within this axis we are not only concerned with the content and expression of assemblage via the materiality of bodies. We are also interested in the ways that these bodies may affect and be affected by each other through affective force so that new and other states of being and relation become possible. Assemblage has the capacity to remain the same, to be drawn into another territorial field (deterritorial) and/or to change into something new and different (reterritorial). The following sections engage these dimensions of assemblage in exploring emotion and affect's circulation.

Building community, claiming injury: affective mobilisations

In this section I describe how affect and emotion have been functional in creating a movement for social change within South Africa. In the response to public events of violence, in the narration of own stories of harassment and violence, affects are assembled that become part of public assembling.[2] Following Deleuze and Guattari, I read event as more than a temporal demarcation of an occurrence that can be relegated to a past, present or future. Rather, a society is caught up in a series of interconnected changes that do not end. The event, then, is an assemblage of 'semiotic flows, material flows, and social flows' (Deleuze and Guattari, 2004: 25), connections that form part of a linguistic, semiotic, material, aesthetic, political and social regime of coding. The nature of the event, its unfolding within multiple and interconnected chains, influences both horizontal and vertical axes of flow of affect and becoming. Through an analysis of events as they unfold and how they are received by the broader public, we can see the process by which events may be mobilised and configured along axes of assemblage, which is part of affective activism.

Event 1

Academic and activist Hlengiwe Ndlovu describes a violent 2016 protest encounter between students and police on the campus of the University of the Witwatersrand (Wits) in Johannesburg:

> At this point I was exhausted. I had already survived three asthmatic attacks, but could not rest because of the situation. I had moved to the Great Hall stairs where there was private security so that I could

avoid running. Comrade Sarah Mukwebo came to me asking that we make an intervention. 'We need a ceasefire. We need to do something,' she said. I was tired and desperate for any action that would stop violence just for that moment. Comrade Sarah seemed to have a plan. She said 'Let's go topless! That's what these men need right now.' In one of the interviews she conducted with media, Sarah discussed the cause and feelings of the moment: 'It was a blur. None of it was planned before that moment … There was very little time to think and reflect, which helped, but we knew that something had to be done to stop the police from injuring us.' … It is important to note that there were different types of violence that we experienced as Black womxn throughout the militarisation … Cdes Sarah and Lerato approached womxn leaders who were on the side and proceeded to inform men who were at the front to hold back the crowd. We took off our tops and charged towards the policemen who were our target. They had perpetuated violence for a while, and someone needed to put an end to that violence. Sarah Mukwebo, Lerato Motaung and Hlengiwe Ndlovu (myself) intervened by charging forward, stripping, exposing our bare chests – and thereby stopped the violence immediately. (Ndlovu, 2017: 74)

Event 2

24 August 2019. Nineteen-year-old UCT student Uyinene Mrwetyana is raped and murdered. Her body is bludgeoned into pieces and dumped in Khayelitsha, a township twenty-nine kilometres from the post office where the attack took place. Weeks of night vigils across campuses in South Africa, community searches and social media awareness about her missing status have come to this moment. Shortly after her death, a man is arrested, a forty-two-year-old postal worker who had attended to her on the day. As the proceedings unfold the public learns the circumstances that surrounded Uyinene's rape and murder: that she had visited the post office to collect a parcel, unavailable at the time of her visit; that she was to be informed when the parcel became available by this postal worker; that, the parcel became available a week later, that she was notified by this postal worker a few days thereafter on a weekend Saturday and that she travelled to the post office on the same day to collect the parcel; that she found the building deserted

and was alone with her assailant; that she fought back in an attempt to escape her attacker; that he hit her over her head with a scale to immobilise her; that he attempted to hide evidence by burning her body. These unfoldings sparked a social movement on the streets and in the digital community. It had women across the country asking '#AmINext?', a real reminder of the precarity of women's lives in a country rife with patriarchal violence. This collective rage, frustration and pain culminated in a march to parliament on 5 September. Several other protest marches across the country were planned. Speaking shortly after the sentencing of Uyinene's murderer, President Ramaphosa would describe the country as going through a 'dark period'.

Event 3

2 May 2018. Karabo Mokoena's boyfriend, Sandile Mantsoe, is found guilty of her murder and sentenced to thirty-two years in prison. During the investigation proceedings, Mantsoe directs police to the scene of her remains where he burnt her body beyond recognition after dragging her from his Sandton, Johannesburg, apartment in a dustbin. News of Karabo's murder sparks outrage throughout the country, with the hashtag #MenAreTrash trending in social media spaces.

Event 4

Sunday 17 April 2016. Eleven men's names are anonymously published on Facebook with the words 'et al.'. Published without description, without allegation, the named men are all students at a particular South African university. The list becomes known as the #RUReferenceList. Those on it have been accused of sexual or GBV, and nothing has been done by the university.

> On the night of Sunday 17 April, the 'Reference List' prompted … students into collective action. They began to grasp what connected the names. A crowd gathered at the student union, and entered one men's residence after the other, intent on rounding up the listed students still [on campus]. The police were called to the campus to intervene – the first of many times. (Seddon, 2016)

Assembling bodies via register of content assemblages

In reading these events through the notion of horizontal and vertical axes of assemblage, what intermingling of bodies are present? Womxn's bodies, men's bodies, black bodies, police (in their varying characteristics of brutality and competency), the president as authority figure. On this axis of materiality of the body's movement in space, we see an intermingling which signals that the disavowal of personhood to some bodies is also present. These bodies are tortured: burnt, beaten, decapitated, raped. These bodies are old and young, trans, gender non-conforming; these bodies also speak back through protest, marching, gathering, nudity; they take up space in their demand to be recognised as embodying persons.

This intermingling of bodies incorporates other objects and sites: *dustbin* – object that provisionally stores waste temporarily houses a young woman's body, dragged away to be burnt beyond recognition; *home* – place where one dwells and makes a life that becomes the battle ground for life and well-being; *post office* – public office responsible for postal services and communication that becomes the violent rape and death scene of a young woman; *police station* – right next door to the same post office; *university* – place of learning and teaching rife with told and untold stories of sexual harassment and sexual violence; *township* and *suburb* – geographical sites of living that continue to reflect the inequalities of a society; *parliamentary building* – office of the highest legislature in the country.

Amidst this intermingling, a rage, fear and frustration integral to the galvanisation of the public body. The ordinariness of spaces (the post office, the campus, the home, etc.) are reassembled as not only unsafe but also spectacular in their mundanity: 'If we are not safe in the post office/homes/campus, where can we be safe?' is the question laid bare to the public body. A social imaginary becomes possible that incorporates different bodies influenced by different affective registers tied to personhood and vulnerability. Through affective registers of fear, rage, vulnerability, the protest marches assemble an ineffectual state and security force that historically and continuously trivialise gender and sexual violence.

Assembling bodies via register of expression assemblages

The affective modes of expression in the machinic assemblage include women marching to parliament with placards that read 'Enough is Enough!' (an expression that tells a *history* of *continued* disavowal of women's bodily integrity). Temporalities converge here – the past's continued interaction with the present and what that might mean for future events: the identity of a nation, the meaning of masculinities and its future are mobilised. African feminist Rufaro Samanga (2017) states that

> #MenAreTrash attempts to do away with the respectability politics that seeks to police the way in which we as women decide to voice out our anger and frustration towards an oppressive patriarchal structure. One needs to understand first and foremost that as women, and particularly as feminists, ours is not to deliver our message prettily garnished in a way that is perceived to be more 'palatable' by men. In short, we are not duty-bound to mollycoddle the men who are a part of the very same patriarchal structure against which we are tirelessly fighting.

The inscription of masculinity as trash is a refusal to speak of gender and sexual violence and harassment with reference to a generic subject. It is an unambiguous *naming of a subject* – men – as a step toward addressing the problem. It is a location of that subject within a broader social, cultural, political and affective system that rewards – materially, socially and psychically – investment in the hegemonic and toxic expressions of that identity.

The juridical regime that includes statesmen and women, police and the law also expresses language that attributes differential and embodied modes of being onto womxn survivors of violence. These include then Police Minister Fikile Mbalula denouncing the murder of Karabo Mokoena with reference to her being 'such a beautiful girl, [a] yellowbone' (*Citizen*, 2017). Elsewhere, Minister of Women in the Presidency, Susan Shabangu, on a televised programme, described Karabo as 'weak and hence she became a victim of abuse. As she tried to deal with her situation in sharing it with other abused women, she ended up being a victim of abuse' (Khoza, 2017). Speaking at Karabo's funeral, Social Development

Minister Bathabile Dlamini said: 'Our children are growing up in a different time than we did. They love money. Our children are materialistic. Our children can't see when they are being abused psychologically, emotionally.' Discursive constructs that caution women not to show too much skin, to dress with decorum, are part of this assembling of women's bodies as both victim and contributor to their own abuse and violation. The language that re-assembles Karabo as weak, materialistic, yellow-bone, re-writes her – and all womxn – in ways that diminish their right to person-hood and agency. Toxic hegemonic masculinity remains unprob-lematised, indeed, seems to enjoy a taken-for-granted status as inevitable and normal.

Assembling bodies via registers of territorialisation, deterritorialisation and reterritorialisation

Part of the characteristic of the machinic assemblage is its capacity for movement and renewal. The inscriptions of the body that are part of both patriarchal violence and part of a resistance against this violence – via refusal – function to deterritorialise and reterritorial-ise meaning. Juridical pronouncements both deterritorise women as victims of violence and reterritorise them instead as bodies *asking for it*. Violent masculinities, in turn, are deterritorised as prob-lematic and reterritorised as normal fixtures of society. Following the aftermath of the Wits student naked protest, much attention was diverted to a discussion of the protestors' bodies. Ndlovu (2017: 75) writes: 'Our hard emotional work at the picket line was reduced to discussions on beauty standards and "hanging breasts". A popular comedian known as Skhumba took to local radio station Khaya FM and body-shamed us'. Collective assemblages of expres-sion such as those uttered by Skhumba function to make womxn's rage in protest irrelevant and apolitical. Through refusal of these linguistic and discursive inscriptions, for example placards held by scantily dressed and nude protestors on campus that read 'Still not asking for it' (Lujabe, 2016), protestors engage in a discursive reclaiming of bodily integrity.

On 6 August 2016 Jacob Zuma, newly re-elected president of South Africa, makes his victory speech. Four young women hold up placards in a silent protest. Standing in front of the podium with their backs to arguably the most powerful man in the country at the time, the posters read 'I am 1 in 3', '10 years later', 'Khwezi' and 'Khanga' (Pather, 2016). These placards signal the crisis of sexual assault against women and children in the country with particular reference to the president's acquittal following a much-publicised rape trial. His accuser, known only as Khwezi and famously reputed to have been wearing a *khanga*[3] at the time of the assault, responded to widespread criticisms from Zuma's supporters on her attire, which was interpreted as inviting sexual attention. Indeed, Zuma, himself used this argument in his defence. In a poem composition titled 'I am Khanga', Khwezi challenges this erasure of women's bodily autonomy through dress code and legitimation of sexual violence (Pather, 2016). Since then, the *khanga* has been taken up by many African feminists as a symbolic reminder of the country's rape culture but also women's capacity to resist and refuse their interpellation as sexual objects (Mushi, 2014; Pather, 2016). What followed this silent protest was perhaps predictable: the president's bodyguards forcibly removed the four women from the scene. But the damage had already been done. Another predictable action was the response of the African National Congress Women's League (headed primarily by female ANC veterans of the apartheid struggle) (Qukula, 2016). In addition to emotive outbursts and scurrying, not only did the president of the league, Bathabile Dlamini, denounce the protest, she also dismissed the agency of the young women to act of their own accord, claiming that they must have been 'put up to' the protest, and decried the lack of respect displayed toward the president (Verwoerd, 2016).

This event exposes formations of women's rage in protest: the silent rage of four young women calling to attention continued violations against womxn's bodies, the loud visceral rage of other women attempting to shut down this call. The affective potential of rage to galvanise social response, to reclaim self, to speak about one's injury and even the cathartic effects of rage cannot be understated. Black feminists such as Audre Lorde (1984), bell hooks (1995) and Patricia Hill Collins (2000) have argued for the empowering use and expression of rage in advocating for personal, social and political empowerment. Part of this call to *express* rage and reclaim it as a necessary tool for empowerment concerns a culture of repressing rage, which forces many women into silence. Soraya Chemaly (2018) and Brittney Cooper (2018) engage women's rage as political, arguing that the concerted and systemic effort at silencing women's anger – whether in the home, within institutions or in broader society – is a deliberate and political practice. They reclaim rage as a powerful force of refusal and re-assertion of personhood that has been denied to women. Rage as affective force includes an analysis of rage as ontological force that disrupts the business-as-usual orientation of society. Rage is thus generative and produces bodies that are in constant motion with each other. This relationality of affective production is an important one to consider in engaging the question of *what social organising does*. Rage assembles bodies in ways that become political, it moves objects to emerge as subjects with political rights via relational arrangements. In this sense, then, rage as affective trope works with another understated affect – love. Hugo Canham (2017, 2018) considers embodied rage in community uprisings as a fight for self-love and love of the other in the struggle for political and community rights. Rage, then, is a revolutionary tool that encompasses knowledge transfer and production about a group's right to exist. Reflecting on Jordan's expressions of rage, Jack Halberstam (1993: 188) considers the fantasy of violence that the poem invites: 'Jordan's place of rage is a strange and wonderful terrain, it is a location between and beyond thought, action, response, activism, protest, anger, terror, murder, and detestation. Jordan's place of rage is ground for resistance'. Through the register of rage, Jordan reclaims a self that has been violated and brutalised. Through the register of rage, she asserts a politics that refuses continued violation. This is 'not the rage that explodes mindlessly and carelessly, but a quiet rage, tightly reined, ever so precise and intent upon retribution' (Halberstam 1993: 195). For Halberstam, this is the return of the gaze, the determination to self-represent and reclaim the power of signification. The affective force that is evident in the technologies of naming oneself, one's feelings, one's body and one's position within society is fundamental to womxn's organising.

Entanglements of silence: affective immobilisations

In exploring what I describe as affective immobilisations, I am interested in how affects and emotions manifest in social organising in ways that foreclose dialogue and collaboration. Three issues are at stake here: 1) What narratives are recognised within the movement as authentic? 2) How does one claim an injury that is *recognisable* as having the capacity to be injured? 3) How does recognition get turned on its head such that perpetrator guilt is absolved?

Through the notion of recognisability, Judith Butler (2009: 5) confronts these conundrums directly in her proposition that to recognise and to be recognised is to concede a recognition of personhood that 'belongs to all persons as persons'. And yet another conundrum is evident here: Who counts as person? If 'existing norms allocate recognition differentially' (Butler, 2009: 6), by what strategies and politics can personhood then be made recognisable? I would argue that in paying attention to the affective dimensions of women's organising this politics of recognition becomes even more visible. In mapping out a landscape of how we invest and engage varying modes of anxiety, resentment, shame, ambivalence, disgust, defensiveness and so on, we can better conceptualise those strategies of engagement that enforce what may be referred to as entanglements of silence within the movement. Through these entanglements some registers of affect are made possible (and therefore recognisable) and others are not (precisely because they are not recognised).

It is my contention that part of the emotional and affective labour is implicitly demanded is that narrators of violence prove both their *legitimacy as persons* and *their claims to injury*. Saville Young (2011: 52) observes that 'for Butler, recognisability comes before recognition; we will only be recognised and mourned if we are recognisable as having a precarious life'. This politics of recognisability, in turn, influences a normalisation of violence against bodies coded as lacking personhood and, therefore, the right to bodily integrity and security. Melanie Judge (2018) has argued that racial repertoires not only produce particular sets of meaning relative to violence but also forms of subjectivity within the South African context. These repertoires of meaning influence how we read violence as normal, spectacular and moral. They also influence how we attach some bodies to normalised enactments of violence. In asking 'why are all rapes not grievable?' Rebecca Helman (2018: 1), a white South African woman, shares her own post-rape ordeal at a Care Centre thus:

A month after I was raped I am sitting in the waiting room of the Heideveld Thutuleza Care Centre waiting to have an HIV test. On the couch opposite me, there is another womxn. She looks about eighteen. She is Black. In her hand she is holding the care package and the information book that I received when I came in a month ago, a few hours after I was raped. The nurse approaches the two of us in the waiting room. She turns to me, 'Who are you bringing for an appointment?' I look at her confused. 'Who is the patient?' she asks. 'I am the patient'. 'Oh', she says. She looks surprised. In a context in which the bodies of poor black womxn are repeatedly constructed as the sites of sexual violence the nurse is unable to recognise my white, middle-class body as the site of such violence.

In *Rape: A South African Nightmare*, feminist scholar Pumla Gqola (2015) argues that the violence of rape includes its differential transgression status relative to different racialised and classed bodies. By this she means that in a country rife with gender- and sexual-based violence against women and children, black women have come to be constructed as *unrapeable* – that is, they have come to occupy a status that fails to recognise their personhood and, therefore, embodies them as subjects that cannot experience harm. The converse of this disavowal of personhood is to be embodied as a subject that Judge (2015, 2018) describes as always already raped. Both these dual and seemingly opposing discursive positions effectively function to erase black women's narratives of sexual and gender violence as simultaneously invisible and normal. In such contexts of entanglement, affective registers are often implicitly and explicitly demanded from many women who tell their stories of violation and violence that is both performative and often made spectacular. In the demand that victims perform their pain and harm, a culture of silence and violence is effectively sustained.

Entanglements of silence that incorporate a struggle to prove one's legitimacy as a person, and in order to be able to make a claim of injury, are also present within women's organising. On 1 August 2018, South Africa watched as womxn from different parts of the country assembled together in a march towards the Union Buildings in Pretoria where the president of the country, Cyril Ramaphosa, received a document highlighting a list of twenty-four demands related to gender and sexual violence in the country. The #TotalShutDown march was the result of planning and organising by womxn through digital and other activism that witnessed the coming together of womxn in their diversity for the shared goal of making their voices heard. Their list of demands included the following:

> Transgender and GNC [gender non-conforming] people have different safety and security needs than that of cisgender womxn based on how laws, policies, practices and systems are conceptualised, based on gender binaries for cisgender womxn and men, as well as for boys and girls. E.g. Transgender womxn and GNC people are raped in correctional facilities and detention centres in the criminal justice system by virtue of their legal gender marker. (*Mail & Guardian*, 2018)

While organised protest against gender- and sexual-based violence in the country has framed itself as intersectional, this has not been a seamless struggle. T. L. Cowan (2014: 501) describes 'the transfeminist kill/joy' as a necessary affective trope that disrupts current and mainstream feminist circles and women's organising which actively exclude and marginalise trans and GNC bodies both in terms of their personhood and their vulnerability to violence. Signalling Sara Ahmed's original framing of the feminist killjoy, Cowan (2014: 502) argues that the transfeminist figure 'works both to spoil feelings of political and social well-being or pleasure that are contingent upon the tacit absence or explicit exclusion of trans women in feminist conceptual and physical spaces'. The assemblage of deterritorialisation during the #TotalShutDown march, for example, included trans women holding placards reading 'Public Cervix Announcement: F*** You' (Dawjee, 2018). The rejection of attachment of material body to gender identity and experience is as much a challenge to patriarchal masculinist society as it is to radical feminist binary constructs of gender and their fallacy of universal gender experience. Cervix does not mean woman. An assemblage of affects includes: the refusal of shame, where shame is a powerful tool of patriarchy in shaming womxn's politics and person; the use of righteous rage in reclaiming one's place in the movement; and the place of love in reimagining a collaboration and coming together of womxn in the fight against violence. The trans figure falls outside of patriarchal and radical feminist imaginings of freedom, even of understandings of violence.

To turn to the question of recognition's subversion, we must ask: What affective technologies are deployed? One of the destructive mechanisms in affective deployment concerns what scholars such as Derek Hook (2005) and Zeus Leonardo and Michalinos Zembylas (2013) refer to as *affective technology*. Engaging Michel Foucault's (1977) idea of technology, these scholars discuss how knowledge, practices, discourse and techniques are assembled as part of broader society's effort to exert influence on each other. Affective technologies are concerned with the circulation of affect and emotions in demarcating boundaries of belonging. Leonardo and Zembylas' work, for example, demonstrates how whiteness may function as affective technology: bad affects such as racist hate and disgust become attached to an Other (bad) white subject. The racist Other is thus always exteriorised: *they are the racists, not me*. Through this affective strategy, whiteness is able to maintain its hegemonic status and not hold itself accountable. Similarly, an affective trope that involves disavowal of systemic toxic patriarchal culture via linguistic strategies of situating violent men as the other is deployed through the refrain of 'not all men'. Understanding the logic of patriarchal masculinities remains an aspect of the unravelling of hegemony, which demands an exploration and critique of its material, discursive and affective features.

Conclusion

In this chapter I have explored some of the features of social organising for women's rights, with attention to gender and violence via affective assemblages that include horizontal and vertical axes of movement and circulation. These assemblages are part of constructive and destructive capacities of affect to produce community and solidarity and to galvanise different bodies into action. Such organising and politics of rage is also evident in some of the formations of the #MeToo movement globally, which remind us of the place of affect in excavating marginalised voices as well as galvanising a social public. However, they may be part of an entanglement of silence that forecloses any possibilities for solidarity and action – both within and outside of the movement.

Acknowledgements

I am grateful to Sharlene Khan, Grace Musila and Grace Khunou for a shared conversation on the possibilities of rage in activism.

Notes

1 Notable formations include #MenAreTrash, #AmINext, #RUReference List and #TotalShutDown.
2 In respect of the confidentiality of these stories, which have largely taken place within online digital platforms, and to honour the meaning of feminist narrative re-telling that refuses the appropriation of another's story, I have only focused on those events and accounts that are explicitly in an openly public domain such as a media report and/or publication.
3 A *khanga* is an African garment that wraps around the body and is widely worn by women across Africa.

References

Ahmed, S. and J. Stacey (eds.) (2001). *Thinking through the Skin*. London: Routledge.
Bansel, P. and B. Davies. (2014). 'Assembling Oscar, Assembling South Africa, Assembling Affects', *Emotion, Space and Society* 13, 40–5.
Brennan, T. (2004). *The Transmission of Affect*. Ithaca, NY: Cornell University Press.

Brown, G. and J. Pickerill. (2009). 'Space for Emotion in the Spaces of Activism', *Emotion, Space and Society* 2:1, 24–35.

Butler, J. (2009). *Frames of War: When is Life Grievable?* London: Verso.

Canham, H. (2017). 'Embodied Black Rage', *Du Bois Review: Social Science Research on Race* 14:2, 427–45.

Canham, H. (2018). 'Theorising Community Rage for Decolonial Action', *South African Journal of Psychology* 48:3, 319–30.

Chemaly, S. (2018). *Rage Becomes Her: The Power of Women's Anger.* London: Simon and Schuster.

Citizen. (2017). 'Mbalula Slammed for Calling Karabo a "Beautiful Yellowbone"', *Citizen*, 13 May. https://citizen.co.za/news/south-africa/15 12831/mbalula-slammed-calling-karabo-beautiful-yellowbone/. Accessed 7 July 2019.

Collins, P.H. (2000). *Black Feminist Thought: Knowledge, Consciousness, and the Politics of Empowerment.* New York: Routledge.

Cooper, B. (2018). *Eloquent Rage: A Black Feminist Discovers her Superpower.* New York: St. Martin's Press.

Cowan, T.L. (2014). 'Transfeminist Kill/Joys: Rage, Love, and Reparative Performance', *Transgender Studies Quarterly* 1:4, 501–16.

Dawjee, H.M. (2018). 'Does not Having a Cervix Make you Any Less of a Woman?' *TimesLive*, 12 September. www.timeslive.co.za/sunday-times/lifestyle/2018-08-11-does-not-having-a-cervix-make-you-any-less-of-a-woman/. Accessed 4 July 2019.

Deleuze, G and Guattari, F. (2004). *A Thousand Plateaus: Capitalism and Schizophrenia*, translated by Brian Massumi. London: Continuum.

Foucault, M. (1977). *Discipline and Punish: The Birth of the Prison.* London: Penguin.

Goodwin, J., Jasper, J. M. and Polletta, F. (2001). *Passionate Politics: Emotions and Social Movements.* Chicago: University of Chicago Press.

Gouws, A. (2019). '#MeToo Isn't Big in Africa but we Launched our own Versions', South African, 3 August. www.thesouthafrican.com/lifestyle/metoo-africa-launched-own-versions/. Accessed 7 May 2019.

Gqola, P.D. (2015). *Rape: A South African Nightmare.* Johannesburg: MFBooks Joburg.

Halberstam, J. (1993). 'Imagined Violence/Queer Violence: Representation, Rage, and Resistance', *Social Text* 37, 187–201.

Helman, R. (2018). 'Why are all Rapes not Grievable?' *South African Journal of Psychology* 48:4, 403–6.

Hook, D. (2005). 'Affecting Whiteness: Racism as Technology of Affect (1)', *International Journal of Critical Psychology* 16, 74–99.

hooks, b. (1995). *Killing Rage: Ending Racism.* New York: Henry Holt.

Jordan, J. (2005). 'Poem About My Rights', in *Directed by Desire: The Collected Poems of June Jordan*, pp. 309–12. Port Townsend, WA: Copper Canyon Press.

Judge, M. (2015). 'Violence against Lesbians and (Im)possibilities for Identity and Politics', PhD diss., University of the Western Cape.

Judge, M. (2018). *Blackwashing Homophobia: Violence and the Politics of Sexuality, Gender and Race*. London: Routledge.

Khoza, A. (2017). 'Karabo Mokoena was Weak, says Susan Shabangu', *Mail & Guardian*, 24 May. https://mg.co.za/article/2017-05-24-karabo-mokoena-was-weak-says-minister-for-women. Accessed 5 June 2019.

Leonardo, Z. and M. Zembylas. (2013). 'Whiteness as Technology of Affect: Implications for Educational Praxis', *Equity and Excellence in Education* 46:1, 150–65.

Lorde, A. (1984). 'The Uses of Anger: Women Responding to Racism', in *Sister Outsider: Essays and Speeches*, 124–34. n.p.: Crossing Press.

Lujabe, N. (2016). 'One Patriarch, 10 Sjamboks, Say Anti-Rape Culture Protesters', City Press, 27 April. https://city-press.news24.com/News/one-patriarch-10-sjamboks-say-anti-rape-culture-protesters-20160427. Accessed 9 September 2019.

Mail & Guardian. (2018). '#THETOTALSHUTDOWN: Memorandum of demands', *Mail & Guardian*, 2 August. https://mg.co.za/article/2018-08-02-thetotalshutdown-memorandum-of-demands. Accessed 9 September 2019.

Massumi, B. (2002). *Parables for the Virtual: Movement, Affect, Sensation*. Durham, NC: Duke University Press.

Mushi, S.A. (2014). *Stains on my Khanga*. Centurion, Pretoria: Hadithi Media.

Ndlovu, H. (2017). 'Womxn's Bodies Reclaiming the Picket Line: The "Nude" Protest during #FeesMustFall', *Agenda* 3:4, 68–77.

Nombembe, P. (2019). 'Luyanda Botha: "This is How I Killed Uyinene"', *TimesLive*, 15 November. www.timeslive.co.za/news/south-africa/2019-11-15-in-his-own-words-luyanda-botha-this-is-how-i-killed-uyinene/. Accessed 29 December 2020.

Pather, R. (2016). 'Four Women, the President and the Protest that Shook the Results Ceremony', *Mail & Guardian*, 6 August. https://mg.co.za/article/201608-06-four-women-the-president-and-the-protest-that-shoock-the-election-results-ceremony/. Accessed 7 September 2019.

Qukula, Q. (2016). 'ANCWL Have Become The Gatekeepers Of Patriarchy – Gender Activist', Radio 702, 10 August. www.702.co.za/articles/15683/ancwl-have-become-the-gatekeepers-of-patriarchy-gender-activist. Accessed 9 October 2017.

Samanga, R. (2017). 'The Real Story Behind #MenAreTrash, South Africa's Response to Domestic Violence', OkayAfrica, 15 May. www.okay

africa.com/real-story-behind-menaretrash-south-africas-viral-hashtag/. Accessed 5 July 2019.

Saville Young, L. (2011). 'Research Entanglements, Race, and Recognizability: A Psychosocial Reading of Interview Encounters in (Post-)colonial (Post-) apartheid South Africa', *Qualitative Inquiry* 17:1, 45–55.

Scott-Maxwell, F. (1968). *The Measure of my Days*. New York: Knopf.

Seddon, D. (2016). '"We Will not be Silenced": Rape Culture, #RUReferencelist, and the University Currently Known as Rhodes', *Daily Maverick*, 1 June. www.dailymaverick.co.za/opinionista/2016-06-01-we-will-not-be-silenced-rape-culture-rureferencelist-and-the-university-currently-known-as-rhodes/. Accessed 5 March 2017.

Verwoerd, M. (2016). 'How 4 Silent Women Became the Voice of this Election'. *News24*, 8 August. www.news24.com/news24/columnists/melanieverwoerd/how-4-silent-women-became-the-voice-of-this-election-20160808. Accessed 7 September 2019.

12

Queer feminism and India's #MeToo

Jaya Sharma

Even as #MeToo in India allowed so many to speak out, to name the sexual violations we face, to say enough is enough, it also raised serious dilemmas and concerns for us as feminists. I am referring here to concerns about how we as feminists were understanding and responding to issues of desire, power and consent as well as the ways in which we were engaging with each other around these issues. I am also referring more specifically to concerns that emerge from a queer feminist lens which make for a particular kind of feminist sensibility – one that readily includes but also goes beyond the frame of heteropatriarchy. While some concerns found articulation in the public realm, many others that troubled us were shared one to one, often in our homes, among trusted friends and colleagues – not all of them, not at meetings and conferences and certainly not online. It is in this context that I hoped that the anonymity provided by interviews might help create a safe space for the raising of concerns that could be placed in the public realm for further feminist engagement. This is why I undertook the research that informs this chapter.

True to how self-critical we can be as feminists, the concerns about our own ways of understanding and engaging in the #MeToo discourse ran sharp and deep. A thread that runs through the concerns is that of contradictions – both with feminism as well as with queer feminism.

For my definition of the word 'queer', I draw on the articulation by Nazariya, a queer feminist resource group based in New Delhi: 'the word queer is normally used as an umbrella term to understand LGBTQIA+ communities and persons. However ... queer also is a lens to understand the structures of heteronormativity … a lens to include perspectives and lives of those who challenge the heteronormative structures of power and binaries' (Nazariya, 2020). This articulation emphasises the importance of the specificity of the experience and location of those who identify in terms of their sexual orientation or gender expression. At the same time, it also allows us not to be constrained by identities alone but to understand 'queer' as perspectives (whether they come from an LGBTQ identified location or not) for which power is key to how desire is sought to be understood. This articulation of queer is appropriate for the research that this chapter draws upon. A majority of those I interviewed identified as queer and often brought to their reflections on #MeToo, individual and collective experiences specific to their location. This enabled, for instance, an alertness to the danger of thinking of survivors as victims who lack agency. It also allowed for self-critical considerations, such as whether we might be approaching the accused in precisely the ways in which we ourselves have suffered as individuals and communities marginalised on the basis of gender and identity. Beyond identities and the experiences related to them, the reflections on #MeToo that emerged from the interviews are queer (whether shared by those who identify as LGBTQ or not) in the sense that they seek to understanding the interplay between desire and power in ways that include but are not limited to gender. The lens is queer, also, because of the recognition of the significance of erotically fulfilling expressions of desire, even as it interrogates and challenges the dimensions of harm. In all these ways, this chapter is not a demand for inclusion of LGBTQ persons into the frame of #MeToo, but an invitation to engage with issues raised by the #MeToo discourse from a queer perspective.

The focus of this chapter is on feminist critiques regarding our own ways of understanding, responding and engaging with #MeToo (not on feminist critiques about how those outside of feminism are engaging with #MeToo). I locate the queer feminist concerns raised in this chapter as part of a trajectory of critical responses to #MeToo in India that have come from a Dalit feminist[1] location as well as an inter-generational one. The significant critiques by Dalit feminists have included bringing to bear a focus on the 'upper'-caste and 'upper'-class nature of #MeToo (Dhanaraj, 2018; Pacharne, 2018). Critiques of the nature of feminist responses were also offered by 'younger' feminists, triggered by one particular public statement by 'older feminists' which was regarded as being in defence of 'due process' (referring to formal, institutionalised systems which investigate claims of violations) (Roy, 2018).

In terms of my own location, I live in New Delhi, India. At age fifty-six, I certainly am an 'older' feminist. I belong to what is considered to be an 'upper' caste. I have been part of what is known as the autonomous women's movement in the county for over thirty years. In India this refers to that part of the women's movement which is not linked to political parties. I have also been a queer activist. I am currently writing on issues of sexuality and politics from a psychoanalytic lens.

The purpose of the interviews, profile of respondents and key themes

The purpose of the interviews was to seek reflections regarding the feminist discourse around #MeToo in India, particularly through a feminist queer lens. The aim was to create a safe space and evoke reflections which have thus far not been able to be articulated in the public realm, including in online spaces. The respondents, whose very honest and generous sharing of insights form the core of this chapter, were known to me. I chose to interview feminists whom I knew because I felt that strangers might not trust me enough to share reflections about #MeToo, which could be considered controversial. The size of the sample was therefore deliberately small. A larger sample size with respondents who did not have this trust would not have been able to evoke the honest, critical reflections required for such an inquiry. The sample is clearly not meant to be representative, but reflective of certain concerns that the chapter tries to explore. Respondents were given the option of remaining anonymous and half of them chose to do so. For them I have used pseudonyms. All respondents were based in Delhi. Seven out of ten identified in ways that could be called queer. Details shared by them are as follows:

Aankhi: cisgender female, queer, scheduled tribe, thirty-seven years

Deepali: woman (female assigned at birth), heterosexual, upper caste, thirty-seven years

Dhamini: cisgendered woman, bisexual/queer, upper caste, thirty-four years

Pavel Sagolsem: gender queer (male assigned at birth), attracted to men, Meitei (dominant community in Manipur, Other Backward Caste), thirty-one years

Priti: woman (female assigned at birth), queer, upper caste, twenty-nine years

Priyanka: cisgender female, lesbian, upper caste, thirty years

Purnima: woman (female assigned at birth), bisexual, upper caste, forty-seven years

Saba: woman (female assigned at birth), heterosexual, upper caste, fifty-four years

Sharda: woman (female assigned at birth), 'straight queer' (sexual orientation so far is heterosexual and political orientation is queer), upper caste, thirty-nine years

Vishal: man (male assigned at birth), gay, Dalit, twenty-four years

In what follows, the reflections around #MeToo shared by respondents have been clustered around four themes. The first theme relates to problems of power. Offered here are concerns regarding the dangers of understanding the interplay of power and desire only along the lines of gender. The second theme relates to the question of justice. Here the reflections of respondents can be broadly articulated in terms of how the demand for justice in #MeToo was retributive rather than restitutive in nature. The third theme relates to feminism on social media. Here the concerns shared relate to how we, as feminists, interact with each other in digital spaces. The fourth and final theme relates not directly to what transpired in #MeToo but points to an important missing piece in the discourse – the realities of messy emotions and desires and the implications for consent.

First, a word on the strengths of the #MeToo movement. The space that #MeToo has created for women to speak about violations has been key. It has created space not just for young women but, according to Mary John (cited in Najib, 2019), also for 'older women who have tried to put the past behind them, have left their jobs or changed professions, and have spoken out years later from a position of relative security'. #MeToo has posed 'an open challenge to the pervasiveness of a culture that allows men to harass women, intimidate and exploit them, with impunity' (Feminism in India, 2018). According to Srila Roy, 'not since the gang rape and murder of a 23-year-old physiotherapy student in New Delhi at the end of 2012, has India witnessed such a surge of mainstream concern with sexual violence, rape culture, and patriarchy' (Roy, 2018). For Mary John, this 'public reckoning of workplace-based sexual harassment' has been accompanied by 'a willingness to believe women's accounts of trauma' (cited in Najib, 2019). Other than the impact on the discourse around gender and violence, feminists have also seen strengths of #MeToo to be in terms of the ways in which it has strengthened us as feminists. It has enabled the emergence of new faces in feminism 'who challenged the old guard of feminist ideology' and a consequent 'decentralisation of feminist ideas' (Thusoo, 2018). It has also 'allowed (a certain section of) women to come together and establish solidarity with each other against a common oppressor' (Vatsalya, 2019).

Much of what respondents shared about what they considered to be valuable about #MeToo in India resonates with the above. Reflecting on what #MeToo revealed about the workings of sexual violations and patriarchy, beyond the significance of individual cases, Deepali said: 'It's like the whole underbelly – hairy, smelly, puckered – of the world turned inside out. The visibilising and naming of behaviour that has always been normalized is amazing.' Second was the significance of #MeToo in terms of the role played by 'younger' feminists. For Sharda, one of the older respondents

(I am using the term 'older' to refer to those who were around or above the age of forty), while decades of activism by the older generation of feminists had contributed significantly to their being able to wage the current battle, in #MeToo, younger feminists had not needed to refer to them. Sharda's reflection resonated with my own experience. As someone who joined the autonomous women's movement at the age of twenty-one, although I felt extremely lucky and grateful to have experienced both comradery and mentorship by those in the movement who were older than me, even when we disagreed with them; the overall frame within which we worked, however, was one that had already been set by those older than us in the movement. In the #MeToo moment, younger feminists were challenging older feminists around core issues, including whether faith in institutional mechanism and due process was justified or not. The younger feminists were also challenging older feminists in terms of their (upper)-caste identity and the implications this had for their politics (Roy, 2018).

Another strength of #MeToo that emerged during the interviews was the tremendous reach made possible by social media. Purnima shared how she was in the market one day and heard a male shopkeeper say, 'MeToo se dar lagta hai' (I am scared of #MeToo). While she found jokes like this to be in bad taste, it showed her that sexual harassment was being recognised as an issue. Sharda spoke about what #MeToo meant for her mother (who did not identify as a feminist) who in her younger days was a nurse in the army but had to leave after the harassment that she had experienced from her seniors went unaddressed. She told Sharda that she wished #MeToo had happened then.

Despite these positive positions, various concerns regarding #MeToo emerged during the interviews. Respondents were uncomfortable with the ways in which we as feminists were understanding the interplay between desire and power, how we were responding to them, and the manner in which we were interacting with each other online about #MeToo. A running thread within these concerns is the perceived contradictions between feminism and queer feminism.

Problems of power

Several respondents felt much of the #MeToo discourse was under-pinned by limits in understandings of power. They pointed to the need to recognise specificities and multiplicities. According to Deepali,

> for all situations to be treated the same, the need to be on one side or another ... how is that possible when you're talking about power and sex and intimacy? There is the absoluteness of patriarchal power and its use and abuse; but there is also the fact that in sexual interactions the play of power is not absolute, linear and unidimensional.

One of the key issues that emerged during the interviews was that, in the context of #MeToo, power was often thought of only along one or, at best, two axes. It was also assumed that power flowed in one direction. Several respondents spoke in the context of the university. Regarding male teachers and female students, some respondents felt that there needed to be an openness to the possibility of consensual romantic or sexual dynamics across such a power divide. Sharda felt it was important to remember how many students and lecturers 'end up as partners or even get married'. Vishal, too, felt that the possibility of mutual desire cannot be ruled out, even in contexts in which there are inequalities of gender, age and roles: 'Of course there are many cases where the teacher has misused their power, but that story should not be a norm for all other experiences. What about those people who want to have a relationship with their professor? They will be left out'. He also wondered about the play of power and desire when the professor is a Dalit gay man or when both the professor and student are women. He argued that a more complex analysis needed to be undertaken. Priyanka felt this was particularly important in the space of academia, which is meant to be 'one in which all views should be acknowledged and addressed'. She also likened the current academic sphere, in which there is no space for such a diversity, to the online space in which also, specifically in the context of #MeToo, she felt that there was little space for debate. The contrast that the online space accords is an issue I will return to later in this chapter.

Priyanka even felt that we should step back from the immediate contemporary moment and recall Greek and Roman contexts, or our own Sufi mystic traditions, in which erotic bonds between the disciple and the teacher were key. Priyanka's reflection adds a newer dimension to the existing #MeToo discussions on the erotic dimension of the student–teacher dynamic. At present this has been limited to how dynamics can involve mentorship, the erotic nature of which lends itself to the teacher exploiting the student. Senior feminist V. Geetha (2017) has described this situation as harassment at universities 'where a young person is made to feel obliged to their mentor on account of the latter's avowed brilliance, political wisdom and rightness'. Priyanka's response draws attention to the possibility that mentorship can have an erotic dimension which is not necessarily exploitative.

So, what are the key aspects of power as it relates to desire that respondents are offering and what might these have to do with their queer location and/or queer perspective? I am teasing apart queer location and perspective here in order to include the significance of the life experiences of those who identify as LGBTQ as well the significance of queer in terms of political ways of understanding desire, whether or not they come from a location within the LGBTQ spectrum or not.

Whether from a queer location or perspective, there are two key aspects of the understandings of power as they relate to desire that emerged during the interviews. One is the recognition of the multiple ways in which power and desire can intersect, and the need to understand the specificities at work in any given situation. The second is an openness to the possibility of mutuality of desire even in contexts of inequality of power. With regard to the first, several respondents, including Pavel, Dhamini and Vishal, drew attention to the strong tendency in #MeToo to see the play of power and desire only along the lines of gender, or rather along the gender binary. LGBTQ as identity necessarily means that, at least with respect to sexual orientation, there is a recognition that there is another axis along which power can flow. Queer as a political perspective is further conducive perhaps to recognition that there are several other axes of power, and that power, particularly when in it intersects with desire, may flow in directions that are specific and unpredictable. A queer location also seems to enhance the ability to be open to recognising the possibility that mutual desire maybe be at play even in contexts in which, along one or more axis, there is inequality in terms of power. This is perhaps not surprising: for those of us for whom marginalised desires are core to our life experiences or identities, other than facing sexual consent violations, there is the reality that – even for desires experienced within the self that harm no one or for desires expressed and acted upon with mutual consent – desire itself becomes the basis of our marginalisation. An openess to the possibility of mutual, consensual desire is perhaps as it should be if one is coming to #MeToo from a queer location.

These responses call for an intersectional understanding of power that takes into account its multiple elements and shifting hierarchies, such as one expressed by Susan Watkins (2018: 74) when she writes that 'an effective feminist politics on harassment needs to recognise its differentiated landscape, varying horizontally, along the course of the life cycle, and vertically, in different social, class and racial situations'. Emily Owens takes us even further to recognise the centrality of power when she forcefully critiques feminist discourses on sexual violence for being limited to consent. Such a focus is premised on the promise of a liberal contract, 'regardless of historical precedent or contemporary institutional forms that curtail the same' (Owens, 2019: 150).

The question of justice

Many of my respondents raised issues around the nature of responses towards the accused within the #MeToo movement. Almost all respondents used the term 'retribution' to describe the manner in which the accused were being considered and several contrasted it with the term 'restitutive' to describe the nature of justice that they felt was more befitting of feminism or queer feminism. The way in which respondents tended to use the term 'retributive' was such that the punishments to them seemed excessive and non-transformatory in nature. The term retributive also referred to the manner in which the accused were constructed as not being capable of unlearning and re-learning, and what they described as a terrible kind of enjoyment in the delivery of justice. Although respondents did not detail what they would consider to be a restitutive approach to justice in #MeToo, some of the elements that were gestured towards included the need for efforts towards education regarding consent and including in such efforts men who might have been accused. With respect to complainants, an element in the vision of desired justice that was evoked by all respondents related to the critical importance of action which might help survivors heal. Relating what the respondents were offering as reflections on how they perceived the existing discourse on justice in #MeToo, they pointed to what they perceived to be inherent contradictions with feminism and queer feminism. These included the unstated assumption that consent is not an object of learning, but a given – that which you either have or do not have.

With respect to the nature of punishment, several respondents pointed to the absence of gradation of acts and claims of how the accused ought to be punished. They also spoke about the extent and length of punishment. In the academic context of which she is part, Sharda asked: 'Do you invite this person to events, do you quote their work, do you allow them to keep awards, do you socially ostracise?' She was not disputing these tactics so much as raising the question of 'for how long' and to what extent. Also, with regard to the academic context, Vishal pointed to the dangers of accusations that could 'scar for life' which, he argued, accusers do not need to explain and no one else is allowed to question. Other than the accused himself, Priyanka felt that it was 'heart breaking' to expect family members, including queer families, to shun the accused.

Several respondents were clear in their critique of the naming and shaming of aggressors. Sharda decreed it 'a double-edged sword', even if it has been used by feminists and other marginal identities in fighting unequal power structures. Some respondents located the current focus on retribution in the #MeToo moment in relation to earlier moments in the women's movement in India. These methods reminded Purnima of those used by rural women's groups she and I were working with in the 1990s – including blackening men's faces, making them wear garlands of shoes, seating them on donkeys and then parading them. The context was one in which there was acceptance of acute violence against women by the family and community as well as a hostile legal system. All of this culminated in desperate acts of collective and public forms of justice, which sought to disrupt public acceptance of this violence. Such acts of punishment were possible because the feminist discourse around violence against women at the time did not take account of the human rights of the perpetrators of violence; did not understand violence as an expression of patriarchy rather than only the fault of individual men; and did not yet recognise the need for a response to violence as a systemic phenomenon not limited to punishment of perpetrators. These perspectives later came to be central to the autonomous women's movement's engagement with violence against women. However, some responses in my interviews suggested that these elements had receded in #MeToo. For instance, Priti felt that the retributive nature of some feminist responses within #MeToo stood in marked contrast with the women's movement that she had known (her age, since it is relevant here, is twenty-nine), which believed in restitutive justice. An example she offered was the passion with which feminists opposed the death penalty for rape, including in the gang rape and fatal assault on twenty-three-year-old Jyoti Singh on a public bus in New Delhi in 2012. Other responses, too, suggested that there was a turn towards earlier feminist ways of understanding and responding to violence, marked by insufficient taking into account of the human rights of the perpetrators of violence; limits in understanding violence as an expression of patriarchy rather than only the fault of individual men; and responding to violence in terms of punishment of perpetrators rather than to violence as a systemic phenomenon.

An impassioned queer feminist critique of the naming and shaming of aggressors came from Dhamini. Naming and shaming, she said, 'is an all-too familiar reality' for LGBTQ folk. 'Shame is an integral part of our lives, and it is often reinforced by those closest to us, whether through the rejection we face by birth families, or the internalised homophobia of our queer partners'. She also felt that, as queer people, 'we owe each other an empathy that is missing in the heterosexual contexts we grow up in'. Making an important distinction, she said: 'This isn't a plea for condoning problematic behaviour, but a radical call to empathise and, thus, not repeat the same cycle of punishment – ostracisation/judgment/opprobrium – that the community as a whole is deeply familiar with'.

Other than the nature of the punishment, feminist responses were considered to be retributive in nature because of the manner in which the accused is constructed, which assumes that men are incapable of learning about consent. Disagreeing with such a view, Pavel suggested that 'we were not born feminist, we have become feminist'. Priti also felt that the focus on retribution ran counter to feminism, because 'feminism was about looking at subjects and how they have been produced by society'. As Priyanka explained, #MeToo discourse focuses overwhelmingly on the accusation: it is all about 'who done it', bordering on the sensational. Similarly, Vishal agreed that the person who puts out their story first will forever be the victim: 'Sadly it has become a war of cards now. Who has more victim cards is the one who wins: Queer, Dalit, Muslim ... – how many cards do you have? Throw them all and you are the winner.' From his location as a Dalit, gay man, he said: 'I can play the Dalit Queer cards too, but I don't want to'.

Some respondents also turned the lens inwards. Pavel, for example, reflected that there might be an unconscious guilt at work, and felt that in vociferously declaring others to be predators, there is an effort to sanctify ourselves. All of us, knowingly or unknowingly, have committed consent violations. If we were to honestly talk about these, the likelihood of others listening to us would be much greater. In this way, Pavel felt, the promise of introspection offered by #MeToo is yet to be fulfilled. Sharda saw guilt playing out in a different sense: 'The guilt about privileges that one has on certain accounts can sometimes be displaced on those who seem to be more privileged than ourselves'.

Some respondents made important observations about what seemed to them to be an excessive charge, in likening, for instance, #MeToo to 'leading mob lynching packs on cases where you have nothing remotely to do with sexual harassment'. Priti went further, saying: 'This is collective vindictiveness and there is pleasure associated with it. Ab humne dikha diya' (Now we have shown them).

Feminist exchanges on social media

Another problematic that emerged during the interviews was the aggression that sometimes marked how feminists engaged with each other in the digital space during #MeToo. Of particular concern was the fierce certainty with which claims were defended. The discourse held little room for diversity or dilemmas. As one respondent expressed it, not only was there the binary of 'for' or 'against' in terms of views, but this also soon turned into battle between those who are 'for us' or 'against us. This is an issue of considerable importance. It also relates to the reality that informs this chapter – the inability of the respondents to share these reflections in the public, digital realm for the fear of being judged and attacked. Why such fear? What is it about the digital space that is conducive to aggression?

In trying to understand aggression among feminists online, we need to go back to the need for certainty, which affects positions articulated online, as well as the glaring messiness of the realities of desire and power. Alongside the clarity that this is what happened is the firmness that this is the right view. The binaries of understanding imposed on the messiness of desire, consent and power continue into the binaries of views articulating online into right and wrong – the battlelines clearly drawn.

Beyond the immediacy of #MeToo, all respondents located the nature of the feminist discourse in the larger context in which online discussions were becoming increasingly aggressive. Priyanka felt that in online spaces, people were less interested in discussion and more interested in voicing their opinion: 'I have an opinion, hence I matter'. The opinions were typically in the nature of attacks and accusations, she said. Many of the respondents no longer engage in online exchanges of views, even if they read what others have written. Saba gave the example of the discussions around the burqa. The insistence from online interlocutors that she declare whether she was 'for' or 'against' the burqa was extremely frustrating for her, as it did not allow for an engagement with the complexities of gender and identity involved: 'Absolute positions become more and more absolute ... We need more complex conversations ... to go closer to the darkness ... If everything is neatly labelled bad ... then how do you deal with it?' Purnima shared her experience of such an exchange which became aligned along two camps of friends who then attacked her and each other: 'These were not only right-wing people but also people like us'.

Temporality is another feature of the digital space that makes it so conducive to aggression. For those engaged in online discussions around #MeToo, the temporality of the digital allowed an immediacy of expression, as though unfiltered (still subject of course to the control of corporates and the state). The pace, conducive to ferocity, left little room for reflection. More generally, too, it is as though the digital offers a quickness as an end in itself. The temporality of the digital also plays out by fixing in time what is said online. This is not conducive to our being able to change views. Respondents also drew attention to the incessant nature of the digital. Priyanka saw social media as 'the online beast that needs to be fed constantly'.

Temporality in the online space also means continuity – of pain for the one who makes the accusation; of stigma for the one being accused. To draw upon Pavel's description of our propensity in #MeToo towards 'fixing and fixating', the digital space is conducive to both. This relates to what emerged as a strong area of concern during the interviews – whether the online nature of #MeToo has helped survivors heal. Almost all respondents felt that while women were able to put their experience out there, healing was not taking place in the online space. Some went to the extent of saying that the online space worsened the possibility of healing. Vishal shared how anxious his friend became after sharing her story online because it did not get as many 'likes' as the story of sexual harassment shared by her friend. It felt as though the experience needed to be 'violent enough' in order to gain validation, which would perhaps never be enough. 'There is also a way in which the narrative online becomes you and you become the narrative. If that narrative is about violence, how will you heal?' As I listened to Vishal, I wondered whether we always necessarily want to heal. Perhaps we require a readiness to heal. Till we have it, the online space might keep us hooked. It is not unlike an addiction, Vishal added, explaining that Facebook, in particular, does not let you forget. One year later, it will literally remind you of what you had posted. In his own experience, some amount of forgetting is necessary in order to heal. Different respondents spoke of what they felt was needed for healing, including therapy and support groups.

Messy emotions, desires and consent

Shades of disappointment that #MeToo did not create the space for deeper conversations about consent, which take into account messy emotions and desires, were expressed by all respondents. The interviews created a space for a queer feminist critique of mainstream feminism's far-too-simplistic understanding of consent as it relates to sexual and romantic intimacies. Some respondents expressed the hope that #MeToo would open up the space to have conversations about consent that are more in sync with the messiness of the realities of sex and love. Whether articulated in terms of disappointment or hope, it is important to underline here that the reflections on consent offered by the respondents pertained to contexts of romantic or sexual encounters with known persons, lovers or partners, and not to contexts in which the person was a stranger or where there was no romantic or sexual interest in the other person. They do not, for example, relate to contexts such as consent violations in public spaces by strangers or by those in the workspace with whom there is no emotional or erotic connection.

One set of issues regarding consent that respondents felt required much greater discussion related to emotional difficulties, such as vulnerabilities and disappointments. Priyanka felt that there is a way in which, when a romantic sexual relationship ends badly, the narrative is often that it, including the sex, was 'all bad'. There is a homogenising of one's own experience, a flattening out at play. The vagaries of love have drawn the attention of too few feminists; Andrea Long Chu is one of the few who have engaged with its messiness. Reflecting on a line of the poem *Lady 45* by Robin Morgan – 'love is more complex than theory' – Chu draws our attention to 'people's attachment to things that are bad for them' (Chu, 2019: 75). Perhaps it should not come as a surprise to us that the irrationality of love can impact the ways in which we experience consent.

Vulnerability with respect to love or sex is all too familiar to us, including us, feminists. The question here is one of how well equipped anyone is to deal with vulnerability. Can we dare to lay ourselves bare to it? To the range of social and economic factors which influence vulnerability and our (in)ability to deal with it, Aankhi made an important addition. She spoke of the aggravating influence of our feminism, since it had always encouraged us to think, at least aspirationally, of ourselves as empowered, not leaving much room to acknowledge our vulnerabilities. In contexts in which we might not have the space to accept our vulnerabilities in love or our disappointments about sex, it can well be that consent violation provides us with the language to hold these otherwise difficult or sometimes impossible to articulate feelings and contradictions.

A second set of factors related to consent to which respondents drew attention related to attitudes towards sex. Despite being 'very modern', we might still be plagued by the idea that 'sex is sacred', said Pavel. Succumbing to those moments of passion with someone who might not be a spouse, a partner or even someone we know might well be followed by inner turmoil. The discomfort around whether to 'give in' to certain desires might be displaced and experienced as having had to 'give in' to the other person without consent. The notion that casual sex is 'bad' can be seen as a taboo that operates in a mainstream, sex negative, patriarchal context. As feminists, we might well feel that we are 'above' such conflicts. However, as Dhamini observed, as feminists, too, we are influenced by our own attitudes towards sex and love. The example that she gave related to the importance accorded to an accused man, if married. This, she felt, stems from a deeply conservative strain of 'this idea of the institution as sacred and the wife a victim of her husband's roving desire'.

A third set of issues around consent that emerged during the interviews related to messy desires. That feeling of being turned on without wanting to be turned on is not an easy place to be. It can also be confusing, including for what it means for consent. This difficulty is compounded by the sense that certain desires run counter to our values or our politics. For instance, if what turns me on is for my boundaries to be pushed, as a feminist I might well experience this as being antithetical to my feminist idea(l)s of dignity and mutuality. Whether such desires do indeed run counter to our politics is an issue which, unfortunately, is beyond the scope of this chapter. I have written about it elsewhere (Sharma, 2017).

In reflecting on the connections between the messiness of our desires, consent and our politics, I would like to draw, in particular, upon the responses of Vishal.

> For me it's very tricky. When I think in that flash of a second, I might have given consent, in a flash of second there were also moments when I didn't want it but it happened, but how do you demarcate, ok, this is what I consent to, this is what I don't consent to?

The BDSM practitioner and activist in me sprang up and said to him, 'the moment you don't like it, just use a safe word'. Vishal's simultaneous feelings of wanting and not wanting is what I term 'yummy yucky', particularly in the context of fantasies and porn (Sharma, 2019), a mix which challenges the neat binary on which consent is assumed to be based. Vishal also spoke about contradictions between our desires and our politics. From a queer male-bodied perspective, Vishal said that while as a feminist he knew that for women sexual harassment in public spaces was a violation, for him it was different: 'When someone paid … attention to me, it's the reverse. This is what I have been yearning [for] all my life'. It does not help matters when others judge the desires as being problematic.

> I went and I had sex, and the guy slapped me and I liked it. I came back and told my friend, 'you know, he slapped me'. Now, if my friend tells me, 'how can he slap you while you were having sex, that's such a violent thing to do' … If I get a similar response from everybody, after a while I also start thinking … ok, how can he slap me.

Vishal is pointing to the important interplay between how we feel about our desires and how others, including other feminists, might regard them.

Messy desire as an important aspect of consent in the realm of the romantic and/or sexual has not received the attention it ought to. Some welcome exceptions include Lauren Berlant and Lee Edelman (2014: vii) who see sex as a site in which 'relationality is invested with hopes, expectations, and anxieties that are often experienced as unbearable'. They also suggest that the experience of our psychic contradictions 'unsettles the fantasy of sovereignty' (Berlant and Edelman, 2014: viii). Drawing on these ideas, Brinda Bose and Rahul Sen (2018) argue, while commenting on India's #MeToo, that the site of sex or intimacy 'undoes us in unanticipated ways, taking away from us all markers of certitude, coherence, and stability'.

The respondents spoke about a lack of engagement with the messiness of our desires and its implications both in the context of feminism and queer feminism. Expressing her disappointment with feminism as a whole, Aankhi asked, given that our feminist mantra of personal is political, how it was that the #MeToo discourse had not taken into account the messiness of desires, which is so much a part of our lives? According to her, even queer politics is guilty of not recognising the messiness of desires: 'We think sexuality is fluid but not that it is also fuzzy'. This is surprising given the many challenges that queer politics poses to heteronormative binaries, including but not limited to the binaries of man–woman and homosexual–heterosexual. Queer politics has questioned and sought to subvert so much – notions of how things 'should' be, what is 'natural' and 'normal'; it has posited lived realities against how things seem to be – such as how happy is the 'happy family' that is built on, and strictly regulates, gender and sexual norms. Some strands of queer politics have also challenged the neat boxes of respectability that others in the LGBTQ spectrum have wanted to inhabit through same-sex marriage. One might expect, then, that queer feminism would be well placed to look through the yes–no binaries and to recognise the messiness of desire at play. Perhaps this potential does not translate because connecting with messy desires, particularly when they seem to run counter to our politics, is not a comfortable place to be. The discomfort in the realm of the personal might inhibit us from moving towards understandings of the messiness of desires in the realm of the political. The way in which discomfort might affect our understanding is, in fact, yet another affirmation of the feminist mantra of personal is political.

Understandings about the nature of desire are of course key to how we understand consent. In terms of more recent feminist discourses in the country related to consent, Aankhi said some thinking has begun which challenges the yes–no binary to include 'maybe' (Agarwal, 2017; Agents of Ishq, 2016). She felt that in the contemporary sex-positive feminist discourse, 'maybe' refers to situations in which the woman is trying to figure out the 'maybe' while the man waits. It is only a matter of time before she moves from 'maybe' to a clear 'yes' or 'no'. However, messy desires might entail greater inner conflict, which cannot simply be resolved in a matter of time. This inner conflict might mean that I am not able to consent to myself. By this I mean I may not allow myself to fully accept these desires and I also may not fully give myself permission to act upon my desires (see Sharma (2020) for a further discussion on the need to widen the existing paradigm of consent).

Conclusion

The queer feminist concerns related to #MeToo in India – whether with respect to the limits of existing feminists' understandings of the interplay of power and desire, the nature of punishment desired, the manner in which we as feminists have interacted with each other online, or the ways in which feminist understandings of consent need to take into account messy emotions and desires – constituted what respondents saw as inherent contradictions with feminism. Our mantra of personal is political should have stood us in good stead to connect with the specificity and multiplicity of the interplay with power and desire, as well as the messiness of emotions and desires in our own lives, to recognise these around us. Our feminism ought to have meant a much greater space for a diversity of views. The value we place on sisterhood should have made us think twice before we laid into each other, no matter how much we disagreed with the stand being taken by others on the feminist spectrum.

Although, as I said earlier, we as feminists are good at self-flagellation, this is neither desirable nor helpful. Perhaps we need to understand why it might be that the principles and values that are so precious to feminism can fall by the wayside and the need for binaries, certainty, retribution and aggression prevail. In the absence of such an understanding, we run the real and present risk of judging ourselves.

It is here, as I draw the conclusion of this chapter, that I would like to invite into this fray the feminist psychoanalytic thinker and writer, Jacqueline Rose. In looking critically at feminism from within, an important frame that Rose uses is that of psychoanalysis. She clarifies that it is not the individual psyche that she is referring to but the collective psyche. 'We are "peopled" by others. Our psyche is a social space', she writes (Rose, 2017: 72). In this space of the psyche Rose looks at sexuality, in particular, since it 'always contains an element beyond human manipulation, however free we think we are'. This is a valuable space because it is in the 'sexual undercurrents of our lives where all certainties come to grief'. Moving from the personal to the political, Rose sees the potential for a feminism which would have 'the courage of its contradictions' (Rose, 2014b). Failure she considers to be unavoidable and 'not to be seen not as the enemy but as the fully fledged partner of any viable politics' (Rose, 2011). Here she is in the company of psychoanalytic thinker Jacque Lacan whose 'Les non-dupes errent' roughly translates as 'Anyone who thinks she or he has got it right is heading down the wrong path' or 'Without mistakes, you are going nowhere'. The kind of feminism Rose calls for 'would accept what it is to falter and suffer inwardly, while still laying out – without hesitation – its charge-sheet of injustice' (Rose, 2014a).

The hope that animates this chapter with regard to #MeToo is precisely this. Can we collectively look within to see where we might have faltered in order to strengthen our feminism? Beyond the specificities of #MeToo in the Indian context, the hope is also that concerns and reflections raised in this chapter point to considerations that might be of some value more generally. The invitation here is for us as feminists to interrogate assumptions, even about the very nature of desire and power. The invitation is also to question retributive justice from a place of radical empathy. There is an urgent need, also, to look self-critically at the ways in which we, as feminists speak with each other online and to be alert to excess in our desire for certainty and to the aggression with which we defend it. Last but not least, the invitation is for us as feminists to focus our

energies on transformation and justice, where messiness, changeful-
ness and contradictions are not bad words but descriptions of life as
it pulsates within and around us.

With the rise of authoritarianism around us, the world over, and
its demise nowhere in sight, perhaps it is more important than ever
that our feminism, in its queer and other avatars, helps us to remain
collectively self-critical, to be open to the possibilities that messiness
offers, and to maintain a watchful distance from the delicious and
terrible sort of enjoyment that certainty and aggression today tempt
us all with.

Note

1 The term 'Dalit feminists' refers to feminists who are members of castes
 which are regarded as being 'inferior' in the hierarchy of the caste-based
 system that still very much stratifies India.

References

Agarwal, M. (2017). 'Understanding Consent beyond a "Yes" and a "No"',
 Feminism in India, 24 January. https://feminisminindia.com/2017/01/24/
 understanding-consent-beyond-yes-no/. Accessed 18 April 2020.
Agents of Ishq. (2016). 'The Amorous Adventures of Shakku and Megha
 in the Valley of Consent'. http://agentsofishq.com/a-lavni-about-con
 sent-the-amorous-adventures-of-megha-and-shakku/. Accessed 18 April
 2020.
Berlant, L. and L. Edelman. (2014). *Sex, or the Unbearable*. Durham, NC:
 Duke University Press.
Bose, B. and R. Sen. (2018). 'Liberal Vertigo, Eros and the University', Café
 Dissensus Everyday, 17 August. https://cafedissensusblog.com/2018/
 08/17/liberal-vertigo-eros-and-the-university/. Accessed 18 April 2020.
Chu, A.L. (2019). 'The Impossibility of Feminism', *Differences* 30:1,
 63–81.
Dhanaraj, C.T. (2018). 'MeToo and Savarna Feminism: Revolutions
 Cannot Start with the Privileged, Feminist Future must be Equal for All'.
 First Post, 18 November. www.firstpost.com/india/metoo-and-savarna-
 feminism-revolutions-cannot-start-with-the-privileged-feminist-future-
 must-be-equal-for-all-5534711.html. Accessed 10 January 2019.

Feminism in India. (2018). 'A Statement by Feminist Groups and Individuals on the Going #MeToo Wave in India', Feminism in India, 13 October. https://feminisminindia.com/2018/10/13/metoo-india-feminists-statement/. Accessed 10 January 2019.

Geetha, V. (2017). Sexual Harassment and Elusive Justice, 52:44, 4 November. EPW Engage. www.epw.in/engage/article/sexual-harassment-and-elusive-justice. Accessed 27 October 2020.

Najib, R. (2019). 'Rage, Uninterrupted', *Hindu Business Line*, 4 January. www.thehindubusinessline.com/blink/cover/rage-uninterrupted/article25908771.ece. Accessed 11 January 2019

Nazariya (Queer Feminist Resource Group). (2020). *Training Manual*.

Owens, E.A. (2019). 'Consent', *Differences* 30:1, 148–56.

Pacharne, S. (2018). '#MeToo and its Aftermath: Notes from the "Margins" of Lists that Name and Shame', *First Post*, 4 December. www.firstpost.com/india/metoo-and-its-aftermath-notes-from-the-margins-of-lists-that-name-and-shame-5619401.html. Accessed 9 January 2019.

Rose, J. (2011). 'What More Could We Want of Ourselves!' *London Review of Books* 33:12. www.lrb.co.uk/the-paper/v33/n12/jacqueline-rose/what-more-could-we-want-of-ourselves. Accessed 9 January 2019.

Rose, J. (2014a). *Women in Dark Times*. London: Bloomsbury.

Rose, J. (2014b). 'We Need a Bold, Scandalous Feminism', *Guardian*, 17 October. www.theguardian.com/books/2014/oct/17/we-need-bold-scandalous-feminism-malala-yousafzai. Accessed 18 April 2020.

Rose, J. (2017). *The Last Resistance*. London: Verso.

Roy, S. (2018). '#MeToo is a Crucial Moment to Revisit the History of Indian Feminism', *Economic & Political Weekly* 53:42, www.epw.in/engage/article/metoo-crucial-moment-revisit-history-indian-feminism. Accessed 24 October 2020.

Sharma, J. (2017). 'The Politics of Fantasy', *Kohl: A Journal for Body and Gender Research* 3:2. https://kohljournal.press/politics-of-fantasy. Accessed 18 April 2020.

Sharma, J. (2019). 'Porn not Erotica', *Plainspeak*, 1 July. www.tarshi.net/inplainspeak/porn-not-erotica/. Accessed 18 April 2020.

Sharma, J. (2020). 'Consent: Not just a No. Also about a Yes, and a Maybe. (Part 1)', Gender Question, *Hindustan Times*, 23 April. www.htsmartcast.com/episodes-listing/society-culture/gender-question-5018007/. Accessed 18 April 2020.

Thusoo, S. (2018). 'From #MeToo to #HerToo: A Feminist Review of 2017', *Wire*, 21 January. https://thewire.in/gender/metoo-hertoo-feminist-review-2017. Accessed 9 January 2019.

Vatsalya, P. (2019). On Sisterhood and Solidarity in Context of the "MeToo" Movement in India: Part II, Youth ki Awaaz, 25 August.

www.youthkiawaaz.com/2019/08/the-me-too-movement-in-india-sister hood-and-solidarity-ii/. Accessed 18 April 2020.

Watkins, S. (2018). 'Which Feminisms?' *New Left Review* 109, 5–76. https://newleftreview.org/II/109/susan-watkins-which-feminisms. Accessed 18 April 2020.

13

Fugitive aesthetics: performing refusal in four acts

Swati Arora

I don't want to die
With my hands up
or
legs open. (Putuma, 2017)

I write this on the winter solstice of 2019, as the darkness in the northern hemisphere slowly begins to recede, amidst an overwhelming feeling of rage and despair. The world is either burning or in mourning, trying to latch on to the last flicker of hope for the new decade.

The season of discontent that began with #MeToo highlighted the widespread misogyny and racism in everyday life. Perhaps those of us belonging to privileged class, caste and race are only now beginning to realise the everyday traumas experienced by Black womxn and womxn of colour from lower classes and castes. On 19 April 2019, a thirty-five-year old woman who worked as a junior court assistant at the Supreme Court of India accused the Chief Justice of India (CJI), Ranjan Gogoi, of sexual harassment in October 2018 (Yamunan and Sharma, 2019). She submitted a detailed report on how she and her family were being punished for refusing his advances. An internal committee that was formed to investigate the matter later absolved the CJI of all charges. More recently, Tarun Tejpal, the former editor-in-chief of *Tehelka* magazine was acquitted of all charges of raping his junior employee after a trial that lasted eight years, even though there are records of his confession of the crime in his email exchanges with the survivor (Baxi, 2021).

On 24 August 2019, Uyinene Mrwetyana went to the Clareinch post office, on the outskirts of Cape Town, to collect her mail. The man at the counter told her that the credit-card machine was not working and asked her to come back later in the afternoon. When she returned, the employee raped and murdered her, and dumped her burned body (Nombembe, 2019). Mrwetyana was nineteen years old and a student at the University of Cape Town. For weeks after this incident, thousands of womxn marched in the streets to show their fury and to demand an end to the growing femicide in South Africa. The convict, Luyanda Botha, was given three life sentences in the trial that followed.

Koleka Putuma's lines above, from her critically acclaimed book of heartfelt poetry *Collective Amnesia* (2017), painfully echo how Black womxn's lives continue to be framed by a close proximity to death. Rape culture and femicide is widespread in South Africa, with mostly Black and poor womxn as victims of sexualised violence (du Toit, 2014; Gqola, 2015; Lewis, 2009). While rooted in contemporary realities, Putuma's poetry also invokes the historical injustices suffered by Black womxn because of the history of colonialism and slavery. Perceived through the prism of an all-pervasive anti-Blackness, her body of work reflects on the fragments and paradoxes of Black citizenship – always distorted, forever fallacious. The refusal Putuma articulates is a refusal to perform victimhood, while simultaneously being aware of the inevitability of an undignified death. This is the curse of the present moment – the refusal does not offer any promises, for repair is illusory. What it does offer is a negotiation with the present – a way to articulate agency and find community through art, activism and performance.

The initial euphoria of the #MeToo movement is slowly beginning to disappear, but the narratives of brutal cases of sexualised violence are not. The celebration and visibility accorded to #MeToo in Euro-America when Alyssa Milano tweeted about it in 2017 overlooked the localised histories of feminist struggles in the global south; the present moment is a moment of its reckoning (Lukose, 2018). Perhaps it was because of the popularity of #MeToo that the junior court assistant in India was able to gather the courage to speak up against the CJI. But even after she submitted evidence, the legal system failed her. In South Africa, too, femicide continues as before, with vague promises and empty speeches made by the government every now and then.

This chapter originates from a place of anger and exhaustion. It is framed by a sense of urgency. #MeToo led to an interrogation of the framework of legal jurisprudence for its immediate relevance to contemporary feminist politics. The workshop on 'Injury and Intimacy' in February 2019 brought feminist scholars, activists and artists from India and South Africa together to consider the meanings of #MeToo in our local contexts, beyond and outside its viral movements in the global north. Springing forth from that workshop, this chapter is an attempt at imagining new languages of freedom and resistance through art and performance, outside and beyond the neoliberal state, as a way of imagining radical hope and practising solidarity.

The failure of legal support and crisis of care for womxn from marginalised communities in the aftermath of #MeToo has exhausted their faith in the state, a faith that was precarious to begin with. 'Perhaps #MeToo can become raw material for more textured (re)considerations of issues, an archive for art and other interventions', writes Lata Mani (2018). Following her prompt, my chapter is an attempt at foregrounding 'layered, intertextual, cumulative encounters with culture, power, narrative frames, pain, skin and soul' through various performances of #MeToo in India and South Africa (Mani, 2018). The body of archive it strives to create is in equal parts devastating and affirmative. 'Think[ing] with and through the intersectional and interstitial of experience', this chapter assembles a few of my thoughts on the different per-formances of refusal in the context of #MeToo in the two countries (Mani, 2018). Refusal by itself is a negation of the performance of victimhood, with a clear-eyed view of the realities of brutal, systemic oppression. I explore fugitivity as a mode of performing refusal in the work of contemporary artists and activists in South Africa and India, a refusal that is rooted in vernacular formations. I discuss the photography of Thandiwe Msebenzi and an art installation by Labohang Motaung in South Africa, and *Vanitha Mathil* (Women's wall), a human chain, and the Blank Noise community art project in India. I articulate what fugitive aesthetics might look like in the face of everyday violence and how it redefines activism and resistance in differing contexts. It translates into a performance of agency – conscious or unconscious political agency – and the finding of joy in a world that criminalises you. It is a form of underground rebellion because it is about refusing to play the role that the state expects of you. Sometimes fugitive aesthetics translate into rage that finds space and visibility in the streets; at other times, it is quiet and consistent and yet invisible on the surface. In the artistic practices discussed below, it is an unstable horizon of the political that cannot be easily contained within the definitions of visibility, recognition and rights.

In the absence of political recognition for precarious communities, Harney and Moten (2013) have called for a joyful celebration of a docile social life that refuses to conform to the idea of a traditional political subject. If the sphere of the political is irredeemably anti-Black, fugitive aesthetics refuse those conditions and coordinates of existence to create new ones. Fugitivity is not an escape or an exit; it is 'separate from settling', they say (Harney and Moten, 2013: 11). It is groundlessness, inaction, exile. After Harney and Moten, Tina Campt (2014) defined refusal as rejecting the big narratives of freedom, instead continuing to imagine – with hesitation and apprehension – ways of being in the world fraught with violence, ways that resist traditional definitions of resistance. Refusal is based on living in the breaks from perpetual wars on marginal lives and finding joy in communities. She highlights the tensions between flights of escape and creative practices of refusal that are nimble and strategic. Campt asks to bring attention back to the minutiae of life, as they are the structures in which we navigate the world.

Faced with the bitter disappointments of post-apartheid South Africa, young Black artists are reimagining the future of the country and their place within it. Their art and revolutionary thought, whether consciously or not, is expressed through vernacular discourses (see Livermon, 2020; Pather and Boulle, 2019). To insist on joy, friendship, sisterhood, community and celebration when the world repeatedly tells you otherwise is a fugitive act of radical politics. Fugitivity is a backlash against the hope promised but never fulfilled, a collective assertion of a corporeal vocabulary that signals a breakdown of the verbal language. Fugitive aesthetics is born from despair and yet imagines a collective future. It refuses state violence in all its forms. Instead of desiring legibility from a system that legitimises racialised capitalism, the artists and activists discussed below engage with and dwell in fugitive modes of existence and refuse belonging. Fugitive aesthetics are gestures of silence that invite us to dwell in the absences, in the withdrawal, incommunicability and flights of abandon and abstraction, while at the same time challenging their bodily erasure from political life.

How do we imagine and focus more attention on things that get overlooked, the artistic and everyday practices that are disruptive? The artists discussed below attempt to activate forms of thinking that exceed the limits of permissible and mobilise the quotidian that is contained by periphery. Their work echoes the painful histories of feminist struggles and leaves behind fugitive traces in the crevices of that history – the breaks that exist between the quiet everyday and spectacular revolutions.

Thandiwe Msebenzi

Thandiwe Msebenzi is a young artist who lives and works in Cape Town. She was born in Nyanga, one of the many townships built after the Group Areas Act of 1950, which reserved city centres, farms, beaches and mountains as White spaces, ghettoising Black citizens in townships on the edges of urban areas. In 2014 Msebenzi studied at the Michaelis School of Fine Art and her photographic work has featured widely in group exhibitions across South Africa. In 2017, she was invited to showcase her work at Documenta 14 and the Dutch Design Week. At present, she is finishing a Master's in Women's and Gender Studies at the University of the Western Cape and works out of the Greatmore Studios in Woodstock.

Her most recent solo exhibition, *Utata Ndiphotha Inwele* (My Father Plaits My Hair, 2019), opened on 10 April 2019 at Smith, a gallery in Cape Town.[1] In the exhibition, Msebenzi addresses the question of masculinity and gendered violence. She places her personal story and experiences at the centre of the narrative and complicates easy definitions of victimhood through her images. The title is inspired by the memory of her father plaiting her hair when she was a little girl, as reflected in the coterminous image (Figure 13.1). Growing up in a violent environment in Nyanga, masculinity was

Figure 13.1 Thandiwe Msebaenzi, *Utata Ndiphotha Inwele* (My Father Plaits My Hair), 2019.

conflated with aggressive violence and men who did not conform were ridiculed and isolated. The image of Msebenzi lying on her father's lap challenges the gendered norms she grew up with through tender evocation of 'soft masculinity' – a subject Msebenzi is also exploring in her Master's thesis. Similarly, the photograph *Usiya Nehobe* (Siya and his Pigeon) shows a pet pigeon sitting in the small of the neck of Siya, her nephew (Figure 13.2). With his back to the audience, the image captures the warmth, kindness and sensitivity of Siya, a lover of birds.

Msebenzi's body is at the centre of most of her images and tells her childhood stories. Violence is a recurring theme and gendered narratives of weakness and strength are complicated through juxtaposition. *Qula* (Stick Fighting) shows Msebenzi armoured with a stick in each hand, looking stern (Figure 13.3). Her grandmother used to hide weapons under her bed, carried them with her all the time and was adept at using them for self-defence whenever she felt the need. When a man laid claim to one of her cows, she challenged him to a stick fight that she eventually won and rightfully reclaimed her cow. *Phantsi Kwebhedi KaNompelo* (Under Nomphelo's Bed)

Figure 13.2 Thandiwe Msebenzi, *Usiya Nehobe* (Siya and his Pigeon), 2019.

displays the overarching fear that dominates women's life in her community (Figure 13.4). Msebenzi started taking photographs of weapons under beds after she learnt from her grandmother that this was a common practice among women. These weapons were meant to be a means of self-protection in the face of intrusion and attacks by men. The photograph is a close-up shot of weapons, placed in a row, which her friend's mother hid under her bed. As the legend has it, one of these weapons is identical to the one that was used to mutilate Black slaves as a punishment in the past. These sharp-edged weapons lie on a blue and white bedcover – the harshness of the metal juxtaposed with the soft background. This photograph complicates the notion of home as a safe space for womxn in their communities by drawing attention to the constant hyper-vigilance

Figure 13.3 Thandiwe Msebenzi, *Qula* (Stick Fighting), 2019.

and trauma that is contained within. It is not just public street spaces that are marked by sexualised violence against womxn; the bedroom is not free from it either.

Kwa Mpengempenge (In the Middle of Nowhere) is a series of photographs that shows Msebenzi dragging a bed across a field, after her grandmother told her that a woman had been raped while crossing it (Figure 13.5). Msebenzi juxtaposes the public and private again by placing the bed – a symbol of privacy and comfort – in the middle of the vast, open, 'dangerous' fields. Invoking anger, despair and strength, this photograph is a form of quiet protest, which explicitly addresses the rampant femicide in South Africa. Her refusal to give in to the patriarchal expectations of a docile and fearful life finds a vivid representation in this photograph. The act of dragging the bed across the field is also an act of taking up public

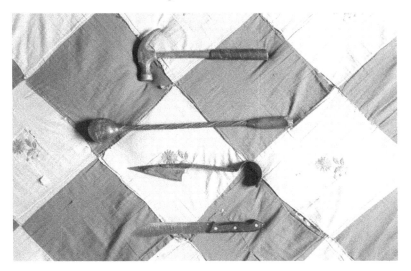

Figure 13.4 Thandiwe Msebenzi, *Phantsi Kwebhedi KaNompelo* (Under Nomphelo's Bed), 2019.

Figure 13.5 Thandiwe Msebenzi, *Kwa Mpengempenge* (In the Middle of Nowhere), 2019.

space that is otherwise not allowed to her. The lines in the mud drawn out as a result create a feminist map – a map that is not based on the masculine notions of flânerie as adventurous and exciting but an embodied experience of violence and trauma (see Arora, 2020).

Ndilindil (I Am Waiting) has Msebenzi seated on the bed in the same field, with her back to the audience, holding a pickaxe in her right hand (Figure 13.6). She is waiting to see who would attack her and is ready to defend herself. There is fear, anger and exhaustion but also an attempt to overpower those feelings with a quiet resolution. Movement and dwelling are present, simultaneously, insisting on lives that refuse regimes of violence and imagine 'new ways to live in the afterlife of slavery' (Sharpe, 2016: 18). The lack of action does not imply stagnation; the intention to wait is itself an act of defiance.

In *Listening to Images* (2017), Campt asks viewers to *listen* to the photographic images created by contemporary Black artists and to pay attention to the erotics of stillness and suspension. These images are haunted by the contexts of their production, she writes. They demand listening, not just hearing. The vocal frequency of these images possesses an intensity and intimacy that commands attention, a haptic relationality with the viewer. Attending to the complexity of the relationship between repetition and routine unveils a vernacular practice of affirmation and a demand for visibility. Msebenzi's photography is a fugitive practice that explores the quotidian as a

Figure 13.6 Thandiwe Msebenzi, *Ndilindil* (I Am Waiting), 2019.

site of rupture and refusal. Her images require an attunement to a world beyond what the vision permits in the first instance, to allow for a deeper connection with the artist. They conjure a possibility in everyday life and articulate a practice of refusal that negates victimhood. Being receptive to the hum of these images is a possible entry into the world in which they were created, to feel the political contexts they are haunted by. The politics and aesthetics of Msebenzi's photography dwells in a fugitivity by prompting its audience to pay attention to the concealed realities beyond the surface.

In the aftermath of #MeToo, sexualised violence has been a recurrent theme in Msebenzi's artworks. In 2017, her exhibition *Awundiboni – You Don't See Me* at the ORMS Cape Town School of Photography dealt with it in a more direct manner (Msebenzi, 2017). The tension between public and private spaces is a visible constant in her work. In the artistic statement for the exhibition, she writes:

> As much as this project is driven by women's fear of sexual violence in both public and private spaces, this work is also a celebration of resistance. It seeks to capture both the women's pain and trauma, but also their immense strength in the face of the sexual violence epidemic that continues to grip South Africa.

Msebenzi's photographs refuse victimhood to seek out quiet, meditative and creative ways of living while acknowledging the precarity of Black life.

Msebenzi continues to explore her engagement with the power of art and photography in addressing representations of gender and violence through her research. Her current work as part of her Master's centres her practice as a photographer while engaging with school students, to understand how the lived realities under the apartheid regime played a role in creating South African masculinities.

Labohang Motaung

Black hair is never 'just hair' – it is about female friendship and solidarity, about love and revolution and about owning one's rightful place in the world. When colonialism and racial capital-ism continue to thrive by fostering a disconnection between Black womxn and their bodies, perpetuating a beauty aesthetic that con-forms to having White skin and straight hair, Lebohang Motaung's *Formation* (2019) tells a different story. Black hair does not need to be straightened or misunderstood, it is a thing to be celebrated and loved, a means of forming and nurturing friendships with other Black womxn.

I witnessed Motaung's *Formation* on 2 May 2019 on my visit to the Youngblood Gallery in Cape Town. It was the first Thursday of the month, when art galleries in the city are free to the general public and open until late. Street spaces that are otherwise perceived as 'dangerous' and 'unsafe' for the middle classes are transformed into social hubs where an audience that would not normally venture into the city late in the evening or would be unable to afford tickets feels welcome. Consequently, the art works that are exhibited on these First Thursdays are chosen with care and political awareness.

Motaung is a young South African artist whose artistic career received a much-deserved boost when she won the Cartier Johannesburg Art Fair competition in 2017. She rose to popularity in 2019 after her installation art piece *Formations* went viral on social media. A trained hairstylist, she combines her braiding skills and artistic vision to tell everyday stories about ordinary women. In *Formations*, head shots of three Black women are arranged in a triptych, looking away from the viewer's gaze, flaunting their hair.[2] Their beautifully done braids hang down from different levels and are tied together in a knot that almost touches the floor. A simple gesture of braiding is an act of bonding between womxn; it creates a safe space where hairdressers and customers have long conver-sations while the hair is being braided. The connection between braids in *Formations* emphasises Black sisterhood and intimacy. Her Instagram page (lebohanglang) is a bounteous collection of her work, showing images of people whose hair she has plaited in real life. All the designs and patterns are her original ideas.

The topic of beauty and Black hair and what is considered acceptable and admirable has been a battlefield in South Africa. Reminiscent of Beyoncé's single *Formation* which invited solidarity for the Black Lives Matter movement and won the Grammy Award for best video in 2016, Motaung's installation draws attention to how South African history is fraught with anthropological perspectives on race, with its roots in biological determinism. Hairstyling practices on the African continent have changed with colonial trajectories, class hierarchies and growth of urban city centres. Influence of the Western ideas of beauty, promoted by the European civilising mission, encouraged hair straightening to acquire social validation in the early twentieth century (Biaya, 1999; Mercer, 1994). Following the Black Power movement in the 1960s in the US, 'Black is Beautiful' became the guiding motto and afro hairstyles became a mode of cultural resistance against White beauty ideals (Kelley, 1997). The Black consciousness movement, strongly rooted in African traditions, rejected all forms of hair modifications as imperialist.

For Zimitri Erasmus (2000), this binary between natural afro as radical, and straightened Black hair as conservative, promotes an essentialised relationship with Black hair that continues to use Western standards of beauty as a reference point. The time spent on straightening one's hair at the weekend, in the company of other womxn, was an opportunity to create a 'gendered cultural space of intimacy' (Erasmus, 2000: 5). The process of tending to one's hair became an important ritual and a site of self-care away from the male gaze; White ideals of beauty were irrelevant. For bell hooks (1995), this time spent with other women was also a space to understand and acknowledge desire by tending to one's body, signalling a journey from girlhood to womanhood.

Motaung's journey as an artist began as a hairstylist, where she experienced the power of intimacy that hair salons fostered in Johannesburg. Finding joy in creating community and a strong sense of self in other womxn motivated Motaung to pursue this craft as an art form. Exploring Black identity in her installations, Motaung portrays ordinary womxn with ordinary desires while focusing on self-expression as an empowering motif in her work. Her installations are rooted in finding ways of creating a strong relationship with one's self, without referring to White standards of beauty.

Black womxn have always exercised power and choice through hairstyling practices, but the art of braiding has been incorporated into surveillance regimes and is increasingly done to 'control' hair today (Banks, 2000). Discrimination based on hair disguises inherent racism and colonial ideas of beauty in contemporary schools and classrooms. As recently as 2017, Windsor House Academy in Johannesburg came under scrutiny after one of its headmistresses asked around ten Black girls to leave after labelling their braids inappropriate. The previous year, students at Pretoria High School were told not to have 'untidy afros' and forced to chemically straighten their hair (Giard, 2016). With its long history of apartheid, discrimination based on skin colour and ethnicity runs deep in South African society and Motaung's installation is a significant intervention that causes a rupture in its hegemonic racist aesthetics.

The relationship with afro hair is never without contradictions, but it is always about complex journeys of self-acceptance and growth for Black womxn. In her fascinating book *Don't Touch My Hair* (2019), Emma Dabiri writes about the tiring, time-consuming and expensive process of chemical straightening that she grew up subscribing to. Having grown up in Ireland to a Black Nigerian father and a White Trinidadian mother, Dabiri had a difficult relationship with her curls and the book is her journey of acknowledging and celebrating them. Refusing to chemically straighten the coils was a political decision she made to re-establish a connection with her body and the natural world. Black hair as a symbol of power and heritage is also a subject for Lucinda Roy's poem 'If You Know Black Hair' (1988). Born to a Jamaican father and British mother, Roy writes about the complexity of relationships that are passed down through one's hair.

> If you know, you really know black hair,
> the way it feels like bunched-up cloud
> or dense-packed candy floss,
> If you know, you really know the smell
> of milky coconut easing through
> the careful braids or the relaxed curls
> of women just as bold with chemicals
> as all the white girls with their tightly perms,
> if you know all this, then you know
> that there is nothing softer sweeter tougher
> than black hair.

Similarly, by celebrating cultural identity and self-worth, Motaung shows how owning and embracing Black hair is a revolution in itself. Her aesthetics highlight a blueprint for resistance that is quietly grounded in building a strong relationship with one's body. Motaung's refusal is grounded in sisterhood and community and is a rejection of racial capitalism's standards of beauty. Her use of labour for aesthetics and bonding with other women is a refusal of performing gendered labour for capitalism.

Vanitha Mathil

> returning daily from the marketplace
> both the fish and she share
> the same path –
> the one through the back door.
> entering through the very same route,
> while hearing the television
> blare the pledge aloud on August 15 –
> all Indians are my brothers and sisters. ('Wasteland', Chirappad, 2015)

What does refusal look like when it challenges the upper-caste hegemony of the state? What form does resistance take when questions of faith and tradition are challenged for their violence? What is the significance of occupying the streets and partaking in its pleasures and perils?

In the state of Kerala in southern India stands the temple of Sabarimala, dedicated to the celibate Hindu god Ayyappa. The site is the destination of one of the largest annual pilgrimages in the world, inviting forty to fifty million devotees each year. But for decades, girls and womxn aged between ten and fifty were barred from entering the temple premises because of the belief that allowing menstruating womxn inside the temple would be disrespectful to the deity. A landmark Supreme Court ruling in September 2018 overturned the tradition when, responding to a twelve-year-old public interest litigation, it decreed that accessing the temple was every Indian's constitutional right to religion. The ruling was a powerful challenge to the centuries-old Brahmanical hegemony that perpetuates itself based on caste and class exclusions.[3]

The Supreme Court ruling of 2018 was not received well. Huge counter-protests erupted when upper-caste men, incited by the Rashtriya Swayamsevak Sangh (RSS), the volunteer paramilitary group of the ruling right-wing Hindu nationalist Bharatiya Janata Party (BJP), blocked the temple as womxn tried to enter after the verdict. In the run-up to the national elections in the summer of 2019, the BJP tried appealing to the more liberal section of the Indian populace by including women's rights in its agenda (Krishnan, 2020). The irony of campaigns like *Beti bachao Beti Padhao* (Save the Daughter, Educate the Daughter) and Selfie with Daughter[4] could not be more evident. Kavita Krishnan's detailed analysis of these campaigns shows how their underlying patriarchal language and ideology continues to paint daughters as a burden until they prove themselves to be good wives, mothers and daughters-in-law. Moreover, the issue of women's rights becomes synonymous with increased surveillance and limiting access to public spaces in the name of protection and safety (see the discussion on Blank Noise in the next section). RSS's violent attacks at Sabarimala is only one example of BJP's fight to consolidate its sexist and casteist Hindutva agenda despite its rhetoric of women's development and empowerment.

On 1 January 2019, around three million women, cutting across class, caste and religion, formed a 620 kilometre-long *Vanitha Mathil*, translated as a women's wall, running from Thiruvananthapuram in the south to Kasaragod in the north of Kerala – a 'model' state in south India with a communist government in power at the regional level. Organised by the ruling Left Democratic Front government in the state with the support of other left-leaning organisations and leadership of lower-caste communities, the human chain protested gender discrimination and state repression. Various sections of society, including students, homemakers, daily-wage labourers and domestic cleaners, as well as famous writers, artists, local ministers and political representatives, participated. The event garnered massive media coverage and was supported enthusiastically by activists nationwide.

Although Kerala became the first state to elect a communist government in 1957, hierarchies based on caste continue to run very deeply. Its efforts surpass those of the BJP government, but Kerala has not furthered gender or caste equality as much as it could. Caste hierarchies are entrenched in the state: caste-based community is stronger than community based on national identity because of the intertwined histories of caste, class and land ownership (see Menon, 1994; Mokkil, 2019). The state does not follow the common four *varna* systems but considers the landlords, Nambudiri Brahmins, as the highest caste and the rest as low castes. Even Iyers – otherwise a high caste – are considered as low caste by Nambudiri Brahmins. Born in Kerala, Chirappad's poetry exposes these hierarchies by highlighting the contradictions and complexities of the state that lays claim to modernity because of its highest literacy rates. The irony in her poem 'Wasteland' is self-evident: the constitution of India grants equal rights to all citizens, but the terrain of gender, caste and sexuality is fraught with violence. The economic, social and psychological wounds of Dalit women render them almost invisible (see Anil 2016; Priya, 2018).

Acknowledging Kerala's complex histories, Navaneetha Mokkil (2019: 6, 200) has argued against grand narratives of 'a quick transition from silence to celebration' and asks that attention be paid to 'flickering moments that cannot be reified'. The event of *Vanitha Mathil* speaks to the lines by Dalit poet Vijila Chirappad above, in their refusal to comply with the gendered and casteist regimes of religious and patriarchal violence. *Vanitha Mathil* was a significant event, which was able to overcome centuries-old caste-based hierarchies – even if temporarily – in the hope of an inclusive society. Sabarimala is now etched in public memory as a site of struggle for gender equality. The memory of collective action created history that is not limited to the written document but is embodied in the form of a 'repertoire' (Taylor, 2003: 20). *Vanitha Mathil* allowed for ways of knowing and being that are grounded in intimacy, participation and connection. Thinking through this event on the basis of Dwight Conquerwood's three *i*'s, this performance of refusal was a work of *imagination*, a pragmatics of *inquiry* and a strategy of *intervention* (Conquerwood, 2002: 152). Coming from varied castes, classes and religions, these women were not the everyday face of protest in metropolitan cities in India and the noise their protesting bodies made continues to 'echo' and reverberate in collective memory (Schneider, 2011: 105), reminding us that feminist struggles take different shape and forms in different spaces.

Circulating as 'reappearance and reparticipation' (Schneider, 2011: 101), performance challenges loss of such moments of collective joy and community.

Chirappad uses poetry as a site of performance of caste and gender to undo all the essentialised narratives of equality and highlight the multiple oppressions that Dalit women experience. Womxn in her poems are not those who are adorned in silk sarees waiting for rain and pining for their lover but womxn who get their feet dirty walking through potholes, earning a daily living. Evoking images of the absence of wealth and other material comforts, confinement to domestic spheres, inhabiting the streets for survival is not a lamentation of a lack but an active effort in Chirappad's poetry to tell the overlooked stories of Dalit women who live in the margins.

> In our home
> there is no TV
> no fridge
> neither mixer
> nor grinder
> no LPG
> not even an iron-box.
> yet my mother knew
> how to operate these
> much before I did.
> because
> like in Madhavikutty's stories
> and the novels of MT
> she is Janu –
> the servant. (Chirappad, 2009)

Chirappad refuses the grand narratives of equality that the state lays claim to and provides an embodied narrative of herself and other Dalit womxn in her community. The quotidian is a site of struggle as well as a source of community.

Blank Noise

The aesthetics of refusal took the form of rest and non-productivity in an initiative by Bangalore-based feminist performance collective

Blank Noise. Formed in 2002 by Jasmeen Patheeja, then a design student at the Srishti College of Art, Design and Technology, Blank Noise uses creative public intervention strategies carried out by young, middle- and upper-class urban women. They started out by calling themselves 'Action Heroes', but now identify as Action Sheroes / Action Theyroes / Action Heroes.[5] Their campaigns and urban projects revolve around female desire to occupy the city without fear. The creative interventions run by Blank Noise were the first of their kind in India and their work has gained an increasing urgency since #MeToo. Blank Noise uses social media to invite testimonies and encourage participation across different cities in India. Their campaign, *Being Idle* (2006), encouraged women to stand idle in public spaces. Blank Noise had collected testimonials of street harassment though their Blogathon in 2006, where several bloggers had shared their experiences of street harassment. These anonymous stories were handed out to strangers on busy streets in the form of bilingual letters titled Dear Stranger, with the hope of inviting solidarity and connection (Figure 13.7). Another campaign,

Figure 13.7 *Being Idle* (2006), a campaign by Blank Noise encouraged women to stand idle in public spaces while they handed out testimonies of street harassment in the form of letters to the strangers they encountered.

I Wish, invited women to share their dreams for a more inclusive city, which were then enacted in a public park.

The campaign *Meet to Sleep* (2018) invited women to sleep collectively in parks. Participants bring rugs and sleep on the grass or on benches (Blank Noise, 2018). They are encouraged to take photographs to share on their website, and Facebook and Twitter pages. The photographs portray women looking directly into the camera, sprawled on the grass, smoking in public spaces, wearing risqué clothes – images that are not routinely associated with 'respectable' womanhood in India. The question of women's mobility in India has acquired a widespread currency following Shilpa Phadke, Sameera Khan and Shilpa Ranade's *Why Loiter?* (2011), which encourages women to take risks in order to experience pleasure on the streets, and has intensified since the anti-rape protests in Delhi in 2012. The initiative challenges BJP's discourse of limiting women's access to public spaces in the name of protecting them by calling on women to take risks for their *azaadi* (freedom) and to loiter on the streets.[6] Blank Noise's initiatives encourage women to refuse the position of victim and assume agency through performative action, and the drive to occupy urban spaces has become increasingly popular (see Arora, 2019; Lieder, 2018; Mani, 2014; Phadke, 2013; Phadke et al., 2011).

While earlier waves of women's movements in India focused on legal reform to counter sexual violence, many of the women who participate in Blank Noise's interventions have adopted a 'do-it-yourself grammar which lays claim to equality as entitlement and seems not to use the vocabulary of women's rights', writes Mitra-Kahn (2012: 113). The focus on individual agency without recourse to legal measures is reflective of India's turn to neoliberalism, argues Hemangini Gupta (2016: 153), where 'individuals are exhorted to take responsibility for themselves and to produce themselves as entrepreneurial citizens'. The circulation and consumption of these images feeds further participation from women with similar middle- and upper-class backgrounds.

In the times of #MeToo, racial capitalism and xenophobia across the world, artists and activists are increasingly exhausted. As the #MeToo movement gained popularity across the globe and womxn began to share narratives of sexual harassment on social media, they also faced having to deal with the male perpetrators either outrightly denying the act or further traumatising the survivor with threats and court cases. The demands for organising, protesting in the streets and shouting slogans overlooks the fatigue it produces in minoritarian bodies. Every act of making the world a little safer requires the emotional labour of making others aware of the different forms of marginalisation and oppression. *Meet to Sleep* challenges – and refuses – the labour required to gain legitimacy and visibility in the eyes of the state by refusing to participate in the economy of production and reproduction. Women's labour, mostly unpaid or underpaid, contributes to the functioning of racialised capitalism; withholding that labour by choosing rest and community is a fugitive practice that ruptures the system. The insistence on rest and sleep, care and mental health is seldom seen in art works of Black and Brown womxn, even when the focus on self-care has become central to resistance vocabularies in White (online) communities. By highlighting inaction and non-productivity, this initiative refuses the capitalist regimes of violence that consume women's bodies. The angularity of the body, existing at 180° instead of the upright 90°, is also a fugitive tactic – a movement that is neither upright nor linear and refuses visibility to the ever-present male gaze.

Meet to Sleep, like all Blank Noise initiatives, focuses on access to the outdoors: gathering women together to loiter, chat and sleep at odd hours of the day, when they would otherwise not be out on the streets. Their practice finds resonance with Msebenzi's photographs as they seek to articulate different forms of quiet resistance outdoors. Loitering on the streets is deemed unrespectable and therefore prohibited for middle- and upper-class women, who invariably belong to upper castes; women from lower classes and castes have always had to use the streets for economic reasons. Domestic workers, sex workers, fruit sellers, financially poor women always inhabit – and, in fact, have to endure – the extremities of the streets: to sleep, rest, earn their daily wage, and to support themselves and their families. The presence of working-class and lower-caste women does not invite surprise or disgust since the urban outdoors has always been their source of survival. When middle-class women attempt to access public spaces as an act of defiance during a performance event, the radicality of the initiative is already defined – and bound – by the temporary nature of that desire (Arora, 2019). After two hours, the participants return home to their comfortable beds. But the homeless poor and the sex workers have no such hope. This mode of 'occupying' the urban through sleeping outdoors, construed as a radical and liberating act, overlooks the concerns of minority women who belong to different castes, religions and socio-economic backgrounds, and who inhabit public spaces in very different ways – either out of 'compulsions of economics' or due to dire infrastructural gaps like lack of toilets (Chatterjee, 2011: 170). Collective participation in sleeping by privileged women also excludes how, under Brahmanical patriarchy, middle- and upper-class women can rest while lower-class and lower-caste women must work.

An upsurge in similar artistic groups and urban interventions across the country in the previous decade, like *Pinjra Tod, Women Walk at Midnight, Take Back the Night* reveals an impatience with the legal reform practices of the state, which have never displayed their solidarities with the feminist movement, leading to digital movements like #MeToo. The imaginations and hope of these young artists are the struggles of Indian feminists after independence. Despite their exclusions at the beginning, these groups are consciously trying to adopt an intersectional approach to their art and activism by trying to be more inclusive (Krishnan, 2020; Lieder, 2018; Roy, 2016). Their dreams of a better future are rooted in a refusal of the patriarchal state and its restrictions in the name of protection and safety, and an insistence on community.

Performing refusal/refusing to perform

'Political vernaculars untethered to the state can help us imagine how we want to live with each other', writes the Kenyan writer Keguro Macharia (2016). 'They create possibilities for different ways of coming together – from short-lived experiments to long-term institution building – and they also impede how we form ourselves as we-formations, across the past, the present, the future, and all the in-between times marked by slow violence and prolonged dying', he says. The four examples discussed above are instances of creative strategies of resistance that are rooted in the quotidian. Each of the artists have imagined a version of fugitive practice that allows for freedom through disobedience.

Sara Ahmed (2010: 592) writes that 'revolutionary forms of political consciousness involve heightening our awareness of what there is to be unhappy about'. Amia Srinivasan (2018: 126), drawing on Lorde, has noted that anger is 'a means by which women can come to better see their oppression'. When we pay attention to modes of action that render certain bodies legible and minoritarian bodies illegible, we realise how the state shapes the lives of Black and lower-caste womxn differently from privileged White, upper-class, upper-caste womxn. But the right to rage and unhappiness is not available to minoritarian subjects who are 'already stereotyped as rageful, violent, or shrill' (Srinivasan, 2018: 136). A 'collective subject', writes Silvia Federici (2018), recognises the collective need for care and mutual support, and refuses the false promises of repair and inclusion offered by patriarchy and racialised neoliberal capitalism. The four artists discussed above argue for a more expansive sense of feminist agency in joy, play and fun – countering the historic ways in which women in the global south have been produced through the lens of development and poverty alone. Rage and anger have always marked the tired bodies of womxn from marginalised communities, but these artists from India and South Africa offer a range of more affirmative affects.

The artists engage in a performance of refusal, which exceeds the textual and the verbal. These imaginative acts defy the delayed and partial justice in that they offer an alternate feminist response outside and beyond the legal jurisprudence system – which favours the upper-class, upper-caste, White, heteronormative subject – and allow for the creation of communities and solidarities rooted in 'a riskier hermeneutics of experience, relocation, copresence, humility and vulnerability: listening to and being touched by the protest performances' (Conquerwood, 2002: 148). They chronicle the everyday forms of inaction, non-productivity, stillness and sisterhood as a structural critique as well as a flight of survival. Msebenzi's photographs are powerful meditations on Black life and survival while refusing the victimhood that is expected from womxn, challenging aggressive notions of masculinity with the delicacy of the images; Motaung's playful renditions of Black hair inspire a revolutionary relationship with one's body – she refuses to perform her labour for racialised capitalism but insists on care and beauty in her work; Vijila Chirappad's poetry and *Vanitha Mathil* refuse to comply with the gendered and casteist regimes of political violence that the state demands; and Blank Noise's *Meet to Sleep* initiative refuses the capitalist logic of labour and productivity by centring rest and community – it asks its participants to pause and slow down amidst the rising decibels of protest marches. Attempting a festivity of fugitivity, as it were, these artistic endeavours invite us to participate in a mode of being in the world that allows for articulating a relationship to ourselves, to one another and to the world in which we live, in tender ways, beyond and against the demands of the racialised, capitalist and patriarchal state.

Acknowledgements

Many thanks to Srila Roy and Nicky Falkof for their helpful comments on the initial drafts of this chapter. Thanks also to the Department of Women's and Gender Studies at the University of the Western Cape for supporting me with an Andrew W. Mellon Fellowship, which facilitated this writing (Grant G-31700714).

Notes

1 The link to Thandiwe Msebenzi's solo exhibition, *Utata Ndiphotha Inwele* (My Father Plaits My Hair, 2019) at Smith Gallery: https://smithstudio.co.za/utata-undiphotha-inwele-thandiwe-msebenzi. Accessed 30 September 2019.
2 Lebohang Motaung's *Formations* (2019) is available to view here: https://sacreativenetwork.co.za/2020/04/creating-works-of-hair-art-with-lebohang-motaung/. Accessed 24 July 2020.
3 Earlier that year, organised religion had already come under the purview of #MeToo when a nun from Kerala accused Catholic Bishop Franco Mulakkal of raping her multiple times between 2014 and 2016. The key witness in the case, Father Kuriakose Kattuthara, was eventually found dead (*Economic Times*, 2018).

4 Prime Minister Narendra Modi launched the Selfie with Daughter campaign to counter the rising numbers of female foeticide and sex selection practices in the north Indian state of Haryana, which became popular in the country. Eventually, Selfie with Daughter was launched as an app to encourage people to send their photographs and create an archive. See the Selfie with Daughter Foundation, http://selfiewithdaughter.world/Default.aspx. Accessed 15 October 2020.

5 The website of Blank Noise has more information about their campaigns: www.blanknoise.org/home. Accessed 2 December 2020.

6 Since the election of Narendra Modi as the prime minister in May 2014, regressive campaigns like the love jihad campaign and the anti-Romeo squad across north India have been prevalent, intensifying, in particular, since the appointment of hard-line Hindutva advocate Yogi Adityanath as chief minister of Uttar Pradesh in March 2017. The love jihad campaign is run by Hindu right-wing groups against what they say is a Muslim conspiracy to convert Hindu girls to Islam by feigning love. The anti-Romeo squad seeks to 'protect' women from suspected youths who harass them. For this, the ruling BJP trains scores of Hindu men who patrol public spaces to prevent the freedom of movement and expression of women, in the name of Hindu nationalism.

References

Ahmed, S. (2010). 'Killing Joy: Feminism and the History of Happiness', *Signs* 35:3, 571–94.

Anil, C.M. (2016). 'For all its Communist History, Casteism is inherent in Kerala society: Dalit poet Vijila Chirappad', *The News Minute*, 18 April. www.thenewsminute.com/article/all-its-communist-history-castei sm-inherent-kerala-society-dalit-poet-vijila-chirappad-41828. Accessed 21 October 2021.

Arora, S. (2019). 'Walking at Midnight: Women and Danger on Delhi's Streets', *Journal of Public Pedagogies* (4). https://doi.org/10.15209/jpp. 1186.

Arora, S. (2020). '*Walk* in India and South Africa: notes towards a decolonia and transnational feminist politics', *South African theatre Journal* 33.1, 14–33.

Banks, I. (2000). *Hair Matters: Beauty, Power and Black Women's Consciousness*. New York: New York University Press.

Baxi, Pratiksha. (2021). 'For the Judge, It Was a Feminist Who Was on Trial, not Tarun Tejpal', *The Wire*, 29 May. https://thewire.in/women/for-the-judge-it-was-a-feminist-who-was-on-trial-not-tarun-tejpal. Accessed 30 May.

Biaya, T.K. (1999). 'Hair Statements in Urban Africa: The Beauty, The Mystic and The Madman', *Codesria Bulletin* 1–2, 32–8.

Blank Noise. (2018). *Meet to Sleep*. www.blanknoise.org/meettosleep. Accessed 29 December 2019.

Campt, T. (2014). 'Black Feminist Futures and the Practice of Fugitivity', Helen Pond McIntyre '48 Lecture, Barnard College, 7 October. bcrw.barnard.edu/blog/black-feminist-futures-and-the-practice-of-fugitivity. Accessed 30 August 2019.

Campt, T. (2017). *Listening to Images*. Durham, NC: Duke University Press.

Chatterjee, D. (2011). 'Dalit Women and the Public Sphere in India: In Pursuit of Social Justice', in *Dalit Rights/Human Rights*, Chap. 7. Jaipur: Rawat Publications.

Chirappad, V. (2009). 'She Who Flew Ahead', in *Amma Oru Kalpanika Kavitha Alla* [Mother is not a Poetic Figment of our Imagination]. Thiruvananthapuram: Maithri Books.

Chirappad, V. (2015). 'Wasteland', in *Pakarthi Ezhuthu* [Copied Notes]. Kerala: Chintha Publishers.

Conquerwood, D. (2002). 'Performance Studies: Interventions and Radical Research', *The Drama Review* 46:2, 145–56.

Dabiri, E. (2019). *Don't Touch My Hair*. London: Allen Lane.

du Toit, L. (2014). 'Shifting Meanings of Postconflict Sexual Violence in South Africa', *Signs* 40:1, 101–23.

Economic Times. (2018). 'Witness against Bishop Franco Mulakkal in Nun Rape Case Found Dead', *Economic Times*, 22 October. https://economictimes.indiatimes.com/news/politics-and-nation/priest-key-witness-in-kerala-nun-rape-case-found-dead/articleshow/66314756.cms. Accessed 8 December 2020.

Erasmus, Z. (2000). 'Hair Politics', in *Senses of Culture: South African Cultural Studies*, edited by S. Nuttall and A. Michael, 380–92. Cape Town: Oxford University Press.

Federici, S. (2018). *Re-Enchanting the World: Feminism and the Politics of the Commons*. Toronto: Between the Lines.

Geetha, V. (2017). 'Sexual Harassment and Elusive Justice', 52:44, 4 November. EPW Engage. www.epw.in/engage/article/sexual-harassment-and-elusive-justice. Accessed 27 October 2020.

Giard, Lelouch. (2016). 'Hair Trends and Racism in South Africa'. *South Africa Today*, 1 September. https://southafricatoday.net/south-africa-news/gauteng/hair-trends-and-racism-in-south-africa/. Accessed 20 August 2019.

Gqola, P.D. (2015). *Rape: A South African Nightmare*. Johannesburg: MFBooks Joburg.

Gupta, H. (2016). 'Taking Action: The Desiring Subjects of Neo-Liberal Feminism in India', *Journal of International Women's Studies* 17:1, 152–68.

Harney, S. and F. Moten. (2013). *The Undercommons: Fugitive Planning and Black Study*. Wivenhoe: Minor Compositions.

hooks, b. (1995). 'Straightening our Hair', in *Identities: Readings from Contemporary Culture*, edited by A. Raimes. Boston: Houghton Mifflin.

Kelley, R. (1997). 'Nap Time: Historicizing the Afro', *Fashion Theory* 1:4, 339–52.

Krishnan, K. (2020). *Fearless Freedom*. Delhi: Penguin.

Lewis, D. (2009). 'Gendered Spectacle: New Terrains of Struggle in South Africa', in A. Schlyter (ed.), *Body Politics and Women Citizens: African Experiences*, 127–35. Stockholm: Swedish International Development Agency.

Lieder, K.F. (2018). 'Performing Loitering: Feminist Protest in the Indian City', *Drama Review* 62:3, 145–61.

Livermon, X. (2020). *Kwaito Bodies: Remastering Space and Subjectivity in Post-Apartheid South Africa*. Durham, NC: Duke University Press.

Lukose, R. (2018). 'Decolonising Feminism in the #MeToo Era', *Cambridge Journal of Anthropology* 36:2, 34–52.

Macharia, K. (2016). 'Political Vernaculars: Freedom and Love', *New Inquiry*, 14 March. https://thenewinquiry.com/political-vernaculars-freedom-and-love/. Accessed 10 September 2019.

Mani, L. (2014). 'Sex and the Signal-Free Corridor', *Economic & Political Weekly* 49:6, 26–9.

Mani, L. (2018). 'We Inter Are: Identity Politics and #MeToo', Feminist Review blog, September 2018. https://femrev.wordpress.com/2018/09/10/we-inter-are-identity-politics-me-too/. Accessed 28 October 2019.

Menon, D. (1994). *Caste, Nationalism and Communism in South India: Malabar, 1900–1948*. Cambridge: Cambridge University Press.

Mercer, K. (1994). 'Black Hair/Style Politics', in *Welcome to the Jungle: New Positions in Black Cultural Studies*, ch. 4. London: Routledge.

Mitra-Kahn, T. (2012). 'Offline Issues, Online Lives? The Emerging Cyberlife of Feminist Politics in Urban India', in *New South Asian Feminisms: Paradoxes and Possibilities*, edited by S. Roy, 108–30. London: Zed Books.

Mokkil, N. (2019). *Unruly Figures: Queerness, Sex Work, and the Politics of Sexuality in Kerala*. Seattle, WA: University of Washington Press.

Msebenzi, T. (2017). 'Awundiboni – You Don't See Me'. Cape Town School of Photography, 1 March. https://ctsp.co.za/artist-in-residence-thandiwe-msebenzi-exhibition-launch-copy/. Accessed 20 August 2019.

Nombembe, P. (2019). 'Luyanda Botha: "This is How I Killed Uyinene"', *TimesLive*, 15 November. www.timeslive.co.za/news/south-africa/2019-11-15-in-his-own-words-luyanda-botha-this-is-how-i-killed-uyinene/. Accessed 29 December 2020.

Pather, J. and C. Boulle. (2019). *Acts of Transgression: Contemporary Live Art in South Africa*. Johannesburg: Wits University Press.

Phadke, S. (2013). 'Unfriendly Bodies, Hostile Cities', *Economic & Political Weekly* 48:39, 50–9.

Phadke, S., S. Khan and S. Ranade. (2011). *Why Loiter? Women and Risk on Mumbai Streets*. New Delhi: Penguin.

Priya N., L. (2018). 'Poetry is Protest: The Contemporary Dalit Female Experience in Kerala', *Annals of Arts, Culture and Humanities* 3:2, 1–8.

Putuma, K. (2017). *Collective Amnesia*. Cape Town: uHlanga Press.

Roy, L. (1988). 'If You Know Black Hair', *Callaloo* 36, 553.

Roy, S. (2016). 'Breaking the Cage', *Dissent* 63:4, 74–83.

Roychowdhury, P. (2013). 'The Delhi Gang Rape: The Making of International Causes', *Feminist Studies* 39:1, 282–92.

Schneider, R. (2011). *Performing Remains: Art and War in Times of Theatrical Reenactment*. London: Routledge.

Sharpe, C. (2016). *In the Wake: On Blackness and Being*. Durham, NC: Duke University Press.

Srinivasan, A. (2018). 'The Aptness of Anger', *Journal of Political Philosophy* 26:2, 123–44.

Taylor, D. (2003). *The Archive and the Repertoire: Performing Cultural Memory in the Americas*. Durham, NC: Duke University Press.

Yamunan, S. and S. Sharma. (2019). 'Chief Justice of India Sexually Harassed Me, Says Former Staffer in Affidavit to 22 Judges', *Scroll*, 20 April. https://scroll.in/article/920678/chief-justice-of-india-sexually-harassed-me-says-former-sc-staffer-in-affidavit-to-22-judges. Accessed 27 August 2019.

Reflection: 'Gay boys don't cry when we're raped' – queer shame and secrecy

Jamil F. Khan

Bodies like mine were never meant to be cared for. They are always to be advertised, yet perpetually hidden. People like me are a warning, warding off wayward, intrusive thoughts of freedom. Pleasure is not meant for us to have – it is taken from us.

I was raped when I was nine. A childhood friend, a few years older than me, did it. He was one of two older neighbourhood boys I started exploring my body with. Until then, our fascination with our erections led us as far as touching and feeling the shame and condemnation building up in our penises at the most inopportune times. We liked the sensations; however premature they were to us.

On the day I was raped, the weather was wonderful. It was the height of summer in Cape Town, on the South African coast, and I had invited my friend around for a swim. As always, we touched and played with each other under the water – incorporating our little explorations into the rules of our make-believe games. When we had enough of swimming, we would lay our towels down on the hot paving and lay on our bellies to dry in the sun. Eventually the sun always got too hot for us and we would seek out shade. Although there was ample shade along the boundary walls enclosing the pool, he insisted that we go to the other side of the house where the garage wall and the neighbour's boundary wall made a concealed alleyway. He told me to stand facing the wall with my hands up. I was not allowed to see what he was doing behind me. He pulled my shorts down and gently penetrated me. The shade suddenly seemed too much, with me still not allowed to see what was being done to me.

I did not make a sound. I didn't say a word. It was nothing like what we are told rape is. Nobody fought, nobody cried, nothing was sore. In fact, it felt nice. To even consider that I had been violated would have demanded many impossible explanations from me, regarding my own participation in it and the fact that I liked how it felt. That I was supposed to give permission for it to happen was a thought I had never encountered before. If anything, the worst thing that happened that day was that two boys had done what is reserved for men and women at best and teenage boys and girls at worst. My shame had not come from the violation but from the sexual affirmation of my queerness.

I was led and instructed by boys older than me to believe that this was a natural progression of the exploration of our bodies. This later happened with the other neighbourhood boy too. What I didn't know was that they, crossing over into adolescence before me, had come to understand my body as a site on which to practice the power they were already being socialised into. In the absence of protest, the only other understanding I could have was consent, even more so because it was not violent. Not only was there an absence of protest, but I started actively seeking it out. They were both latchkey kids, so after school, under the guise of going to play, I would seek them out at their homes so we could do it again. I suppose, to repeat it made it valid or acceptable. I understood myself to be desirable to boys, which allowed me to normalise my queerness. In those moments I was not repulsive for liking boys. It was the validation I kept seeking. These experiences laid the foundation for an enduringly insecure relationship with sex and consent for me.

The sex I was going to have, although I denied it to myself for years, was always going to be a secret. How does one seek help for being violated during an act you are not supposed to be partaking in, in the first place? Even when I was no longer trying to hide my queerness, I was still hiding my sex. Nobody wants to hear about gays having sex anyway, right?

The years that constituted my openly queer explorations of sex hardly alerted me to my entitlement to consent. The power dynamics of my first experience of penetrative sex informed me that sex is something that is taken from me, whether I agree to it or not. That first instruction not to look behind me to see what he was doing remained the rule with which I conducted all sexual relations. For most of my adult life I have not felt able to stop sex or intimacy due to discomfort, nor refuse sex after participating in flirtation. Even when it felt violent or painful, I did not believe I could stop it because, in the same way as then, I knew myself as an object without a desire for pleasure and that initiation meant unconditional commitment to the experience.

I had never seen an example of queer sex, normalised and acceptable as a form of pleasure. What it should have been was a mystery to me. The insidiousness of heteronormative gender roles ensured that I performed the submissive, passive role becoming of my femininity while serving only as a receptacle of a man's desires. The lack of reference to healthy queer sexual practices and the long shadow of shame and secrecy around queerness breeds the perfect conditions for queer men to be sexually violated over lifetimes; robbed of language and support to defend ourselves.

Throughout my life, men have raped me multiple times and I made sure to cover it up. I did not know that I could say 'no' or 'stop'. For most of my sexually active life, sex has been painful and harrowing and to me, that was just the way it was. The residues of self-recrimination for practicing unnatural sex, combined with violence and force as my only frame of reference, told me that sex served to punish me and pleasure someone else. It was the price I paid for being desired and entertaining flattery.

My innocent exploration of my body bore down under the weight of shame for my queerness – things children are not supposed to know about. It still shakes me to realise that the conditions under which I came to sexual awareness were designed to be so unsafe and shameful that I could have spent my entire life knowing only violation. Violation that was my responsibility. It is with this realisation that I contemplate just how deeply enmeshed we are with the violence of rape and sexual assault. So deeply that one can go their entire lives not knowing that they have been raped, save for the lingering of a deep despair nobody cares to notice, until we say: 'Yes, me too'.

A map of sexual assault

I go to the wall behind the house
Index finger stretched in purpose
Waving meaning through the air
Here is the place I call the first time
I was nine
This is the place my eyes gasped
This is the place my heart dropped
That is where my guilt talked
Here is where my soul walked
There was the way the child laughed
He was soft
To the left is where his laugh stopped
In between is where the light docked
There was the way he grew up
Here was the way he sought love
The roads don't finish here
To walk on them is to run out of air
Just enough to take a shallow breath
Not quite loud enough to say
No

Index

Note: 'n' after a page reference indicates the number of a note on that page
Literary works listed under author name

South Africa Demographic and
Health Survey 78
South African Law Reform
Commission (SALRC) 77
South African Male Survivors of
Sexual Abuse 161–2,
170n8
South African Medical Research
Council 31
sovereignty 155–9, 165–8, 303
Soweto 28, 97n5
speakability 123–5
spectacle 165, 212
spectacular 13, 273, 279, 313
stalking 85, 140
Statement *see* Kafila statement
statistics 4, 11, 33, 79–81, 90, 162,
170n1
Statistics South Africa (Stats SA) 240
Steenkamp, Reeva 9, 12, 28–9,
37–9, 40–1n1
Stellenbosch University 215
Stemple, Laura 162–4, 169
stereotypes
of black (African) women 212,
214
cultural 216
of women 211, 331
workplace 143
Students' Federation of India (SFI)
53–4, 63–4, 68n8
students' hostels 48–9, 51, 54–5,
59, 69
Supreme Court of India 14, 47,
104, 122, 223–4, 226,
262n2, 309, 323–4
surveillance 141, 321, 324
SWEAT *see* Sex Workers Education
and Advocacy Taskforce

Tata Institute of Social Sciences
(TISS) queer collective 48,
68n2

technologies 1, 6–7, 15, 132–3,
145–6, 214
affective 277, 281
Tehelka (magazine) *see* Tejpal,
Tarun
Tejpal, Tarun 132, 142, 257,
309
temple 110–11, 121, 323–4
temporality 270, 274, 299
tertiary education *see* education:
higher
Tlhabi, Redi 15, 158, 161
TMC *see* Trinamul Congress
toxic 274–5, 281
trans 60, 70, 103–4, 189–90, 212,
273, 281
gender 17, 96, 178, 210, 280
people 2, 69n13, 103, 105,
280
phobia 105
transexual 178
women 7, 97, 105, 261, 280
transformation 61, 66, 105, 182–3,
209, 214–15, 217, 223,
227, 269, 294, 306, 320
transgression 10, 154, 211, 218,
230, 234–6, 259, 279
transition 156, 170n2, 216, 325
translation 15, 94, 97n7; n11,
154–5, 211, 303, 305, 312,
324
transnational 2–4, 8–9, 20, 199,
208, 213
Trinamul Congress (TMC) 53, 55,
68n9
Twitter 139, 142, 144–5, 177–8,
183, 218, 224, 254, 328

UCT *see* University of Cape Town
UGC *see* University Grants
Commission
United Nations (UN) 41n2; n5, 76,
225

Milton Keynes UK
Ingram Content Group UK Ltd.
UKHW011812120324
439387UK00021B/360